MW01140754

The Prickly Pair

To Anne, for so many things,
and now a new skill in indexing,
with love.

The Prickly Pair

Making Nationalism in
Australia and New Zealand

DENIS MᶜLEAN

OTAGO

Published by University of Otago Press
PO Box 56/56 Union Street West, Dunedin, New Zealand, Fax: 64 3 479 8385
email: university.press@stonebow.otago.ac.nz

First published 2003
Copyright © Denis McLean 2003
ISBN 1 877276 47 2

Cover: Rosalie Gascoigne, *Cow Pasture*, 1992, 171.5 cm x 137.4 cm, torn linoleum,
synthetic polymer paint on corrugated galvanised iron on composite board.
Collection of National Gallery of Australia, Canberra.
(c) Copyright Estate of Rosalie Gascoigne.
Licensed by Viscopy, Australia, 2003.

'High Country Weather' reproduced by permission of J.G. Baxter.
First published in *Collected Poems* by James K. Baxter,
Oxford University Press, Australia and New Zealand, 1980.

Printed in New Zealand by Astra Print Ltd, Wellington

Contents

Part I: THE ANTIPODEANS

Part II: GLOBALISM v NATIONALISM

Part III:
AUSTRALIAN AND NEW ZEALAND NATIONALISM

Preface

As a New Zealander, I grew up neither knowing nor caring about Australia. I assumed that, as in identical Russian dolls, New Zealand was simply a smaller replica of its neighbour. For that very reason, Australia was uninteresting and taken for granted. When I finally took ship to England, working as a galley boy on a freighter, two wet days in Hobart loading apples did nothing to fire my interest. I went to a lecture by the famous Antarctic explorer, Sir Douglas Mawson, and was excited not by Australia but by Antarctica. The wide world was where I wanted to go, and Australia was not it.

Thirty-five years later, I was fortunate to spend a year as a visiting fellow at the Strategic and Defence Studies Centre at the Australian National University in Canberra. It was disconcerting to be overtaken by a sense of estrangement. Walking in the crackling eucalypt woods on subdued round hills amid the din of raucous Australian birds, glimpsing something of the vast reach of a strange antique land, New Zealand seemed very far away. Easy, unexamined assumptions about the fundamental character of trans-Tasman ties, the eternal bond of ANZAC and so on, began to shrivel in the harsh light. Canberra itself was already a stylish expression of national self-confidence and very different from comparable half-hearted statements of nationhood across the Tasman. For all that my hospitable Australian friends and I had in common, it became clear that vague, almost mystical essences of land, cultural identity and historical interpretation had long since been working to set New Zealand and Australia apart. Why was this so, when the two countries were intertwined in so many ways, had the same origins and shared so much history?

Nationalism is for all seasons and conditions. Even at the low end of the scale, and as between Australia and New Zealand, two countries with so much that is shared, it resonates. In theory the formation of a united Australasia should be the way to go. Because it is extremely unlikely to happen, the evolution of New Zealand and Australia throws a new light on one of the most potent issues of our times – the enigma of nationalism. The one simple, ineradicable fact about nationalism, is that we are what we are – or what we choose to be; few escape the landscape of the mind painted in for us from that beginning. Globalisation will never carry that away. Obviously, I write as a New Zealander and should apologise in advance for any offence to Australian sensibilities, or for crass generalisations.

Australia and New Zealand figure in this text as 'down under', the 'Antipodes', the Southland, the Tasman pair, 'neighbours', the ANZACs, the odd couple and even the 'prickly pair'. I shall be caught out using 'Australasian'; although, on my side of the Tasman Sea, this is generally thought to be used only in Australia about a successful New Zealander. No one term is inherently satisfactory. 'Southland' has been taken already by a New Zealand province. 'The Antipodes' is Eurocentric and, like 'Australasia', now rather dated; 'Australasia' was coined by an eighteenth-century French geographer, De Brosses, to encompass Australia and outlying islands, which, in a nutshell, is why New Zealanders do not like it. As a general purpose collective noun, ANZAC now transcends the strictly military connotation to stand for ties of blood. It has been suggested that a common currency might be called the 'ZAC': an excellent idea, echoing ANZAC and the slang word for a 'sixpence', an old coinage common to both countries. The problem is, a common currency seems unattainable. 'Trans-Tasman' – that is, what takes place across the Tasman Sea – accurately describes the current state of inter-connectedness. I have tried to use it in this sense, although it is hardly elegant. Perhaps the absence of a generally agreed collective term for the two countries is a measure of the furtive character of the sense of common identity. Indeed, this is one of the points of the book.

I wish in particular to thank the then Australian Minister of Defence, later Leader of the Opposition, the Honourable Kim Beazley, who secured for me that fellowship to the ANU which set me off on this trail. I am also most grateful to the Woodrow Wilson International Center for Scholars in Washington DC, which gave me the opportunity to continue. The friendship and contributions to my thinking of Dr Richard Solomon, President of the US Institute of Peace, and Dr Desmond Ball, of the Strategic and Defence Studies Centre in Canberra, were most helpful. The book mostly draws on my own professional experience as a career officer in the foreign ministry of an active smaller country, plus some years of engagement with national and international defence and security issues. The insights and thinking of many friends and colleagues, all in various ways fellow toilers in the field of international relations, have been invaluable. Among them, I am especially grateful to Hon Michael Bassett, Paul Dibb, Alan and Robin Burnett, Hon Paul Cleveland, Frank Corner, Roderick Deane, Bryce Harland, Professor Gary Hawke, Gerald Hensley, Sir Frank Holmes, Colin James, Sir Ewan Jamieson, Kerry McDonald, the late Ralph Mullins and Hugh White. This book has been such a long time in the making that I fear I have left out some of my many interlocutors, and to them I apologise.

I am also most grateful to Ian Grant, Executive Chairman of the New Zealand

Cartoon Archive and the Alexander Turnbull Library, for arranging at short notice the publication of cartoons. I also wish to acknowledge with gratitude and respect the cartoonists (or their copyright representatives) whose work has been reproduced in this book: Bob Brockie, Peter Bromhead, Eric Heath, Jim Hubbard, Sir Gordon Minhinnick, the late Bill Mitchell, Alan Moir, and Bill Wrathall.

A peripatetic career has given me a look at nationalism from other perspectives. Having lived for most of the 1990s in the United States, I have no doubt that modern nationalism is shaped by calculations of prestige and power or the reverse – lack of power and the need to be noticed. The United States is driven still by a strange fable called 'American Exceptionalism'. This may be the exceptionalism that proves the rule; nationalism arises and flourishes because all nations, by definition, believe themselves to be exceptional. Americans invest the many roles of the United States in the world today, and the globalising forces their country represents, with the same values they themselves hold dear. It is assumed their own perceptions of themselves are shared by others. Few of them comprehend that in other countries, where the sense of being put upon by the United States can be strong, these things may lead in exactly the opposite direction – as cause for differentiation, fuel for nationalism and the need to define the nation in ways distinctive from the United States.

DENIS McLEAN
Wellington, June 2003

"AUT CAESAR AUT NULLUS"

CHORUS OF FEDERALISTS : "Don't you want to come aboard of our ship?"
Hon. R. S. ... : "What? Give up my position as skipper of this 'ere little craft to be a bo'sun's mate along of you?
No thanks." (Proceeds to paddle his own little canoe.)

Incorporation in the Australian Commonwealth did not appeal in 1899; New Zealand attitudes have not much changed since.

'Aut Caesar Aut Nullus', Ashley Hunter, *New Zealand Graphic*, 8 July, l899.
Source *The Unauthorized Version*, Ian F. Grant.

Introduction

D r Watson reported to Sherlock Holmes, 'The dog did nothing in the night-time'. Holmes concluded, 'That was the curious incident'. Like Dr Watson, we tend to think that when the dog of nationalism is quiet, and makes no noise in the night-time, nothing is happening – its presence is unimportant. This book sides with Sherlock Holmes: even when the dog is not making a noise, it must be taken into account. Nationalism is everywhere and is the essence of modern life. The absence of nationalism from international relations would constitute a truly curious incident. Nations and peoples wrap around themselves qualities which range from the downright dangerous to the pompous and prejudicial, and out to the merely silly and ordinary. There is, it seems, no end to the capacity of human societies to lay claim to distinctive identities, exceptional characters and beliefs. The notions on which these beliefs are based are many and mystical. Whatever the perception, the upshot is to promote senses of difference, to foster separatism.

The Australia-New Zealand story is about two adjacent peoples – of the same kind, and mostly from the same place on the other side of the world – who have grown apart rather than together. In both places high hopes and ambitions soon came up against hard realities; from the first clank of chains in the wilderness and raw confrontations with peoples who were there before them, the realisation did not match the dreams. The pilgrim fantasy that they would plant New Jerusalems, or at least improved versions of the Britain they left behind, had to be reconciled with the situation in which they found themselves – isolated and in very different surroundings from anything they had previously known. An important strand in their sense of identity was then fashioned by the swagger of the British Empire at the height of its power. This much was shared. The very persuasiveness of the British heritage stunted personality growth, leaving the two countries almost desperately dependent on an Imperial connection, for want of anything else. In both, more so in the smaller, the British Empire put the striving after national identity in the shade for a long time, while completely eclipsing the notion of an Australasia.

Clinging to the past, it is always difficult to face the future. Australians and New Zealanders seemingly did not want to know, during most of this time, that their new countries were not set down in some remote 'new world', but hard up against the old and very different, difficult world of Asia. A fast developing and dynamic east Asia has now become a region of great promise and profound challenge for both countries. The emerging great power of China will obviously be a major influence. Will the United States long continue to maintain policies of forward engagement? Can Australia and New Zealand build themselves in as integral, respected partners of the countries of the region? Can stability be sustained in the face of fracturing and extremism in Indonesia and elsewhere? What will be the long-term effect of a seemingly almost complete failure to build stable modern nation-states across the arc of islands to the north of Australia and New Zealand? Benjamin Franklin famously warned the representatives of the separate American colonies, as they signed the Declaration of Independence in July 1776, 'We must indeed all hang together, or, most assuredly we shall all hang separately.' Australia and New Zealand, one would think, would make this philosophy a foundation for their relationship – in the face of shared global trading problems, regional insecurity, international terrorism, the danger of being marginalised by developments in Asia, and so on.

Ben Franklin's homespun wisdom is absent. The advantages of making common cause would be huge for New Zealand and far from unimportant for Australia. If nationalism had not got in the way two relatively small societies would by now be focusing hard on how best to achieve economies of scale and how to become more effective and competitive in the world through the pooling of resources, assets and talents. There would be harmonisation of effort in pursuit of shared strategic objectives and productive economic as well as political relationships with Asia and the Pacific. Working closely together it would be possible to iron out anomalies from the past to do with the relationship with the British crown and to achieve effective integration of judicial, educational and professional systems. A broader and deeper research and development base could be developed in response to the demands of the modern knowledge-based global economy. Removal of all impediments to trade and financial exchange would be capable of triggering new economic dynamism to match the potential of the region. Merger would create a vast Exclusive Economic Zone of great potential. With focused foreign and defence policies and re-jigged political systems, the new Republic of Australasia could become something not seen before – a dispersed modern nation-state held together by shared commitments to western ideals and commitments but straddling both the eastern and western worlds, at ease in both.

The head can accept the rationale; the heart, in the guise of nationalism, says otherwise. Philosophers down the centuries have thought in terms of human beings eventually disporting themselves on the sunny uplands as one universal family. If the joining of hands is to take place anywhere, it should surely be here, as between New Zealand and Australia. These two have more in common with one another than either has with any other country on the planet, they are probably simply more alike than any other two separate nations. The Australian Department of Foreign Affairs and Trade website puts it succinctly:

> Australia and New Zealand are natural allies and friendly rivals with a strong trans-Tasman sense of family. At a government-to-government level, the relationship that Australia has with New Zealand is better developed and more extensive than with any other country.

There are strong personal and social affinities between the two peoples and close links by modern transport; both are liberal, moderate democracies, fortunate and successful states with a far-reaching network of co-operation between them; there are no divisive legacies of bitterness or war: there is nothing of a racial, religious, ethical or linguistic character to provide any pretext for apart-ness.

For all that, the two countries have developed as separate entities with firmly differentiated ideas about themselves. The incomers in both places may have been more or less of the same kind. Their new identities, however, were shaped not by inheritances from the past but by the exigencies of the present, by the new circumstances in which they found themselves. British models may have set the scene, but the two immigrant societies were soon marching to their own music. The Australians derived theirs from the sweep and promise of the 'wide, brown land', an assertive, disrespectful individualism and some well-polished legends. For the New Zealanders, the pursuit of reconciliation with Maori, fewer social cleavages and a country of great natural beauty, established very different local rhythms.

Many assume that recent economic consolidation will eventually build up such momentum that political convergence will follow. But it is, to say the least, an open question whether other more metaphysical considerations to do with history and national pride, affinities with places and peoples, cultural identities and sporting loyalties will ever be broken down by closer economic relationships or intensive day-to-day interactions. There are, it seems, some irreducible commitments to one's own.

The technology revolution is, nevertheless, an obvious counterweight. For the first time in history there are virtually no impediments to dialogue and understanding, making it possible to look in a new way at the world. By breaking down barriers of distance and understanding, the new technologies offer new opportunities for overpowering nationalism and self-centredness in world affairs. Yet globalisation is provoking violent protest and deep, if unspecific, unease. The imperative of the market place is seen by many to be running out of control, threatening jobs, imposing standards over which people have no say, remorselessly consuming natural resources and polluting the environment. It is a more open world, but individuals are fearful of the loss of old national touchstones.

The superior weight of Australia will inevitably continue to make itself felt in New Zealand as globalisation gathers pace. But there is nothing to suggest that New Zealand's sceptical, prickly independence will in the process be extinguished. In a world of nation-states a sense of nationalism has become indispensable to the business of government, simply because it is necessary to define the national interest internally as well as against other states. All countries, great or small, democratic and stable or xenophobic and unpredictable, demonstrate it in one form or another. Globalisation does not seem to be leading ineluctably in the direction of a surrender of identity or sovereignty. Age-old divisiveness and strife are still with us in the new globalised world.

The famous photograph of our 'blue planet' from space shows no political boundaries. It would be an imperishable optimist who supposed that this is how it might be. Yet the boundaries are being overcome; international collaboration is real, productive and expanding all the time. The irony is that this very process has now triggered alarm at the homogenisation of things and an incoherent revolt against the agencies of global change. What we have is a two-way stretch: globalisation and nationalism – harmonisation and fragmentation. The astronauts' view of our shared world was made possible only by courtesy of a nationalistic enterprise in which the United States flag was hoisted on the moon. NASA also actively promotes international co-operation. Yet nationalism thrives – even under the banner of togetherness and collaboration. The evidence from the quiet South Pacific is that it is easily conjured up, even between friends, and will work against 'best-laid plans' for more enlightened co-operative international effort. The New Zealanders and Australians have taken on separate identities and cling – without any good cause – to idiosyncratic happy-go-lucky nationalisms of their own. Nationalism is, by definition, exclusive. Where each is taken up with self, there is little room for mutual accommodation.

This book is not intended to be a definitive, comparative study. It does not pretend to be a survey of all aspects of the trans-Tasman relationship. Such a vast project would lead well beyond the issue of nationalism, and how it happens, into thickets of sociology, psychology, identity politics and cultural history outside of my experience, let alone competence. Rather, this project springs from the simpler thought that analysis of some of the ways Australia and New Zealand have diverged may help fill in a few blanks on the map of nationalism. This is about the fingerprints at the crime scene of nationalism. Understanding what has happened to set the two countries on different tracks should give clues to the chances for serious convergence in the future. As we are often told, we must think about the past in order to understand the present and prepare for the future. In the interactive, interdependent world of the twenty-first century the sets of beliefs the nations and peoples had about themselves in the nineteenth and twentieth centuries still ring in our ears. In many countries such reverberations have sprung from bloody revolutions, battlefield triumphs or pretensions to glory. In the case of Australia and New Zealand, more mundane considerations apply – to do with the character of the respective lands, native peoples, early history, isolation, evolving political and economic relationships, military experience, political and administrative systems, divergent strategic perceptions, emerging trends in literature, cultural styles and sport. Contrary to any conventional wisdom that the two countries are like peas in a pod, the record suggests that separatist and localised notions have prevailed from the outset.

New Zealanders assume their Australian mates will always take them for a ride. Prime Minister Fraser stuffs New Zealand Prime Minister Muldoon into his kangaroo pouch.

Bob Brockie, *National Business Review*, 17 March 1976. New Zealand Cartoon Archive, Alexander Turnbull Library, Wellington.

Part I

THE ANTIPODEANS

The rough Aussie thinks only of again having his wicked way with the tremulous and unwilling New Zealand maid.

Bromhead, *The Auckland Star*. New Zealand Cartoon Archive, Alexander Turnbull Library, Wellington.

HOW WE SEE IT

THE OGRE: "Come into these arms." NEW ZEALAND: "Nay, sir, those arms bear chains."

New Zealand delusions about the convict 'stain' and their own supposed enlightened partnership with Maori were, it seems, sufficient grounds for repelling the Australian ogre.

'How we see it', Scatz, *New Zealand Graphic*, 20 October 1900. Source *The Other Side Of The Ditch*, Ian F. Grant, New Zealand Cartoon Archive Collection, Alexander Turnbull Library, Wellington.

chapter one

Antipodean Attitudes

Those two women will never agree; they are arguing from different premises.
– *Sydney Smith (1771–1845), on seeing two Edinburgh women hurling insults at one another across an alleyway.*

One of the first laws of magnetism is that like poles repel, and unlike attract. Australia and New Zealand are alike in very many ways and accordingly the more effort is devoted to pretending otherwise. Two-way name calling and mutual belittlement are incessant. New Zealanders pretend to look down on their Australian cousins; Australians find it hard even to admit New Zealanders to their league. To most Australians, New Zealand is simply out of sight and out of mind, a butt for truly bizarre jokes about sheep, a backward and unkempt provincial place. Since Australia itself is only a middling-sized country, New Zealand – being even smaller – serves the useful purpose of providing ballast against feelings of inadequacy. New Zealanders are unable to ignore Australia, but fall over themselves to be dismissive. Barry Humphries, the insightful Australian entertainer, equips his wonderful character, Dame Edna Everage, with a New Zealand acolyte called Madge. Whereas Dame Edna is exuberant, loud and irreverent, Madge is plain, mousy and dull, proclaiming that her boring clothes were produced by one of New Zealand's foremost fashion designers. Humphries has caught the stereotypes each side has of the other. Australians are quite happy to be thought pushy, translating pushiness into boldness and dynamism; they see irreverence as coincident with assertiveness and disrespect for authority. New Zealanders think Australian exuberance equates with flashiness – boastful and crass. Whereas Australians pretend to find New Zealanders dull and boring, New Zealanders believe that if Australians were not so shallow they would see that the virtue lies in New Zealand steadiness and good sense. What Australians regard as national strengths, especially when set against the pathetic inadequacies of their Kiwi cousins, New Zealanders see as laughable pretension – and so on and on, seemingly forever. Is such trivial attitudinising important? Of course! These are the basic building blocks of nationalism.

Divided by a Common Culture, Common Origins, Common Just About Everything

Oscar Wilde's famous crack about Britain and America being divided by a common language applies in spades to Australia and New Zealand. The basic attributes of culture, history, institutions and beliefs intertwine and overlap. Yet New Zealand was moved as early as 1901 effectively to declare its independence, not from Britain, but from Australia – by declining to join the new, united Commonwealth. Not dreaming the same dreams, each looking at the world from different perspectives, not hard-pressed by external enemies, the two countries give scarcely a thought to notions of a unified 'greater South-land' community. Blame the empire, or the good fortune of two countries able to develop, happy-go-luckily, sequestered in a quiet corner of the world, but Australasia never bloomed.

One explanation was offered, unwittingly, by Edward Heath, the former British Prime Minister. In Britain, he observed, it is always 'Australia and New Zealand in one breath'. After three weeks travelling all over Australia, he was mystified that he had heard no mention of New Zealand. 'How do you account for that?' he asked. 'There was a long pause. "Perhaps because it is irrelevant", volunteered one of his Australian escorts.'[1] In choosing to stand aside from the long march of Australia, New Zealand became unimportant in Australian sight. The larger and better endowed country then proceeded to consolidate a sense of its own destiny. Australia can never be irrelevant to New Zealand, but a surprising amount of energy goes into pretending otherwise. Australian leaders still make it clear that New Zealand is welcome to join Australia, or to continue to go its own way; but New Zealanders shouldn't delude themselves about the character and worth of the 'special relationship' between the two countries, unless it is founded in genuine and profound commitment. New Zealanders, for their part, think more in terms of jogging along with Australia from time to time, as the spirit moves, but cannot contemplate a permanent engagement.

Well over a century ago, in 1890, Wellington's *Evening Post* proclaimed its opposition to union with Australia: 'New Zealand would be the Cinderella of the federal family ... The Australian people rather look down on New Zealand and New Zealand absolutely refuses to look up to Australia or accept a subordinate position.' This is still the nub of the issue. Both governments devote considerable efforts to bolstering the official relationship; increasingly, and in various ways, New Zealand coordinates many aspects of the business of governance with Australia. There is no talk of commitment to making common cause. The elegant crack by the New Zealand nationalist historian Keith Sinclair is still sustaining to some of his compatriots. In Sinclair's view, what remained in the relationship between the two countries – after the cursory examination by New Zealand of the advantages of joining the federation in the late nineteenth century – was 'a feeling of comradeship and a friendly rivalry in which the Australians regarded the "Kiwis" as genteel country cousins, while the latter profess to see the "Aussies" as coarse fellows, whose ancestry, in the interests of courtesy, should be ignored.'[2] Sinclair was convinced that New Zealand was destined to be a 'place apart'. Wisecracks about class and convictism are, however, no longer relevant.

In the two hundred plus years since the two countries first impinged on one another, hostilities have been confined to fist fights between drunken soldiers in Cairo and hard battling on the sports field. Set against the history of struggle between, say, Britain and France or Japan vis-à-vis China or Korea – to take two other island nations that have had to define themselves against continental neighbours – the association between New Zealand and Australia is innocuous. So why has inclusiveness not taken hold?

To begin with, things are not what they seem. The population base in the two countries is no longer dominated by the 'Anglo-Celtic' immigrant communities which set the tone of apparent similarity in the nineteenth and early twentieth centuries. As nationalism has taken hold, the respective populations overwhelmingly identify themselves as 'Australians' or 'New Zealanders' – with all that implies by way of notions of separatist and distinctive sentiment. Equally, each community has diversified its population base in different ways over the past fifty years. Both have gained substantial numbers of peoples from other places than their traditional source of immigrants – the British Isles.

In 1947 81 per cent of Australians traced their origins to the main English-speaking countries (British Isles, New Zealand, Canada, South Africa and the United States); by 1997 this proportion had fallen to 39 per cent. Only 10 per cent of the Australian population was listed as 'overseas-born' in 1947; of that group, the overwhelming majority were traditional immigrants from the British Isles. Fifty years later, in 1998, 23 per cent of the total population identified themselves as 'overseas-born'; 27 per cent of those born in Australia had at least one parent who was 'overseas-born'. In effect, 50 per cent of Australians are now first or second generation Australian. Since the Second World War, six million migrants have come to Australia – from 170 countries. This is a higher per capita intake over this period than in Canada or the United States. The pattern was set in the immediate post-war years when large numbers from Southern Europe, especially Greeks and Italians, were recruited for major Australian development projects. (The war and the threat of Japanese attack had also shocked many Australians into thinking that a small population in a large continent on the edge of an unstable region may be a prescription for future insecurity.) In the 1980s and 90s, in turn, Asian immigration made an important impact: 6 per cent of Australians are now of Asian origin. In 2001–02 the five countries (other than New Zealand) which provided the most migrants to Australia were Britain

(15,320), China (9380), India (7620), South Africa (7220), and Indonesia (5730).

In 1999 almost 80 per cent of New Zealanders still listed themselves as of European origin – predominantly tracing their origins back to the British Isles, but with significant numbers from the Netherlands, Germany and former Yugoslavia. It was not clear what proportion of these 'European' New Zealanders were recent (first or second generation) arrivals. Polynesian and other Pacific island migration from the 1960s onward has made a significant contribution to New Zealand life; about 6 per cent of New Zealanders classify themselves as Polynesians. Together with the 14–15 per cent who class their identity as Maori, there is an increasingly distinctive 'Pacific' character to New Zealand demographics. New Zealand, too, is now attracting significant numbers of Asians and is certainly no longer a place of largely British immigration. Auckland is increasingly a city of Asian as well as Polynesian influences.

All this means there are increasing numbers of people on both sides of the Tasman with none of the connections with Britain and Empire that for so long served to identify Australia and New Zealand as countries of the same stamp. New immigrant communities in Australia do not have any feel for a special ANZAC bond and have been the source of political complaints about special immigration concessions for New Zealanders. The make-up of the two societies is changed. Traditional assumptions about an inherently firm foundation for the relationship arising from a shared history and culture have to change also. In this sense, the common presumption that New Zealand is still a more 'British' society than Australia perhaps has meaning, but not much.

The conventional wisdom would suggest that cross-migration would lay the foundation for political consolidation. For over a century flows of Australians into New Zealand and New Zealanders into Australia switched according to economic circumstances in either country. Until recently, there have effectively been no impediments to nationals of the one country travelling to or taking up residence in the other. If this process has had any political consequences it would seem to be counter-intuitive. Australian statistics now suggest that there are 450,000 New Zealanders living in Australia, over one tenth of the population of New Zealand. Many New Zealanders have made major contributions to many sectors of Australian life; the reverse is of course also true. Australian complaints have nevertheless become loud and shrill. In an interesting example of what the English eighteenth-century author Horace Walpole observed (speaking of the French) as the *vulgar antipathy between neighbouring nations,*[3] New Zealanders in Australia have been widely dismissed as 'dole-bludgers', income tax fraudsters, petty criminals and cheats against sacrosanct Trade Union rules and codes. Like the France-Britain relationship, closeness seems to stiffen the sense of difference rather than the reverse.

The presumption that these are two predominantly agricultural societies also no longer holds up. In both countries, about 85 per cent of the population live in urban areas. The great Australian cities are not only distinctive and striking, in large measure they set the tone and style of the country. In New Zealand, the cities reflect the drawn-out character of the land, lush in the north, austere in the south; being smaller, the cities flow readily on to the sheep-strewn green countryside, which is the template for the 'clean, green' image the small nation has set for itself. The legendary 'outback' still chimes in the imagination of Australians, few of whom have direct experience of its demands. Likewise, New Zealanders still pretend to identify with the sterling family farmers, making their own way on their own land, when in fact the rural proportion of the population is very low. In the realm of myth, New Zealanders like to think that drought-stricken, bare-bones farming in the featureless outback sets the tone for Australian life; in the same way, Australians are determined that New Zealand is a nation of scarcely articulate peasant farmers. The economic realities are what count: almost 30 per cent of the Gross Domestic Product (GDP) of New Zealand derives from exports from an efficient and competitive agricultural sector; the comparable figure in Australia is 8 per cent. Agriculture is still important in both societies; more so in New Zealand than in Australia, where there is more depth to the economy. In neither country, however, is it any longer relevant to think that agriculture sets the tone of national life.

The Metaphysics of Place and Space

For Australians looking at New Zealand, size must be the launching pad for notions of relative importance. There is no getting away from the lop-sidedness of the relationship. Australia (3.67 million square miles) is about thirty times larger than New Zealand (104,454 square miles). The smallest, or island, continent, Australia is almost the size of continental United States – the 'lower forty-eight' states (excluding Alaska and Hawaii). New Zealand is a couple of islands, a continental outrider parked off to one side – as Australians would see it. In fact, if the nations are to be ranked in terms of geographic scale, New Zealand is small only in comparison with its nearest neighbour. Britain is smaller and the entire British Isles, including Ireland, is not much bigger (126,824 square miles) than New Zealand; Italy is 116,290 square miles. Australia is not only big but empty; geographical size and scale are offset by the limitations imposed by climate and a harsh hinterland. New Zealand, too, is hardly over-populated when compared to countries of similar size and topography, like Japan and Italy.

In relation to the land masses of the two countries, people are scarce. There are almost five times (4.9) as many Australians (19.6 million – estimate March 2002) as New Zealanders (3.9 million – March 2002). The Australian population is increasing at a steeper rate – although neither do too well in the reproduction department. Migration flows largely determine population growth in both countries. There is approximately one Australian to every fifteen Americans. At

1.4 per cent of the US population, New Zealanders are out-numbered 70:1 by Americans! (Colorado, the twenty-eighth most populous state in the United States, is the same size and has about the same number of people as New Zealand.) The proportion of Australians to New Zealanders is more manageable: somewhat less than 5:1! Approximately 75 per cent of the population of Australia is concentrated on the south-east of the continent in a narrow zone more or less coincident with the area of New Zealand.

Relative wealth favours Australia with a GDP of $A556.9 billion for the 1998–99 year, almost seven times that of New Zealand ($A80.5 billion). Australia's relative economic advantages stem, largely but not entirely, from an unearned windfall: a continent which, although giving a passing imitation of a desert, proves a treasure trove of minerals.

Distance rules. It is a longer journey, by about 600 miles, to travel from Auckland, New Zealand, to Perth, Western Australia, than from New York City to San Francisco. Perth is further from Canberra, the capital of Australia, than is Wellington, the capital of New Zealand. The distance between Canberra and Wellington is more than from London to Moscow or Algiers. Both countries are a long way from the centres of Western life and influence on which they draw. Europe is closer to the east coast of Australia by way of Suez than by way of Panama. Although the Greenwich meridian line passes just to the east of New Zealand ports, the easterly route to Britain is the shorter for New Zealanders. (The sea approaches to the British Isles correspond effectively with the 165th degree of longitude, which more or less bisects the Tasman Sea.) In sum, New Zealand turns east to get to Europe, Australia goes west-about.

Geography plays more tricks. Australia, the tourist brochures say, is washed by the waters of the Pacific, when in fact the Tasman and Coral Seas do the washing along Australia's east coast, while New Zealand looks out into the open spaces of the Pacific. Australia, by contrast, is brought hard up against (literally so, in a geological sense) the islands and archipelagos of South East Asia to the north and also looks out to the Indian Ocean to the west. The difference in geo-political outlook imposed by the distinctive geographical settings of the two countries was established early and impacts on policy-making to this day. New Zealand has traditionally regarded itself as a country of the South Pacific; this has nourished a widely held belief that the country can concern itself principally with what was once a relatively tranquil environment there. In point of fact, like Australia, New Zealand has extensive economic and political connections with Asia and further afield. The security of New Zealand is bound up with that of Australia, although many subscribe to the comforting fiction that in its splendid isolation the country can define its defence and security efforts in ways which largely take no account of Australia. On the other hand, the Australian world-view is not exclusive and also takes in the South Pacific. Whichever way they look, both countries are impaled on the reality of their remoteness. Perceptive outsiders are struck by an almost chilling sense of loneliness – the impact of the wide skies and blank 'red heart' of Australia and of the encircling seas dashing against the empty shores of New Zealand.

Relative bigness begets condescension; the large presume there is a pecking order and that the small are on the wrong end of it. No one who has considered French attitudes to Belgium, or New Yorkers to New Jersey, or Trinidadians to Tobago, and so on, could be surprised to find that Australians mock New Zealanders: in a competitive world it is always a comfort to turn a smaller neighbour into a mere satellite. For their part, the smaller will always be only too ready to try to cut their bigger neighbours down to size. Like the Canadians towards Americans, New Zealanders try hard to insist on their differences with the Australians. Both smaller partners in fact gain immeasurably from their association with the larger country. The nationalistic difficulty arises when it comes to admitting this. Unlike the Canadians, the New Zealanders can pretend that a wide and stormy sea allows them to keep their distance from their neighbour and thus maintain their presumptions of self-worth.

Nationalism is oppositional. It is not merely a statement of identity, of national belonging; it is also a matter of defining these things in relation to others. Nationalists need a measure against which to assess themselves. New Zealand's sports victories against Australia are achieved thanks to true grit in the face of great odds; its losses are a matter of going down fighting despite being outnumbered and outgunned. Strangely, New Zealand equally serves as a useful touchstone of Australian superiority: the reassurance of being able to whip New Zealand regularly seems to give Australians the confidence to take on the much larger forces in the wider world. It is a war of siblings in their own backyard, fought without regard to differences of size and strength. No matter that playing fields of sport are generally pretty level and that matches are won or lost thanks to factors that have little to do with national qualities or the size of the pool of national talent. What is important is that through such interactions the smaller partner presumes equality despite the size differences; in contrast, the larger player expects deference, because of those same differences. As a mark of inherent worth, the small will hoard its tally of triumphs (even of the most arcane or marginal kind) over its larger rival; the latter will simply assume that on that day, in that matter, Homer merely nodded.

In neither New Zealand nor Australia is the disposition to hide the national light under a bushel an abiding or evident characteristic. Indeed, both revel in the art of thinking well of themselves. New Zealand is drawn ineluctably into the Australian orbit; at the same time, Australia is stuck with New Zealand. In each country the prevailing assumption is that there is little need of the other; but the reality is that their interdependence is now highly – if disproportionately – important to both. What is it that apparently makes these two young and vigorous societies impervious to thoughts of making common cause?

"UNION IS STRENGTH."

A LESSON BETTER LEARNT LATE THAN NEVER.

An anonymous cartoon to mark what became Australia Day makes an early point about the advantages of union between the seven British Australasian colonies, including New Zealand.

'Union is Strength', *Melbourne Punch*, 26 January 1860. Source *The Unauthorized Version*, Ian F. Grant.

chapter two

In the Beginning: Places Apart

Land of mountains and running water, rocks and flowers
and the leafy evergreen, O natal earth,
the atoms of your children
are bonded to you for ever[1]

The basic building blocks of nationalism are primordial. They are to do with the land and the sense of belonging to the native earth. In Australia and New Zealand, variations on these themes have helped to establish ideas about unique national identities and circumstances, almost from the first. This is the food of nationalism in new societies as in old. New countries also need foundation myths – the stories of exploration and the dramas of establishment in the wilderness; the encounters with the original inhabitants, their character and identity and their mythologies. Hopes and dreams carried over the oceans by the incomers must also be factored in. The dynamics of the mix of social and racial factors, associations with the land, folk memories, the ideals and hopes of immigrants and the effect of the struggles to get established were obviously different as between New Zealand and Australia. There was much overlap. There was also more than enough that was singular to each to found and foster protestations of difference.

Gondwanaland

If the grain of the native earth inspires nationalism, the differences between New Zealand and Australia are as old as the hills. As geological constructs, Australia is ancient, New Zealand is young (relatively speaking); each has evolved in its own and separate fashion – a continent and an offshore island chain; a stable core and its mobile outlier. Both offer haunting and wonderful landscapes of unique and radically different moods and form. Mineral resources are distributed in unequal fashion. Yet, for much of traceable geological history, New Zealand developed in association with parts of Australia. Scattered rock sequences, dating from the early Palaeozoic era (c. 225 to 600 million years ago) along the western side of the South Island can be correlated with similar deposits in south-eastern Australia. New Zealand looks newly minted, marked at every turn by the constantly and literally shifting scene. In marked contrast, Australia seems – and is – old, a land subdued and stable. Nevertheless, the two land masses have close and very long-standing connections. When they were joined together they shared plants, dinosaurs and small sea creatures. When they separated, New Zealand established itself with chips (many thousands of cubic kilometres of chips) off the Australian (and Antarctic) blocks.

Australian and New Zealand separatism started in a bust-up of planetary dimensions. Beginning 160 million years ago, the vast mega-continent of Gondwanaland, which was made up of Africa, South America, India, Antarctica and Australia and New Zealand, began breaking apart over a period of about 70 million years. Australia was a core component of the whole structure. By contrast, New Zealand developed along the south-eastern margin of Gondwanaland on a now-you-see-it-now-you-don't basis. Sedimentary rock shorn off the mountainous margins of Gondwanaland was deposited, contorted, pushed up, eroded away again, stretched out, submerged once more and then rebuilt in response to continuing and intense pressures within the earth's crust. Present-day New Zealand straddles a major boundary in the earth's crust, where the Indo-Australian Plate crunches up against the Pacific Plate. The country's convoluted structures, high alps along an extended mountain spine and deep offshore troughs are the result of ongoing geological tumult.

The geological action that formed Australia took place much further back in time. Crystalline rock found in Western Australia has been dated to a staggering 4200 million years ago and may have been derived from the first primeval continent, now known as Pangaea. Formed before the moon separated from the earth, this rock gives Australia – or, more accurately, some bits of it – claim to have been in at the creation, give or take a billion years or so. The gneisses, schists and granites spread across the Great Western Plateau are also astonishingly ancient, belonging to the earliest geological period, the Archaeozoic (from more than three billion to about 2500 million years old). Sands and coarser fragments from these rocks were deposited, either in shallow seas or as desert sands, to make the typical 'red bed' rocks of north and central Australia. Several times they were rucked up into great mountain ranges only to be worn back down again. A flight across the desert wastes of central Australia reveals folds and breaks of strata, now often worn completely flat, which signal the ancient contortions. Brooding Uluru (Ayers Rock) stands as a symbol of the grandeur and antiquity of the red heart of Australia. A surface remnant of vast sedimentary deposits reaching as much as eight kilometres beneath, its now almost vertical beds of massive sandstone were laid down in a delta 600 million years ago, around the time the first recognisable fossils appeared. Pushed about by the inexorable forces of the sliding continents, Uluru has been sculpted by frost, wind and rain as mountains rose and melted away around it, as forests formed and disappeared and seas spread and ebbed away. At the Olgas, only thirty kilometres away, it is possible to walk into the deep ravines of worn red rock, which the random pressures of the earth have here left lying almost flat, and see the ripple marks and cross-bedding that reveal its origins in ancient shallow seas.

Australia did well out of this stage in its history. Huge deposits of sedimentary iron ore were laid down in the Hammersley and Middleback ranges on Eyre Peninsula. Extensive mineralisation – successively 2400, 1900 and 1700 million years ago – created gold at Kalgoorlie, silver and lead at Broken Hill and Mount Isa, and copper as well, along with tungsten, silver, beryl, mica, tin, tantalum, among other useful things, at many other places. Ancient rifting of the continent created diamond pipes in the north and west. The oldest marine fossils of the world were entrapped 600 to 700 million years ago at Ediacara in South Australia. Major economic deposits of uranium formed at about the same time are now mined in Queensland and the Northern Territory. Substantial oil deposits are being exploited in the centre of the continent and along the north-west coast. This is Aladdin's cave geology. By comparison, the New Zealand yield is meagre indeed. There is coal in both the North and South Islands and sufficient oil and gas in the area of Taranaki to provide about a half of the country's needs. Gold deposits, associated with granites of relatively recent age in both islands, have been productive and have recently been reworked to advantage.

The Gondwanaland connection seems to explain many things held in common by New Zealand and Australia: the shared presence of the flightless (ratite) birds, for example, and the podocarp and fern forests, all widespread either in the fossil record or in current fauna and flora in Australia, Antarctica, New Zealand and South America. Dinosaurs walked the southern earth and one or two species reached the New Zealand land mass before it disappeared again for one of its periodic submergences. The fossil record shows that there were communities of early marine life shared between New Zealand and Australia. Essentially, however, the pattern was cut early in the Cretaceous period (the culmination of the age of the Dinosaurs) about 112 million years ago.

Australians jibe that New Zealand is 'the shaky isles' and they are right. Ruaumoko, the Maori god of the underworld, who can make the earth move, is a continuing presence. Moreover the plate boundary so splits New Zealand that all of the North Island, the north-western part of the South Island, plus the sliver down the West Coast are part of the Indo-Australian Plate, while the main, more easterly, mass of the South Island rides on the Pacific Plate. The junction lies in a deep buckle of the sea floor off the east coast of the North Island and can be traced down through the South Island as the Alpine Fault and on south-westwards into another undersea trough. The Pacific Plate is being thrust under the North Island and up and over the western part of the South Island. All of this triggers the activity and the seismic shiftings that fit New Zealand into the belt of instability known as the 'ring of fire' running around the Pacific basin.

As the 1989 earthquake in Newcastle, New South Wales, demonstrated, Australia is not immune to seismic disaster. Yet the land has an immemorial solidity: lying back from the zone of crustal confrontation around the rim of the Pacific, earthquakes are shallow, volcanoes superficial, and the landscape is austere, worn down and sparse. Like the North American Mid-West, Australia is at base a stable continent, or craton. Unlike North America, the margins of the continent have not been violently disrupted – at least in relatively recent geological times – by the incorporation of large chunks of other land masses and by the present dynamic forces that determine the shape of things around the Pacific Rim itself – as in New Zealand. Ultra-nationalists in New Zealand may be discomforted by the knowledge that at least the northern part of the country is inescapably being propelled towards Australia, at the rate of about 2.5 centimetres or so a year. Political union may seem unlikely, but geological union is inevitable, in some seventy-six million years. As is the case with Japan, the unyielding pressures of the sliding plates will one day end a vaunted separateness. Cataclysmic collisions of this kind have shaped both coasts of North America and changed the character of that continent almost beyond recognition. As in the American state of New Mexico, vast volcanic events seem to be symptomatic of territories in this interesting condition. In New Zealand's case, very recent (the latest less than 2000 years ago) and hugely explosive rhyolite eruptions, which have shaped much of the central North Island, were among the largest of such events detected anywhere. Pending physical merger, then, New Zealand will remain very much its own place. When merger happens, neither side will be the same.

What is the City but the People?[2]

Australia has been a homeland for people for perhaps as long as 100,000 years, while in New Zealand there is not much of a record beyond 800 years. The New Zealand Maori are a subset of the Polynesian race, with a culture and language linked closely to the islands of the central Pacific. The Aborigine of Australia may even be *sui generis*; they have affinities with the Austronesians of New Guinea and adjacent islands, but in essence they are uniquely Australian. Maori and Aboriginal are not only very different races, established at different times. They came to their homelands by different means and from different directions. They never met before the Europeans came.

The Polynesians, an oceanic people, spread by awe-inspiring voyaging over little more than 3000 years to occupy the islands of the Pacific. The dates of departure for the journey or journeys that brought them from central Polynesia to what came to be called Aotearoa, also called New Zealand, are not known for sure; the passenger lists are recorded only in legend. However, several ports of embarkation in the Cook and Society Island groups have been identified by archaeological research. Polynesian navigation was not haphazard. Recent studies and remarkable re-runs of the classical voyages have demonstrated that the Polynesians had highly developed ship-building and navigational skills.

Tantalising scientific analysis of pollen and the distribution of a species of native rat suggest that they may have first reached New Zealand 2000 years ago, perhaps on an exploratory expedition (which would confirm, in a remarkable way, the legend of the voyage of a pioneering navigator, Kupe). While it is generally accepted that scattered occupation could have begun about 800 to 1000 years ago, firm archaeological evidence goes back no further than the thirteenth century, and the storehouses of knowledge represented in Maori genealogy also suggest that several ocean-going canoes reached the country at this time. Even a comparative handful of progenitors could have built the succeeding generations. A founder population of three pairs would have had almost an even chance of establishing a viable community.[3] In 800 years, twenty people could, in theory, expand to 100,000 at a population growth of 1 per cent per year.[4] What we know for sure is that from exiguous beginnings Maori developed as a complex, highly evolved and structured society at the south-western corner of what has become known as the Polynesian triangle, comprising the islands of the Polynesian culture (the other corners being Hawaii in the north and Easter Island in the east).

Whether the first Australians came in one or several waves is not known. It seems clear, however, that lower sea levels during periods of glaciation made it possible for early migrants to travel by way of the now submerged Sahul Shelf, crossing such water gaps as there were by rafts or dug-out canoe. The last ice age – from 30,000 to 10,000 years ago – offers a correlation with a generally accepted date for a major influx, 25,000 years before the present. But the archaeological record of human activity in Australia is now being stretched back – perhaps into the time of a precursor race to modern *homo sapiens.* Successive levels of human occupancy at a site about 320 kilometres south of Darwin on the western side of Northern Territory have been tentatively dated back to 176,000 years ago. Ochre found in the sequence suggested to some researchers that artistic endeavour was taking place there from 75,000 to 116,000 years ago. Although these datings have provoked scepticism, some comparisons are informative. The earliest known cave art in Europe is dated back 30,000 years, while the theory is that modern *homo sapiens* emerged in Africa 100,000 to 150,000 years ago. If dates can be verified, Australia will take its place as one of the founts of human art and in at the beginning of the origins of the species.

Whether or not their forerunners were of more ancient lineage than *homo sapiens,* the Aborigines who occupied the Australian continent at the time of the European onset were unique. It is assumed that the race derived from within and beyond the south-east Asian region, but it is not known whether from a single or several racial stocks. Semi-nomadic hunters and gatherers, the Aborigines endured while the climate and the relationship between land and sea literally changed around them. Australia was not extensively glaciated, but the lower sea levels of glacial times provided people who were then predominantly coastal with extensive rivers and estuaries for relatively easy food-gathering. The associated moist climate made what is now the dry centre a grassy place with lakes and water courses alive with birds and fish. Probably twice in the last 20,000 years or so dry conditions took over to drive back the vegetation and force radical revisions of lifestyle.

Maori society evolved rapidly in New Zealand, the last previously unsettled land on earth. In the classic phase of Maori culture, from about the sixteenth century until wide-scale European settlement in the mid-nineteenth century, Maori lived mainly in family groupings in fortified villages with associated gardens; the warrior spirit was strong and young men received specialised instruction in the arts of warfare. In the absence of the written word, the oral tradition prevailed and great store was set by the ability to recite genealogy and a facility in the arts of poetry and song. With some regional and tribal variations, the same language was spoken throughout the country and never evolved far from the common language of Polynesia. Identification centred on the iwi, the people of a particular tribe recognising common ancestry; iwi (of which there were about forty) gave allegiance and authority to arikinui, a paramount chief or chiefs. The tribes had deep affinities with place and territory. Tribal warfare was endemic and internal migration, enforced by the victors, not uncommon. Primary loyalties were to the family communities, or whanau, within the tribes. There were seasonal routines for the maintenance of their food gardens, for hunting, fishing and war; by way of ritual public debate on marae, tribal meeting places, the tribes developed formalised dispute settlement procedures. Nevertheless, with a well-developed sense of mana, personal or tribal dignity, insults were long remembered and a cause of war.

The nomadic lifestyle of the Australian Aborigine could hardly have been more different. Speaking approximately 260 distinct, but inter-related, languages and divided into some 500 tribes, each with recognised territorial affiliations but on the move for much of the year, the indigenous Australians developed deep relationships with the natural and supernatural worlds. Dependent as they were on sparse water supplies and animal and vegetable food stocks from the wild, the paths taken by the mythological heroes of the group were of determining importance in establishing the itinerary of their year. They incorporated other species and water into their own moral and social order, developing a ritual relationship with the forces of nature. Aborigines see their place in the world as defined by elusive notions of a 'Dreamtime' – when the land was formed, various species were created and human life and culture established. All things are interdependent, so that kinship extends outwards from family and tribe into the natural and supernatural worlds. Aborigines do not journey through life alone, but in mutually sustaining company with the inhabitants of the 'eternal Dreamtime'. Infusing a vast and seemingly empty landscape with these heroic ancestors gave continuity and meaning to the cycles of life.

The European Upheaval

The global interconnectedness of our times was ushered in by the development of the long-distance sailing vessel some 600 years ago. With the Renaissance, European thought was liberated from the constraints of narrowly interpreted doctrine; scientific enquiry and technological progress were opened up. These movements, coupled with restless political ambitions and social pressures in Europe, set the clock for the inevitable ending of the geographical and human isolation of New Zealand and Australia, three and four centuries later. Complex native societies – formed in intimate association with local deities, grounded in the hills and rivers and sacred places of the two separate southern lands for hundreds and thousands of years and woven together by separately evolved myths and notions of history – were brusquely cast into the wider river of humanity. New political ideas, religious beliefs, the notion of nationalism itself, would almost flood out what had gone before. Nothing would ever be the same again, in either place.

For centuries European philosophers speculated about a great South Land in the lower reaches of the Pacific; there must be, it was reckoned, a geographical counterweight to the land masses of the Northern Hemisphere. The Polynesians, the true pioneers of navigation in the Pacific, could have told them it was nonsense. The first Europeans to venture into the great ocean were too tentative and sailed too far to the north to pierce the fog of speculation. It was very late in the human story before the truth was out. Northern Australia may have been sighted by Portuguese and Spanish navigators early in the seventeenth century; the Dutch, sailing from Batavia (present-day Djakarta), were the first to anchor the philosophers' speculations in reality. Their tracings of parts of the western and southerly coastlines revealed a barren land, which they called New Holland. In 1642 the merchants in Batavia despatched Abel Tasman, with sailing instructions that were strong on avarice, if weak on geographical logic, and that signalled their disappointment with what they had found so far:

> For all which reasons we, the Council of India ... have determined no longer to postpone the long contemplated discovery of the unknown Southland. [Because there were] found many rich mines of precious and other metals, and other treasures [in northern countries in similar latitudes], there must be similar fertile and rich regions situated south of the equator ... so that it may be confidently expected that the expense and trouble that must be bestowed in the eventual discovery of so large a portion of the world will be rewarded with certain fruits of material profit and immortal fame.[5]

Tasman landed on what he called Van Diemen's Land, later renamed Tasmania, and was disappointed by what he found: an inhospitable mountainous place, inhabited by threatening and very black people. He then sailed eastwards, across what we now know as the Tasman Sea, to fall in with the west coast of what he described as a 'large land uplifted high'. Again the reality did not fit the dream. In the course of a tentative run along the west coast of the two islands of New Zealand, four of Tasman's crewmen died after a ship's boat was intercepted by Maori war canoes. He sailed away. Believing he had discovered the west coast of the fabled 'South Land', he applied the same name that his compatriot Jacob Le Maire had bestowed on the land lying to the west of the channel at the southern tip of South America: Stadten Land. On his return, the Council of India called it Nieuw Zeeland, after the Dutch province. New Zealand, far from being the edge of the great southern continent, was an island chain. A 'new sea-land' indeed.

During his three world-changing expeditions to the Pacific, James Cook, the great eighteenth-century English navigator, visited Australia once, making the first recorded transit along the east coast. Not only was he the first European to circumnavigate New Zealand (1769–70), but he refitted his ships there four times prior to launching out again on new phases of his explorations, which finally revealed the daunting emptiness of the Pacific. According to the American historian Daniel Boorstin, Cook was 'the world's greatest negative explorer', the thesis being that discovery is as much about putting speculation and dreams to rest as about finding new worlds to conquer.[6] Thanks to James Cook, philosophical speculation about geographical symmetry and covetous dreams of wealth and empire gave way to the awkward reality of two very isolated – and seemingly unwealthy – countries: the one large, brown and apparently not very productive, the other so much smaller, mountainous and complicated by the presence of a resolute and industrious people. The rest of the vast area was ocean, for 6,500 kilometres on either side. The New Zealand poet Allen Curnow makes the point that what emerged was not what was expected:

Still as the collier steered/ No continent appeared;
It was something different, something/ Nobody counted on.[7]

If history – and nationalism – is what lies in the minds of men and women about their past and their struggles for place and identity, it had been going on for a long time in the two neighbouring lands of the South Pacific before the Europeans arrived. The European incomers had to deal with the awkward reality that they must usurp possession from those who were there before them. Ancient lifestyles and formidable cultures slipped away in the face of more potent technology. Yet for all the fateful damage inflicted by European diseases and European weapons, something new would be born. Diverse local societies and cultures were not buried and lost. Much survived; the sense of separate native cultural identities has remained strong in both countries – if demonstrably different from past forms. The two hitherto isolated races on either side of the Tasman Sea were brought into contact with one another, and with the world.

Strange New World

In January 1788, eleven British ships carrying 1,030 people, of whom 548 men and 188 women were convicts, entered a beautiful harbour in a southern land. A major expedition had been mounted and despatched safely across the world, not in pursuit of dreams of empire and glory but in response to a political hue and cry about prison overcrowding. There was no serious planning, no time for reconnaissance, no prior preparation of the site; these first settlers were simply required to make do in a land that was weirdly different from the place of their birth and upbringing. They would hardly even have known where they were; the shape of the continent, called New Holland, would not be mapped for another fifteen years; the name, Australia, was not officially adopted until 1817.[8] At the end of a tenuous supply line stretching halfway round the world, the convict settlement was soon starving, in what would become a land of plenty. Tools were inadequate, the land difficult to work and their few farm animals began to disappear – wandering off into the bush or poached by convicts or Aborigine alike.

By contrast, New Zealand was known to have a temperate climate and fertile soil. Even further away from Britain and more isolated than New South Wales, the great gardens maintained by the Maori made it obvious that a convict community there could soon have been self-sufficient. Cook and Joseph Banks, the scientist on Cook's first voyage to the Pacific, had reported extensively on New Zealand. Yet the convicts were sent to Botany Bay in New South Wales – where Cook's party had spent a mere eight days, at what was by chance a favourable time of the year when the land looked more productive than was actually the case. Cook had not been impressed by Australia.

> The land [he wrote] naturly produces hardly anything fit for man to eat and the Natives know nothing of Cultivation … the country itself so far as we know doth not produce any one thing that can become an article in trade to invite Europeans to fix a settlement upon.[9]

At the time, Banks thought Botany Bay 'barren … in a very high degree'. Ten years later, in 1779, Banks – by then a great man of the new scientific age driven along by British industrial innovation – was called before a special committee of the House of Commons, convened to recommend a site for a new penal colony, needed after the American Revolution put an end to disposal of convicts in the Carolinas and Virginia. His recommendation that the convicts be sent to 'Botany Bay, on the coast of New Holland, in the Indian Ocean' had to stand, uncorroborated since Cook had, unbeknown to the committee, been killed that year in Hawaii. Banks's testimony skated past previous doubts about the place, expressed both by himself and Cook, with qualifying phrases:

> the proportion of rich Soil was small in Comparison to the barren, but sufficient to support a very large number of people … [More pointedly, he] apprehended there

would be little Probability of any Opposition from the Natives, as, during his Stay
there, he saw very few [and these] were naked, treacherous and armed with Lances,
but extremely cowardly.

Cook, more charitably, had reported of the Aborigine, 'I do not look upon them
as a Warlike People, on the Contrary I think them a timorous and inoffensive
race, in no ways inclinable to cruelty.'

The fierce reputation of the Maori spared New Zealand the joys of convict
settlement. From the beginning, the country and its people were seen to be
different. Cook had felt threatened by the Maori and used his weapons in
response. In three separate incidents at what is now Gisborne, during the first
weekend of the *Endeavour*'s presence on the New Zealand coast, four or five
tribespeople were killed. Cook would soon see that the Europeans could maintain
their position in the new country only 'by the Superiority of our firearms ... in
what other light can they ... look on us but as invaders of their country.' In the
years following Cook's first visit to New Zealand, Maori fearsomeness even
brought on a burst of philosophical revisionism. Jean Jacques Rousseau had
conjured up the notion of the 'Noble Savage' out of the romantic fancies brought
back by the first European voyagers to reach the exotic island of Tahiti: innocent
of the pressures and lusts of so-called civilisation, native peoples would redeem
humanity with their uncomplicated character and artless integrity. After the
French explorer Marion Du Fresne was massacred with some twenty of his men
at the Bay of Islands in 1772, his second-in-command, Julien Crozet, wrote a
vehement denunciation of such unworldly intellectualism. 'Is it possible,'
Rousseau is said to have murmured, 'that the good children of nature can really
be so wicked?'[10] The earthy truth that peoples of different cultures speak to
each other across huge gulfs of understanding does not seem previously to have
dawned on the great philosopher; wickedness was not in it. But the disposition
to leave New Zealand alone would have been reinforced in 1774 when the
Adventure, one of the ships on Cook's second voyage to the Pacific, returned to
England to report that ten of the ship's crew had been killed and eaten by Maori
in Queen Charlotte Sound.

New Zealand was nevertheless seen as a potential source of strategic raw
materials for the Royal Navy. Banks had observed that the Maori made their
fine mats and other clothing, their enormous fishing nets and the sails of their
larger canoes from the New Zealand flax. Persuading himself that 'so useful a
plant would doubtless be a great acquisition in England', he sponsored the idea
that similar flax products could be turned out at the new convict settlement. The
operational plan for the 1788 voyage of the 'First Fleet' to Australia accordingly
noted, almost as an afterthought, 'that considerable advantage will arise from
the cultivation of the New Zealand hemp or flax-plant ... the supply of which
would be of great consequence to us as a naval power' since experts believed
that 'canvas made of it would be superior in strength and beauty to any canvas

made of European material'; likewise a 25 centimetre rope from the flax would be 'superior in strength' to one of 45 centimetres made of Baltic hemp.[11] One of the few inland expeditions that Cook had made in either New Zealand or Australia, was a trip of 20 or so kilometres up the Waihou River, at the head of what he named the Firth of Thames in New Zealand. Banks noted the concentration of kahikatea trees, growing alongside the river, 'the streightest, the cleanest and what I may say the largest I have ever seen'. Thus the British plan for the proposed convict settlement also observed:

> It may also be proper to attend to the possibility of procuring from New Zealand any quantity of masts and ship timbers for the use of our fleets in India, as the distance between the two countrys is not greater than between Great Britain and America. It grows close to the water's edge, is of size and quality superior to any hitherto known, and may be obtained without difficulty.

Lord Sydney, the Secretary of State for Home Affairs, was not being serious. His plan for the convict settlement allocated neither military resources to extend British dominion to New Zealand, nor supply ships to carry the timber, nor even the expertise needed to dress and prepare flax. This was a penny-pinching enterprise, totally inconsistent with the pursuit of military, or strategic, supply objectives. Only two ships of the First Fleet were naval vessels; the other nine were chartered merchant ships, which had to return as soon as the settlement was established. The infant community was provided with a military establishment of only two companies of marines (about 106 men) 'not only for the protection of the settlement, if requisite, against the natives, but for the preservation of good order'. As Robert Hughes has put it, 'In London's view, Australia was [to be] a land-based hulk, the size of a continent'.[12] William Pitt the Younger, the British Prime Minister, never thought of it as anything else. Arthur Phillip, the first Governor, presumably out to curry favour with his minister, named one of the most splendid harbours in the world after the Home Secretary responsible for penal policy. J. R. Seeley, a nineteenth-century historian, famously observed that 'We [the British] seem to have conquered and peopled half the world in a fit of absence of mind.' In the Antipodes, the fit was more like a deep-seated dementia. New Zealand seems to have excited the interest of Governor Phillip only as a suitable place to send murderers or sodomites: 'For either of these crimes I would wish to confine the criminal until an opportunity offered of delivering him to the natives of New Zealand, and let them eat him. The dread of this will operate much stronger than the fear of death.' The first white man to hold office in Australia set the tone for succeeding generations of Australians in un-neighbourly thoughts about New Zealand!

Norfolk Island, two weeks' sail from Sydney and 800 kilometres north-east of the northern tip of New Zealand, a brooding place bound by cliffs and reefs, had also been reported by Cook as a source of the New Zealand flax and tall pine trees seemingly suited for ships' spars. Within a couple of months of arrival in 1788, concerned that the French explorer La Perouse might make a prior claim to the island, Governor Phillip despatched Lieutenant Philip King and twenty-one others to take possession. By putting convicts to work making canvas for the Royal Navy from the flax, Phillip thought that the penal colony would begin to pay its way in the world. Two years later, in 1790, when starvation threatened the main settlement in Sydney, Phillip sent a third of the people there to Norfolk Island. The Norfolk Island pine proved to be too soft and resinous for naval purposes: if he were to establish a flax industry, he needed expertise.

Thus, the first official interaction took place between Australians and New Zealanders – a hijacking. In 1793, two Maori were seized by the Royal Navy off the east coast of the far north of New Zealand and taken to Norfolk Island, to teach the convicts there the art of flax dressing. This historic encounter was a commercial flop. The two men, chiefs, were greatly insulted by the manner of their removal and by the very idea that they should know about flax dressing, which was women's work. But the New World opened for them. Lieutenant King was courtesy itself; he gave his guests the run of his cruel domain, and saw to it that they would be impressed by the advantages of commerce between Sydney and the Bay of Islands. They, in turn, told him of their world: Tuki Tahua drew a remarkable and moving map of the two islands of New Zealand, replete with spiritual significance. When he and Ngahuruhuru were returned home after six months or so, they were equipped with artefacts of the industrial age, iron tools and the techniques of European agriculture. These goods, and their travellers' tales, excited the imagination of other Bay of Islands chiefs, who soon grasped the commercial opportunities of the new era and the need to deal with the power established across the Tasman.[13] Younger Maori took ship, more or less voluntarily, as crew on trading vessels. The hitherto isolated New Zealanders, the tangata whenua or people of the land, travelled out to make contact with other peoples and other places. Sydney was their first port of call; it became Poihakena, as close as the Maori tongue could get to Port Jackson.

chapter three

Foundations

Bands are playing, flags flying and the Red Cross of England floats supremely over the rest … Emigrants in their best are off to build a new Albion at the world's end.

– London Morning Chronicle, *reporting the departure of the first New Zealand Company ships from Gravesend, 16 September 1839*

N o high-mindedness, no pilgrim ships out to establish new kingdoms of God, attended the first wave of Europeans into Australia and New Zealand. The two places were colonised in very curious and distinctive fashions, each in its own way and to a different rhythm. From the first, both were simple off-shoots of Britain to which transplanted British people came in markedly idiosyncratic style. They were dedicated not to the establishment of new freedoms, or the creation of new nations, so much as to the extension of the old realm. The modern history of Australia opened on 26 January 1788, when the First Fleet discharged its passengers at Sydney Cove. New Zealand had no such inaugural moment: 6 February 1840, when the British crown concluded the Treaty of Waitangi with Maori chiefs at the Bay of Islands in the north of the North Island, is usually regarded as New Zealand's inauguration day. But it wasn't. Europe had broken in on the Maori world decades earlier as commerce, sprouting in the bizarre colony of New South Wales, took root across the Tasman and escapees from an evil penal system found sanctuary. The stage was then set for settler government and for the tidal wave of new immigrants which then transformed both countries – and in the process shaped separate and distinctive societies.

At the End of the World[1]

The idiosyncrasies of the two new countries was beyond all previous European experience. From the first, the character and fierce reputation of the Maori would shape perceptions of New Zealand. To this day, a shop in St Martin's Lane in London carries the sign, 'We buy … New Zealand and all savage countries curios etc.' Nevertheless, James Cook, a severely practical man who literally put the land on the world's map, had been able to see beyond the fascination with the exotic to realise that the climate and terrain of New Zealand were admirably suited to settlement. 'In short was this Country settled by an Industrus people they would very soon be supply'd not only with the necessarys, but many of the luxuries of life.'[2] By contrast, Australia was enigmatic and challenging. 'Here nature is reversed,' wrote Major Ross, an officer with the First Fleet. The earliest convict settlers almost starved because of their inability to make the hard earth productive. Even the indigenous animals were eccentric and strange. The sense that things were not as they seemed struck Lieutenant Southwell, another officer of the First Fleet:

> ... nothing can be conceived more picturesque than the app'c of the country while running up this extra[ordinary] harbour. The land on all sides is high, and covered with an exuber'n of trees; towards the water, craggy rocks and vast declivity are everywhere to be seen ... [and] the labyrinth of inchanting glens that so abound in this fascinating scenery. Tis greatly to be wished these appearances were not so delusive as in reality they are.[3]

It took years to break the spell of strangeness, desolation and the sense of confinement. As the Australian novelist Thomas Keneally puts it, 'The rule Australia imposed on everyone from the start was that you had to take it on its own terms, and they were very individual terms.'[4]

In true New World style, a handful of commercial opportunists – ex-convicts, soldiers, wandering traders – came up out of the struggling penal settlement of Sydney Town to kick-start an Australian economy and try their trading luck with the British colonies in India and around the Pacific. By 1800 they had put Sydney on the mercantile map of the world, a primitive entrepôt for local ventures in selling sandlewood from Fiji, sealskins from Bass Strait and smoked sea cucumbers from north Australia. Sydney soon became a regular port of call for American and British whaling and sealing ships and the sleek New England vessels involved in the famous China trade. On the other side of the Tasman Sea, Maori life went on much as before. The New World only began to press in gradually as ships, from America and Britain and later Australia, began to arrive at the Bay of Islands. The lonely whaling ships, which often stayed at sea for years, their sails grimy from boiling blubber, came as much for rest as for trade. They were supplied with water and wood for their fires, and sex for the sailors; the Maori discovered alcohol, flour, iron tools and commerce with the wide world, and would be changed forever. New Zealand – ever since dependent on exports – became a trading nation; the oldest professional activity in the world may well have been the start of it. But, absent an administration, a justice system or an economic structure, New Zealand commerce could be only of the most rudimentary, barter kind.

In Sydney, meanwhile, a complex, curious and dynamic European society was developing. Most of the new arrivals were – often literally – chained to the place. Commitment to the new country and a sense of national identity would hardly have sprung into being lightly. The convicts were confined to the immediate area around Sydney and the subordinate penal colonies in Van Diemen's Land, Norfolk Island and Brisbane. Back in England, the reputation of what was popularly known for a long time as 'Botany Bay' was not one to attract free settlers. No more than a hundred willing immigrants came in the first twenty years. Yet, if nothing else, transportation is a forced migration scheme. More white people – 1,030 – arrived on the First Fleet in 1788 than would be living in all New Zealand forty years later. Governor Macquarie, who reached Australia in 1809, found the New South Wales colony to be 'barely emerging from juvenile imbecility'[5]; yet it was already an economic powerhouse compared with New Zealand, where the handful of Europeans would have seen themselves as birds of passage, hoping to secure advantage from rudimentary trading enterprises before moving on or returning home. Kororareka (Russell) would become an infamous, iniquitous port of call at the Bay of Islands in the north of New Zealand in the 1820s and 1830s, but even then it was essentially still a Maori place.

Within days of their arrival at Sydney Cove, convicts were trying to escape their cage. The French commander, La Perouse, who arrived in the adjacent Botany Bay a few days after the First Fleet, sent back runaways who pleaded to be allowed aboard his ships. They were flogged, but they were in luck, for La Perouse's two ships were later wrecked on a reef in the New Hebrides; there were no survivors.[6] Over the years, benighted souls struck out northwards from Sydney, hoping to walk to China. A better way to go was to take ship, by stowing away or striking a deal with the crew; despite stringent controls, it happened so regularly as to suggest an organised racket. Some 10 per cent of the 30,000 prisoners sent to Sydney, Hobart or Norfolk Island up until 1820 slipped away from their gaolers in some way or another. The Bay of Islands became, according to Robert Hughes, 'a veritable rookery of absconders' from New South Wales. Recent enthusiasm for research into family has turned up a few surprises for New Zealanders finding that respected hard-working forebears were graduates of 'the system'.

New Zealand was soon drawn into the Australian sphere of influence in other ways. Sealing was the first major Australian enterprise. In 1803 operations were extended to Dusky Sound, on the west coast of New Zealand's South Island. An American captain then reported in Sydney that there was another likely killing ground, in what is now called Foveaux Strait off the southern South Island. Joseph Foveaux – a corrupt monster, a military man with a truly vicious record when he was in charge of the Norfolk Island penal settlement[7] – was responsible, as Lieutenant-Governor of New South Wales, for authorising the first official extension of the sphere of interest of New South Wales merchants to an area of New Zealand. His reward was to get his name on the map – among other things. For ten years, Australian sealing gangs worked Foveaux Strait; when the slaughter there was complete, attention was switched further south to inhospitable Campbell Island, which had been discovered in 1810 by a Sydney ship and named after Robert Campbell, one of the most successful of early

Sydney merchants. The white man came to New Zealand tentatively, and with justified caution. A tough trans-Tasman breed (called 'Tasmen' by the New Zealand historian James Belich[8]) of runaway convicts, American and British seamen, Maori adventurers, and other vagrants and scallywags came into existence. They were, in more ways than one, the true founding fathers of modern New Zealand. They manned the ships, cut down the mighty kauri trees, were left behind on barren shores to hunt the seals and whales, established the fragile trading outposts among the Maori tribes and took up with Maori women. Thus was the meeting of East and West consummated on the farthest shores of the known world.

Inspired no doubt by the observations of James Cook on the suitability of New Zealand timber for masts and spars, Sydney merchants also sent their agents to quiet bays around the northern North Island coasts to secure anchorage rights and the labour to extract kauri logs from the local chiefs. A New Zealand timber wharf was opened at Sydney in 1828 and a fluctuating trade worth many thousands of pounds a year was maintained during the 1830s. Shore whaling – the pursuit of the migratory southern right whale in longboats from coastal stations – became another trans-Tasman commercial connection. Australian whaling firms established a number of shore stations along New Zealand's east coast, especially in the southern South Island in the 1820s. Ancillary trading outposts adjacent to the whaling stations were opened for commerce with local Maori.

Joseph Banks's vision of a flax trade finally came to fruition as Maori were offered barter in exchange for dressed fibre, for spinning into rope. Banks had mused about the potential of the fibre to make sails for warships; in the event, flax provided the trigger for devastating warfare in New Zealand. 'By 1820 the Bay of Islands Maori had decided that "the great god of the white man" was the pu, the gun. He was the first new god to make converts. By about 1815 they were carried away with desire for guns.'[9] When they got them, the northern tribes raided southwards to settle old tribal scores, setting off a train of destabilisation and unrest: thousands died as the new way of making war was put to unequal test against the old. Naturally, the victims wished to convert to pu in their turn. Demand for weapons became all-consuming. Missionaries, dependent on trade with the Maori for their food, found that tribespeople would accept only one currency: guns. They, too, were then drawn into the arms game. Coastal tribes exploited their own trading advantages by establishing extensive flax production arrangements and outlets so that they could buy their own guns, which the Sydney traders were happy to supply. The market was brisk – in both directions. At its peak in 1831, the flax trade was valued at £26,000. By then, the number of guns which could be absorbed had reached saturation point and that particular trade began disappearing. The spasm of inter-tribal violence passed. Maori had again demonstrated their avidity for commerce, but at tragic cost.

In the end, the evangelical takeover was even more portentous. Samuel Marsden – chaplain, magistrate and successful sheep-farmer in New South Wales – opened a new chapter in the overlapping histories of Australia and New Zealand when he preached the gospel at the Bay of Islands at Christmas 1814, to an orderly crowd of curious Maori. Marsden was the earliest trans-Tasman Pecksniff. The 'bringer of light' into the 'heathen darkness' of New Zealand had meted out sadistic punishments from the magistrate's bench in New South Wales. Dispensing large sums of his own money on schooling and evangelising Maori, he seemed to have been indifferent to the lot of convict and Aborigine alike at home. At the Bay of Islands, he established an exiguous band of missionaries, dispatched from London by the Anglican ('low-church') Church Missionary Society. He bought land to establish model farms and basic enterprises and did his best to help patch up quarrels among the chiefs. He was sympathetic to Maori, offering them education and instruction in agriculture at his farm at Parramatta, near Sydney. He also had to deal with missionaries caught up in the gun trade and in their own often-spectacular internal jealousies, and their lapses from the paths of moral righteousness, with Maori women.

The British government was almost embarrassingly uninterested. In 1817 New Zealand was cited in British criminal justice legislation as among 'places not within His Majesty's dominions', and therefore beyond the reach of British courts. It made for administrative tidiness to give the governors of New South Wales a watching brief insofar as concerned New Zealand. No resources were provided, nor policy formulated. New Zealand was not a major preoccupation of the merchants – or the administration – in New South Wales. Nevertheless, the economic nexus centred on Sydney provided the framework for an Australian web of mercantile interest that would, in turn, spark the creation of modern New Zealand. Australian traders dominated New Zealand commerce, but had no monopoly: of eighty-nine vessels which called at the Bay of Islands in 1833, thirty-nine were Australian colonial traders or whalers and two were colonial government brigs; the rest were British or American.[10] Even in the 1830s – good years for the timber and flax trades – imports from New Zealand ranked no higher than third in order of importance in New South Wales, well below goods from Britain. They also usually trailed the products of the South Pacific fisheries (ocean whaling) and imports from 'China', British India and Mauritius.[11] Seal and whale products, much of them derived from New Zealand, were nevertheless the mainstay of Australian exports – ahead of wool – through until 1835.[12] There was overlap between the developing communities on either side of the Tasman but the push all came from New South Wales. New Zealand was no more than an extension of the Australian frontier, on the receiving end of irresistible forces for change: the missionaries, traders, gun merchants and adventurers of the New World fanning out from Sydney. In the Shakespearean sense, the 'onlie begetter' of modern New Zealand was Australia.

Yet the pattern was different from the first. In its first half-century, New South Wales life was determined by the systems prescribed to govern crime and punishment, and relationships between convicts, their descendants and the various social grades of 'others'. The willing settlers, administrators and, above all, the military, gained mighty pretensions to superiority over their fellows tainted with the 'convict stain'. Soon prisoners were being 'emancipated' for good conduct – freed, but not yet able to return to Britain; others were awarded a 'ticket-of-leave', given permission to work for themselves; still others were hired out to work in factories or farms or as domestic servants. Land grants, given to military officers and administrators and even to free settlers, were supplemented by the supply of a convict workforce. As the 'emancipists' took their places in the community, they married and raised a generation who were themselves unable to escape the mark of convictism – indeed, tended to embrace it actively in contempt for the governing classes. These were the 'currency lads and lasses', native-born and in a curious, cockney-slang kind of way identified with disputes over the establishment of a 'native' currency for the colony. They were Sydney's 'larrikins', free-wheeling, disrespectful and edgy. Many were of Irish descent, doubly alienated from the respectable world of the 'exclusives' – the non-convict element in a strange society. Students of Australian life and culture associate the 'currency' strand with the origins of a characteristic 'Aussie' style.[13]

Because the 'currency/emancipist' grouping constituted about 60 per cent of the population of New South Wales, at least through into the middle years of the nineteenth century, a lively sense of disaffection persisted. By 1851, there were 76,530 'free' settlers and only 2,693 (1.5 per cent) convicts; yet convict descendants and emancipists constituted 58.5% of a total of 187,243. In 1828, just under one in three of the population of New South Wales was Catholic, a reflection of the high proportion of Irish transported to Australia. Contrary to received wisdom, they were guilty, for the most part, of no more than the thievishness and larceny of the suffering poor rather than political disobedience. A relatively high proportion of Roman Catholics compared with Protestant denominations would be built in to Australian society. The Irish dimension from which it was derived would lend further bite to political life and add another colour of difference with New Zealand – and indeed with 'Home' (the British Isles).

A community of free spirits this was not. Rather than drawing together in exile, the landed gentry of New South Wales established their very own caste system. Since prior possession by Aboriginal tribes was not recognised, the squatters had either taken up land grants from the authorities or simply occupied land for their own purposes. It was an easy road to power and influence. At the top of the heap were the 'pure merinos', free landed settlers with no 'convict stain'. 'Exclusives' and 'pure merinos' joined in pursuing dreams of a privileged, plantation society. In a non-representative political community, dominated by an appointed governor, such a combination of interests could, for a time, hold effective power – keeping the rising commercial class, dominated by the 'currency/emancipist' element, at arms' length. Their loyalties were to 'England, home and beauty', and they desired nothing more than to see Australia emerge as a model appendage of the British crown. The opposite, and more boisterous, political current was borne along by reverse sentiment – held by the 'emancipists' and their ilk – to do with repudiation of the past and the establishment of a distinctive Australian identity. Out of this clash of interests between classes, between town and country, and landed and commercial interests, would spring much of the vibrancy of Australian political life. It was a rowdy disconnect that would not be matched across the Tasman.

First Stirrings of Nationalism

The onset of Australian nationalism is linked with the name of William Charles Wentworth. English-educated but Australian-born, Wentworth was the son of a convict woman and a minor sprig of the English aristocracy, who had opted to serve as a prison doctor in New South Wales in order to escape being sent there as a convict for debt. The father made money in Australia and sent his son to Cambridge University, where William developed expansive ambitions. He gained second prize in the Chancellor's Medal poetry competition for an offering entitled 'Australasia', in which it seemed that New Zealand was to share in his vision of a new Antipodean order: 'And Australasia float, with flag unfurl'd, A new Britannia in another world.' Wentworth launched the first non-official newspaper in New South Wales and entered the political lists as an advocate for representative institutions. He was a mixture of patrician and street radical, an intellectual with the common touch, wanting to bring the 'emancipists' into the political life of the colony while living in the grand manner as a sheep baron. The Australian Patriotic Association, which Wentworth helped found in 1835, became a focus for the advancement of 'Australia', the 'New Britain of the South'. Wentworth's undergraduate notions of 'Australasia' later developed into an idea that New Zealand would serve as a handy extension of Australian squatter-dom. As Robert Hughes describes it,[14] 'he and some associates gulled seven Maori chiefs into selling them about one third (most of the South Island) of New Zealand – the largest land deal in history'. The British government, exasperated by the pretensions to power and influence of Australian squatters, stopped the deal. Ever afterwards, Wentworth was said to describe New Zealanders as his defaulting tenants.

In New Zealand, the sun of the British Empire had hardly even risen. There, beyond the reach of British administration, it was possible to live the life of the outcast in scattered sealing camps or whaling stations, at timber mills or trading posts set up alongside Maori tribes. In this society, as James Belich has put it,[15] 'The missionaries were fewest but they had the busiest pens, and they divided this wave of Europeans into two; themselves, the agents of virtue; and almost everyone else, the agents of vice, who very often came from Australia.' The Europeans, however were merely floating on the surface of a Maori world. It was by no means Arcadia. But it was delicately in tune with the fact of continuing Maori dominance and proved remarkably cohesive in the face of disturbing and disruptive influences from outside. Maori were attracted to the material things available from the Europeans, disporting themselves in bizarre cast-off clothing and keen to acquire trading goods, especially tools. Their society was structured, secular and flexible. The chiefs had an eye for symbolism. In 1833, two years before William Wentworth founded his Australian Patriotic Association, the Bay of Island chiefs spent a pleasant afternoon while the British agent put forward various designs for the first New Zealand flag. Had it survived, their choice – a red cross on a white ground with a blue field and red cross plus stars in the upper left quadrant – would have headed off much complaint in our times about having a national flag with the Union Jack stitched into one corner. It was recognised by the British Admiralty and the administration in New South Wales as the first New Zealand flag – and was flown on Maori as well as European-owned ships trading with Australia.

New Zealand was thus first represented to the outside world thanks to the Maori – the first New Zealand nationalists – to whom the concept of mana, implicit in a flag, would have been important. A 'Confederation of Chiefs and Tribes of New Zealand' was proclaimed in 1835, when thirty-five northern chiefs signed a declaration of independence at the Bay of Islands, at the instigation of the same British agent. Fifty-four signatures were eventually obtained for this document, including those of two important chiefs from elsewhere in the North Island. This, too, was a first: a definitive statement of a New Zealand national interest. The independent chieftainship of Maori was asserted, along with the sovereign collective authority of the chiefs meeting in assembly once a year. However, it was mostly cockalorum on the part of a British representative denied the usual perquisites of power and needing a treaty to wave in the face of a possible French pretender to authority in New Zealand. If the chiefs had seriously intended to unite in pursuit of independence they would not have required British mediation nor would they, at one and the same time, have sought British protection and independence. Those who signed on were not representative of the country as a whole; the proposed congress never met. Nevertheless, from then on, there would be no escaping the need to define New Zealand in Maori as well as European (British) terms. European New Zealanders did not get around to establishing their own version of Wentworth's Australian Patriotic Association until the 1890s, when New Zealand-born Europeans formed New Zealand Natives Associations.

Unlike Maori, the Aborigine had no use for settled ways and could not understand that commitment in others; trade and acquisition of material things did not interest them. In 1815 Governor Macquarie encouraged a group of Aborigine to farm on an island in Sydney harbour, equipping them with huts and a boat: 'They lost the boat, ignored the huts and wandered off into the bush.'[16] Europeans could not come to terms with the elusive, spiritual basis of Aboriginal life and culture. Nomadic ways, without settled villages and agriculture, were interpreted as deficient, a mark of a low order of civilisation, rather than a subtle adaptation to a harsh environment. Some Aborigine at first welcomed the white intruders, as returning spirits of the dead. Few among the Europeans were as insightful or lyrical as James Cook:

> ... they may appear to some to be the most wretched people upon Earth, but in reality they are far more happier than we Europeans; being wholy unacquainted not only with the superfluous but the necessary Conveniences so much sought after in Europe, they are happy in not knowing the use of them. They live in a Tranquillity which is not disturbed by the Inequality of Condition: The Earth and sea of their own accord furnishes them with all things necessary for life ...[17]

Early administrators in New South Wales tried to follow instructions and treat the native inhabitants well. But their charges knew no such charity. The convict outcasts, as Robert Hughes points out, 'desperately needed to believe in a class inferior to themselves. The Aborigines answered that need. Australian racism began with the convicts, although it did not stay confined to them for long; it was the first Australian trait to percolate upward from the lower class.'[18] Presumptions of racial superiority were of course unshakeable. The Maori were thought redeemable; the Aborigine beneath consideration. In 1827 the English artist Augustus Earle, who travelled among and painted the native peoples of both New Zealand and Australia, could find only the language of unadulterated racism to describe the Aborigine: they 'seem of the lowest grade – the last link in the great chain of existence which unites man with monkey'. By contrast, having obviously drunk deep of 'noble savage' theory about the Polynesians, Earle found the Maori to be 'cast in beauty's perfect mould; the children are so fine each might serve as a model for a statue of the Infant Hercules: nothing can exceed the graceful and athletic forms of the men, or the rounded limbs of their young women.'[19] Earle could anticipate 'the glorious prospect of beholding a clever, brave, and I may add, noble race of men, like the New Zealanders, rescued from barbarism'. Across the Tasman no such prospects were held out for the Aborigine. The nomads reacted sharply against inroads into traditional territory and interference with long-used natural resources; their skill with the throwing spear was put to lethal use. Their reprisals were silent and bloody. In the hilly country of Tasmania and along the continent's eastern shoreline, the odds were for a time on the Aboriginal side; serious damage was done to intruders and their stock. As the frontiers of pastoral farming and settlement were pushed out into the dry, open, lightly forested land beyond the Great Dividing Range and northward into the

Queensland hinterland, however, there was nowhere to hide. No sweating lines of redcoats were marched out against them. When Aborigine resisted, settler cohorts simply rode them down: '... by the 1830s ... a hardening of attitudes to the Aborigines ... meant their virtual extermination in Van Diemen's Land (Tasmania) and their decimation along the eastern seaboard.'[20]

The Imperial Net Goes Fishing – for New Zealand

In 1831, in response to a proposal by Governor Darling, the jurisdiction of New South Wales was extended to New Zealand. The Governor was authorised to appoint a British resident at the Bay of Islands. James Busby took up this impossible charge in 1833. His job was to protect 'well-disposed settlers and traders', to prevent outrages by Europeans against Maori, and to apprehend escaped convicts.[21] It was a sleight-of-hand act which did not work. Busby was a busybody, but he was on his own. London refused to allocate a warship to back his authority; he had no treaty-making powers. He was derided by critics in London as a 'man-of-war without guns'. For pay and expenses, Busby had to look to the Government of New South Wales. The Governor's council, however, made 'parsimony its watchword'[22] in all matters to do with Busby's precarious mandate. For the first – but by no means the last – time, New Zealand affairs caused extreme irritation in Australia. In 1833, Wentworth savaged Busby as a placeman, 'soon to strut about in a gold-laced coat for the savages in New Zealand to gape at and perhaps the next day be turned into a roast meal for the savages to eat'.[23] (Wentworth's Australian nationalism was more than a little tinged with Australian racism.) Governor Bourke, Darling's successor, reported the Sydney press as 'openly hostile' to the appointment: 'That salary [£598.10s in 1839] ... is universally regarded as a prodigious grievance in New South Wales.' The merchants of Sydney were clearly able to put their profits from a not inconsiderable New Zealand trade in one pocket and their grumbles about taxes in the other. By 1839, the value of New Zealand exports to New South Wales of flax, timber, whale products, fish and farm produce was £71,707, while exports to New Zealand were valued at £95,173.

Australians could have afforded to be more generous to poor James Busby. Already in the 1830s they owed him more than they knew. He had studied viticulture in France and published a book on the subject in 1825. The next year he bought land for grape growing on the Hunter River, north of Sydney. In 1831–32, before going to New Zealand, he collected vine cuttings in France and Spain, which he subsequently distributed in New South Wales, South Australia and New Zealand. Although grape growing had been attempted in Australia almost from the time of the arrival of the First Fleet, a very successful wine industry developed largely thanks to Busby's efforts to produce varietal wines, especially in the Hunter Valley. In New Zealand, Busby's pioneering viticulture brought less immediate success. Again, he was first in the field, but conditions at the Bay of Islands, where he made his plantings and produced wine, were not the most suitable and the industry has developed elsewhere, with spectacular results, in recent years.

By the late 1830s, New Zealand affairs were raising the political temperature in London. A group of 'respectable settlers' in the Bay of Islands petitioned for legal protection; in an evangelical age, missionary interests, genuinely concerned about the fate of the Maori, had the ear of government ministers; a colonisation lobby – proposing to export surplus British population and social problems, and confer practical investment opportunities for British capital – was also influential. At the same time, Australian land speculation in New Zealand was becoming a matter of serious concern to Governor Darling in Sydney.[24] As the Australian pastoral industry fell on hard times in the 1830s,

> squatters and would-be squatters began to turn to New Zealand in search of land where they might prosper temporarily free from licence fees and variable taxes on their flocks. Almost every ship crossing the Tasman Sea brought land-hungry passengers from New South Wales.[25]

Nicely balancing liberal sentiment with pragmatic financial concerns, a Whig government accepted that it was time to 'do something'.

The instinct was to do as little as possible. The first half-hearted expedient was formally to extend the Commission of the Governor of New South Wales to include authority 'within that group of islands in the Pacific Ocean commonly called New Zealand'. The new colony of New Zealand thus 'began not as an independent possession of the Crown but as a lowly appendage of the more politically mature Colony of New South Wales.'[26] A lieutenant-governor, Captain William Hobson R.N., was appointed, subsidiary to the Governor in Sydney. Hobson moved quickly to conclude the Treaty of Waitangi with Maori chiefs at the Bay of Islands in February 1840. New Zealand was annexed in the name of the young Queen Victoria; the Treaty made it possible to cut the exiguous administrative ties with New South Wales and Australia, formally and forever. In 1841 the new imperial possession was established as a crown colony in its own right. New Zealand was set on a course of its own. In the imperial scheme of things, New Zealand would remain for a time part of a broad southern realm which overlapped, and in many ways coincided, with the spheres of interest of the Australian colonies. A complex of linkages with Australia – in maritime concerns, trade, shared security preoccupations, business and banking connections – would grow in importance and shift in focus down the years. But essentially – and to the regular, intense annoyance of both parties – since 1841, New Zealand and Australia have had to deal with each other as separate and independent national entities.

When the tide of settlement hit New Zealand, the first Europeans had hardly marked the place. Victorian values and presumptions about a British destiny to rule would be planted raw, without preliminaries. Whereas Australia retains a lingering feel of the eighteenth century, a touch of the restlessness and sense of destiny of the United States, New Zealand still carries the marks of the high days of the British Empire. The New Zealand colonists took on silly and wrong-headed pretensions to superiority over their Australian brethren from the convict legacy. Moreover, a broadly middle-class settler society in New Zealand could write as though on a clean page; conservative interest groups – centred on large landholdings – were not given the time to consolidate before a liberal reformist strain took over public life. It still exists. In New South Wales, Victoria and to a large extent Queensland, by contrast, rampant inheritances by way of class and privilege, radicalism and disaffection from the first period of Australian history would be in conflict well into the second half of the century and would make lasting impact on Australian life and character.

Goodbye To All That

By 1840, 115,000 convicts had been despatched to Australia. Although the system was officially ended in 1839, another batch was sent to New South Wales in 1846. Victoria was pleased to have 1700 or so switched its way for five years until 1849. Van Diemen's Land took even longer to rid itself of the narcotic economic justification for an evil system – the wish to have cheap labour; the last ship-load of convicts reached Hobart in 1853. As a mark of separation from the dark convict era, the island took the name Tasmania in 1855. That same year, convicts were sent to Norfolk Island for the last time. Meanwhile, an assertive squatter class in Western Australia had gone in the other direction and been pleased to embrace the convict system in 1850, holding to the practice until 1868.

The factionalism inherent in the system would not easily be expunged. The free immigrants were caught up in it. According to Manning Clark, 'To the alarm and disgust of the free the convict community gloried in their past and boasted of it. "Thank God I'm not a bloody immigrant", they cried. "Thank God I come out 'onorable".'[27] In opposition to the 'exclusives', the merchant community, with roots in the 'emancipist' strain, became deeply engaged in the struggle for representative political institutions. In the burgeoning cities, the 'currency/emancipist' influence, especially in the small trading and labouring sectors of society, would help set a turbulent tone. Many new immigrants were also influenced by the Chartist reform movement in England. A small-farming element would emerge from their ranks, at odds not only with the sheep barons but with the roving 'bushmen', the landless agricultural labourers of Australian legend who had close sympathies with the convict system. Russel Ward concludes that there is a great deal of evidence about this period to show that the whole of colonial society, including even the purest of 'pure merinos', was deeply affected by 'the system' ... certain distinctively Australian attitudes may have then been formed, and have become stabilized enough to persist through the more real 'swamping' of the felon strain by the tidal wave of immigrants which arrived during the subsequent decade and later.[28]

Among the skyscrapers in the centre of the modern metropolis of Sydney, little evidence now remains of the convict era. Where the convict transports discharged their unfortunate passengers, pampered tourists now descend from great white liners; across the head of the little cove in a wonderful harbour where it all began, an ugly elevated highway gets in the way of any thoughts about what it was like to be marooned here, a 'Prisoner of Mother England'. But at sequestered Port Arthur in Tasmania, and along the pounding shoreline of lonely Norfolk Island, in the clusters of roofless stone buildings (many rather grand), an almost palpable air of human misery hangs over otherwise pleasing places. What went before has not been swept away, but merely transformed: the convict 'stain' has become a badge of honour. What remains is intangible, an assertive, splendid manifestation of the human spirit in lifting above such beginnings.

People Experiments

Edward Gibbon Wakefield, an uncomfortable, charismatic ideologue, had a grand design for systematic colonisation. He had edited the works of Adam Smith, and turned a three-year term in Newgate prison (for abducting an under-age heiress) to advantage by writing *A Letter from Sydney* and other works advocating systematic colonisation based on the establishment of a 'sufficient price' for land. Wakefield was a conservative parading as a colonial reformer. As such, he put an idiosyncratic mark on both Australia and New Zealand. He believed that by making fixed plots of land available at predetermined prices, stable and structured immigrant communities would emerge, with the different levels in the new society being determined by what each settler family could afford to pay for its land. By selling land at a fixed price, the organisers of the new colony could offer free migration and vest government in the hands of free citizens, who would ensure free institutions and freedom of religion. These were ideas attractive to social reformers, political radicals and religious dissenters alike. Politicians were also receptive to the notion of shipping out the urban poor while finding a productive outlet for capital investment in the colonies.

In 1836, an area of unclaimed virgin land around the mouth of the Murray River in South Australia became the site for the first Wakefield experiment. Within five years, 12,000 assisted migrants had arrived, most with only the haziest ideas about what to do with their plots of land. Not surprisingly, and with an enthusiasm foreign to the detached Wakefield philosophy, they speculated instead of working the land for productive purposes. Prices rose and the colony's credit collapsed. Spirited men and women, with the hopes and dreams to carry them halfway round the world, were scarcely to be confined by pathetic attempts to recreate the English class system in a new country. The settlers soon broke out from a land-based scheme to establish themselves as they chose in South Australia and elsewhere. Those who wanted to farm moved beyond the established boundaries to squat on land which they took for their own; others built the towns and cities, as might have been expected.

When the Wakefield vision was applied on the other side of the Tasman, the authorities in London were more sceptical and were obliged by increasing public interest in the well-being of the Maori to be cautious about private settlement schemes. While the government procrastinated, trying to reconcile conflicting interests, the New Zealand Company, formed by the Wakefield group in 1837, launched a private pre-emptive strike by way of an expedition to find suitable sites for settlement before British authority was established. Their first settlers arrived in Wellington in 1840 and in Nelson in 1841. Dodgy, and in some cases downright dishonest, land purchase schemes were entered into with Maori. Unfortunate settlers found their allocated plots of land to be steep mountainside or soggy bush. A parallel settlement at New Plymouth, in the Taranaki district, proceeded on sadly mistaken assumptions: inter-tribal warfare had displaced local tribespeople, but they did not see their exile as permanent. Returning, they found themselves in bitter conflict over land with the equally desperate incoming settlers.

In the end, European hegemony in New Zealand would be built on the ashes of Wakefield's blithely capitalist notions about land – the most intensely spiritual element in the being of any indigenous people. Following the Treaty of Waitangi, the crown assumed all rights for the resumption of land from the Maori chiefs. Land for settlement by the incomers was obtained in huge lots by crown purchase from Maori. Various leasing arrangements were also entered into by the tribes. All transactions were given the cloak of legality through the newly established Maori Land Courts and formal registration arrangements. But the entire process by which Maori were finessed out of so much of New Zealand land was not pretty. Nothing that must be settled by war can ever be that – or in any way satisfactory. The best that can be said now is that things would have been a great deal worse if the early – and largely uncontrolled – land grabbing, which marked the onset of the expansion phase of European settlement in Australia, had been replicated in New Zealand. In retrospect, the Wakefield schemes in South Australia and New Zealand had the merit of putting a market valuation on land, which worked against large-scale buy-outs for derisory sums. Moreover, settlement schemes provided at least the semblance of a structure for the incomers; land titles were established and the basis for a rudimentary administration put in place. The interests of small-scale farmers could be provided for and government could proceed without having to contend with a politically influential squatter class. In both New Zealand and South Australia, this has left a legacy of reliance on government for securing the basics of society, which distinguishes the two places from the more free-wheeling character implanted from the beginning in New South Wales and Victoria. Wakefield, who came to live in New Zealand in 1853, had a hand in two more controlled colonisation experiments there: on behalf of the Free Church of Scotland in Otago in 1848 and the Church of England in Canterbury in 1850. Both succeeded in setting a distinct denominational and social tone to important parts of the country.

Give Us Your Huddled Masses

With mass immigration, the European population of New Zealand rose by 50,000 per cent in fifty years, from about a thousand in 1831 to approximately 500,000 in 1881.[29] By the 1850s, Europeans already outnumbered Maori: as the settlers poured ashore at Wellington, Te Wharepouri, a great chief of the Te Ati Awa, is said to have wept as he realised that the old ways were doomed. In Australia, the populations of New South Wales and Victoria increased by 103 and 520 per cent respectively in the twenty years from 1841 to 1861. The population of the country as a whole trebled in the decade to 1861 – from 405,356 to 1,145,585 – when the gold rushes began.[30] Much of it was 'follow-the-leader' emigration, from particular communities within the British Isles to particular places in the Antipodes. The famine of the 1840s and 1850s drove numerous Irish to migrate, especially to Australia. Gaelic became the preferred tongue in the expressly Scottish community established in Otago, New Zealand, but also in places in inland Victoria. Presbyterians from Northern Ireland and from counties Roscommon and Cork in the south, the descendants of the transplanted Scots of the seventeenth century, went in large numbers to New Zealand. Irish Catholics became concentrated in Victoria and New South Wales, and also Southland in New Zealand. The percentage of Catholics in Australia was as high as 30.4 per cent in 1851, slipping back to 20.7 per cent by 1947. The Cornish tended to identify with New Zealand, as did Shetland Islanders. Scottish migrants 'did well' in both countries and generally had a higher education level than their English counterparts. The numbers of declared Presbyterians in Australia remained steady at between 9 and 10 per cent from 1841 until after the Second World War. There were Europeans too: German Lutherans established farming communities in South Australia and small groups of Germans set up in the South Island of New Zealand. And the Chinese arrived, generally to work in the lonely gold diggings in both countries – and racial prejudice reared its ugly head

What was the cause of all this immigration? Why endure the long voyages and huge separations inherent in transferring to the other end of the world, when America was nearer? Technological changes and the impact of free trade were convulsing British life; at the same time, a new spirit of empire was enlarging horizons and giving new scope to the ambitious and the restless. America temporarily lost its attraction in the lead up to and during the Civil War. The British, at the forefront of the industrial revolution and confident in their military and political predominance in Europe, were swept up in a heady nationalism. Expansive dreams came easily; the idea of a 'Greater Britain' of white colonies over the seas, chimed nicely with notions of racial and British imperial supremacy. There would have seemed to be opportunities galore in an apparently ever-expanding universe. By the 1860s, New Zealand and the separate Australian colonies were in the market in Britain for both settlers and capital. They did more than launch a direct appeal to potential migrants; their propaganda shaped the British public's perceptions about their new imperial possessions. Australia and New Zealand, previously little known and less well understood, gained their positive place in the British mind thanks to well-organised public relations programmes for immigrants. New Zealand was pleased to promote itself as the 'white man's country', equable and green, another England – in contrast with parched, snake-ridden Australia. Australians could with justification tout opportunity – to get rich from gold or sheep or to acquire land in an apparently boundless continent.

Both communities, it was soon noted, believed themselves more British than the British, true children of the empire. In the book about his travels in Australia and New Zealand published in 1873, the British novelist Anthony Trollope found that 'The New Zealander among John Bulls is the most John Bullish', because he [sic] so roundly asserted that everything there is just like England, only with better crop yields, a more benign climate and improved scenery. The New World propensity for what the American historian Daniel Boostin calls 'boosterism' was endemic in both countries, however: 'And I would observe to the New Zealander generally, as I have done to the other colonists,' Trollope lectured, 'that if he blew his trumpet somewhat less loudly, the music would gain in its effect upon the world at large.'[31]

Even so, the English historian J. A. Froude, when he made the circuit of the 'white' colonies in 1884 to 1885, was told by the ship's captain that 'emigrants were generally discontented'.[32] The duration and tedium of the voyage – it took three to five months before the advent of the steamship in the 1860s – would have underscored the completeness of their separation from all that they had known. While the colonists were striking out to new worlds and new experiences, beyond the ken of those they left behind, change at home would inevitably distance them even further from the past. This is the lot of immigrants: to be suspended between two worlds, at ease in neither. The imperial connection was a useful life-line, but there was nothing static about it. A reassuring link with Britain, presumed to be stable, would become something different in face of the need to carve a new life – while the homeland itself changed behind them.

The Land is a Mother That Never Dies

Settlement, by definition, involved staking claims and cultivation of land long since in customary use by the tribes; the incomers' hunger for land would inevitably translate into commercial and political value. The flood of immigrants would put their imprint on the face of the two countries in different ways, depending on the generic character of soils, climate and the lie of the land itself, and on the political issues – the inevitable disputes as to entitlement. Differentiated responses to these questions helped shape the distinctive characters of Australia and New Zealand. Land would become the catalyst for strife. Ultimately, colonial expansion must degenerate into a struggle for power.

In the late 1830s, people began to move out overland from across the Blue Mountains and northwards from what was still Van Diemen's Land, to take advantage of the splendid grazing land reported by the first European explorers in the south-east. Others moved north into what would become southern Queensland. For a brief time the horizons seemed limitless. But Australia was not America. The desert heart of the continent set limits to notions of ineffable expansion. Soon there was not enough land to accommodate both the aspirations of the squatter class and the immigrants' demands for land for small farming. There were large economic, political and social interests at stake as the small farming hopefuls (called 'selectors' – from their 'selections' of land as parcels of country were opened up for subdivision)[33] fanned out onto the open range lands which many 'squatters'[34] had simply taken as theirs by right. In Wyoming these stresses led to small-scale warfare. In Australia, adjustment was achieved more peaceably, but the tensions were real enough. Again, like the American west, the character of the land itself soon wrecked many a dream of sturdy independence as a yeoman farmer. For the selectors and their families, if the heat and pests eating out their hard-planted crops weren't bad enough, the isolation and oppression of a monotonous landscape often brought despair; poor communications to market brought bankruptcy. The hardness of life in the outback entered Australian legend.

In New Zealand, the onset of mass settlement soon tore apart the delicate generalisations about the balance between British authority and that of the Maori chiefs, inscribed in deceptively simple language in the Treaty of Waitangi. The New Zealand Wars originated in systematic fighting between the British and northern tribes in the 1840s; war broke out again between the government and Waikato and Taranaki tribes in the 1860s. A tough and tragic struggle continued over much of the North Island for over ten years. Maori campaigning and military skills severely shook European presumptions of natural superiority, especially in the art of warfare. British regiments and settler militia did not have an easy time of it. The issues, ostensibly to do with land, were at base about sovereignty; these were colonial wars, fought to establish British authority. They have left legacies similar to those of other frontier wars: bitterness at loss of ancestral lands and feelings of marginalisation and despair as the old tribal structures collapsed in the face of the brisk new order – leaving a foundation for political activism in pursuit of redress for later generations. Not all tribes resisted; some used the advent of the white settler to settle old tribal scores by aligning with the government, which in turn gave them influence and helped them hold on to land. In turn, tribal antagonisms within Maoridom were exacerbated. New Zealand was deeply scarred. Swiftly, in a matter of years or so, Maori were separated from a great deal of land: by purchase from the tribes or conquest, or – as in several parts of the North Island – by punitive expropriation for having had the temerity to resist.

Reserves of 'native' land were established, so that not all tribal holdings were swept away. The disagreeable business was not as disagreeable as the westward expansion in the United States, where the increasingly discombobulated tribes were forced back on to wastelands the white settlers did not want. The Maori tribes were not simply ignored, as in Australia. They retained portions of their ancestral turangawaewae, standing grounds, even as the surrounding lands passed into European hands. From these remnants, Maori were able actively to enter into New Zealand political life and maintain their place to a degree. Disputes about ancestral title to land and efforts to seek redress of grievances about the means deployed to dispossess the tribes of their lands are a staple of national politics, over two centuries after the Europeans first appeared on the scene. In the meantime, Maori life has of course been transformed, in particular by migration to the cities, although tribal affiliations remain strong for many.

Differences between Australia and New Zealand in the way farming would develop were inherent in the climate and the terrain. New Zealanders have long since been pleased to compare their 'moist' climate and 'moderate' temperatures, 'which allow the grass to grow the year round' – with the 'unrelenting' heat, dust and flies of Australia. Most of this belongs to the list of great New Zealand fables, which are difficult to sell to local farmers who are often drought-stricken or to anyone caught out in the icy blasts of a New Zealand southerly storm. But a smaller scale to sheep farming was feasible from the outset. The 'mixed' (that is, cattle as well as sheep) 'family' (owner-occupied) 'hill country' (usually not mountainous, but by no means flat either) farm on freehold land is the classic model in New Zealand agriculture. Almost every other aspect of the New Zealand sheep-farming industry – the first merino sheep let out on the native tussock, the financial structure, the lay-out of farms and buildings – was adapted from Australia. Both countries, but especially Australia, rode to prosperity on the sheep's back. Thirty Spanish merinos, imported into New South Wales in 1797 from the Cape Colony in South Africa, in due course turned a number of pioneer squatters into 'sheep barons' on a scale of grandeur to make subsequent New

Zealand activities puny by comparison. Today, Australia is a world leader in the sheep industry (which makes silly sheep jokes about New Zealanders even sillier).

In both countries the land was always a factor in calculations about how best to achieve economic growth. However, in New Zealand, questions of equity were uppermost – for Europeans, if not Maori. Scottish immigrants, who would prove to be as influential in New Zealand life as the Irish in Australia, had not crossed the world to put up with 'plantation' style farming on behalf of the rich. Highlanders Donald Reid and then John McKenzie shaped the political landscape in New Zealand in favour of the small-holders. As a boy, the angry McKenzie had seen wretched victims of the Highland clearances huddled in a churchyard; as a politician in New Zealand he was the guiding spirit behind far-reaching programmes, initiated in the 1890s by an innovative and radical Liberal government, to break up large holdings and open up the land for the small farmer. He bruised Maori interests and those of absentee Australian run-holders in the process. Large estates were progressively squeezed by graduated taxation; a state right of compulsory purchase or development of crown land was also established in respect of land held on behalf of Maori. Pastoral farming on the grand scale undoubtedly made some large fortunes in the early days of New Zealand. Nevertheless, democratisation of the land became a prevailing ethos and a New Zealand family farming tradition was established.

The pleasant, open, rolling, hill country farmland of today belies the great effort and loss involved in the assault on the vast tracts of New Zealand sub-tropical rain forest. Erosion and the proliferation of plant and animal pests are indicators of the massive cost of disturbing the natural order of things. Similar orders of difficulty faced settlers in the drier parts of eastern Australia, where the desert has come back after the water table was disrupted. Rabbit plagues in both countries have destroyed countless farming dreams. In the North Island of New Zealand, Maori raiding in the 1860s left isolated settlers fearfully exposed. Easy country, as in Western Victoria and South Australia, swiftly imposed the logic of smaller-scale arable farming. It was no accident that South Australia and New Zealand were able to ensure that large landed interests did not get a controlling interest in affairs – although in both places large landowners quickly took a prominent place in public life. New Zealanders also learned from Australian experience some of the techniques needed to deny political power to a landed ascendancy. The New Zealand Land Act of 1877 drew from precedent in Victoria to give small farmers practical help, including a form of hire purchase for land[35] and provision of favourable loan terms for development. The government also provided the necessary investment in the infrastructure of rural life. Perhaps as a result, the farming stream has flowed more calmly through New Zealand life than has been the case across the Tasman. For all the toughness and hardihood needed to tame the back country, there was little of the drama of confrontation between landed proprietors and small farmers, conservatives and radicals, over land questions which had marked rural development in Australia.

Equally, no chronicler of the hard life of the New Zealand farmer gained a hold on the national imagination to match Henry Lawson and 'Banjo' Paterson, who enshrined the rough language, tall stories and harshness of the Australian 'outback'. New Zealand is the poorer for it. Nothing has been handed down comparable to the heady legends of the Australian bush-ranging tradition. There was no New Zealand mythological Ned Kelly, the 'decent' jail-bird who takes to murder and mayhem, when he finds that his old mother has been worn to death working an unproductive farm, and becomes, in his suit of home-made armour, the epitome of the common man defying authority and 'polite' society. In the company of the swagmen, the stock-drovers and bushmen, the bushrangers have been deep-woven into Australian beliefs about national identity and character. New Zealand up-country mythology is centred on elusive, lone sheep-stealers, in the 'man pitted against nature' tradition; fortunately Maori legend is more colourful and more helpful to New Zealanders wishing to people the land with larger-than-life characters.

Crocks of Gold

The two Antipodean communities were for a time bound by threads of gold. Fabulous discoveries in New South Wales and Victoria in 1851 unveiled suddenly magical places with strange names, like Ballarat and Bendigo. Rowdy hopefuls from around the world poured into Australia. Ten years later, gold was found in the South Island of New Zealand by the Australian, Gabriel Read. Where Melbourne had been catapulted to wealth by gold, Dunedin followed. The Kawarau and Shotover rivers became the new magnets for the miners, who moved on from Australia to New Zealand. Gold helped put the two countries on the world map and established a pattern of trans-Tasman vagabondism in pursuit of fickle fortune, which has persisted to this day. The pattern began in the 1850s as early settlers, disillusioned with the travails of establishment in New Zealand, responded to the excitement over the bonanzas struck on the Victorian goldfields; in the 1860s the flow was the other way.

In Australia, mining licence fees and the tactics of goldfields police became prodigious sources of grievance; diggers agitated for the vote and land reform, swelling reformist movements in Victoria and New South Wales, which had in turn been inspired by the English Chartists. Ancient Irish grievances also surfaced; in the heady atmosphere of the diggings 'authority' came to be equated with 'English' oppression. When miners openly took up arms and erected what they called the Eureka Stockade, a few kilometres from Ballarat, the 'whiff of revolution' suddenly became real – and tragic. Four hundred state troopers attacked 150 miners on the morning of 3 December 1854, leaving thirty mostly hung-over diggers and five police dead. The shots at Eureka may not have been heard around the world, but they certainly focused the minds of the politicians. Progress towards more fully representative government followed; the diggers gained representation in the Victoria State Assembly, and went on to be influential in the Australian radical movement. In a more lasting sense, Eureka became a proud symbol of Australian resistance to authoritarianism; the diggers' marvellous black flag decked out with the Southern Cross stands still as a token of the Australian spirit of independence.

Alarmed that the Australians would bring their miners' radicalism with them, the New Zealand authorities quickly appointed administrators in the Otago goldfields, who had experience in Victoria of the discontents of miners. Regulations for management of the fields – which the Victorians had adopted in the aftermath of the show-down at Eureka – were applied across the Tasman. New Zealand miners gained voting rights with their licences and were given access to leasehold land. They proved tractable; even the instinctive diggers' phobias about their Chinese fellow-toilers, which had been brutally demonstrated in New South Wales and Victoria, were less rampant along the Kawarau and the Shotover. Further discoveries along the West Coast of the South Island in 1865 led to a further surge of hopefuls from across the Tasman, and left a residue of non-conforming Irishness, which has not lost its appeal, even today. Again the authorities were able to draw from Australian experience the political nous to keep the diggings under control.

The (Near) Fatal Impact

In neither country were the settlers magnanimous. The Darwinian precept that only the fittest survive was misappropriated to demonstrate that the two native races were doomed. The European responsibility was expressed as smoothing the pillow for dying races – with due expressions of regret. The consequences were obviously huge, on both sides of the Tasman. European onslaughts, diseases and that tragic, bewildering wasting process, noted wherever tribal cultures were destabilised by European incursions around the world, soon cut at the roots of Maori and Aboriginal life. In 1769–70 James Cook estimated the Maori population in New Zealand to be about 100,000, which was perhaps on the low side. Less than a hundred years later, the first New Zealand census of 1857–8 recorded only 56,000 Maori. By 1897, the slough of despond for Maori, there were 42,000. Improving social circumstances then led to a marked renaissance: numbers doubled in twenty-five years from 58,000 in 1926 to 116,000 in 1951, then doubled again in the next twenty-five years to 234,000. Passing along the eastern coastline of Australia in 1770, Cook made what can only have been an extremely unscientific guess that the Aboriginal population of Australia was of the order of 500,000. If it were anywhere near accurate, the subsequent European impact was very nearly the crack of doom. The first Commonwealth census in 1911 put Aboriginal numbers at 79,000; by 1954 the situation seemed even worse, at 74,000; in 1981 numbers of people of Aborigine or Torres Strait Islander origin had reached 160,000 or approximately 1 per cent of the Australian population.

At the 1997 census, 16 per cent of New Zealanders claimed to have some Maori blood, no matter how distant; 14.5 per cent registered themselves as 'Maori'. Constituting a substantial proportion of the population and with well-developed political skills and strong military proclivities, Maori have been able to insist on their place in New Zealand life. The Native Rights Act 1865 and Maori Representation Act 1867 conferred political and electoral rights early. Across the Tasman, the constitution was amended only in 1967 to provide that Aborigines be treated as Australians in matters to do with civil rights and to secure the pre-eminence of the federal government over state governments in Aboriginal policy. Until then, aboriginal rights, especially in the matter of land tenure, remained a largely buried issue in national politics. As a relatively small component of the entire society, and lacking a cohesive tribal structure through which to deal with the government, the Aborigine had little political clout. The first Aborigine was elected to the federal parliament in 1971. The right to hold reserve land in parts of the Northern Territory was not given until the Aboriginal Land Rights Act of 1976.

If development of coherent and strong feelings of national sentiment depends on redressing the rights of minorities – and there is much evidence, especially from the United States, that it does – then both New Zealand and Australia have some way to go. But at the turn of the twenty-first century, the circumstances of the two indigenous races could hardly be more different. The two countries may even be on different courses in the matter and the implications could yet drive a further wedge between them. On the one side of the Tasman, the Maori are active in the political arena, strongly contending for a fair and economically viable place in New Zealand life. The Treaty of Waitangi is enshrined as a fundamental constitutional document. In Australia, the challenge is that much the steeper for the handful of Aborigine taking an active part in political life. Change is coming, but not in ways that will put any strong Aboriginal stamp on modern Australia. The reverse is true in New Zealand.

chapter four

Companions of the British Empire

C is for Colonies. Rightly we boast
That of all the great nations, we have the most.
– *from 'An ABC for Nursery Patriots', published in Britain in 1890[1]*

For a time, Australians and New Zealanders drank deep of the glories of the British empire and of the companion brew of imperial confidence and chauvinism. The empire offered scope for brash colonial politicians to play on a global stage and, in the process, to score points off one another. Trade, communications and emotional ties went instinctively back to the 'mother country'. A narrow view of local interests prevailed. Colonies that were spread so far apart naturally pushed for their differing concerns and perspectives in their dealings with London, which then worked against ideas about an integrated trans-Tasman community. Technological changes progressively reduced the significance of the 'tyranny of distance', without generating any groundswell in favour of a break with empire and the construction of a radical and different united Australasia. The movement to create a federation of the Australian colonies never strayed from the premise that the new Commonwealth of Australia would continue to belong to the British Empire. New Zealand was interested for a time, when it seemed that what might emerge would be a regional imperial council, but fell out when it became plain that the outcome would be subordination within a new federal state. New Zealand was happy with its own lot and not much interested in Australia's. The constitution of the new Commonwealth of Australia, which came into effect on 1 January 1901, notes that New Zealand is eligible for membership but specifies that the terms of entry for new members will be determined by the federal parliament.

Family

There were no revolutions or defining events that would precipitate either Australians or New Zealanders into separation from Britain. On the contrary, they inherited membership of the British empire. They belonged to the extraordinary global realm of a Greater (white) Britain and wanted nothing else. An imperial web, centred on London, above all represented continuity; it was also about racial identity, solidarity – and economic survival. Moreover, two remote countries could be part of the ferment of the times. British success, American expansionism, the imperial ardour of the other European states, were all to be wrapped up in 'white' triumphalism. The Antipodean countries were very much part of that parade.

With no cause or capacity to organise alternative systems, the Australian and New Zealand colonies simply transferred what they needed from Britain: crown, Westminster-type parliaments, bewigged judges, red-tabbed generals, Hansard, Bellamy's meat pies – the lot. New South Wales had gained a limited form of self-government in 1842; similar arrangements were made for Victoria, South Australia and Tasmania in 1850. In 1852 New Zealand took a larger leap forward to an ungainly provincial system of full self-government, which was put on hold for two years while the governor tried to sort out Maori policy. South Australia became effectively self-governing in 1853, Tasmania in 1854, Victoria in 1856 and Queensland in 1859. Western Australia, which barely survived an ill-conceived first attempt at settlement in 1829, struggled to achieve representative institutions much later (1893). These were – with Canada and later, more ambiguously, South Africa – the 'kith and kin' empire, places apart from the spreading welter of 'native' colonies, protectorates and territories, with India the jewel in that segment of the imperial crown. To what would become the 'white dominions', the self-confident British transferred systems of government and concepts of the civil society – and people in great numbers and, with them, deep-rooted beliefs in the supremacy of British civilisation.

The second British Empire was very different from the first. For the British themselves, the maintenance of close affinities with their colonies of settlers made pleasing contrast with the humiliation of the Treaty of Paris, which recognised the independence of the United States of America in 1783, only five years before the First Fleet arrived at Botany Bay. Perhaps recalling their rough handling (which transformed the world) by the stroppy North American colonists, but more likely in response to the currents of liberal reform then sweeping British life, governments in London were indulgent about responding to calls for self-government within the second empire. More than that, by the mid-nineteenth century, Britain had become the workshop of the world, an undisputed great power, with the empire as its crown jewels. The 'greater Britains' strung across the world were the focus of strong national interests and emotional commitments.

For the Australians and New Zealanders, Britain was principal trader, banker and insurer, defender and arbiter of standards in all aspects of public – and private – life. While 'Britannia ruled the waves', their long life-lines to the heart of empire were secure. Handling their own affairs, they competed with each other for the attention and favour of London. Robert Peel's conversion to free trade in 1846 transformed the economic and strategic environment in which the Antipodean colonies would come into their own. As the focal point for world trade, British demand for industrial raw materials and food made it possible for the Australian and New Zealand economies to get away to good, secure starts. A window of opportunity opened, thanks, in large part, to an apparently insatiable demand for fine wools for the British textiles trade. Colonial gold, especially from Victoria, then helped consolidate London as the financial hub of the world. With the introduction of steamships from the 1860s on, Australia and New Zealand entered global trade calculations. The development of refrigeration in the 1880s then fostered investment in meat and dairy production for the British market, and in due course Australian wheat made a further contribution. Eventually, places such as Broken Hill and Mt Isa would make Australian metals mining yet another factor in the global economy. Minerals and the extraction of extensive deposits of iron ore and coal would eventually underpin the Australian economy and give a platform for industrial development.

It was a comfortable youth. Increasingly, enthusiastic endorsement of their good fortune to be part of the imperial plan provided a common foundation for New Zealand and Australian senses of identity. Bickering with the imperial government in London, and with one another, would however set the pattern for future separateness. Together or separately, the Antipodeans would proffer advice – and, often enough, robust criticism – about the conduct of empire affairs or solicit support for the pursuit of their own regional interests in the Pacific. Certainly, the British were accommodating – perhaps brilliant is the better word – in so managing imperial business as to convey the illusion of partnership. London would, however, never concede on the hard realities: Britain alone, not just as the senior, but the dominant party, represented the empire in all dealings of international life. New Zealand and Australia would develop their own ideas about power-sharing, centred essentially on various concepts of an imperial council or even – at its most optimistic – of a federation. But they would discover that authority in the conduct of imperial foreign policy would not, indeed could not, be shared.

Another Kind of Manifest Destiny

In their 'new' countries, pragmatic, fresh-minded politicians would turn settler aspirations to build 'new' societies – purged of tawdriness from the 'old world' – into national objectives. Through legislation one could change the world. A strong trade union movement in New South Wales and Victoria produced Labor[2] parties determined to push for social and political reform. A Liberal government in New Zealand in the 1890s made the country a by-word around the world for political innovation. In fact, the stark realities of place and space should have put a dampener on their expectations from the first. In America after the revolution it was possible to dispense with imperial fandangle and start afresh. Territorial enlargement by way of the Louisiana Purchase (1803) and the Mexican War (1846–8) laid the vast potential of a rich continent open for development. There were to be no such tantalising pointers to a 'manifest destiny' for the New

Zealanders and Australians. For all the vast size of Australia, and the excitements of sudden wealth from gold, it was soon evident that there were harsh limits to expansiveness there, and New Zealanders were up against them from the start. The empire was a crutch against the reality that these were small and very isolated fledgling countries, a long way from home.

Many, on both sides of the Tasman, took exception to overheated imperial loyalty. Populist politics, arising from struggles against the landed interests, anti-establishment inheritances from the convict era and goldfields radicalism, had a strong hold in New South Wales and Victoria. Republicanism was in the air from the 1850s, when the excitement of gold made everything seem possible. The State Legislature in Victoria was split down the middle over the New South Wales decision to send a contingent off to fight in the Sudan in 1885; blind imperial loyalties were offset by mistrust, among many people, of the new jingoism, dislike of a nascent Australian militarism and concern about foreign reactions to enlistment in the imperial cause. Victoria – belying the name – was the least likely of the Australian states to bend the knee. An assertive Australian-ness was also being fostered by the Sydney periodical, the *Bulletin*, founded in 1880, under the masthead of 'Australia for the Australians'. Well before the 1880s, egalitarianism and republicanism had begun to mark Australian political life; the trappings of empire – royalty, hereditary privilege, titles, a stratified society – were publicly and vigorously repudiated in some quarters. The Australian Natives Association (that is, the native-born Europeans) established in Melbourne in 1871, from an earlier New South Wales movement with the same objectives, pursued a basic equity in society – federation, one person-one vote, women's suffrage, Aboriginal welfare and 'buy Australian-made' – which, for many members, did not sit with imperial pretensions. And the Australians were discovering themselves in the writings of Henry Lawson, in the romantic legends of the battlers of the bush and in the expansive, illusionary promise of the outback.

A republican league was founded in 1888 to promote a federation of the Australian colonies under republican government. Empire Day was celebrated by the *Bulletin* as 'Vampire Day'; nationalist journals such as the *Republican* and the short-lived *Boomerang* provided an outlet for writers of a radical bent, such as Henry Lawson. During the 1880s, rows with the government in London over colonial policies towards the New Hebrides and New Guinea fired up anti-imperial sentiment. It was discomforting to budding nationalists to find that Australia lacked the clout to ensure that it had influence in its immediate region. The imperial system rather than the facts of relative power got the blame. Disagreeable phobias were also at work. Early Australian nationalist sentiment was seeded with large doses of racism. Ugly beatings of Chinese diggers on both the Victorian and New South Wales goldfields showed a sad residue of white bigotry at the heart of Australian egalitarianism. The *Bulletin's* 'Australia for the Australians' was replaced in 1908 by 'Australia for the White Man' – not removed until 1960 – which expressed the foundation for nationalist beliefs for many.

New Zealand, too, while fostering immigration in great numbers from Britain, placed restrictions on Chinese immigration. This was one topic on which the southern colonists were in agreement with one another and at odds with the British government. London's attempts to encourage a broader and more humane view were bitterly rejected, as in this attack by the Agent-General of New Zealand in London on 'this very spirit of English business, which while poisoning China with opium in the interest of India, is ready to take up the cause of the Chinese if only there is money to be made in flooding Australasia with yellow barbarians'.[3] The New Zealand Agent-General of the time, William Pember Reeves, made brilliant contributions to New Zealand life as journalist, principal innovator in the reformist Liberal government of the 1890s, historian and poet; in England, he became a leading light in liberal intellectual circles. There need be little doubt of the prevalence of anti-Chinese racism in New Zealand if Reeves was an advocate. Working and middle-class interests, predicated on the belief that 'European' standards and livelihood would be threatened by 'cheap' Chinese labour, were in the ascendant. Behind it all there was, perhaps, a growing awareness of the strategic exposure of the two 'white' countries on the margins of Asia.

New Zealand nationalism was also brewing and was something different from the imperial extravaganza enjoyed by the politicians. 'New Zealand for the New Zealanders' was as potent a slogan on the eastern side of the Tasman as its equivalent was on the western – and with the same, unstated, anti-Asian codicil. Nativist feelings were also stirring. A sincere, if slightly precious, commitment to things New Zealand was evident; Maori names of birds and places were bestowed on the children of immigrants. New Zealanders started calling themselves 'Maorilanders'. The natural wonders – the mountains, lakes and geysers – of the new country were promoted as unique in the world and served as a foundation for a developing sense of identity and national pride. New Zealand Natives Associations were formed, after the Australian models, in the 1880s and 1890s. It was all a little contrived and forced. Nationalism and republicanism barely surfaced as factors in New Zealand political life; in small and scattered communities, the depth and vitality needed to sustain contrarian politics were hard to marshal. Even during the 1890s – when the country was in radical and innovative mode under the Liberal government – New Zealand nationalism was tentative and difficult to separate from imperial jingoism. New Zealanders were mostly committed to Britain, secure in the unshakeable presumption that Britain would continue to want to underwrite their loyalty, by paying for their defence and providing the capital needed for development. The stir of political debate was less disruptive than across the Tasman; New Zealanders were less moved by the issues of the times, more pragmatic, and – to Australians at least – duller.

Staring at the Pacific with Wild Surmise

The Pacific became the cockpit for the ambitions of the settler governments. This was an area seemingly to their scale and was, moreover, not yet fully 'flagged' by the European powers. From the earliest days of settlement, New Zealand liked to see itself as the lynchpin in a mini-empire in the Pacific. On the evangelical front, as early as the 1860s, a Melanesian mission based in Auckland had endeavoured to develop New Zealand as the missionary hub. In 1874, Julius Vogel, Treasurer in the New Zealand government at the time but prompted by Auckland business interests, proposed the formation of a Pacific colonisation company. The New Zealanders were discomfited by the British refusal to award them Fiji, which London annexed in 1877.

The first stirrings of an Australasian nationalism were set off by concerns about the competitive colonialism of rival European powers in the Pacific. The first-ever joint Australia-New Zealand exercise in foreign policy was to try to get a British response to power plays by France and Germany in the region. The inter-colonial meeting that addressed these international issues was held in Sydney in 1883, and was elevated to the status of a constitutional convention in order to consider the question of a federation of the Australasian colonies. On the foreign policy front it was agreed that

> further acquisition of Dominion in the Western Pacific, south of the equator, by any Foreign Power would be highly detrimental to the safety and well-being of the British possessions in Australasia, and injurious to the interests of the Empire.

The Antipodeans petitioned London to forestall their rivals and take possession of New Guinea and the New Hebrides; a protest was lodged about the continuing presence of French penal colonies in the region.

Their concerns, if inflated, were not absurd. The Indonesian Archipelago to the north was controlled by the Dutch and Portuguese; half of New Guinea was under the Dutch; the other half, plus New Britain and New Ireland (both now part of Papua New Guinea) had fallen, or was soon to, under German control; the French were established in New Caledonia and in 1887 joined the British in taking over the New Hebrides (now Vanuatu). Yet there was no denying Antipodean colonial aspirations. The Colonial Office, as Keith Sinclair observed, 'was too shrewd not to see that the colonists were calling on Great Britain, in the name of the British Empire, to pursue imperial interests of their own'.[4] After disgraceful expeditions to recruit (more by foul means than fair) the indigenous people of the New Hebrides and Solomon Islands to work their plantations, the sugar 'kings' of Queensland made an abortive attempt to annex south-eastern New Guinea in 1883. The Queenslanders were working to their own subset of strategic considerations: the journey to Suez and London by way of Torres Strait was much shorter and more convenient than via Sydney or Melbourne, and their bid for a private empire in New Guinea was motivated by the wish to protect this spur line to the imperial route against unfriendly powers. The British established their own protectorate in New Guinea, but eventually persuaded a by-then reluctant new Commonwealth Government of Australia to take it over. The New Zealanders offered to take over Samoa in 1884 and were rebuffed by London. Then, in the 1890s, the New Zealand Premier, Richard Seddon, was said to have told the American President William McKinley that his country, not the United States, was the logical candidate to assume control of Hawaii. In 1899 Samoa again became the focus of New Zealand's interests: Seddon offered to send New Zealand troops to uphold imperial interests, as Britain confronted Germany and the United States. New Zealand ambitions were eventually brought down to scale in 1901, with the offer of administration of the British protectorate in the Cook Islands. Antipodean aspirations were less than fulfilled. But it was all simply a manifestation of the age; colonists too were colonisers, but power politics called the tune.

Australasian opinion was unlikely to sway London greatly. By the 1880s, colonial rivalries were being played out on a wider stage. Colonial interests had become part of the bargaining coin of power politics, to be competed for, swapped or otherwise manipulated in the attempt not only to satisfy the urge to occupy and exploit, but to maintain the balance of power in Europe. In the Pacific, Germany and France, as well as the British, were players and the United States was already on the scene. As far as the policy-makers in Whitehall were concerned, the Australians and New Zealanders were welcome to a slice of the colonial action – if they were prepared to pay for and run territories themselves. On this basis, in due course Australia assured its position in Papua and New Zealand in the Cook Islands; after the First World War (under the League of Nations mandate systems), Australia and New Zealand respectively added to their mini-empires the former German colonies of New Guinea and associated territories, and Western Samoa. Co-ordination of Australasian interests in the Pacific was not attempted.

The Australian and New Zealand colonies represented something new: assertive mini-states insistent on their own autonomy but far too conscious of the economic and political advantages of operating within the British system to want to throw it aside. Moreover, they could use the empire to project themselves. They were content to have the British shoulder most of the burdens of defence and the conduct of international relations while proclaiming their own unique contributions to empire. Nevertheless, by the turn of the century, they were well aware that their interests and those of the mother country often diverged. At the Imperial Conference in 1907, Alfred Deakin, the Australian Prime Minister, complained about the difference in attitude between 'those who live by the Pacific Ocean, as in our case, and those on this side whose shores are washed by the North Sea'. New Zealand Prime Minister Seddon had earlier told the British that their muddling and mistakes over Samoa had done irreparable injury to New Zealand. Even so, nothing would precipitate a break for independence.

Hands Across the Tasman – Tentatively

For all their imperial brouhaha, the Australian and New Zealand colonies could not ignore the facts of life: they had limited resources and were situated at the end of long lines of communication across the world. Faced with common problems, there would be obvious advantages in collaboration, if only to reduce costs. As early as the 1860s, it was obvious that the colonial administrations should meet to explore what the New Zealand Premier, Edward Stafford, called their 'community of interest'. The issues were humdrum – lighthouses, overseas mail services, harmonisation of statistics, trade and tariff arrangements and the establishment of the new cable linkages – but vital. Localism, however, already ruled.

Manning Clark gives a glimpse of the workings of the colonial parliaments of the day:

> The minds of the colonists were not called to rise above the level of the parish pump. Every time a question of general interest was raised a torpor descended on the proceedings of a colonial parliament. By contrast, every time a question of local interest was raised, the proceedings deteriorated to that point where they were 'unworthy of the dignity of parliament'. As soon as the question of a road, or a bridge, or a school was raised the business of Assembly degenerated into 'a scramble' for a share of the government plunder.[5]

The larger picture was filled in by the 'grand design' of empire, colouring and shaping all issues of local interest. There was no room for the development of an alternative strategic vision, in the shape of a united 'Australasia'. More than that, introspection thrives on isolation. Leadership and vision – plus a clear appreciation of the issues involved in looking to the larger interest – are needed to rise above the level of the parish pump. Easier said than done.

The political reality was that Western Australia and New Zealand may not share either the perspectives or the interests of south-eastern Australia, the political 'heartland' of 'Australasia'. They were likely only to be exasperated by the apparently eternal rivalry between Victoria and New South Wales, which would always be at the heart of the politics of an 'Australasia'. By the same token, the other parties all had specialised interests in relation to one another.

Transport connections highlighted the problem. The initial route out in the age of sail was long and uncomfortable: from west to east around the Cape of Good Hope, calling at Australian ports as needs be, with New Zealand the last stop. The onward journey eastward was even more challenging, making the turn northward at Cape Horn. A more direct, partly overland, route to India via the Mediterranean was introduced in the late 1830s. Australia was hooked in with a connection at Ceylon (now Sri Lanka) in 1852, thanks to a hefty subsidy paid by the British government to the P&O Line. Steamships were plying this route by 1856. But it was still agonisingly slow. It could take fifty-four days for a letter to reach Melbourne, fifty-seven to Sydney and sixty-one to New Zealand

– if there were no mechanical breakdowns, missed connections or storms at sea.

Victoria became the focal point for the overseas mail service, under the British subsidy system. But there were few satisfied customers elsewhere, least of all in New Zealand. Transit times were further reduced when the Suez Canal was opened in 1869 and better designed steam engines improved both the reliability and speed of passage of the ships themselves. Even so, the mail service was a perpetual source of grievance to the colonists. The bulk of traffic and cargoes through into the 1880s continued to follow the traditional route across the southern Indian Ocean. The flames of 'us' and 'them' politics were readily stoked up over the issue of how each colony could take best advantage from the subsidies they and the British paid for a mail service. As early as 1862, the New Zealanders opted for a service via Panama. Officials from both sides of the Tasman met in 1866, but failed to iron out their problems in the face of British interests.

The Premier of Victoria then proposed a conference to focus on the mail service issues of most concern to Victoria – the slowness of the P&O service – but failed to invite New Zealand. Miffed, the New Zealand Premier set out to garner wider financial support for his preferred Panama service, which had just begun to operate. At a further conference in 1867, with all six colonies represented, the delegates agreed to establish a federal council to arrange matters in ways satisfactory to all: subsidies for the Suez and Panama routes as well as Torres Strait for the Queenslanders. The assertive and cross-grained Henry Parkes of New South Wales, who would become a guiding spirit in the move towards Australian federation, wrote that, 'For the first time in the history of these Australian colonies, they have all, including New Zealand … met with nothing but the desire to effect a common will, to suit the views of all.' This was surely a sign of things to come: 'the time has arrived when these colonies should be united by some federal bond of connexion.' Alas, out of their very enthusiasm, the delegates sewed further discord. Their plans went nowhere, against the declared ambition of Victoria and an understandable British disinclination to subsidise three different services. The signs of things to come, which Parkes had detected, were pointing towards disunity, not unity.

Things became unstuck again over New Zealand's pet project for a mail service down the Pacific, linking in this time with the newly completed American trans-continental rail link. Unfortunately for the New Zealanders, Victoria, Tasmania and South Australia found that the new Suez Canal worked well. New Zealand's expectations of support from New South Wales and the British failed to materialise. Then New South Wales attempted to run a rival service and did not even invite New Zealand to a conference of the Australian colonies to discuss postal services in 1871. 'A perfect feud with regard to postal matters seems to exist between New Zealand and New South Wales,' a Victorian postal official observed in 1872.

Vogel, the New Zealand Premier, stated the obvious to Henry Parkes: that each colony had been 'doing its best for its own interest in its own way'. He hoped they could be more friendly in future. Rivalry over the postal service surfaced again between Victoria and New South Wales in 1872, when a British offer of enhanced subsidies was taken up precipitately and without consultation by Victoria. Parkes was upset on behalf of New South Wales, and presumably because of dreams of Antipodean federation. Another conference was called early in 1873. New Zealand was caught in the middle. Practicalities butted against the pieties about a 'community of interest'. The trans-Pacific connection was faltering and New Zealand could not afford to jeopardise its still vital linkage with the Suez route; for fear of getting offside with the Victorians, it did not support the New South Wales objective of Sydney being the terminus for the Suez link. But this stand in turn compromised New South Wales support for the Pacific venture. In exchange, Victoria offered no more than an agreement in principle to help with the San Francisco as well as Torres Strait services. Victoria came out on top as the terminus of the imperial route and New Zealand's dream of a separate (jointly subsidised) Pacific link faded.

The twin but opposing forces of dependence and inter-dependence, nationalism and supranationalism, were at work. For all their pretensions, the Antipodean colonies could not stand alone; they needed each others' business as well as support for their own legitimate, separate-but-shared, interests in establishing the most effective mail services for each colony. There was, to that extent, a community of interest. Politics, however, is the fly in the ointment of nationalism. In a situation like the conference in Sydney in 1867, which so raised the hopes of the federalist Parkes, it was possible for hard-headed local leaders to abandon thoughts of their narrow local and/or national interests and ambitions to come up with solutions in the broad collective interest. But when they returned home, local politics (that is, nationalism) again enveloped them. (To this day, delegates to international conferences are at risk of this disease.) The nationalist grist in the mill of politics has very human components: local or national pride, ambition, the irresistible temptation to score points off rivals, and the need to push local interests and prospects. Against this, the Premier of Victoria was behaving predictably in asserting a dominant place for his state in the developing construct of a satisfactory mail service for the scattered Antipodean colonies; equally, New Zealand could hardly be blamed for pushing a Pacific route.

The difficulties in the way of establishing mutual commitments were then compounded by the introduction of the submarine cable. In 1870, South Australia (then the putative master of the entire central wedge of an empty continent, north to south) took the initiative to build a telegraph line from Port Augusta to Darwin to tie in with a cable line from Singapore. A telegraph link between Sydney, Melbourne and Adelaide had been established long before – in 1858.

When a wire had been looped across the desert heart of Australia, with heroic telegraph operators established in little citadels every 160 kilometres or so to repeat the Morse code messages on down the line, the modern world opened. A message from London cost the amazing sum of ten shillings a word and took, in the beginning, several days to transmit from London. But commerce and investment were transformed:

> British investors were more likely to finance the building of Australian railways and reservoirs, the developing of Australian mines and pastoral houses, and they were more likely to lend money to Australian banks and governments, once the telegraph gave them a swift newsline to the distant country in which they were risking their savings.[6]

New Zealand felt left out on a limb and tried to work with the similarly isolated Queenslanders to set up another cable route through Torres Strait to Brisbane and on across the Tasman. The other Australian colonies, however, were hoping that New Zealand would continue to support their schemes while paying for the onward link on its own account. Vogel thought he had New South Wales signed on to help guarantee the cost of the spur line across the Tasman, which he said had given 'great satisfaction in New Zealand'. The New South Wales parliament, however, was reluctant and would not agree to support a hook-up with New Zealand until 1875. Vogel, an activist and a moderniser, had recognised the importance of the cable link to his plans for investment and development. The New Zealand parliament, however, was largely indifferent to being at the end of a line via Australia and, when completed in 1876, the connection failed to generate much excitement.

There was another vexing question on the agenda – the respective rights of each colony to grant tariff preferences to each other and to foreign countries. At New Zealand's initiative, a conference was arranged in late 1869. When they arrived in Melbourne after a tedious journey across the Tasman, the New Zealand delegates were told that the conference in Sydney was off because the Premier of Victoria thought it a waste of his time.[7] Instead, they settled for tripartite talks with Queensland and New South Wales. Although the right of the Antipodean colonies to establish preferential trading arrangements with one another was widely supported; there was plainly advantage in boosting economic links in the neighbourhood. Principal trading connections were, however, with Britain; inter-colonial trade was of marginal importance. Moreover, the Australians were actually barred by Imperial statute (the Australian Colonies Government Act of 1850) from using tariffs to promote trade with one another. Once again local interests and concerns did not sit well with each colony's perception of its place in the Imperial scheme of things. New Zealand was not so constrained; Vogel even wanted to go further and negotiate over trade with foreign powers, notably the United States.

When another conference was called in 1870, New Zealand declined to attend. The Australian colonies favoured a common external tariff and removal of barriers to internal trade in locally produced goods. But they were at odds over which trade items could be removed from internal tariff protection. In fact, they each wished to be able to negotiate for themselves on such matters. It was agreed that the separate colonies would make representations to this end to London. The British, however, did not like what they regarded as a trend away from unquestioning empire loyalty, even though they themselves were divided between unqualified free traders and those who thought that small concessions would help hold the empire together. The free trade lobby (led by the redoubtable William Gladstone) was dismayed that colonial administrations wished to establish tariffs that could disadvantage British suppliers; the empire loyalists were upset at a prospective loss of cohesion in the imperial system.

In 1873 London was prepared to go only as far as authorising the Australian colonies as well as New Zealand to establish preferential trading arrangements among themselves. Vogel's desire for the colonial governments to be given the discretion to negotiate trading arrangements with foreign countries was repudiated, both by the Australian colonies and the British. Vogel was regarded as a nuisance by the Australians and several of them worked their own British connections to dissociate their colonies from what was being proposed. There is no magic wand which creates a 'community of interest' when each community has divergent interests. Nationalism is localism. Large issues were looming – for the British as for the colonists. In the 1890s and on into the early years of the twentieth century, Joseph Chamberlain would lead a full-scale political battle in Britain in favour of an imperial trading bloc protected behind its own tariff walls (a kind of 'All-British' common market). Behind it all lay a concept of an imperial federation. Faced with such drastic proposals for restraint on trade, many liberal free-traders began to wonder whether the empire was really worth the candle.

Federation

Perhaps the most significant national decision New Zealand has ever taken was to jump off the bandwagon of Australian federation, which began rolling in earnest in the 1880s and 1890s. Yet it was hardly a decision at all – more an option treated with a resounding absence of interest. New Zealanders had already developed a sufficient sense of their own separate national identity. Arguments about political, economic, strategic or merely social advantages of merger with a larger, more dynamic, diverse and potentially richer neighbour fell on deaf ears. New Zealand politicians had already learned how hard it was to secure their interests in the clash of differentiated concerns represented by the other colonial leaders; they had experience of the difficulties of travel and communication which would be involved. Rather than seeking avidly to exploit the wider opportunities offered by a larger population, New Zealand business people were mainly concerned with protecting their own local market. A solidly middle-class establishment in New Zealand was sniffy about Australian egalitarianism and 'mateship'. The great cities of Melbourne and Sydney had not developed in ways which made them poles of attraction – commercial or social – for small town, small farming New Zealand. Despite a two-way flow of people, no sense of a common destiny had emerged.

The comparison with the history of the American Revolution is instructive. Having brusquely severed their imperial relationship with the British, the thirteen American colonies were obliged, during the 1780s, to come to terms with one another and thus to lay the foundations of a new political entity: the United States of America. They did so in two stages: first, through the adoption of the Articles of Confederation in 1781 and, second, by establishing an authoritative national government and federal structure laid out in the constitution drawn up by the Constitutional Convention of 1787. By contrast, the Australian and New Zealand colonies could continue, through the high days of empire in the latter part of the nineteenth century, to sublimate their local interests in the global. In one respect it was an old story – the bright lights of the imperial stage would tempt ambitious and activist colonial politicians more than the hard slog needed to reconcile conflicting interests 'back home'. More than that: all roads led to Rome. The origins of all things in their new societies, incuding trade, political instincts and affections, were caught up in the linkages with the mother country. Where all the satellites revolved around the 'sun of empire' their own inter-connections had little force.

Some of the preoccupations on which the colonies founded their notions of separate identity were arrogant and intrinsically absurd – such as the belief in New Zealand and South Australia that they were free of the convict 'stain'. The early escapees, people looking for work due to depression in one place or the other, the gold rushes, developing business and farming connections had already thoroughly mixed up the Australasian peoples. Other assumptions were less forgivable. In the late nineteenth century, Queensland tried to stand aloof from political connections with the other colonies, which it thought might block the flow of low-cost Kanak workers for the canefields. Western Australia approached the question of federation with care, out of fear that a vulgar democracy of the goldfields might undermine an oligarchy of leading families. Hard political issues soon emerged, too. In New South Wales and Victoria, developing industrial interests and associated trade union issues soon became part of the stuff of politics, whereas other colonies had different, predominantly pastoral, perspectives. In New Zealand, Maori and land questions were central to the political process.

Politics will out. The issues of federation were tested against local perceptions and interests as expressed in vigorous-minded colonial assemblies. The differences of style and character between New Zealand and Australia, which began to emerge during the latter part of the nineteenth century, did not have to be substantial. All they had to be, in the somewhat fevered circumstances of the time, was enough to give freight to part-formed ideas about national identity. Nationalism is as much about fancy as fact.

In Australia the railway was pulling together what had previously been isolated communities; increasingly evident riches, agricultural and mineral, provided a tangible basis for mutual commitment. The continent itself gave promise of a grand future. The New Zealanders had but islands to occupy and technological developments did little to help bridge the barrier of the Tasman Sea. The grandeur of the landscape, the challenge of creating a society so completely cut off from others and the drama of the confrontation with the respected Maori fostered a strong sense of local identification. William Pember Reeves's poem, written in the form of an interrogation with a friend in London, to justify his life in exile in the colonies, can almost stand as a rationale for the politics of separatism.

> 'No art?' Who serve an art more great
> Than we, rough architects of State
> With the old earth at strife?
> 'No colour?' On the silent waste
> In pigments not to be effaced
> We paint the hues of life.[8]

On both sides of the Tasman, the challenge of creating and shaping new societies was all-absorbing. The colonial leaders represented a common imperial type. Their ambitions were shaped by the arrogance of empire and the certitudes of the British mission; but their platform was assertive, small-country chauvinism. As early as 1854 the editor of the *Sydney Morning Herald* was pointing out that the differences between the Australian colonies 'were only perceptible to minute investigation'. Writing under the pseudonym of John Adams (presumably the reference is to the conservative, but staunchly unionist, second president of the United States), John West poured scorn on 'those attempts we have sometimes witnessed to form new and minute nationalities in particular colonies'. For all the size and scale of Australia there was, he wrote, 'no aspect incompatible with their unity'.[9] The same, in practical terms, could be said of the New Zealand colony vis-à-vis the Australian colonies. Nevertheless, for Australia the spreading railway lines carried political as well as commercial or human freight. In 1876, the Premier of Victoria predicted that as the colonies were connected by railway the imaginary boundaries would disappear and Australia would be under one government and form one dominion – which would be the dominion of Australia.[10] The insightful bush balladeer Henry Lawson could also see what was happening, as local interests lost relevance,

The golden days are vanished,
And altered is the scene;
The diggings are deserted,
The camping-grounds are green;
The flaunting flag of progress
Is in the West unfurled,
The mighty bush with iron rails
Is tethered to the world.[11]

Could any modern activist against globalisation distil the issues with such accuracy – and poignancy?

Towards the Australian Commonwealth

When the New Zealanders came to decide whether or not to join the movement towards federation of the Australian colonies, they did not have their feet on such solid – or at least common – ground as their Antipodean colleagues. They were unmoved by the majestic possibilities of the 'great brown land' and had little feel either for Australian history or politics. The conventional bromide was that New Zealand would be swamped by Australia and that, in any case, the 1200 miles (1800 kilometres) across the Tasman Sea were 1200 reasons why it couldn't happen. Perhaps, too, the mind-set of islanders is different: 'Always to islanders, danger is what comes from over the sea,' the New Zealand poet Allen Curnow has written.[12] Islanders are inward and readily feel threatened by the world beyond; more than that, islanders have an advanced sense of their own importance – finding it difficult to relate to the size and scale of others. To political establishments, danger also comes in whatever form threatens their own hegemony in their own patch. When that threat too comes from over the sea, it seems the more comprehensive and the less compassable. Although the distance across the Tasman Sea is no greater than the distance from, say, Brisbane to Melbourne, the ocean crossing presents barriers in the mind. (Few would deny the barriers in the mind established down the centuries by the twenty-two miles between England and France.) The argument about relative size and weight in fact loses force when the respective distributions of population are considered. Geoffery Blainey has pointed out that, in this regard,

> the two countries are similar in shape. While New Zealand is a long finger of land, the Australia where eight of every ten people live is a slightly longer and wider finger stretching from South Queensland to Melbourne with a bend of the forefinger extending to Adelaide.[13]

Thus, the mass of Australians live opposite the New Zealanders and – essentially – live like the New Zealanders. The Australian commentator Phillip Adams remarked after a visit to New Zealand in 1985 that it was impossible 'to imagine two societies more boringly similar'. In the last few years, the economic boundaries, like the challenge of distance, have likewise lost all significance: if the will were there, this concentration of people could readily become the focus for an interactive political relationship. Yet the notions of difference got, and continue to get, in the way.

At the 1883 Constitutional Convention, its two delegates spoke in favour of New Zealand becoming a member of a proposed federal council. But was such a grouping to lead in the direction of an imperial federation or to be a step towards political convergence of the Australasian colonies? There was support in New Zealand for the former concept, less for the latter. Clichés such as 'selling our birthright for a mess of potage' predictably made their appearance in the New Zealand press; there were misgivings about being 'governed from Sydney or Melbourne'. (Again there is a parallel with modern British attitudes to 'government' from Brussels.) No strong advocates for merger with Australia appeared on the New Zealand political stage. Sir George Grey – who was something of an early trans-Tasman person, having been twice governor and briefly premier of New Zealand as well as an early governor of South Australia – emerged from his retirement on a sequestered island near Auckland to speak for the idea. He supported it only as a step towards greater union of the empire and the English-speaking peoples. The New Zealand government gave no lead one way or another, and the electorate sent them no strong signals.

Almost a third of the House of Representatives did not want New Zealand even to be represented at the critical Australasian Federation Conference in Melbourne in February 1890. In the event, the government sent Sir John Hall, premier from 1879 to 1882, and a conservative empire loyalist, and Captain William Russell, then Colonial Secretary and Minister of Defence. Amid great fanfare about the Queen and empire, Sir Henry Parkes, the father of the Australian Commonwealth, proposed that it was timely to move firmly toward federation. The New Zealanders' heads were not turned. Alfred Deakin, later to be prime minister of the united Commonwealth of Australia, tried blandishments: 'New Zealanders are just like us' and 'nothing should separate the two countries'. Stolidly, Hall responded with what has become New Zealand's stock answer about the 1200 miles (1800 kilometres): transport was inadequate and what New Zealanders knew about Australia was little better than their knowledge of Africa. Hall was a successful farmer on the rich Canterbury Plains, a representative of the New Zealand landed gentry. Yet he insisted New Zealand was too tough a country to field an élite band of squatters wealthy enough to spend five months in Australia every year servicing a federal system.

Russell, who had made a fortune on some easy, open and beautiful sheep country in mild Hawkes Bay, put it to the convention that New Zealand 'was likely to develop a very complete individuality – a distinct national type', because New Zealanders had been obliged 'to struggle against … a more boisterous climate than Australia' and in the process had shown qualities of 'self-denial …

to an extent of which the people of the Australian continent have no conception'. Piling one patronising remark upon another, he remarked that the New Zealand settlers had also had to contend with 'a proud, indomitable, and courageous race of aborigines', who had of course been treated better than any 'other native or savage race on the face of the globe ... Their right to their lands was recognised from the first.' (Russell's first extensive land purchases in Hawkes Bay were challenged in the High Court by the Maori owners; his further acquisitions were found to be 'not illegal' by a Native Lands Alienation Commission.) By contrast, according to Russell, the Australians knew little and cared less about Maori and could not be entrusted with their administration. Moreover, they had treated their own 'native races in a much more summary manner than we have ventured to deal with ours in New Zealand'. (Manning Clark, the Australian historian, drily comments on this embarrassing performance, that 'the minds of the New Zealanders nourished a great delusion about past and present relations between Pakeha and the Maori'.[14]) Russell concluded with the thought that federation could be a 'marriage of affection', as between the Australian colonies. For New Zealand it could only be a marriage of convenience'; New Zealanders would accordingly have to scrutinise the terms carefully before signing and would want the Married Women's Property Act to apply 'in case of any little dispute occurring hereafter'.

Manning Clark described Russell as one of those 'maddening New Zealanders', an adjective which perhaps represents Australian views to this day. The bombast in Russell's interesting speech is often enough echoed today in unofficial comment on the subject of Australia-New Zealand relations. However, his principal and most substantive point was neither pompous nor self-deluding: 'It has been said,' he argued, 'that we cannot federate without fiscal union. As a free-trader, such is my opinion. The true basis of Federation is that interchange of products which leads to the expansion of trade, and a consequent rapprochment between the peoples of different communities.' Such questions touch deep political chords. It would be nearly a century later before a New Zealand prime minister – Geoffrey Palmer – could concede monetary union as a necessary further step towards further harmonisation of economic interests between Australia and New Zealand.[15] In between times the two countries had felt able to move only slowly towards open markets; the first stage in this process – the establishment of free trade in goods across the Tasman – was achieved just over a hundred years after the 1890 Federation Convention. As for monetary union, in 1989 Palmer would go no further than to say that it would be being given serious consideration by the year 2000 (and he was right; in 1999 the two prime ministers agreed to a joint examination of the pros and cons of a common currency. Three years later, nothing has come of it).

When the Australasian Convention reassembled in 1891 in Sydney, New Zealand again registered its caution by sending only three delegates (Sir George

Grey, former premier Sir Harry Atkinson, and Russell) whereas the other colonies accredited seven. The New Zealanders were instructed by their parliament to give no commitment that New Zealand would join any eventual federation. It was already a dialogue of the deaf. Russell had a point of a kind: 'the great question ... is not the creation of one large colony on the continent of Australia, but ... so to frame a constitution that all parts of Australasia should be able to attach themselves to it should they now or hereafter think fit to do so.' The constitution would have to be a loose one. Apart from anything else, the Hawkes Bay autocrat advised the convention, 'in New Zealand there is a very strong section of public men who are beginning to doubt the wisdom of responsible government'.

What it all boiled down to, however, was that New Zealand had no liking for being tightly bound into Australia, but might in due course consider joining some wider and looser union. This was plainly a bit rich for Australian delegates, who had more immediate political problems to face. Thomas Playford of South Australia interjected that 'there is a disposition to be embraced'. Russell replied that the embrace shouldn't 'be a bear's hug!' Alfred Deakin found that the New Zealanders were offering 'that Irish reciprocity which is all on one side'. Russell, he said,

> was careful to tell us that we must not at the present time expect anything from New Zealand; but he laid down with great fullness and freedom the duties which we immediately owed to that most beautiful, wealthy and important colony, whose position, he led us to understand, was that of a coy maiden, not unwilling, indeed expecting to be courted, and whose consent would be granted by and by as a favour.

That courteous squelch delivered, Deakin rubbed salt in New Zealand sensibilities by saying he would pass by Russell's heresies about 'responsible and democratic government'.

It was all shadow boxing. Many Australians – and indeed a large number of New Zealanders – since Deakin have assumed that the New Zealand 'maiden' would eventually give its consent to pairing up with Australia. As Russell discerned, the terms would never be right, the country has wished to live its own life. There has not been a temptation to give that away and to lose its identity in a marriage over which it could expect to exert little control. Almost a century after Deakin, with due Victorian circumspection, spoke as though federation were all a matter of the way of a man with a maid, David Lange, Prime Minister of New Zealand, put it more bluntly. New Zealand, he said, would be 'always a mistress, but never a wife'.

New Zealand stayed away from subsequent conventions to draft the constitution, never throwing itself into the arena of Australian politics in which the great issues of governance under federation were thrashed out. For a decade, from 1890 to 1900, the Australian colonies grappled with questions of power, and the division of power, between the federal government and the states, between the House of Representatives and the Senate, between executive and administration. What was at stake for the colonies, which were to become states, was no less than the preservation of their identity in the face of the new Commonwealth. The process was not easy. Landowners in Western Australia were especially reluctant – fearful of the democratic and trade union linkages with the eastern states imported by the goldminers crowding to exploit the new fields at Kalgoorlie. And contending political interests in New South Wales and Victoria – trade unions, the free-traders and protectionists – found it hard to concede power and to get a grip on how they would be able to influence a central government. No less than nine referenda were held in the various states – in one of them, in 1897, New South Wales voted against federation – and the Western Australians did not commit themselves until 1900. New Zealand stayed aloof from these battles, as it has stayed to one side of Australian political life ever since. By 1899, as an English observer noted, an 'immature' nationalism prevailed in New Zealand. Few New Zealanders would entertain 'the suggestion that the most vigorous national individuality of the southern hemisphere should forego its splendid prospect of independent evolution' by involvement with the Australian Commonwealth. New Zealanders, he contended, were 'no longer "Britons of the South", nor Australasians, but Maorilanders first'.[16] He was right – on all three counts. An obstreperous, not very thoughtful, instinctive sense of national identity was by then already well in place. Australia, too, at the turn of the twentieth century, was indulging its own taste for the 'immature' nationalism of enthusiastic imperialists. The federation of the Australian colonies forming the Commonwealth of Australia was proclaimed on 1 January 1901, in ceremonies which demonstrated an unwavering commitment to the British imperial system. In the quizzical prose of Manning Clark,

> Queen Victoria … was the lady in whose sovereign name the crowning word of union came. Australians might live under different stars, but their hearts were the hearts of yore. England had loyal sons beneath the Southern Cross.[17]

And nowhere more loyal than in that unquenchable imperial enthusiast across the Tasman Sea. At the last knock in 1899, there was a brief flurry of interest in federation in New Zealand. Then in 1900 – when the die had been cast as far as Australia was concerned – the New Zealand government appointed a royal commission, which recommended against federation because it was believed that the rights of Maori would be infringed and development would be compromised, through a loss of financial autonomy. In a not uncharacteristic bid to have it both ways, Richard Seddon then attempted to intervene as the Commonwealth of Australia Bill was being formulated in London for consideration by the British parliament. He proposed three amendments: giving New Zealand right of entry on the same terms as the other original colonies at any time; appeal rights to the High Court of Australia – in addition to the Privy Council; and permitting the two countries to be able to unify their defence forces as required. This egregious attempt to short-circuit what had been a laborious political process in Australia produced little more than an early outbreak of bad blood on both sides of the Tasman.

The issue of political union has not been given any official currency since that time, in either country. The Australians made a smooth transition to federation. No blood was shed, there were no life-or-death struggles. What had been achieved was an essentially pragmatic response to the growing interdependence of the Australian colonies, now states in the new Commonwealth. They could cohere around a federal arrangement with instinctive commitments to such notions as: state intervention to ensure fair treatment for all, protection of developing industry, a 'white' Australia, and continuing loyalty to the British Empire. New Zealand could proceed to pursue its own versions of these Antipodean lodestars. The two countries would be steady, reliable, comprehensively democratic, hard-working and, for almost another half-century, dependent. The British period of global ascendancy had stamped them both in very similar fashion, but had not forced them into the same mould.

chapter five

Brothers in Arms

From this day to the ending of the world,
But we in it shall be remembered;
We few, we happy few, we band of brothers;
For he to-day that sheds his blood with me
Shall be my brother ...[1]

P aradoxically for two countries so isolated from the storm centres of the world, military associations have hugely influenced links between Australia and New Zealand. Yet King Hal's beliefs in the imperishable bonds of military brotherhood have not been reflected in the development of a true ANZAC bond. Numerous shared campaigns round the world during the twentieth century – from South Africa to East Timor – have left an inheritance of genuine mutual respect and confidence in military circles. The focus, however, has been on participation in foreign wars rather than preparation of combined capabilities for regional defence purposes. Shared, even integrated, action in the field is not the same thing as a determination – at the political level – to join together for strategic purposes. Military respect does not equate with political. Moreover, passages at arms, as so often in history, have been transmuted into the stuff of separate national legend, rather than woven into integrated battle honours. From the carnage of the First World War, New Zealanders and Australians would each hew out new estimations of themselves. What emerged was a maimed nationhood for each, rather than any deep-rooted sense of collective identity. Gallipoli and the first ANZACs have left a confused legacy, at once a kind of blood brotherhood and prideful separate nationalisms.

Imperial Nationalism

The war in Southern Africa at the turn of the twentieth century, which pitched the Boer farming nation against British interests, tipped empire loyalty and 'British' patriotism over into assertive colonial nationalism. Colonial societies on both sides of the Tasman were already saturated in imperial nostrums. An Australian historian's description of the education system of the day gives the picture: 'Throughout the system, indoctrination was aimed at British-Australian loyalty. History, geography and literature were British, jingoistic and openly racist; loyalty to Queen and Empire was axiomatic and further encouraged by the cadet system and the drill manual.'[2] Confidence was high; there was little room for doubt about the splendours of empire. The Australian and New Zealand colonies had each been represented in the imperial panoply deployed for Queen Victoria's diamond jubilee celebrations in 1897 in London. British exuberance over their empire was itself virtually out of control. The empire's children had toy soldiers arrayed in the splendid uniforms of multitudinous colonies, and read the adventure yarns of the empire's heroes; at school they were subjected to military drill. British nationalism was bound up in military grandeur and the heroics of the great British battlefield successes – and failures. All of this was absorbed seemingly with the mother's milk in Australia and New Zealand.

When a tenuous political arrangement between British colonial interests and the Boers broke down in 1899, New Zealand and all six of the Australian colonies, plus the newly minted Australia itself (after 1 January 1901), rushed to commit mounted riflemen to the British Army's fight on the veldt. There was much talk of the lion's cubs coming to the aid of their dam. New Zealand, in an early manifestation of nationalistic rivalry with the Australians, offered a contingent two weeks before the war began. Prime Minister Seddon's bombastic speech to parliament neatly defined the paradox of a self-preening New Zealand nationalism set firmly within the frame of Empire. He poured scorn on a famous image of the inevitability of decline of empire, evoked by the English historian Thomas Macauley ('some traveller from New Zealand shall, in the midst of a vast solitude, take his stand upon a broken arch of London Bridge to sketch the ruins of St Pauls'.[3]) Far from it, said Seddon,

> I am sorry for Macauley, he little knew the New Zealander. The history ... will show that the New Zealander will not recount the downfall of Empire, but will fight to maintain it. ... I say our strength lies in being an integral part of this mighty British Empire, and that we should help to maintain its unity intact ... If we take responsibilities and share the burdens and expense of maintaining the Empire ... we shall, before many years have elapsed, be represented in the council of the nation at home – the New Zealander will be advising in council, not croaking on London Bridge.

This was the first leg of belief: military contributions would buy influence at the heart of empire. The second leg was that to get in ahead of the Australians was the measure of being a New Zealander: 'other colonies have made offers [of troops] but this is the first colony in which the representatives of the people in Parliament assembled have been called upon to give a vote upon this question. Let this vote be practically unanimous'. Britain declared war on the Boer republics in South Africa on 5 October 1899; the first New Zealand contingent was despatched amid scenes of wild enthusiasm on 21 October; the first New South Wales contingent marched to the docks one week later.

Australian loyalties were more tangled. Emotional links and ties of loyalty with Britain vied with the affection and political commitments most felt for their own colony, while recognition of a common Australian identity gathered increasing force. There were stronger anti-war feelings in Australia – stirred up by a continuing strong streak of anti-establishment feeling and by republican dismay that the new Commonwealth of Australia should still revel in the embrace of Queen and empire. The Boer War was the last hurrah for competition in imperial fealty among the separate Australian colonies. The decision to establish the Australian Commonwealth had been taken before hostilities opened. The first units representative of Australia, as such, could, however, not be put into the field until the federal government was inaugurated at the beginning of 1901. The colonies, soon to become states in the new Commonwealth, meanwhile remained the focus for everyday life. They rushed to send off their own contingents. Although perhaps few recognised it, for New Zealanders this was also the end of an era – the last occasion in which the seven South-land colonies would be competing on more or less even terms for the attention of the mother country. In future it would be 'little' New Zealand and 'big brother' Australia. Moreover, in South Africa itself, the New Zealanders were discovering for themselves a separate identity as 'Maorilanders' – something different from the Australians and certainly not to be confused with the British.

Wider strategic concerns were also having an impact on thinking in both countries. Edmund Barton, first Prime Minister of the new Commonwealth of Australia, put his finger on the underlying issue about the war in South Africa. Addressing the federal parliament in January 1902, he noted that

> the bond of Empire is not only one of mere patriotism – on which terms I think the bond of itself ought to be maintained if there were no ulterior considerations – but also one of self-interest ... in the event of Britain at any time losing control ... of the Suez Canal, the [trade] route by South Africa would become most important ... to ... Australia.[4]

In future, Australia, not the former colonies (and new States), would be responsible for international affairs. When the first battalion of the Australian Commonwealth Horse went off to war in February 1902, it was an inaugural showing on the world stage. But the change of gear would be almost imperceptible. To Seddon, on the other side of the Tasman, Asian-Pacific regional concerns were another cause for an active New Zealand engagement. The Sino-Japanese War of 1894–5 and a developing confrontation between Russian and Japanese interests in the north Pacific, alongside the predation of the European powers (and Japan) in China, were clearly on his by-no-means-trained-mind when he made his speech urging commitment to the South African War: 'See what is going on now in the way of division of territories in the Far East. Look at the nations which are established in China and in the Pacific.' For a small nation, 'security lies in being part of this mighty British Empire'.

Imperial Illusions

Visiting New Zealand in 1904, an acute French observer, André Siegfried, could see that drinking deep of the glories of empire was no preparation for the real world. 'Anxiety over external relations,' Siegfried observed,

> only weighs on New Zealand to the extent that she desires ... This colony is, in fact a spoilt child which never suffers for its sins, for a helping hand is always there to redeem its faults. It may then be asked what advantage New Zealand could possibly find in shaking off this yoke which is not a yoke?

The motivation for a shrill, but circumscribed and pragmatic, sense of national identity was found to lie in the need – in such a small and remote country – to be noticed and admired in the world at large. Siegfried discerned that policies were influenced not so much by 'imagination and sentiment' as by 'a curious form of a patriotic vanity, which makes the New Zealanders believe that the world expects much of them and that they must not be false to their destiny'. The guiding consideration appeared to Siegfried to be 'a blend of a too practical outlook with a too exalted sense of apostleship'. He could see that these were the sorts of reasons why 'New Zealanders have never dreamt, at any moment in their history, of political separation from England'. What is more, by way of such attachment New Zealand could steer clear of 'Australian suzerainty ... which would wound the New Zealanders' pride to its very roots ... In this way may be explained, quite naturally, the line of conduct followed by Mr Seddon's Government: resistance to Australia by drawing closer to England.' [5]

A few brave souls on both sides of the Tasman questioned the rationale of joining the British cause in South Africa, and its (distinctly questionable) morality, and were mostly pilloried. When Henry Lawson, already the bard of Australian-ness, said that the jingoism made him ashamed to be Australian, few listened. But at least in Australia there were, from the recently formed Australian Labor Party, strident notes of political opposition to the war. William Morris Hughes, who would be Australian prime minister during the First World War, condemned this colonial war as immoral and unjust. By contrast, in New Zealand – although a doughty pacifism was heard against the patriotic clamour – Seddon's Liberal government at one and the same time embraced the war and its likely radical opponents; imperial conformity was to all intents and purposes thus ensured and complete. The lessons of war are always disquieting, even for the most ardent of patriots. In South Africa the mass displacement of Boer people into atrocious camps and the razing of farms to 'clear the countryside' and the harsh, punitive campaigning took some of the gloss off the glories of empire. British military leadership was often incompetent and the British Army's performance in the field a great deal less than brilliant. Over 16,000 Australians and about 6500 New Zealanders served in South Africa in a succession of contingents. In the overblown language of the day, they would be 'proving themselves in the sternest test' on the battlefield. Ironically, as was to happen in later twentieth century wars, the chief consequence of enlisting in an imperial cause seems to have been that the Australians and New Zealanders separated themselves off from their British counterparts. They learned to look down on them, as less tough, less well-conditioned by the rigours of an outdoor life to the hardships of campaigning on the veldt. Enduring mythologies were established: about being intuitive soldiers, disinclined to accept orders without question, more democratic and therefore more successful and, indeed, 'better at the game' than their British cousins. Kipling, the poet-laureate of the new empire, took up the theme, contrasting the manly colonials with the effete English:

> And ye vaunted your fathomless power, and ye flaunted your iron pride,
> Ere – ye fawned on the younger nations for the men who could shoot and ride.
> Then ye returned to your trinkets; then ye contented your souls
> With the flannelled fools at the wicket or the muddied oafs at the goals.[6]

It was a pleasing conceit for the 'younger nations' to be recognised as effective, 'as the men who could shoot and ride'. As nationalism blossomed, New Zealanders revelled uncritically – not least in respect of the Australians – in such praise as was voiced by the pillar of the imperial establishment, *The Times* of London: 'they were, by general consent, regarded on the average as the best mounted troops in South Africa'.[7] Australians could point to the award of six Victoria Crosses as evidence of the conspicuous gallantry of Australians under fire. Behind the flag-waving, more focused local nationalisms were blossoming. It was not seen as paradoxical to be parading, at one and the same time, an uncritical and immature commitment to British interests and a resounding confidence in themselves as Australians or New Zealanders. The empire obviously was a security blanket and, in large measure, a substitute for thought. It was also a vehicle for activism. Support for 'Queen Victoria's Little Wars'[8] could be accommodated within their emerging economies – especially after the 1890s, when recovery from the depression of the previous decade boosted development. Engagement of this kind was politically profitable at home. What is more, New Zealand or Australian troop contingents could be fitted without difficulty into overall British command systems and would undoubtedly have been thought useful. Relatively easy engagement in colonial wars would then lead on to the bloody slopes of Gallipoli in 1915 and the terrible battles of the Somme in 1916. The price of empire escalated.

Australians drew another lesson from Boer War experience which put them ahead of the New Zealanders on the path to nationhood and identity. The 'Breaker Morant' affair – the trial by the British high command and subsequent execution by firing squad of three Australian officers for squalid war crimes – caused an uproar at home. Morant had been something of an outback celebrity, a 'bush' poet, horse-tamer and rural philanderer. The case was, however, principally seen as an affront to newborn 'Australian' national dignity. The Prime Minister told parliament that justice had been done. The real point, as expressed by Manning Clark, was that the execution by the British of three Australians was 'part of the price Australians paid for the British connection'.[9] (New Zealanders in South Africa tended to agree with the verdict, given the nature of the crime.)

Command and control of smaller national units within a large allied force is always a vexed military issue. Henceforth, Australian military leaders would insist on national disciplinary and courts martial arrangements. When the two countries joined with the British in their next and more serious engagement in the First World War, New Zealand had made no such provisions. Five New Zealanders were executed by firing squad on the Western Front between 1916 and 1918, and no Australians (with three to four times as many troops engaged). The New Zealand government, too star-struck by empire, had failed to take the elementary step of encompassing its own soldiers within its own disciplinary procedures. It was an inexcusable New Zealand lapse and the cases of the five soldiers executed still caused heart-ache eighty years later. (The outrage is generally directed at the British, when it was clearly the New Zealand government of the day which had failed to assert a necessary national authority.)

For all the empire enthusiasm on display during the Boer War, that engagement would expose deep-seated issues which lie at the heart of national assertiveness: how to define national interests within the broader canvas of empire (or alliance); how to secure those interests within much larger allied forces; who is responsible for what? Australia and New Zealand were as likely as not to approach such issues from different angles. The one would try the harder to assert an expressly national point of view; the other, and smaller, partner would be the more content to ride on imperial coat tails. Bizarrely, both could conclude that their respective approaches appropriately defined them. As André Siegfried had noted, New Zealanders would play the British card in preference to going in with the Australians. The Australians would grasp every opportunity, within the overall setting of imperial defence, to take the wider view by putting a distinctive national stamp on their role.

Naval Engagements

The Royal Navy was the prime instrument of British power. Security of trade links was vital to the continued well-being of its colonies and, of course, to the wealth of the United Kingdom itself. The strategic dilemma for Australia and New Zealand essentially boiled down to supporting a centrally controlled fleet able to be despatched to different parts of the world as required – 'one empire, one flag, one fleet'; or, devolution of naval responsibilities, permitting the member countries of the empire to look after their regional interests on their own account while joining together for collective security as required. Needless to say, London held most strongly to the 'one fleet' doctrine. Their partners in empire pushed variously for: local squadrons within the 'one fleet' concept; regional fleets, committed to the centralised navy only in the event of trouble; or outright endorsement of the pure doctrine of the centralised imperial navy. Behind it all lay a fundamental issue: are the interests of smaller regional countries better served by upholding the central power of an alliance or by making their own dispositions to uphold security in their own backyard? What if their own military wherewithal is inadequate for protection of their own interests? What if the great power cannot spare the resources to look after its regional partners? These are issues that plague Australian and New Zealand defence thinking to the present day.

As early as 1859, the Royal Navy established an Australian station 'for the general protection of the trade of the Australian Colonies and of Tasmania and New Zealand'. A local squadron of British ships would be maintained in the area, under British command. 'In the event of war,' the Admiralty noted, it may be necessary, 'to give periodical convoys to treasure ships proceeding home either by the Cape of Good Hope or Cape Horn.' The boon of empire had to be freely transferable both ways, to Mother as well as offspring; colonial gold must make it back to the imperial coffers in London. A separate 'Australian' command area was carved out from the zone of responsibility of first, the East Indies station based in Colombo and, later, the Far East station established at Shanghai. Almost casually, Australian and New Zealand defence interests were taken under the imperial cloak. There was no discussion. The Admiralty in London simply decided on arrangements suited to its own interests. Only six years later, in 1865, under the Colonial Naval Defence Act, London passed the hat: the colonies should help by sharing the costs of naval defence. Some local ships were acquired and a beginning made on the construction of harbour defences.

In 1887, the Australian and New Zealand colonies, for the first and only time, agreed to join forces in creating a combined 'Australasian' naval force to supplement Royal Navy units of the Australian squadron. It would be a hundred years before any similar exercise in naval togetherness would be attempted again.[10] Colonial dudgeon about the weakness of the imperial effort to meet regional preoccupations moved even the New Zealand authorities to agree to make the necessary funds available to build a quasi-independent combined regional force to supplement what the British might be willing to provide. The extra ships were not to be removed in wartime without the consent of the colonial authorities; New Zealand insisted that two vessels be stationed in its waters in peace-time. Sadly for the spirit of Australia-New Zealand togetherness, nothing much came of this scheme.

Instead, the pendulum swung back from the regional towards the global. A new naval agreement in 1903 re-established the principle of 'one empire, one flag, one fleet'. Antipodean concerns about security in the Pacific had been, at least partly, allayed by the Anglo-Japanese Naval Alliance of 1902, which effectively countered Russian pressures in northern Asia. Japan proved the point convincingly with its crushing defeat of the Russian fleet at Tsushima in 1905. The naval alliance with Japan was a smart move for the British. As a result, the Admiralty felt able to withdraw units of the fleet from the Pacific for service in the North Sea and Mediterranean as a counter to the developing German threat. But this strategic balancing act was not applauded in Australia and New Zealand. White supremacist feeling was strong and few were comfortable with the thought of a Japanese proxy for British power. Moreover, the demands of the central balance in Europe were clearly taking precedence at a time when Japanese expansionism was beginning to lend weight to regional strategic anxieties. Then the United States entered the lists with a deliberate display of naval power, masterminded by President Theodore Roosevelt, to remind Japan that it did not have the field to itself. The cruise of the 'Great White Fleet' was wildly popular in both New Zealand and Australia and an important harbinger of things to come.

In Australia, Alfred Deakin, second Prime Minister of the Commonwealth, applied an independent and subtle mind to what he saw as the central problem in imperial affairs: how to reconcile the unity of the whole empire with the self-government of its parts? Policy co-ordination was essential and this could only be achieved by effective participation of all in the government of the whole. These were novel and challenging notions to the authorities in Whitehall, not least in matters of imperial defence policy. Deakin's sense of a growing Australian nationalism did not sit easily with London's view that the countries of the empire should help pay for 'one navy', which would be despatched their way when needed. But Deakin reasoned that it was better by far to build up regional maritime forces in ways that could amplify the strength of the main battle fleet, if needed, while securing a large measure of local self-reliance. When Deakin first attended a Colonial Conference in 1887, Lord Salisbury, then British Prime Minister, had condescendingly dismissed the strategic concerns of the distant and isolated British communities in the Pacific. At the 1907 Imperial Conference Deakin noted that in their dealings with the Colonial Office, Australia encountered 'A certain impenetrability or a certain remoteness, perhaps geographically justified; a certain weariness of people much pressed with affairs, and greatly overburdened'. (Any Australian or New Zealander who has had dealings in Washington in the late twentieth century would respond to that remark.) As early as 1905 he had understood that 'any defences, if they are to be appreciated as Australian must be distinctively of that character. At present we are without any visible evidence of our participation in the Naval Force towards which we contribute.' On his return from the conference he announced the intention to abandon the subsidy arrangement and establish what would become the Royal Australian Navy.

There were stirrings of a regional kind in New Zealand, too. James Allen, a prominent member of the opposition Reform Party, wanted the country to throw in its naval lot with Australia. Allen, born in Australia and raised in England, proposed that New Zealand's Royal Navy subsidy be devoted to the purchase of extra units for a combined regional fleet, an 'Australasian navy'. The Prime Minister Joseph Ward had also been born in Australia, but he was an empire man and saw no future in trans-Tasman collaboration. New Zealand's future destiny, he roundly asserted, was as 'distinct from that of Australia as the light to the dark'. (No prizes for guessing which Ward thought would be which.) Allen rejected Ward's surreal rhetoric; the Australians, he proclaimed, were New Zealand's 'brothers in the Pacific', and had adopted the 'right policy' in forming their own navy. He shared Australian concerns about the rising power of Japan and was less sanguine than his colleagues about the wisdom of total reliance on the timely arrival of the Royal Navy in the event of trouble.

Whether out of sentiment, practical estimation of how a small country could best project itself in the world, realistic strategic assessment of where the real threat lay, or chauvinistic determination not to follow an Australian lead, New Zealanders opted to build the defence connection with Britain. Ward thought in terms of: 'One Imperial Navy with all the Oversea Dominions contributing, either in ships or money, and with the Naval stations at the self-governing Dominions supplied with ships by and under the control of the Admiralty.' New Zealand, accordingly, increased its subsidy payment to the British towards the maintenance of the Australian Squadron (which was maintained while Australia's own naval force was under construction). Allen's thinking, like the earlier attempt in 1887 to join with Australia in naval matters, was out of key with gathering national sentiment in New Zealand. There was no political mileage in strategic collaboration with Australia. Trans-Tasman rivalry was not far below the surface. Ward courted British favour by stipulating that – unlike the new Australian navy – New Zealand would place no constraints on the deployment elsewhere, if needs be, of Royal Navy ships stationed in its region. In March 1909, he upped the stakes even further: in response to clamour in Britain that German naval building programmes would undermine the Royal Navy's supremacy at sea, New Zealand gave the British a battle-cruiser. Funding was offered for 'at least one, and, if necessary, two first class battleships of the Dreadnought or latest types, to be completely under the control of the Admiralty'. HMS *New Zealand* would in due course enter Royal Navy service, paid for by the New Zealand taxpayer. (It took eighteen years, until long after the ship had gone to the scrapyard, to pay off the loans.)

Public opinion in Australia was going the other way. The new Australian Commonwealth should have its own national defence capabilities. At the same time, the New Zealanders were not to be allowed to steal Australian thunder in London. In August 1909, Deakin, at heart an empire man – representative of what Manning Clark defined as the governing class of Australian-Britons – offered an Australian Dreadnought to the empire. The offer was made, moreover, against the expense of the orders already placed for ships for the new Australian fleet. For all the individuality implicit in the notion of the new Commonwealth, Australia could not disengage from the inherent framework of empire.

Not surprisingly, the New Zealanders duly earned high marks in London, and were gratified. Winston Churchill, who became First Lord of the Admiralty in 1911, was of the view that, 'No greater insight into political and strategic points has ever been shown by a community hitherto unversed in military matters'. But Churchill, the grand strategist, had his own axe to grind. Writing to the Colonial Secretary in 1912, he was of the view that 'the 1909 arrangements made with Australia were not very satisfactory as far as British naval interests were concerned. The whole principle of local Navies is, of course, thoroughly vicious …' Churchill was not one for devolution of power. James Allen became Minister of Defence in New Zealand in 1912 in the Conservative Reform government led by William Massey. For all his enthusiasm for the regional approach while in opposition, Allen could read the signs in government, and seems to have let the matter lie. Allen and Massey wanted to build up national naval capabilities; indeed, Allen had a testy interview with Winston Churchill to this end. But the New Zealand view remained that regional forces should not compromise imperial unity, and that centralised command and control should continue. New Zealand even rejected the Australian position that naval forces in the Pacific should not be transferred without the consent of local governments.[11]

The establishment of the Australian Commonwealth in 1901 had changed the mix of Australia-New Zealand naval calculations – and everything else. Australians got on with the business of developing national defence capabilities. Meanwhile New Zealand, by supporting the principle of empire defence, could score marks if not in heaven, at least in London. Yet Australia, too, wished to take its place within the imperial system, for the same sorts of reasons as New Zealand: instinct and limitations of size and scope. In all this there lay the essence of the Australia-New Zealand defence relationship through to the present day. One tries to side-step confining connections with its larger regional partner by striving after an alternative – first in the empire and now in the United Nations. The other grandly proceeds on a regional tack, despite the twin aggravations of knowing that it cannot, if push comes to shove, go it alone and that it must accordingly also throw in its lot with a larger partner, first the empire and now the United States.

Naval policy mirrored the contradictions of empire. The Royal Australian Navy came into being in 1911. In 1913, when the battle-cruiser HMAS *Australia* and six other fighting ships steamed into Sydney harbour for the first time, the fleet was under Australian, not British, command. Australian pride was stirred. Yet with it went 'avowals of loyalty to England and of the determination to maintain responsibility for Australia and thereby contribute to the "fabric of Empire" which was held to be the guarantor of peace in the world'.[12] Nor were things all one way in New Zealand. While still committed to the concept of the single imperial navy, the New Zealand government also wished to show that the payments it was making produced something tangible in its own region. Thus, at the 1909 Conference it was envisaged that under the subsidy system, two cruisers, three destroyers and two submarines would be allotted to what was to become the New Zealand Division of the Royal Navy. But as war loomed in Europe, such a redistribution of resources simply could not happen. The New Zealand approach had all the weakness of dependency. Five years later, the admiralty had allocated to New Zealand a single, 1890s light cruiser, which was in transit when war was declared. The empire's Pacific fleet never eventuated, as the fateful build-up of forces in Europe proceeded unchecked. When war came, national interests were subordinated to the 'decisive battle' thesis. All effort was devoted to trying to ensure that the centre of empire would hold. And when that decisive naval battle was fought at Jutland in 1916, HMS *New Zealand* was in the battle line; HMAS *Australia* was not, having been damaged during night manoeuvres a few days beforehand in a collision – with HMS *New Zealand*.

Together But Separate

Before the First World War, no less a personage than Field Marshal Lord Kitchener, the apotheosis of British military glory, saw the defence of Australia and New Zealand as a whole – at least in terms of requirements for land forces. He recommended that military arrangements should be brought together. An officer training establishment should be established to which both countries would contribute; there should be exchanges of officers and planning discussions between the respective staffs. Subsequently, it was agreed that the two countries should, if required, provide the empire with a joint infantry or mounted horse division – two Australian brigades, one New Zealand. Staff officers were charged with standardisation in matters of supply, planning, intelligence, and so on. Had there been the political will, truly integrated forces could have been worked up and in due course put in the field. Such tentative military togetherness developed before the war did not, however, overcome New Zealand sensitivity about subordination of its interests and identity in a larger Australian effort. The New Zealanders did not regard themselves as committed to forming a joint force with the Australians; the greater priority was to go with the British, as a New Zealand element in an empire army.

On the outbreak of war, the two Antipodean countries immediately supplied what London described as a 'great and urgent imperial service' – the capture of German establishments in Papua and Samoa. A powerful German squadron was known to be at large in the Pacific, but the empire's fleet, including HMS

New Zealand, had been concentrated in the North Sea. New Zealand's commitment to the 'one fleet' doctrine proved an embarrassment. With no ships of its own to escort its troops, New Zealand was obliged to depend on the Australians, whose advocacy of a regional navy proved to have been the right call – HMAS *Australia* escorted the convoy to Samoa. New Zealand's first independent military action proceeded under Australian cover. Caution had been justified, as a German squadron appeared off New Zealand-occupied Samoa a fortnight later but failed to investigate. The Australian regional fleet was also available to escort their own expedition against New Guinea; landing at Rabaul, the Australians suffered casualties in subduing the German garrison, beating the New Zealanders to be 'baptised' by fire in the First World War.

An inability to deploy effective naval forces was again an embarrassment to New Zealand in September 1914, when the first army units raised for service in Europe were to be despatched. Determined to be in the vanguard as the 'loyalest of the loyal', the government sent the transports off without any escorting warships. The Australian Naval Board, reinforcing advice given by the Admiralty in London, suggested that the risks were too high when the whereabouts of the German Pacific fleet was not known. The troopships were recalled from halfway across the Tasman Sea. The German fleet then revealed itself by bombarding Papeete, over 3000 kilometres from New Zealand. Both the Admiralty and the Australians prodded the New Zealanders to proceed, since the danger was past. However, New Zealand Prime Minister Massey, having been rash once, became over-cautious, waiting for the arrival of a British and a Japanese cruiser – provided under the same Anglo-Japanese naval agreement which had caused such racial disquiet in the Antipodes ten years before – before letting the convoy sail, three weeks late. It was a lesson that naval capabilities are not divisible and should be at hand, not subject to the needs of a great power on the other side of the world. In the event, on 1 November, Admiral von Spee's ships demonstrated that they were to be reckoned with by routing a British squadron off the Chilean coast, before being heavily defeated five weeks later at the Battle of the Falkland Islands. With that, the maritime challenge in the Pacific was effectively ended, and the Australians could commit their 'regional' navy to the 'global' battle.

In late October 1914, ten transports carrying 8500 New Zealanders met up with the Australians, over 20,000 strong in twenty-eight ships, in King George Sound, near where Australia turns to face the Indian Ocean. It was a stirring event. According to the official New Zealand war history, which to the sceptical modern eye sometimes reads like *The Boys' Own Paper*, as the New Zealand ships entered, 'The cheering and counter-cheering, the Maori war cries and the answering coo-ees would have moved a stoic'.[13] This was not quite the first time in history that soldiers of the New World had set off to come to the aid of the Old. Canadians were already in action in Belgium. But it was close. Perhaps a few sensed the significance of Australians and New Zealanders joining in a common cause. But for most, it was all just plain exciting, a high adventure: escape from the ordinariness of life. Manning Clark's survey of attitudes aboard the troopships was probably close to the mark:

> The men on the convoy who were longing for a chance to 'get at 'em', the men who were on board because they feared they would not be able to look a mate square in the eye again, the men who needed the six-bob-a-day, the men who wanted to get away from their wives, the men who believed they owed the Empire a life, and the men who could never find words to explain anything they did in life, were about to have their opportunity.[14]

But excitement blended with solemnity. On the way across the Indian Ocean the cruiser HMAS *Sydney* intercepted and destroyed the German warship *Emden*. 'How the New Zealanders envied the Australians this momentous achievement of their young navy,' the New Zealand official history recorded.[15]

Be that as it may, some New Zealanders were already creating the mythology that they were more serious soldiers, more dedicated to their responsibilities, than the Australians. After they had been at sea only a few days, Lieutenant Colonel W.G. Malone (an austere disciplinarian who would become a figure of legend for New Zealanders after he was killed on the summit of Chunuk Bair less than a year later) wrote in his diary that he had a prejudice against Australians. He found fault with them for failing adequately to black-out their ships in the convoy: 'There is evidence of slackness on their part and a comparison unfavourable to them can be made every day.'[16] Nevertheless, the sense of occasion was strong. Describing the convoy entering the Red Sea, Malone wrote:

> I went up on the bridge and saw a rare picture; the sea full of ships moving into position with the two Adens silhouetted against the sky ... the rocky land stern and rugged ... It was most impressive; magnificent. I am glad that I have seen it; nay, see it and live to take my part in the action.

Despite sharing this great adventure, there is little evidence that the New Zealanders and Australians developed any sense of common identity along the way. They went into separate camps on arrival in Egypt; there was little by way of integrated training; their uniforms were distinctive. Australian folklore, built around the wide, open spaces of the outback and the roaming life of the free-spirited bushmen, contemptuous of authority but ever solicitous of their 'mates', was transmuted into a national style in the army. It was like no other. For the first time, the new Australian Commonwealth was deploying a national army; all were members of the Australian Imperial Forces (AIF), and wore the insignia of the rising sun and the famous slouch hat turned up on the rifle-firing side. Their collective identity was defined. The New Zealanders had little of this. They did not adopt their own 'lemon-squeezer' hat until after Gallipoli and, for the most part, were deployed in units with regional names, such as the 1st Otagos or the Wellington Regiment or the Manawatu Mounted Rifles. The regional labels were important to them, not to be submerged beneath any explicit fostering of the notion that they belonged to a national army.

The usual games of national stereotyping and myth-making went on. New Zealanders were 'colourless', according to the Australian war historian C.E.W. Bean; Australians tended to think of New Zealanders as a 'pale imitation' of themselves.[17] A New Zealand trooper's judgement of Australians in general would have found a wide echo among his compatriots: 'The Australian, and more especially the town-bred man, is a skiting bumptious fool, who thinks nobody knows anything but himself.' There seem to have been plenty of fights: 'If we meet or see them in a restaurant or anywhere in town, there is generally a row of some kind.'[18] Australians tended to think the

> New Zealanders were 'soft on the blacks'. They were far too inclined to treat them as they would a Maori, without recognising that New Zealanders were demeaning themselves as white men by not recognising that the 'gyppo' was a lesser being on the human scale.[19]

When they finally went to war, the extraordinary circumstances of the ANZAC toehold on Gallipoli would, if anything, reinforce rather than diminish the sense of difference.

The New Zealanders, too, were egalitarian by instinct and disliked much of the military ritual, especially the obligation to salute officers whom they did not necessarily respect. They were also far from always being well-behaved. But the national style was already low-key and unexuberant; in the military context, the New Zealanders were regarded as more accepting of the rigours of army discipline than the Australians, and more willing to accept British precepts about successful soldiering. Whereas the Australians in Egypt made much of being different, a new breed, the New Zealanders simply strove to be the best. 'The Australians walk about as if they own everything,' a New Zealander wrote home.[20] By contrast, New Zealand national myth was still centred on the conceit that New Zealand was the most favoured of the British dominions and New Zealanders were the 'select' among overseas Britons. They felt no need for swagger. Their identity as New Zealanders was plain to them; they were, apart from anything else, not Australians.

In deciding not to federate with Australia, New Zealand and New Zealanders were thrown back on the need consciously to define themselves in their own way. The First World War was indisputably an important stage in that process. W. P. Morrell, a New Zealand historian of the 1930s, made an important distinction between empire and national identity:

> The men who fought, fought for the Empire, but also for New Zealand. The Empire belonged to the realm of imagination: New Zealand belonged to the realm of experience. They thought of it as their country. By the very fact of coming to the old world and coming in a body, they could not but realize that they had as New

Zealanders, their own individuality, that they were not ... merely Englishmen living overseas.[21]

The New Zealand identity may be obvious to New Zealanders, but the articulation of such notions, in terms of grand national dreams or large themes about 'mateship' or solidarity, is rarely attempted, even to this day. For the soldiers of the First World War, their nationalism would have been more than a little self-conscious, low-key and contained – British, only more so, New Zealand-British. They identified themselves as 'Fernlanders'; 'Kiwis' came later. After their return from Gallipoli, where a Maori unit had performed most creditably, a new respect for the place of Maori in New Zealand life was evident. 'The last and most spectacular stage in the grand reorganization [to incorporate all New Zealanders into the 1st New Zealand Division] was the arrival of the 2nd Maori Contingent.' The Maori ceremonies of welcome and tribute were watched by the entire division:

> The emotional meaning, the elegy for the dead and the exhortation to the living, came through with no need of translation ... Last of all the old Maoris filed along the ranks of the new and greeted and shook hands with each. Next morning veterans and newcomers were indistinguishably assimilated.[22]

For the most part, the Australians and New Zealanders who took part in the Gallipoli campaign were native-born, not themselves immigrants, but sons of immigrants. Away from home, they would learn where home was. The rootless empire loyalism that led many of their compatriots to call England 'home' would have little meaning as they came up against the British and found that they had little in common. On Gallipoli itself, the commitment of Australian and New Zealander alike to the 'greatest empire in the world' would also be shaken by the disorganisation, poor planning, skimpy support systems and, above all, by the aloofness and incompetence of British staff officers. In other words, they did not come together as members of an imperial cohort. Rather, they each saw themselves in their own 'tribal' terms. 'It seems great', a New Zealand soldier wrote, 'to be such a long way from home but we are all New Zealanders and now that we are away from our own country we all stick together like glue.'

ANZAC

Before the first landings at Gallipoli on 25 April 1915, the Australia & New Zealand Army Corps was constituted in Egypt with two divisions: the 1st Australian (there were eventually two Australian divisions at Gallipoli) and the New Zealand and Australian Division (with two brigades of New Zealanders and two of Australians plus a New Zealand artillery brigade) – 'New Zealand coming first, as it is the nucleus on which the Division is built and all the staff is New Zealand'.[23] (The acronym 'ANZAC' entered the language out of a lowly administrative decision at corps headquarters to have a rubber stamp made to facilitate correspondence.) Australian and New Zealand mounted brigades were not incorporated at the outset because their horses were not likely to be useful among Gallipoli's crags. However, they were soon required to leave their horses behind and join as infantry. The New Zealand and Australian divisional structure was maintained throughout the Dardanelles campaign, under the command of an austere Anglo-Irishman, Alexander Godley, who knew New Zealand and New Zealanders well, having been charged with the establishment of national forces before the war. The Australians were ahead of the New Zealanders in securing national command of national forces and in fanning nationalist sentiment from the campaign. When William Throsby Bridges, who commanded the 1st Australian Division, was killed at Gallipoli, his body was returned to Australia for a hero's burial. Paradoxically, Bridges had opposed the formation of separate Australian national forces before the war. In life, according to Manning Clark, he was 'one of those Australian-Britons who saw no difficulty in being both an Australian nationalist and a loyal son of King and Empire'. In death he became a symbol of Australian patriotism.

ANZAC, the legend, was not born in any formal military structure, but out of the near-breakdown of such structures in the truly extraordinary circumstances of the Gallipoli landing. As the ships left Lemnos for the Gallipoli landings, a young Sydney clerk was in no doubt that theirs was an Australian – not imperial, not Australasian, not ANZAC – cause: 'Today most momentous in Australian history – Australian force moves forward to attack Turkey from the sea. Now the world can watch the success of Australian arms. The officers and men are very keen. Sir Ian Hamilton expects a lot from us.' The general feeling was one of confidence: 'Who could stop us?' another Australian wrote, 'Not the bloody Turks!' Put ashore in the wrong place and faced with steep and confused country, the Australians clambered for the high ground. The New Zealanders, who followed a few hours later, were unstinting in their praise: 'All along the beach were dead and dying Australians (3rd Brigade) who had landed at dawn with splendid courage and drove the Turks back over the ridge of hills.' The New Zealand historian of the campaign, who cited this account, noted that 'Every [New Zealand] letter, every diary, records the praise and admiration for the Australian effort: "No orders, no proper military team-work, no instructions. Just absolute heroism".'[24] Once ashore, national and unit boundaries broke down in the chaotic terrain. The dour Malone noted the consequences: 'As the New Zealanders landed they were rushed up to the heights, mixed up higgledy-piggledy among themselves and with the Australians with the result, in the case of my men anyhow (in my opinion), in serious avoidable loss.' The units more or less sorted themselves out. Eventually three divisions of the ANZAC held right (1st and 2nd Australian) and left (the New Zealand and Australian) sections of the line. However, the line was not much more than two-and-a-half kilometres long; and the enclave never more than 1000 metres deep, stretched across broken, precipitous barren hills. Continuing interaction and interdependence was a fact of life. For the first and only time, a true sense of trans-Tasman community grew on the desperate slopes of the Dardanelles Peninsula. Out of a shared intense experience there came a deep sense of fellow feeling, but hardly an interwoven ANZAC military – let alone political – fabric.

Malone, an effective and decisive commander, made an impact on the conduct of the campaign by securing a major strong-point and making it impregnable. His intolerance of the independent Australian style bordered on the ludicrous. On his sector, 'I insisted on the Australians being all withdrawn. General Walker asked if I could get on without them. I told him they were a source of weakness.' On being transferred from the ANZAC sector at Gallipoli to the British lines at Cape Helles, he wrote, 'It is a relief to get in where war is being waged scientifically and where we are clear of the Australians. They seem to swarm about our line like flies ... They are like masterless men going their own ways.'[25] The Australian legend, however, was of a dashing soldiery, free spirited – not at all inclined to conform to traditional military discipline – but capable of great daring and initiative; not so much masterless as men of initiative and independence of mind. (For example, in May, delicate high-level talks with Turkish emissaries were held in a cave on the beach to establish the basis for a cease-fire, for both sides to bury their dead. It is recorded that the solemn proceedings were interrupted by an Australian soldier bursting in to say, 'Have any of you bastards got my kettle?')

New Zealanders had only supporting parts to play in the great Australian drama of creating a nationalism. Thus, Manning Clark, writing in 1981 about the lead-up to Gallipoli: 'Australians, aided by the gallant New Zealanders, and guided by more experienced British and French forces,' were to be employed to deliver a strategic knock-out punch.[26] The Australians fashioned the ANZAC legend out of Australian clay from the outset. The diary of the war historian Charles Bean, who was present for much of the campaign as a war correspondent, cemented the Australian role into the national consciousness. Even before the war Bean had been articulating implausible, high-flown notions of Australian destiny, founded in a vigorous model of a 'new man', a 'utilitarian but clean, a very "square" man who valued frankness highly, a man who owned no class distinctions'.[27] Writing in the *Sydney Morning Herald* on 22 June 1907, Bean had maintained that the constant struggle of life in Australia, against drought, fires, strong men, unbroken horses and cattle – 'fierce as any warfare, has made of the Australian as fine a fighting man as exists'. Embarrassing mythologising of this kind, about the stamp of a rural inheritance on what was already predominantly an urbanised country, prepared the way for the national legends of the 'Aussie digger' woven around the Gallipoli campaign. Bean's war reporting established the 'digger' as the type of manly hero, the unyielding fighter, disrespectful of tradition, that an ambitious new country demanded. Later in the campaign, a young but influential Melbourne newspaperman, Keith Murdoch, visited the peninsula and reported the courage, endurance and spirit of the Australians in glowing terms. According to Manning Clark, Murdoch was 'impressed by the affection of these fine Australian soldiers for each other and for their homeland. Australianism had become among them a more powerful sentiment than before'.[28] C.J. Dennis, the bard of Australian larrikinism, contributed in his own way to the legend. His collection, *The Songs of a Sentimental Bloke*, published in October 1915, left no room for doubt that the war would make Australia a land fit for heroes.

> An' each man is the clean, straight man 'is Maker meant 'im for,
> An' each man knows 'is brother man at last.
> Shy strangers, till a bugle blast preached 'oly brother'ood;
> But mateship they 'ave found at last; an' they have found it good.

The military framework exists because of the fundamental importance of co-ordination, clearly defined command and control procedures, and the development of integrated responses to the problems of the battlefield. Australian and New Zealand units were manoevred in support of one another. In the August offensives, the Australians on the right were committed to attacks, including the almost-suicidal assaults on the covered Turkish trenches at Lone Pine and the Nek, as counterpoint to the efforts of the New Zealand and Australian Division on the left, in which the Wellington Regiment, under Malone, achieved the greatest gains of the campaign – holding the summit of Chunuk Bair for a day. At the deepest and most fundamental level, the two countries were engaged together in literally a life-or-death enterprise. Of actual troop numbers deployed on the peninsula during the campaign, the ratio of Australians to New Zealanders was almost three to one. Casualties from the whole doomed enterprise were in the same proportion: 7594 Australians and 2721 New Zealanders died; 18,500 Australians and 4752 New Zealanders were wounded.

Few among them would have known, or cared, that they were fighting across the Dardanelles from the same shore of Asia Minor as the Greek expedition against Troy, reported on by Homer in that first war history, *The Iliad*, written some 3500 years earlier. In their more prosaic way, they too would create a legend. Like their predecessors, they found themselves tied down together in a precarious foothold on an alien coast, and could not discover anything in the grisly business of fighting that overcame their separatist instincts in peace-time. Indeed, the reverse. They had no national grievances with, and little knowledge of, the Ottoman Empire. What united them was what Homer described as bringing the 'multitudinous tribes' of Greece together: the straight-forward military need to operate in a combined way. Like the Greeks before them, they were moved essentially by the spirit of their tribe: they joined together to make a combined force not out of friendship or mutual respect but in response to military need. The assemblage of the tribal armies of Greece on the plains of Troy all those centuries before was little different.

After Gallipoli, the Australians and New Zealanders were reconstituted into two army corps – I and II ANZAC – for consignment to the battlefields on the Western Front. Within those two formations, the New Zealanders established their own separate New Zealand Division, with a New Zealander in command. To this day, there is an unusual closeness to the military relationship and a mutuality of confidence between New Zealand and Australian military people. (In Vietnam, for example, the two national forces were even able to field a combined infantry battalion, representing a degree of military intimacy perhaps previously unknown in the annals of warfare.) An Anzac mounted division, with one New Zealand and three AIF brigades under the command of an Australian, Major-General H.G. Chauvel, fought with great success against the Turks for the rest of the war in Sinai and Palestine. In France, I and II ANZAC were maintained for a time; then, after the two formations had been separated in different field armies on the Western Front, an Australian and New Zealand Corps command was re-established, with the New Zealand division alongside two Australian divisions. But the dreadful circumstances of the war, first on the Somme in 1916, in Flanders, then back in northern France in 1918, gave few opportunities for operating in tandem. With the home-grown Australian, John Monash in command, the ANZACs helped turn back the German offensive in March 1918 in what was the last combined operation by the Australians and New Zealanders. A post-war citation issued to the New Zealand Division by the French War Council makes official mention of what became another ANZAC legend: 'its reputation was such that on the arrival of the division on the Somme battlefield during the most critical days of March 1918, the flight of the inhabitants immediately ceased.' For the final and decisive battles of the war, the Australian divisions were reformed into a single Australian Corps commanded by Monash. The Australian priority was to establish a national chain of command rather than to persist with the ANZAC combined arrangement.

Military systems are allergic to divided loyalties. They are certainly a poor vehicle for the carriage of supranational notions. The divisions, brigades and battalions, within which the individual soldiers find themselves, foster national identity and separatism. At unit level the emphasis is on cohesion, discipline, teamwork, on generating – in the most fundamental way – a spirit of 'all-for-one and one-for-all'. This purely military necessity in no way serves to diminish the sense of national identity inherent in the national formations concerned. Indeed, the reverse happens. Operations in close proximity with, or alongside the national formations of other countries, serve to reinforce prejudices about 'us' and 'them'.

Out of a harsh shared experience would come a new and brilliant talisman – ANZAC – to stand for the combined purposes of Australia and New Zealand. The Australians, however, would take possession of the ANZAC myth. A member of the Australian parliament recently surprised New Zealand officials by not knowing that the 'NZ' in ANZAC stood for New Zealand, or that Gallipoli was a shared story. A fine new suspension bridge across the Parramatta River was opened a year or so ago in Sydney and christened the ANZAC bridge; the Australian flag was flown above both arches. It took gentle reminders from New Zealand that Australia had no pre-emptive right to 'ANZAC' before it was agreed that the New Zealand flag might be flown at one end. Ignorance was hardly surprising. Exclusivity set in early. Even in late December 1915, only days after the evacuation from the Dardanelles, Major-General I.G. McKay, speaking at the Melbourne Town Hall had no doubt but that ANZAC and Australia were synonymous:

> the first great sacred spot in the history of Australia was the ANZAC beach and the heights above it ... There were 20,000 of us on a 380 acre selection for several months, under fire all the time. Small as it was that bit of Gallipoli would forever be part of Australia.[29]

New Zealanders' exasperation with such Australian self-absorption and conceits would become a large element in their own sense of identity. It has remained so. Many were bitter. A wounded New Zealand soldier hospitalised in England after the war wrote home on 26 April 1919:

> Yesterday, ANZAC Day, was commemorated here by a march through London of the Aussies. The New Zealanders were not represented. They didn't land on Gallipoli, although you might have thought so once. The Aussies did all the work and here the term ANZAC is applied exclusively to them in spite of two of the letters in the word.[30]

Gut nationalism springs from such slights. No one appreciates being taken for granted – least of all the inhabitants of a smaller country in respect of a larger. Yet there is a pecking order in these things – Australians no more like being patronised by the British or Americans than New Zealanders by Australians. New Zealanders have long since learned a series of defensive mechanisms. The official war correspondent Ashmead Bartlett, drafted his report of the first day of the Gallipoli landings on 25 April with no mention of the New Zealanders at all. By chance, a naval officer friend of General Godley, the commander of the New Zealand and Australian Division, censored the despatch and added the words 'New Zealand' or 'New Zealanders' as appropriate after 'Australia' or 'Australians'. A British member of parliament, Aubrey Herbert, who served on Gallipoli as a roving intelligence officer to the division, put his finger on New Zealand fatalism:

> I admired nothing in the War more than the spirit of these sixty-three New Zealanders, who were soon to go on to their last fight. When the day's work was over, and the sunset swept the sea, we used to lean upon the parapet and look up to where Chunuk Bair flamed, and talk. The great distance from their homeland created an atmosphere of loneliness. The loneliness was emphasised by the fact that the New Zealanders

rarely received the same recognition as the Australians in the Press, and many of their gallant deeds went unrecorded or were attributed to their great neighbours. But they had a silent pride that put these things into proper perspective. The spirit of these men was unconquered and unconquerable.[31]

The New Zealanders, when they went to France, called themselves the Silent Division – whether to make a trans-Tasman comparison or simply to establish taciturnity as the rule, is not recorded. Certainly, there were no New Zealand war correspondents to report from the front. Neither Gallipoli nor the notable subsequent performances of New Zealand soldiery in the First World War became sounding boards for New Zealand nationalism. New Zealand emerged, scarred but reticent. Yet as O.E. Burton, a New Zealand infantryman – who turned pacifist in the Second World War – wrote,

> Somewhere between the bloody ridge of Chunuk Bair in August 1915 and the black swamp in front of Passchendaele in October 1917, New Zealand quite definitely found individuality and nationality.[32]

The ANZAC legend owes much to the accidents of the campaign that enabled the Antipodeans to stamp their own identity on a corner of a desperate enterprise. The British high command, doubting the calibre of the Australians and New Zealanders, had allocated them their own separate sector of the Gallipoli front, confident that the main thrust from the south would be decisive. Neither succeeded; not the British or the French or the ANZACs ever broke out of their tightly constrained perimeters. If they had, the ANZAC experience would have been more comprehensively shared with other allied units. But in the process of failure two new countries, strong in differentiated beliefs about themselves, caught up with old messages about the global character of toil and trouble. French, British and Indian losses at the Dardanelles were far greater than those of the ANZACs. The Turkish defence cost them more dearly than the entire allied attack. More inured to triumphs and disasters, these 'old' countries have relegated the affair to history. In New Zealand and Australia it is still necessary to revert systematically to the ANZAC story. Each year thousands of young New Zealanders and Australians journey to Gallipoli for the dawn service to mark the anniversary of the landing on 25 April 1915. Many carry the medals earned by their grandfathers and great grandfathers on those rugged slopes – almost as an offering, a token of personal and national pride.

Mutual respect between New Zealand and Australia is higher on Anzac Day than at other times during the year. But it is impossible not to see that single-country chauvinism has largely taken over. Despite the closeness of the confinement of the original ANZACs on a singularly inhospitable bit of land, and the obvious community of pain represented by the campaign itself, each year's commemoration ceremonies are more to do with national feelings and national pride than with a sense of common identity. It is not about Gallipoli or ANZAC; it is about national identity and nationalism and a consequent felt need to insist on special qualities – apartness at the expense of togetherness. Both countries, in the years since Gallipoli, have become more than confident enough of their own separate histories and character. Profundity and sensitivity is needed to call into existence genuine feelings of community of interest and shared history. For the present, it seems that two pragmatic countries cannot reach far enough to give such a commitment their attention. Nationalism and separatism are easier chords to pluck than songs of unity.

chapter six

Rivalry in Patriotism

Our researchers into public opinion are content
That he held the proper opinions for the time of the year
When there was peace, he was for peace;
When there was war, he went.
– *W.H. Auden, 'The Unknown Citizen' (1940)*

The First World War was a turning point in the histories of Australia and New Zealand. Dissent at home about conscription during the war and developing nationalism – especially in left-wing politics – afterwards showed that presumptions of continuing unquestioning commitment to empire might be misplaced. The two countries gained an important measure of international recognition from their roles in the war and both signed the Versailles peace treaty. But there was no attempt to separate from the empire: they had nowhere else to go. Politically, the two were at odds and pursuing different courses as the world fell apart during the 1930s. There was no effective defence co-operation between them and little consultation. During the Second World War wartime commitments were once again arranged separately through the British, and were focused on British strategic interests in the Middle East and Europe. Then, when the Japanese attacked in the Pacific, the two countries were drawn into a regional war for which they were ill-prepared. They fell out with one another, and also with the Americans and in the end with the British. Their difficulties with their allies then fostered a major commitment to one another – the Canberra Pact of 1944.

Cohorts of Empire

Presumably because they perceived few differences between them, New Zealanders and Australians freely enlisted in the armed forces on whichever side of the Tasman they happened to be during the 1914–18 war. The interconnections are everywhere: Horace Moore-Jones, whose watercolours of the ANZAC positions at Gallipoli now hang in the Australian War Memorial Museum was a New Zealand war artist; his most famous painting *Simpson and his donkey* used a New Zealander called Henderson, who was doing the same work as the Australian Simpson, as a model. A New Zealander, Alfred Shout, won one of the seven Victoria Crosses awarded to members of the Australian forces at Gallipoli. The sad saga of the Gallagher family of Auckland was typical.

David, the eldest, was famous in New Zealand – and wherever rugby football is played – as captain of a New Zealand team that swept all before it on a tour of the British Isles in 1905–6, and was over forty when war broke out. Yet, in 1916, he enlisted after his younger brother was killed on the Somme serving with the Australians. Dave was killed the next year when the New Zealanders attacked through the mud at Passchendaele; a third brother, with the Australians, was killed on the Western Front in 1918.

The statistics of New Zealand and Australian contributions to the allied war effort in 1914 to 1918 are hardly bearable.[1] When it was over, both took part in the 1919 peace conference and signed the Treaty of Versailles as dominions of the British Empire; the British signed for the empire. To Australian historians, the Versailles peace conference was a springboard from which the country vaulted into the international arena. William Hughes, the Australian Prime Minister, is presented as having seized the occasion to project Australia and Australian interests. His famously grim response to President Woodrow Wilson, when asked what grounds he had for speaking so forthrightly about Australia's claim to German territory, certainly spells out an unequivocal nationalism: 'I speak for 60,000 Australian dead.' By contrast, the Versailles conference seems to have left little impression on New Zealand historical memory. The dour Massey was not one for hyperbole. Yet, by persistent advocacy, the two Antipodeans achieved what they wanted: more influential roles in the Pacific, with Australia gaining administrative responsibility in German Papua and New Zealand in Western Samoa. Both campaigned strongly against having to exercise that control subject to outside international supervision through the mandate system. In this regard, Hughes seems to have antagonised President Wilson the more, but perhaps that merely reflected the difficulty the United States had in recognising either country as sovereign entities, independent of Britain.

After the war, debate opened as to whether the dominions should move on to become independent states within the Commonwealth. Instead of loosening the bonds, New Zealand and Australia wanted a greater share of responsibility for running the empire. Having invested so much of their national identity in membership, they would find it hardest to concede that its glory days were over. In agonised and querulous notes, written on his way to the 1921 conference, William Massey underscored the dilemma of a loyal 'Greater' Briton faced with changing times and changing imperial circumstances.[2] 'We did not wrest our present status by force from the statesmen of the United Kingdom.' New Zealanders, in other words, had never seen the need to make a break from the empire. Indeed, it was the reverse. New Zealand wished to continue to anchor itself within the larger system precisely because New Zealanders could not conceive of their having any identity outside it. Independence was a frightening proposition; the physical loneliness of New Zealand cried out to Massey.

New Zealand [is] alone in the Ocean ... the Dominions have everything to gain by remaining in the Empire and everything to lose by going out. A Dominion has the protection of the Army and Navy [British] as part of the Empire but on its own would be only a third or fourth rate power ... even in the case of trade it would be [at] a tremendous disadvantage as compared with its present position.

(Only six years after Gallipoli, Massey seems not to have considered the advantages of an ANZAC partnership as an offset to isolation.) From this conclusion he drew his central argument: 'we must have unity ... and political organisation ... of Empire ... 17,000 New Zealanders died to save this Empire and as many more came back incapacitated.' For South Africa and Canada, unity on such terms would have been a poison pill for their domestic bodies politic. For the British it would have posed irreconcilable demands. Devolution of power within an empire is a contradiction in terms.

The exigencies of war caused the British to offer the crumb of consultation to Empire leaders, but they certainly had no intention of sharing power. An Imperial War Cabinet, formed in late 1917, engaged the prime ministers of the dominions in continuing discussions about war aims and future peace settlements, but gave them no handles on decision-making. The British considered the cabinet to be an imperial conference, not an executive body. Twenty-five years later, the British Foreign Office grandly noted that it been 'admitted by the UK Government that in view of the part the Dominions were playing in the (1914–18) war, their governments were entitled to be heard when decisions ... were being taken'.[3] Dominion leaders based themselves in London for long periods during 1917–18 but were offered little or no opportunities to influence strategic or even tactical decisions, even those involving the use of their own forces. Overall command of forces in the field remained in British hands. It was thin gruel. The empire's contribution to the war effort was about one to four.[4] Yet member countries did not participate in the decisions of the War Cabinet. The British would consult, but not delegate.

Cracks in the Façade of Loyalty

For New Zealand as well as Australia, the strains of war exposed class and sectarian antagonisms; to many, empire came at too high a cost. In Australia, the loyalty of a large Irish-Catholic community was severely tested by the violence of British suppression of the Irish uprising of Easter 1916. Australian Prime Minister Hughes attempted to introduce conscription but was thwarted by a deeply divisive national campaign against it, in which the Cardinal Archbishop of Melbourne played a leading role. The split in the governing Labor Party left scars that would not entirely heal for fifty years. Two national referenda were held on the issue, in 1916 and 1917, and conscription was defeated both times; even the soldiers at the front were about equally divided on its merits. In New Zealand, the government introduced conscription in 1916, but only after several militant labour leaders were gaoled for sedition. (In the next war, one of them would be prime minister and several others would be cabinet ministers responsible for the introduction of conscription.)

By the early 1920s, domestic politics in both countries no longer cohered around unequivocal support for the empire; indeed, imperial issues became something of a political football. When the British asked for help over the so-called Chanak crisis at the Dardanelles in 1922, New Zealand had offered a brigade of troops before the Australians and Canadians had read the message: the New Zealanders had the time zone in their favour and key ministers were dining at Government House when the telegram came in. Hughes was annoyed by New Zealand's imperial claim-jumping. Convinced of the need for a positive Australian response, he found his parliament to be sceptical. The Labor opposition wanted a referendum before any commitment, and even on the conservative side there was gathering opposition to the traditional notion that the empire was at war if Britain was. Not long afterwards Hughes, the empire man, received a vote of no confidence from the electorate, and he left political life. In New Zealand, the fledgling Labour Party also flew its internationalist colours in the Chanak affair, wanting to refer the incident to the League of Nations. Like its Australian counterparts, it thought the people should be consulted before any commitments were made about sending troops overseas. It was all a storm in a teacup; the Chanak crisis soon blew over. Nevertheless, a newly minted national awareness in Australia and New Zealand had introduced new notes of caution and even dismay about the implications of the British connection.

Yet it was still all they had. Through until the beginning of the Second World War, neither country was developing independent foreign policies – there were no national intelligence organisations, no networks of embassies, no strategic assessment programmes or national defence planning structures independent of the British. Like it or not, and many didn't, the key elements of national life – economic, political, social or cultural – continued to be shaped by the British inheritance. Equally importantly, both countries were dependent in the classical sense used by Machiavelli:[5] they did not have the power to look after their own interests and accordingly were obliged to look to others for protection. Dependency on Britain was total.

The Singapore Base

London accepted that after the First World War a major base should be built at Singapore to underpin British global strategic interests. Australia supported the Singapore policy, but gave priority to building its own naval capabilities. New Zealand tilted the other way: while still wishing to have some Royal Navy units in its own area, Wellington – consistent with the basic New Zealand commitment to a single imperial navy – came out strongly in favour of the Singapore project, contributing the then large sum of £1 million towards construction. The Australian contribution would be provision of maritime security in the broad area and naval support for the approaches to Singapore, from a base to be built at Darwin. Anxiety about Japan began to weigh on both governments during the 1920s, and the rationale for the Singapore base concept was increasingly questioned, especially in Australia. The issues were to do with strategy and discrepancies in size and power between states. Was the 'citadel' concept a sound one in the twentieth century? If war came in the Pacific, how long would it take for a British fleet to arrive in Singapore? If there were a war in Europe at the same time, would a fleet be released at all? In Australian military circles, it was argued that priority must go to the defence of Australia, and its immediate approaches, against the possibility of a direct threat. This group, dubbed the 'invasionists', argued that there were too many questions about the reliability of the imperial defence concept for it to be a viable basis for planning.

Short-lived Labour governments in Britain in 1924 and 1929–31, led by Ramsay MacDonald, introduced a new dimension to the debate. Mistrustful of traditional defence and security thinking, MacDonald's Labour governments wished to refer all international differences to the League of Nations or the International Court of Justice. The Singapore project was put on hold. Such thinking found a ready echo in left-wing politics in Australia and New Zealand and would be vigorously espoused by New Zealand after 1935. But the governments in power in the two southern countries at the time Labour was in power in Britain had different ideas; they wanted firm British commitment to the Singapore project. New Zealand, in particular, vigorously criticised British backsliding.[6] Construction proceeded by fits and starts. The base was finally opened in 1938 and, when put to the test against the Japanese invasion in December 1941 and January 1942, proved a tragic failure, meeting neither the needs of regional nor global security.

Muddling as to War

As concerns about Pacific security mounted during the 1930s, there was little by way of hands across the Tasman. In 1933, the Australians proposed 'active co-operation and co-ordination' between the two defence establishments, coupled with New Zealand participation in Australian defence supply and manufacturing arrangements. The response was lukewarm. Knowing their New Zealanders, the Australians then recruited an influential Briton – the Secretary of the Committee on Imperial Defence – to push the cause of trans-Tasman defence co-operation. Limited arrangements were made for New Zealand to make use of Australian repair facilities and sources of supply. However, in a New Zealand economy still deeply afflicted by the depression it was difficult to make the case for defence expenditure. Besides, why promote Australian industry, much of it in competition with New Zealand and with a cost structure that other suppliers could be expected to undercut? After 1935 the two countries were on opposite sides of the political fence: the newly elected Labour government in New Zealand was against the Singapore strategy and wanted to develop a basis for a regional commitment; in Australia a coalition government was swinging away from the regional focus, back towards emphasising empire defence. Australian Prime Minister Joe Lyons would have been regarded as a turncoat by the leaders of New Zealand's Labour government. Some of them were Australian by origin and committed trade union socialists, completely out of sympathy with a Labor leader like Joe Lyons who had agreed to lead a national coalition in response to the crisis of the depression. The Australian coalition government, instinctively conservative, aligned itself with a British coalition in which Ramsay MacDonald, who like Joe Lyons abandoned his old party, had again become prime minister. The Australians also followed the British Conservative governments of the late 1930s in refusing to advocate intervention against the rising tide of fascism. The New Zealand Labour government was led by the Australian-born Michael Savage. New Zealand soon found itself playing a lone hand at the League of Nations and in empire circles urging the need for collective action to stand up to the dictators.

Dealings descended to the level of near farce. As late as September 1938, Savage noted to Lyons 'that … liaison with Australia … is not as good as is desirable … Our problems, both in peace and war, resemble each other's even more than they resemble those of the United Kingdom.'[7] (This may well have been the first formal acknowledgement of the strategic interdependence of the two countries.) Yet Australia and New Zealand continued to deal with one another through the Committee of Imperial Defence in London. Returning from a visit to Australia, the Secretary for the New Zealand Organisation for National Security described the absence of co-ordination as 'really absurd'. Savage proposed an exchange of decisions on defence policy: copying of communications with the British likely to be mutual interest; exchange of copies of war books and related data, and of course full exchange of data about enemy activities in time of war. The Australians took six months to reply and were grudging in the extreme. In March 1939, six months before both countries were about to be precipitated once again into global war, the Australian government solemnly agreed with its neighbour and imperial partner, 'in principle [that] the exchange of information between the parts of the Empire cannot be other than beneficial to mutual understanding and cooperation in Empire Defence'.[8] But there should be 'no hard and fast rules' as to classes of documents; while the two governments should keep one another informed as to policy and plans, 'the conclusions reached, rather than the documentation relating to their evolution is all that it is necessary to transmit'. In response to the specific suggestion from the New Zealand side that any documents either country sent to the Committee on Imperial Defence should also be exchanged directly, the Australian response was a masterpiece, not only of bureaucratic gobbledegook but of the disdainful brush-off: 'This can be arranged on the basis determined by each Government, as to the particular document to be forwarded.'

In 1937, Savage proposed Britain, Australia and New Zealand enter discussions on the strategic importance of the Pacific islands; a year later this idea was widened to embrace the strategic situation in the western Pacific, especially in the event of simultaneous war in both Europe and the Pacific. Canberra was condescending: questions of higher policy should be discussed in London not Wellington; Australian ministers would be too busy and chiefs of staff likewise. What was called the Pacific Defence Conference was finally convened in Wellington in March 1939. The Australians sent relatively junior officers. The British told the two Dominions not to worry: in the event of a war in the Pacific coincident with a struggle in Europe, Singapore would hold, although it may take six months for a relieving force to reach the base and it may be a case of 'fighting their way in'. The most Australia and New Zealand would have to fear would be 200-man raiding parties directed at their territories. The ANZACs were less than reassured. Little did they know it, but the British, aware that they could probably not cope with war in the Pacific as well as in Europe, had already proposed to the Americans that the United States Navy provide naval forces in the region. In the absence of heavyweight Australian representation, the conference did not serve to advance trans-Tasman co-operation or understanding of the regional defence issues. The British could not descend from the global to the regional in their thinking; instead, they made the traditional request that in the event of war the two southern partners make available army divisions for 'operations overseas, where ever they can be employed most usefully'. As the last time round, it was confidently expected that this would be at the main battle front in Europe. As for the Pacific, the conference produced agreement between Australia and New Zealand on joint naval and air patrol responsibilities; arrangements were made for New Zealand to undertake airfield and harbour defence work in Fiji, while preparing to garrison other islands against the projected 200-strong raiding parties. Singapore remained the lynchpin of policy.

Lonely Loyalists

When Australia and New Zealand entered into a state of war with Germany in September 1939, both were well and truly out on a strategic limb. A war on the other side of the world commanded their attention because the very core of both societies, and the mind-sets of both peoples, were consumed with Britain, things British and the British Empire. Yet the prospect of a direct threat in their own region was looming large. Japan was on the rampage in China; great power interests, American included, were seriously at risk in Asia and the Pacific. But the spirit of ANZAC was absent: the two countries dealt separately with the British and made no attempt at a joint assessment of their shared regional concerns. Yet their overlapping strategic dilemma was never so stark. Both suffered equally, as New Zealand historian F. L. W. Wood wrote, 'the embarrass-ment of an inescapable dualism: tied at once to Europe and the Pacific ... deeply committed to Britain, yet ... situated in an area where American was replacing British dominance'.[9] Military forces in both countries were seriously deficient. In the early days of the war, each separately agreed to participate in an extensive Empire scheme for the training of aircrew. New Zealand consented to a squadron of light bombers ordered from Britain remaining there for duty in the European sector. A New Zealand cruiser was sent, at British request, to the South Atlantic, where it played a significant part in the Battle of the River Plate in December 1939. Australian ships were summoned for service in the Mediterranean. Each country got on with the business of training land forces for service overseas, without any establishment of priorities or consultation as to where they might go. The opportunity for full-scale collaboration in wartime, which could have changed the histories of both countries, was never grasped.

In the game of the 'loyalest of the loyal', the troop commitment card would be played for all it was worth. (This game had gone on ever since the Boer War and was, in a way, still being played by New Zealand in June 1982, when the then Prime Minister, Robert Muldoon, offered the British a frigate for patrol duties near the Gulf, so that a Royal Navy vessel could be released to take part in the Falklands War.) Nearly three months into the war, the Australian Prime Minister, by then Robert Menzies, wrote to Savage about the deployment of troops overseas.[10] He rehearsed 'some real uncertainty about the position of Japan' and the 'feeling' that with nothing happening on the Western Front in Europe, there was no particular urgency about making a commitment there. 'We do not wish to be out of step with you as we think that from every point of view the closest co-ordination between our policies is essential.' This put New Zealand on the spot. Savage was obliged to reply the next day saying that New Zealand had advised the British authorities, the day before Menzies's message had been received, that the First Echelon of a 'Special Force' would be despatched overseas, and that he had proposed to tell Canberra as soon as a date of announcement had been arranged with the British.

There was no official New Zealand representative in Canberra at the time, or vice versa. The absence of reciprocal diplomatic representation between the two neighbours at the outbreak of war was in itself an astounding reflection of strangulated nationalism, expressed uniquely through the relationship with Britain. Perhaps it was just as well. The British High Commissioner in Canberra reported to London that Menzies 'was ... highly incensed at the New Zealand Government',[11] and had told him that 'there was rivalry in patriotism between New Zealand and Australia which, while perhaps foolish, had to be taken into account'. In an interesting commentary on the degree to which the two political systems in fact intertwine, Menzies had explained that the New Zealand decision would generate pressure in Australia to send forces overseas 'at least as soon as New Zealand'. If the Australian government then responded to that pressure, 'it would be incontestable that their hands had been forced and that they were merely following New Zealand's lead'. This in turn would have domestic political consequences for the Menzies government, since the Labor opposition were opposed to the despatch of forces overseas, and it was 'particularly undesirable to provoke them unless there was real necessity'. (Besides, no Australian, in government or out, would wish to be seen as merely following passively behind New Zealand.)

Menzies noted the regional strategic challenges for Australia. In an early indication of the importance of what would become Indonesia in Australian strategic thinking, he observed: 'If Germany invaded and conquered Holland this would leave the Dutch East Indies masterless and they might prove too tempting a bait for Japan.' Best to get on with training in Australia. Shipping was short and the government believed that at that stage in the war it was 'more important to ship commodities than to ship men'. The Australian government understood the proposed Empire air training scheme to be 'infinitely more important than despatch of one or two divisions overseas'; but once the news was out that the army was being sent, there would be a 'clamour' to join it rather than the air force.

Menzies let a week pass before replying to Savage on 28 November.[12] He pointedly recalled earlier correspondence about exchanging information on each country's defence policy decisions – although he did not mention Australia's lukewarm commitment to the proposal. 'I regret earlier consultation was not possible,' but there should be scope for pausing and considering matters 'without prejudicing our strength here or later co-operation when forces are ready to take the field.' He would announce the next day that Australia's 'Special Division … will proceed overseas when it has reached a suitable stage in its training … early in the New Year'. There should, he suggested, be consultations in London about co-ordination of shipping requirements for the two forces. As in the First World War, the two contingents left together in January, in a single combined convoy, bound for the Middle East.

New Zealand had accepted British reassurances about the reinforcement of Singapore should Japan enter the war. The idea of co-ordination with Australia seems not to have occurred. The decision to send forces overseas had been largely driven by the most mundane of considerations at home. There were simply not the facilities in-country to provide for training of more than about a brigade at a time. Once one echelon of troops had been given basic training – and it was very basic, given the almost complete absence of modern equipment[13] – they had to be moved on to provide space for the next. In the Middle East, they could be consolidated for major unit training with the equipment necessary for effective preparation for battle. There was no scope for this in New Zealand. No doubt, too, New Zealand politicians were driven to make a virtue of necessity by showing once again that the smallest and most distant was first in loyalty.

It all seemed like empire business as usual. But the two countries were in uncharted waters. It would be another two years before the war spread to the Pacific, but already the aggressiveness of Japan and its looming confrontation with the United States were lifting the curtain on a completely new Asian-Pacific world. Little though Australia and New Zealand knew, the easy times of dominance of their region by European colonial interests were over. When the war ended, the time of anti-colonial struggle began. In future, the complex intersection of interests of the rising nations of the Pacific rim would dominate the strategic horizon. The relationship with the United States would come to be fundamental. In the meantime, Australian and New Zealand nationalism and their national interests would continue to be expressed in the British context. Given the close-grained character of Australian links with Britain, and the strength of Menzies's own personal feelings on the matter, there was never any way his government could have held back for long from the commitment of major army forces to the struggle in Europe. At that stage of the war, the regional was never in with a chance against the global. It would be different later.

No Revival of ANZAC

In March 1940 Australia rehearsed the Gallipoli spirit, suggesting to the British War Office the formation of an ANZAC force in the field.[14] There was perhaps more to this offer than met the eye. Canberra would shortly make clear to London the principles under which the Australian Expeditionary Force would be deployed: it would be

> an Australian Force under its own commander who would have direct responsibility to the Commonwealth Government and the right to communicate direct with that Government ... No part of the force was to be detached without Australian consent ... Policy as to use of the Force was to be decided by the UK and Commonwealth Governments in consultation.[15]

The British interest would have been to preserve maximum flexibility of deployment of all forces. Being presented with an integrated ANZAC force, at that early stage in the war, would have limited Britain's ability to respond to the strategic problems ahead. Someone in the War Office deleted from the telegram welcoming the Australian proposal the caveat that Britain would not wish to commit itself until it could 'foresee more closely best method of using Australian and NZ divisions.' Presumably they were concerned not to put their partners on notice about a looming difference of opinion over command and control of forces in the field. New Zealand was at first naively forthcoming about joining an ANZAC force. Such a move, Wellington commented, would be inspiring to national morale of Australia and New Zealand in particular and empire in general. There is also a close psychological affinity between our troops. Effect of such a decision would certainly not be encouraging to the enemy and would be a further demonstration of solidarity with the United Kingdom.

But the proposal soon bogged down. New Zealand, too, insisted on direct control, so far as feasible, over its own forces in the field: it had more strongly developed ideas about its own separate national responsibilities and identities than in the 1914–18 war. The formations in the field of both countries were not to be regarded as part of the British Army; they would be national armies, with their own distinct styles and character. More importantly, they would be subject to national direction and control. Each government, New Zealand as well as Australia, would give its commanders express instructions about communicating with it and the importance of holding full national control over its forces at all times; piecemeal deployment was not to be permitted except in special circumstances. Dreams of supranationalism go by the board when each party in a wartime alliance claims its own. Neither government wished to concede national control to the British. At the same time, it would have been obvious that, within an ANZAC structure, New Zealand, as the smaller partner, would have to concede command and control over its own forces to Australia. With the larger country contributing two or three divisions to New Zealand's one, the commander would have to be Australian.

New Zealand would be more comfortable going to war alongside the British once more. After the German successes in France in May and June of 1940, the New Zealand general, Bernard Freyberg, advised Wellington that New Zealand's role should be to help in the way 'best conforming to the British war effort. New Zealand may not wish to be associated automatically with a possible aggressive Australian attitude regarding strategy.'[16] The government in Wellington agreed and turned down a revival of ANZAC. Indeed, in the absence of any political co-ordinating mechanism between Canberra and Wellington, it is hard to see how the concept could have worked. In Greece a year later, in April 1941, the New Zealand Division under Freyberg and a division of Australians were briefly consolidated into an Australian Corps under the command of General Thomas Blamey; when the Australians were consolidated into a second Division, the famous name of ANZAC was resurrected for the final stages of a parlous withdrawal. A week or so later on Crete, Freyberg was given overall command of British forces, which included a brigade of Australians and two of New Zealanders, although again no combined ANZAC force was formed. At the military level, there were recriminations between the Australians and New Zealanders about aspects of the conduct of these two reckless British campaigns. The principal focus for Antipodean resentment, however, was the Middle East Command and the British government, for failures of consultation and a continuing presumption that Australian and New Zealand forces could be regarded and deployed as integral units of the British army. The experience was salutary. Both governments would not compromise on the issue of national control in future.

As with political devolution within the empire, it took time for British commanders and British politicians to come to terms with the insistence of the Australians and New Zealanders on separate national command and control. The British high command in the Middle East wanted to break up their formations for use as dispersed units to fill gaps elsewhere. Whereas the Australian commander, Blamey, was uncompromising, in the early stages of training in Egypt in 1940, Freyberg yielded to a British request to detach his signals unit; he soon found that it was assumed that other elements of the New Zealand Division could be extracted, more or less as the high command chose. He finally put the matter to rest with a firm letter to Middle East Headquarters:[17] 'The New Zealand Forces are not an integral part of the British Army – they are a distinct New Zealand Force, proud of their own identity. They cannot be split up and used piecemeal except with the consent of the New Zealand Government.' He was disconcerted, as he later wrote, 'to be treated as a "black sheep" by one's old friends in the British Army. But the British generals greatly misunderstood my character if they thought that I and the New Zealanders would allow ourselves to be bulldozed.' Blamey also expressed his own frustrations on the topic: 'It seems quite impossible for any English officer to appreciate the position from our point of view, and once any Australian unit gets into the command of the UK formation, it's like prising open the jaws of an alligator to get them back again.'[18]

In a way, it was all shadow-boxing. The two Antipodeans had never contemplated moving out from under the British mantle in shaping their defence and strategic postures. They could satisfy their own nationalism and fend off domestic criticism by insisting on national command and control. In reality both countries fought as components of the British war effort. The boot, ironically enough, readily shifts from one foot to the other on the issue of national command. In 1918, the Australian battlefield commander, Monash, threatened to call off a major Australian attack on the Western Front if an American brigade, which had trained with the Australians, were not employed under Australian command. The American commander, General John ('Black Jack') Pershing, was famously resistant to use of his troops as subordinate units in British and French divisions. The Americans, he insisted, must be deployed as independent national forces under American command. In the next war, it was the Australians who would baulk at taking part in the Philippines campaign of 1944 unless they could have their own independent corps command. General Douglas MacArthur refused.

Global versus Regional

A collective security alliance is more complex than the ancient proposition of 'one for all and all for one' suggests. If the collective is to survive, the centre must hold. This proposition would be taken as read by the world-weary arbiters of power at the heart of empire (or, later, in Washington); it is less comforting for anxious regional partners faced with perils of their own. While the empire was being challenged only in Europe, its junior partners could reasonably be expected to agree that their own fundamental interests required them to offer help. From London, this much must have seemed beyond question during the dangerous summer of 1940, and was broadly accepted in Wellington and Canberra. As Japan engaged in a particularly brutal war in China and began to look southward towards Indo-China, this rationale for imperial defence began to look rather less compelling. Regional threats to the outlying partners were secondary; the centre could not weaken itself vis-a-vis its main enemies in order to help out at the periphery. This is the flaw in the logic of empires, coalitions and alliances. Unless the guardian of the centre has true global capabilities, it will be obliged to relegate its regional interests to second priority. By the same token, each of the regional allies such as Australia and New Zealand will define its own separate relationship with the senior partner in its own terms. Reflex acquiescence in the interests of others is not for this world.

As early as June 1940, after the collapse of France, the War Cabinet in London delivered a thunderbolt, advising that in the event of simultaneous war in the Pacific, it is 'most improbable that we could send adequate reinforcements to the Far East. We should therefore have to rely on the United States of America to safeguard our interests there.' Earlier reassurances from Churchill, that British commitments to their 'kith and kin' in Australia and New Zealand were second only to the defence of Britain itself, became so much rhetoric. The Middle East, and with it defence of the Suez Canal, the approaches to India and the oil fields of the Arabian Gulf, again emerged as a focal point of British strategic interests. Without willing it, the United States was beginning to loom large to the Australians and New Zealanders. As Churchill advised Roosevelt soon after becoming prime minister, it was central to his thinking that an American role in the Pacific would be needed 'to keep the Japanese quiet, using Singapore in any way convenient'. Washington never took this bait; Singapore was a British problem. Moreover the United States did not share with the British any sense of responsibility for the security interests of Australia or New Zealand. For Washington, the rising power of Japan, and the threat this posed to the strategic balance in Asia and the Pacific, was the key strategic issue. The British Ambassador in Washington accordingly reported that although Australia and New Zealand were little known to Americans, United States strategic interests would ensure their protection. Even so, it is now known that as early as November

1940 it had been agreed in Washington that should the United States become engaged in war in Europe and the Pacific the main effort would be to defeat Germany first.[19]

Dealings with London, especially for the Australians, became increasingly strained, even embittered. At the same they had to do what they could to bring themselves to the notice of the Americans. When the first Australian Minister to Washington, R.G. Casey, presented his credentials to President Franklin D. Roosevelt in March 1940, the distance to be covered in gaining recognition in the United States was bluntly confirmed. When asked about his attitude towards Australia, Roosevelt said that the United States could not be indifferent to an attack on Canada, nor probably on the republics of Central and South America, but as far as Australia and New Zealand were concerned 'the element of distance denoted a declining interest on the part of the United States'. New Zealand was negligent in allowing nearly two years to go by before following suit and accrediting a Minister of its own to Washington, in February 1942. Meanwhile, Casey worked to raise Australia's profile in Washington to such effect that by mid-1941 Roosevelt could reassure the Australian Prime Minister, Menzies, that the United States would not stand idly by if Australia was attacked. By that stage, New Zealand had also been slotted into American strategic thinking.

While Washington failed to respond to British inveigling over use of the Singapore base, Australia and New Zealand had no option than to stick by their commitments to Singapore. The Australians, in particular, did so with reluctance and anxiety that smaller powers must forever dance to their larger partners' tunes. In upholding imperial defence, Australia sent three infantry divisions to the Middle East and England in 1940 and New Zealand one; in addition, through their endorsement of the Empire air training scheme, both governments were in effect underwriting eventual diversion to the European theatre of trained aircrew, rather than developing their own air forces for regional defence purposes. Naval units were despatched as determined by the British Admiralty. Protestations to London about the need for effective consultation and for some understanding of their own exposed strategic position aroused little more than impatience among British officials consumed by worry about the threat to their own security. 'I think Australia will have to be mauled a little,' Mr Churchill, who would not concede a place in his War Cabinet to a Dominions' representative, told Menzies in February 1941. Menzies was then and would remain the epitome of Empire loyalism among Australians, yet he too became exasperated by Churchill's high Victorian notions that the imperial children should offer only unquestioning obedience in times of crisis.

Australians and New Zealanders were on a steep learning curve. Both were, in effect, dragged willy-nilly into two serious and costly campaigns in Greece and Crete, for which they were given no opportunity to contribute either political or military advice. With the bulk of their forces on front-line service in the Middle East, they had to cope with British reluctance to commit military supplies of aircraft or ships to shore up their own defences against Japan. London's confidence that the 'impregnable' Singapore fortress would hold was high, and respect for Japanese military capabilities low. Australia committed two infantry brigades and air force units to Singapore in early 1941. New Zealand sent a squadron of obsolete fighter aircraft; it had little else to offer. As agreed at the Wellington Defence Conference in 1939, New Zealand also posted an infantry brigade to Fiji and undertook airfield and gun battery construction there. The contributions of the two smaller partners in Empire counted for little against the inability of the senior partner to provide the substance of regional security.

The Japanese assault on Pearl Harbour in December 1941 drastically and summarily dropped the scales from the eyes of Australians and New Zealanders. Furthermore, simultaneous landings by the Japanese in Malaya, and the destruction of two major British battleships, the *Prince of Wales* and *Repulse*, dented the credibility of the theory of imperial defence, to say the least. The Australian Prime Minister, John Curtin, issued a New Year message that turned the country almost obsequiously towards the United States – and infuriated Winston Churchill in the process. There was no longer anything theoretical about the question of a global commitment as against the regional focus. When Singapore fell in February 1942, 15,344 Australians were captured and committed to the miseries of Japanese prisoner-of-war camps; 4783 did not survive their treatment at Japanese hands. Two major Australian warships were sunk in the initial naval battles. Desperately difficult fighting – first during Japanese advances in Malaya, in the Java Sea, Timor, Ambon, New Guinea, Rabaul and the Solomons, and then in the effort to push them back – imposed severe casualties and heavily imprinted the forbidding defence problems of the region on the Australian national consciousness. The immediacy of the military threat, and the need to contend mightily within allied councils in order to ensure that Australia's own interests were upheld, likewise made a deep and lasting impact on the country's foreign and security policies. Japanese forces penetrated almost to within sight of Australia across the Torres Strait, in eastern New Guinea, and the Australian mainland was repeatedly attacked by air and sea.[20] The place of Australia at the foot of the strategic chain of islands projecting out from South-East Asia was all too plain. Distance did not confer immunity. Australia, which had seen itself as cut off from the world of its origins and instinctive connections, was now plainly not separate from its own region. Two of the three divisions in the Middle East were at once pulled back from the desert war; the third division was withdrawn in January 1943 after joining in the key Battle of El Alamein in late 1942. A commitment to the global interest was retrenched and the emphasis was given to the regional.

The distinction is not quite apt. The Pacific War was part of a global struggle;

quite understandably, Australia gave it first priority. Shortages of shipping, strategic imbalances, the need to hold the line elsewhere, were all advanced as reasons why Australia should adhere to global planning rather than transfer its experienced divisions from the Middle East to the direct defence of Australian interests at home. But John Curtin, the new Prime Minister, and Herbert Vere Evatt, Minister of External Affairs, were Australian nationalists of a new breed. They chose not to subordinate Australian interests to those of the global collective, represented by the senior allied powers, Britain and the United States. Rather, the prime consideration was what was in Australia's interest; from that should be derived the Australian contribution to the global partnership. This put a new gloss on Australian notions of independence and self-reliance that was to leave the New Zealanders struggling to catch up. It united Australians as never before.

In February 1942, Australia found itself at odds with the British over a request that one or both Australian divisions, returning from the Middle East, should be diverted to Burma. Winston Churchill enlisted President Roosevelt's help to pressure John Curtin into agreeing to take part in what would certainly have been a disastrous last-minute effort to defend that flank of the allied position. Curtin refused. Although it was subsequently agreed that two brigades of the returning soldiers should disembark at Ceylon in order to secure that key place in the Indian Ocean, Australia established its own priorities. The British were incensed, and the Americans only slightly less so. By this stage, Australia and New Zealand had been swept up in the strategic planning of the United States – not in response to their own representations so much as thanks to a convergence of their interests and those of the new, and unmistakable, power in the Pacific. Agreement to the use of New Zealand as a base, if required, was signalled before Pearl Harbour; at the same time, Australia had agreed to American construction of air bases in New Guinea and Rabaul. As early as 14 December 1941, the US Chief of Staff, General George Marshall, approved a plan prepared by a Colonel Dwight Eisenhower to maintain lines of communication across the Pacific, from Hawaii through Fiji to Australia, and to convert Australia into a staging post for the defence of the Philippines. New Zealand, too, should be garrisoned to secure these links and as a reserve base. When US army troops began to arrive in strength in Australia and marines in New Zealand, the Americans had already been evicted from the Philippines and Japanese forces had reached almost to Port Moresby in New Guinea, while pressing south into Solomon Islands and New Hebrides to threaten American supply lines. The next stage of the struggle would involve not only hard campaigning against the Japanese but sharp in-fighting among allies about their respective roles in the Pacific War.

A Single Strategic Entity?

New Zealand was more fortunate than Australia in escaping direct assault by the Japanese. Although it obviously shared strategic interests and was part of the same sector, the immediate concerns were not the same. In the stress of events over December 1941 and January 1942, the Washington Conference between Winston Churchill and Franklin Roosevelt designated command areas for the Pacific which would eventually put Australia and New Zealand in separate camps for the duration of the war. In the same way as there should be no taxation without representation, so there should be no drawing of military maps without the participation of those whose strategic interests are being bandied about. The Joint Chiefs of Staff in Washington had other matters to contend with than the interests of New Zealand and Australia; more particularly, they had to accommodate severe wrangling between the US Navy and Army about control of the ultimate direction of the Pacific War. First, New Zealand was placed in an ANZAC area, a subset of the Pacific command, under US Navy control. Australia was put to one side as a separate command area. The New Zealanders suggested that an exclusively naval focus for the ANZAC area might be inappropriate, since there were land and air forces in Australia and New Zealand and the various adjacent islands to be considered. Australian planners then developed and extended the notion of an ANZAC area to provide a basis for a solid and integrated trans-Tasman wartime partnership. Admiral Ernest King, the US Navy Commander-in-Chief, thought the Australians were too preoccupied with 'continental defence'. Accordingly, a South-West Pacific Area was accordingly created to cover Australia and adjacent areas to the north. New Zealand, because it lay across the sea approaches to Australia from the east, was placed in a separate South Pacific Area and would remain a US Navy responsibility. The army, under the flamboyant and potentially difficult General Douglas MacArthur, would have the command of the South-West Pacific, the navy of the South Pacific Area. MacArthur operated from Melbourne and then Brisbane; the US Navy commander was established at Auckland and later moved forward to Noumea.

New Zealand and Australia protested strongly to Washington. The Australian chiefs of staff reported that: 'it is essential to Australia that New Zealand, Fiji and New Caledonia should be in the same command area as Australia: they were interdependent and, from every point of view must be considered together.' New Zealand Prime Minister Peter Fraser sent Curtin a copy of his message to Washington, commenting, 'Australia and New Zealand were inevitably one strategical whole in which already a substantial degree of cooperation both economic and military had been achieved.' It was all to no account. When Japanese naval forces were turned back from the South Pacific by the US Navy, with valuable assistance from the Australian Navy, at the Battle of the Coral Sea in May 1942, the threat of invasion of New Zealand and Australia was removed.

At the Battle of Midway in June, the United States reasserted its overall dominance of the Pacific, which has never been in question since. There would never be any doubt as to who was running the war against Japan.

In the event, the conduct of the Pacific War through different command areas reinforced the separateness of Australia and New Zealand where an integrated approach would perhaps have laid the foundation for a post-war convergence of interest. Unlike Australia, New Zealand had the luxury of choice as to where to make its strategic commitments. More fundamentally, the leaders of the allied cause were able to maintain pressure on New Zealand to stick with the broader objectives of the war, whereas the Australian case for focus on the Pacific was harder to rebut. The upshot was a major row between Australia and New Zealand, which has perhaps cast a shadow over the relationship ever since. After anxious deliberation, in March 1942 New Zealand agreed to heed the call of the great powers and not press for withdrawal of the New Zealand Division from the Middle East, where it was deemed to be making a major contribution. Without consultation with New Zealand, Churchill had arranged a strategic swap, whereby an American marine division would train in New Zealand for operations in the Pacific, while providing the key component of local defence if needed, allowing the New Zealand division to remain in the Middle East. The issue was considered again in November–December 1942 after the Battle of El Alamein, in which New Zealand made perhaps its strongest contribution to world history, breaking through (with the Australians) in the first phase of General Bernard Montgomery's famous attack, and leading the final break-out as the German positions collapsed. Churchill knew how to flatter and cajole, saying that he would be reluctant to have the division 'quit the scene of its glories'. The New Zealand wartime leader Peter Fraser was not susceptible to such blandishments. He told Churchill that the place of the division was 'in the South Pacific'. He noted that nearly a half of the New Zealanders who had served in the Middle East had been killed or wounded – 18,500 out of 43,500 – and that once all three Australian divisions had returned it would be very difficult to resist public pressure for New Zealand to do likewise. After reference to the Combined Chiefs of Staff in Washington, Churchill turned this argument by saying that Australian withdrawal made retention of the New Zealand Division in the Middle East more necessary. After a secret session of the New Zealand parliament, it was decided that the division should remain meanwhile.

By April 1943, when the campaign in North Africa was drawing to a successful conclusion, the New Zealand authorities were deeply concerned to augment their military efforts in the Pacific in order to ensure an effective future political stake in the region. Indeed, the Pacific political imperative was becoming uppermost. However, once again New Zealand's arguments were countered by heavy pressure from London and Washington to leave the division to contribute to the overall objective of victory in Europe before turning to the Pacific. In the event the global argument was accepted. Fraser felt obliged to solicit a message of support from Churchill, which was duly sent, strong on emotion: 'it is the symbolic and historic value of our continued comradeship in arms that moves me.' It was decided, with very mixed feelings, that the Division should remain to see out the war in Europe.

The Australians were scathing. Sir Frederick Shedden, Secretary to the Australian War Cabinet, wrote John Curtin a memorandum, which must stand as a memorial to Australian official dismissiveness of – and occasional bitterness about – New Zealand. The New Zealand decision 'was another manifestation of that acquiescent attitude to United Kingdom policy rather than the development of a National Dominion Policy, which has brought them so much applause as the "curly headed boys of the Empire".' Shedden was an empire man, a friend of the long-serving Secretary of the Committee on Imperial Defence, Sir Maurice Hankey, a respected student of strategic affairs and very influential with successive Australian governments. The failures of liaison between the New Zealand Labour and Australian coalition governments immediately before the war had obviously slipped his mind. It had always been Australia, he wrote, which placed 'the emphasis in Imperial Defence policy on the strategical needs of the Pacific ... exemplified by the development of the Royal Australian Navy as part of the scheme of Pacific Naval defence which centred around Singapore with a capital ship fleet based thereon'. Australia had developed secondary industries and established a munitions, aircraft and shipbuilding industry, whereas New Zealand had been 'tardy' in such matters and had 'not hesitated to call heavily upon us for coal, fabricated materials, manufactured products and munitions essential to the maintenance of her National economy and war effort'.

Shedden made no mention of small-country nationalism. But he put his finger on the essence of the issues between Australia and New Zealand when he commented,

> Either ... New Zealand is less co-operative towards Australia than to the United Kingdom, notwithstanding our common interests in the Pacific, or ... they feel they are overshadowed by Australia and show up better by playing a lone hand, even if it is really prejudicial to their vital interests.

The matter of the formation of an ANZAC force was mentioned as an example of unwillingness to co-operate. Not neglecting the chance to draw a wider moral – for Australia as much as for New Zealand – he concluded,

> A Dominion will never find its destiny as a Pacific Power if it is not prepared to think for itself as to what are its true interests and stick out for them. It may bring criticism from those abroad who do not get their own way or from a section of our own people who look for their leadership overseas, but it is the only way to build a nation with a strong national sentiment.

Shedden was right, but perhaps not in the way he thought. New Zealand could in fact – and justly – interpret its interests in different ways from Australia. Further back from the line of battle in the Pacific, the danger of direct attack had in fact receded for New Zealand with the Battle of Midway in May 1942. In the absence of any platform for practical political or military collaboration with Australia, New Zealand could properly interpret things strictly in terms of its own strategic interests and perceptions.

Curtin would have remembered his own battles with Churchill and perhaps accepted Shedden's facile analysis that New Zealand wished merely to curry favour in high places. He sent a severe message to Fraser:

> ... if we had not insisted on the return of the AIF, New Guinea would have been lost and we would have now been fighting on the mainland of Australia. (2) For every soldier New Zealand keeps away from the Pacific theatre either an Australian or American has to fill his place. (3) Australia has rendered substantial material aid to increase and sustain the war effort of New Zealand on the basis of our common defence in the Pacific. This has, in effect, amounted to an export of our limited manpower ...

Curtin regretted that the two governments had not consulted 'before this important decision was taken'. He then went on to rehearse the difficulties both countries had in achieving effective co-ordination within 'the set-up which governs global strategy and operations ... particularly as the commanders of the South and South-West Pacific Areas are not directly responsible to the New Zealand and Australian Governments'.

It was a cry from the heart. Behind it lay vexing issues, close to the core of beliefs about the separate national destinies of Australia and New Zealand. When all is said and done, do two such isolated countries constitute an integral strategic area? Is it rational to face a complex and demanding strategic environment without effective co-ordination of policy and of military effort? Such questions bear on deeply held political beliefs and entrenched attitudes. They still reverberate. New Zealand and Australian officials would return to the issue in the 1970s and 1980s, with New Zealand at that stage the more assertive that the two nations constituted a 'single strategic entity'. The election of a Labour government in New Zealand in late 1999 has raised the issues again. New Zealand has since striven to assert strategic detachment, and the present Prime Minister, Helen Clark, expressly denies the notion of a 'single strategic entity'.

The failure of attempts to place the two countries in the same command area in early 1942 undoubtedly compromised subsequent wartime collaboration. Attitudes were frozen into mutual indifference and misunderstanding. It is still widely assumed in Australia that New Zealand was so firmly committed to the European theatre as to have taken no effective part in the Pacific War. Because they were in different command areas, neither country was well informed about the other's role. In fact both countries made mammoth efforts in the allied cause and New Zealand's role was far from confined to the European theatre. As well as its efforts to develop Fiji as a focal point for the defence of the South Pacific, New Zealand raised a second army division which played a role in the recapture of Solomon Islands in 1943–44; New Zealand naval forces were actively engaged throughout the region; the Royal New Zealand Air Force (RNZAF) took a prominent part in air operations in the Solomons, New Hebrides and New Britain, including Rabaul. The supply of New Zealanders was stretched to the absolute limits to provide manpower for these efforts. In January 1944, the Minister in Washington, Walter Nash, reported to President Roosevelt that of 600,000 male New Zealanders between the ages of fourteen and sixty-four, 560,000 were in the forces or engaged in war production; 87,000 were in the army, of whom 31,400 were at home, 21,900 in the Pacific and 33,500 in Italy; and that a further 40,500 were serving in the air force and 8,350 in the navy. At a comparable period, the end of 1944, Australian military strengths were: army 411,300, air force 179,500, navy 34,500. After 1942, the Australian army was almost exclusively focused on the South-West Pacific command area, as was the navy; the Australian Air Force continued to make major contributions to the European and Middle Eastern as well as the South Pacific sectors throughout the war. It was a strange legacy from an Empire in which all effort was focused on the centre, that two regional nations equally enmeshed in a global struggle could get to be so out of touch and out of sympathy with one another.

The ANZACs often seem to waste more
shot firing at one another than forming up
together in support of wider shared
objectives.

'The Spirit of ANZAC', Wrathall, *Truth*, 1979
Source *The Unauthorized Version*,
Ian F. Grant.

chapter seven

Ties that Bind

… this land is not the sweet home that it looks,
Nor its peace the historical calm of a site
Where something was settled once and for all: A backward
And dilapidated province, connected
To the big busy world by a tunnel, with a certain
Seedy appeal, is that all it is now? Not quite:
It has a worldly duty which in spite of itself
It does not neglect, but calls into question
All the Great Powers assume; it disturbs our rights.
– *W.H. Auden, 'In Praise of Limestone', April 1948*

W artime alliances represent power politics in action – literally. The military, logistic and strategic preponderance of the great powers leaves little room for smaller allies to assert their place in the grand scheme of things. The war in the Pacific, from 1941 to 1945, required Australia and New Zealand to deal with the power of the United States for the first time; and, equally, Washington would have to fit two hitherto little-known countries into its frame of reference. It was a tough learning curve – especially for Australia. Alliances are fertile breeding grounds for nationalism – triggered as much by the difficulties of dealing with friends as foes. In the ANZAC Agreement of 1944 two smaller allies put their great power partners on notice about their interests in the Pacific. It was also a first – the establishment of a formal collaborative arrangement between Australia and New Zealand. More an unfurling of flags than a formal alliance, this inaugural diplomatic initiative largely misfired as it came up against great power presumptions. Australia and New Zealand came out of the war with reinforced convictions about their respective independent nationhoods and about the overlap of interest between them. Yet within six years of the ending of the Pacific War, they were pleased, faced with the transcending threats of the Cold War, to sign on to a formal collective security treaty: the ANZUS Pact.

Fighting with Allies

The war in the Pacific was an American war. Australia and New Zealand found it difficult to find and hold their place within it. Pacific War Councils established in Washington and London proved not to carry much weight. The London council was soon redundant, as Washington became the focus for the conduct of events in the Pacific; indeed, the British also had to scramble for influence with the American Joint Chiefs of Staff.[1] For the Australians, the appointment of General Douglas MacArthur as Commander South-West Pacific Area almost guaranteed difficulties of co-ordination and clashes of personality. In an attempt to create an integrated command, General Blamey became Commander Land Forces, and deputy to MacArthur. Differences of operational and military style, comparative American military inexperience – often coupled with beliefs about superiority of American military standards and distrust of Australian senior officers, most of them greatly more battle-hardened than their American counterparts[2] – made command relationships difficult at all levels. Almost from the first, Blamey found himself sidelined; integration of military effort on the ground proved elusive and, accordingly, Blamey assumed the appointment of Commander Australian Land Forces. His, and Australia's, position was invidious. The idea that General MacArthur's headquarters would function as a combined US-Australian military command soon withered. Instead, MacArthur preferred to deal with Prime Minister John Curtin on a personal basis, and it became increasingly difficult for Australian planners to have any input in overall strategic decision-making. By the end of 1944, Blamey had six divisions and an armoured brigade under command for operations outside Australia. But the Australian government was dependent on MacArthur for broad oversight and strategic direction as to their deployment. The first successes against the Japanese in New Guinea were Australian; heavy and extremely difficult fighting in that campaign during late 1942 and 1943 was then closely shared between United States and Australian forces and laid the platform for the bold leap-frogging campaigns which MacArthur made his speciality.

An Australian corps with two infantry divisions was then withdrawn back to Australia for training in amphibious operations on the understanding that they would be employed for the next stage, the advance against the Japanese in the Philippines – the 'return', which was MacArthur's overriding obsession. Other Australian units were designated to relieve United States forces for garrisoning and what MacArthur called 'neutralisation of Japanese pockets on the various islands'. For all their demonstrated effectiveness and preparedness, Australian ground forces were not employed in offensive operations towards Japan after the New Guinea campaigns. The two designated divisions were held back from the assault on the Philippines, partly because of a clash over command arrangements. The Australians had insisted that they should be commanded and controlled as an integral Australian corps-strength force. MacArthur claimed not to be able to accommodate this arrangement and wanted them as single divisions under American operational command. When planning for the invasion was accelerated, the operation went ahead without bringing the Australians forward. First-class troops were available, and the Australian government was eager to make a contribution to forward operations, after the years of bitter slog in New Guinea. However, its insistence on Australian command in the field and giving priority to repossession of the mandated territories in and around New Guinea and other British islands made it impossible to argue, when General MacArthur left the Australians to 'tidy up' while he made his own dispositions to use United States forces for the offensive operations.

In other ways, Australia was stymied by classical problems – political and military – of alliance management. The Chiefs of Staff in Washington were too preoccupied with their own battles – between the navy and army; between General MacArthur and the Chief of Naval Operations, Admiral Ernest King; between a central Pacific approach to Japan versus the retaking of the Philippines – to be able to accommodate allied interests.

The amphibious-trained Australian corps was eventually employed for the attack on Borneo in the final two months of the war. After the event, there were doubts as to whether the struggles of attrition waged against Japanese forces left behind by MacArthur's spectacular strategy had been worth the effort and the losses involved. Justifiably or not, there was more than a suspicion that Australia had been deliberately relegated to a secondary role, which was hard to take given the prominent front-line roles Australia (and New Zealand) had always been allocated in British operational planning. Consequently, both New Zealand and Australia were happy to return to the British fold for operations against Japan in the final months of the war. A considerable Commonwealth Naval Task Force was assembled and brought into action a few weeks before the war ended, and Australia and New Zealand joined the British in a Commonwealth division for the occupation of Japan after the peace treaty was signed.

New Deal Washington was notoriously unsympathetic to a post-war restoration of the European colonial empires. New Zealand and Australia would inevitably be suspected – not without cause – of acting as stalking horses for the British. Earlier in the war, Admiral King had ardently upheld the need to provide effective defence for Australia and New Zealand: 'we cannot in honour let Australia and New Zealand down. They are our brothers and we cannot let them be overrun by Japan.'[3] Even so, he was an Anglophobe opposed to the resurrection of British ambitions in the Pacific. It was not only the Australians and New Zealanders who struggled to assert their interests. As the end of the war in Europe came in sight, the British too were anxious to re-establish their position in the Pacific. The US Chiefs of Staff, however, were never helpful about British participation in operations against Japan in the last months of the war. At the same time, Australia and New Zealand were not wrong in their suspicions that some in Washington had imperialistic ideas of their own: as early as March 1943, the General Board of the US Navy recommended that the United States should have:

responsibility for the Pacific area extending as far South and West as is necessary to cover all islands and water areas to the shores of China, except limited contiguous areas naturally under the control of the British Dominions and the Netherlands

The necessary bases should be taken 'without regard to sovereignty'. Specific mention was made of the New Hebrides, Solomons and New Caledonia. United States claims to sovereignty in relation to outlying islands in the Cook and Tokelau groups already overlapped in some cases with those of Britain, for which New Zealand had assumed responsibility. Early in 1943, the United States Secretary to the Navy, Frank Knox and the influential Senator Arthur Vandenberg, asserted that the United States should take over Pacific islands administered by Commonwealth or European countries in return for lend-lease military assistance. In December 1943, the Australian High Commissioner in Wellington reported New Zealand 'concern regarding the future control of bases constructed and occupied by U.S. forces in the Pacific'.[4] In the event, excessive big-power swagger was repudiated at higher levels in Washington. On 7 January 1944, President Roosevelt approved a circumscribed statement to the effect that the United States should have exclusive military rights in islands north of the Equator and participating rights in the existing base structure in the South-West Pacific, including Papua New Guinea. The Canberra Pact, concluded by Australia and New Zealand only two weeks later, proclaimed a 'regional zone of defence comprising the South West and South Pacific areas'. Not only the timing but the definition of the ANZAC area of interest was unfortunate. The terminology was the same as that used for the command areas the Americans had established for what they had come to see as their war in the Pacific. The ANZACs were regarded as making waves in what many in Washington already viewed as an American lake.

For all that there will always be differences of size and scale of contributions to great collective enterprises, each participant must equally be expected to view its role in its own national terms. Nationalism arises easily from national assertiveness and pride about such things. Australia had particular cause to believe that it had shouldered a major part of the burden of the war in the Pacific. New Zealand, too, had made a major effort. And both countries had legitimate interests in the character of the post-war dispositions in the Pacific. More than that, Dr Evatt, nothing if not an activist Minister of External Affairs, believed that Australia was destined to be an important actor in the post-war world. He took the initiative with a major foreign policy speech in Parliament on 14 October 1943, proposing to exchange views on 'the problems of security, post-war development and native welfare [with] ... the various Governments interested in the South-West Pacific'. His was no exclusive vision: 'I regard permanent collaboration with New Zealand,' he went on, 'as pivotal to a sound post-war Pacific policy.' The New Zealand High Commissioner, reporting a subsequent conversation with Evatt, confirmed the Australian's wish for a preliminary meeting with New Zealand. According to Evatt,

Australia and New Zealand in co-operation should be the foundation of the British sphere of influence in the South-West and South Pacific and that the future safety and prosperity of these two Dominions depend on their having a decisive voice in these areas.

Britain would, he thought, be well advised to transfer its colonies in the region to the two Antipodeans, who were 'particularly qualified' by 'special knowledge and experience'.[5] Evatt was nothing if not a nationalist.

Australian and New Zealand nerves had been jangled when on 1 December 1943 the 'big three' powers – Britain, the United States and China – announced after a conference in Cairo that Japan would be stripped of all its island possessions in the Pacific, Korea would be independent and former Chinese territories would be returned to China. The then-head of the New Zealand Department of External Affairs, Alister McIntosh, later confirmed that both Evatt and New Zealand Prime Minister Peter Fraser had been 'dismayed and affronted' to read about the Cairo statement in the press.[6] Lonely smaller allies, quite properly believing they were making important contributions to the establishment of a new international order, found that the global powers grandly made their post-war dispositions about matters clearly concerned with the security of the Pacific – and the Antipodes – without troubling to consult or even inform. In the background lay a series of cross-grained preoccupations: frustration with the difficulty of establishing a working relationship with the United States; annoyance with the British for joining in formulations of post-war objectives in the Pacific without consulting them; an understandable wish to assert their respective interests in their own region; and a shared wish to again involve the British in the Pacific. Such concerns went together with unease about American strategic ambitions in the central Pacific, centring on speculation about future bases and the development of international aviation in the post-war period. During this period, Dr Evatt was thinking aloud to United States officials about his perceptions of post-war arrangements: the United States and Australia should divide up the region or should work in collaboration with existing colonial powers and the New Zealanders, he suggested. Evatt's enthusiasms were suspect in Washington. Several months before, the United States Minister in Australia had translated Evatt's ambitions for a new post-war Pacific order to the State Department as an intention to create an Australian 'sphere of inluence' and to oppose American 'interference'. It was wartime and the Americans didn't have too much of a feel for Antipodean puffery. Even so, there was a certain giddy over-reaction in the Minister's interpretation of Evatt's proposed 'zone of security' in the South West Pacific as 'the first Imperialistic peace terms yet made by any leader among the Allied Nations of this war'. In retrospect, it can be seen that Evatt's tendency to over-egg things doomed the 1944 Australia-New Zealand Agreement from the first. On top of that, New Zealand would for a long time yet be uncomfortable if it found itself out of step with the British.

Towards an ANZAC Sphere of Influence

Evatt and Fraser were the two principals at the meeting which opened in Canberra on 17 January 1944.[7] New Zealand was by no means an unwilling partner. Fraser shared Evatt's resolve to stake a claim for more consideration in working out the future of the South Pacific. Although he had been ill for two months, Fraser actively interested himself in preparations for the conference; he was reported by an Australian source in Wellington as saying that New Zealand would be looking for 'some definite conclusions and agreements on policy'. The New Zealanders took with them a War Cabinet Secretariat paper on post-war security which formulated strategic aims and objectives in the region, but were expecting little more than sustained discussions leading to agreed conclusions. The Australians had taken their thinking further. On arrival in Canberra the New Zealand team – to their discomfiture, according to McIntosh – was presented with an annotated agenda, drafted by Evatt, which the Australian side envisaged would be the basis for a formal agreement. Fraser doubted that the delegation had the powers to conclude an agreement as well as the wisdom of doing so.

McIntosh has noted, however, that from the first Fraser was keen to use the Canberra meeting to inject warmth into the trans-Tasman relationship after Curtin's frosty reaction to New Zealand's 1943 decision not to withdraw its division from the Middle East.[8] Accordingly, Fraser contented himself with arguing the point on about a quarter of Evatt's proposals and accepting the rest. Nevertheless, the New Zealand delegation toned down Australian proposals in several important particulars: they refused to endorse an explicit statement of an Australian intention to take over responsibility for administration of Solomon Islands and to assume the British place in the New Hebrides condominium; likewise, they ruled out an express reference to rebutting any American notions of establishing condominium arrangements in New Caledonia or other island groups of the south-west Pacific. McIntosh later said that Fraser did not share Evatt's exaggerated suspicions of United States territorial ambitions in the region. Fraser objected to signing a formal treaty or pact; the conclusions of the conference were drawn up as an agreement, which was signed on 21 January 1944 for later ratification by governments.

New Zealand's attempt to diminish the significance of what had been done, by insisting that it be known as an agreement, not a treaty, was avoiding the issue. For the first – and so far the only – time, Australia and New Zealand had formally staked out common strategic interests. Soon by-passed by the rapid expansion in international diplomacy in the post-war world and long since buried beneath the multitude of informal contacts and means of doing business that have burgeoned across the Tasman, it is hard to understand now why the agreement could have caused such a fuss. Naïve perhaps, and certainly ill-timed, it was a first foray into the field of international diplomacy by two countries with little experience of acting alone, but strong convictions about the necessity of articulating their shared national interests in the face of the apparent indifference of their senior allies. Quite aside from the issues of wartime alliance management, it represented a statement of a new-found determination by Australia and New Zealand to step out from their previous role as acolytes of empire.

It was unexceptionable that the two countries should have committed themselves to joint action in matters of common concern in the South West and South Pacific. Rather more surprising, in view of their manifest incapacity to cope with such a complex far-flung region on their own account, was the proclaimed intention to establish 'a regional common zone of defence comprising the South West and South Pacific areas ... based on Australia and New Zealand, stretching through the arc of islands North and North East of Australia, to Western Samoa and the Cook Islands'. The provisions in the agreement for the establishment of a permanent secretariat in the capitals of the two countries to facilitate liaison, consultation and the fullest co-operation in defence and external policies were innovative, and for a time served actively to promote trans-Tasman interaction. So far so good. What gave the agreement notoriety, however, was the forthright way in which the two countries asserted their own points of view about issues that would come up for decision after the war. The pact spelt out a firm espousal of the trusteeship principle for administration of all non self-governing territories in the region and proclaimed the right of Australia and New Zealand to participation in all decisions relating to the south-west and South Pacific and, further, made the point that wartime arrangements should not prejudice future decisions about sovereignty and control over Pacific territories; finally, the two countries stated their intention to convene a conference of all allied countries with colonial interests in the Pacific.

These latter provisions caused a ruckus in both London and Washington. The British government was not amused by public pronouncements by the two Dominions, which might prejudice future plans for its colonial territories in the Pacific or anywhere else. The United States was affronted that two junior wartime partners should presume to make the post-war running in the Pacific before the struggle was over. For the previous eighty years, at least, Australia and New Zealand had been insisting on the importance of their interests in the Pacific. The British were well used to that. This time round, however, the United States was the principal actor in the Pacific strategic setting. Washington did not know how to deal with two independent-minded British dominions beginning to feel their oats in international affairs.

Where Japan's rampage into the South Pacific had failed to provoke an effective regional ANZAC partnership, ambition to have a full say in post-war settlements did the trick. As the allies took the offensive in late 1943, the two British Dominions began to look to their options. Neither country was well versed in the conduct of international relations; McIntosh subsequently commented that 'the two countries acting in concert (in strategic matters) tended to overplay their hand ... the Canberra Pact with its emphasis on Pacific regionalism and its apparent anti-Americanism so far as that region was concerned, could have been more felicitously drafted'.[9] Nevertheless, the frustrations that gave rise to this play for the attention of the great powers were real. At its core, the agreement lays down regional interests, in the teeth of the global preoccupations of their great power allies. Later in 1944, the United States Minister in Australia reported that Dr Evatt had told him that the Australian and New Zealand governments were convinced that they had been 'constantly brushed off' by the United States and Britain in discussions about the Pacific.[10] Within the imperial framework, informal processes of consultation and exchange of views had at least given them a chance to speak up and be heard; the United States had neither the inclination nor the experience to provide them with any comparable opportunity. The Pacific War Council had been a vehicle for President Roosevelt to tell the assembled company what was going on rather than solicit their advice. For a long time, both countries had tried to claim a say in the management of the British system; now, it seemed, the Americans would prove to be even less amenable to according them what they believed was their due place. Small-country nationalism often reflects frustration at an inability to gain the respect nations – or, more precisely, national leaders – believe they deserve. On such matters there is a gulf in perceptions between the major powers, with their global preoccupations, and smaller countries, with their narrower interests. For both Australia and New Zealand, the Canberra Agreement was a manifestation of an emerging nationalism.

Big Power Backlash

Nowadays, smaller countries almost routinely fly diplomatic kites, more as distress signals than as firm statements of intent. But this was before the era of independence: the small fry were expected to know their place. On his return to Wellington, Peter Fraser conceded to the British High Commissioner that 'New Zealand Ministers were rushed by Evatt'. He denied that there was any

> anti-British intention in the Agreement or in the attitude of Curtin or Evatt, if there had been he would not have signed. If it was anti-anything, it was anti-American and he himself was somewhat nervous as to American reactions. In view however of American pretensions in the Pacific it was necessary to speak plainly ... he referred especially to question of bases and alleged determination of the United States to retain New Caledonia.[11]

The heaviest shots did indeed come from Washington. At first they were aimed at the proposal (article 34) that Australia should call a conference relating to security and other matters in the South Pacific. The Secretary of State, Cordell Hull, made it clear that Washington wanted no part of this:

The President and I have some fears that a formal conference of the interested powers for the purpose contemplated would possibly do more harm than good … might well arouse suspicions and possibly bring into focus conflicting opinions on matters which do not require decision at this time.

The Americans were also concerned that regional security arrangements must follow rather than precede establishment of 'a general international security system'. Otherwise others would move to make their own regional security arrangements, which might 'seriously interfere with efforts to achieve a general system of world security'.[12] These criticisms were easily turned. Australia and New Zealand supported the concept of an over-arching international security system; the agreement said as much and they were happy to accord it priority.

The State Department nevertheless did not let up. When Fraser and Curtin visited Washington a few months later they were each taken to task by Cordell Hull. Curtin was told that 'we frankly do not appreciate the attitude of Dr Evatt on this and other matters'. According to Hull, the United States had been 'almost flabbergasted' by the agreement, especially by the assertion of a wish to be involved in discussions about future sovereignty of territories in the Pacific. The American note of Hull's conversation with Fraser states he was told Washington had become convinced that aspects of the agreement were 'clearly directed at the United States'. It had 'almost shocked some of us' and seemed to be all Evatt's idea. Fraser is said to have agreed with a far-fetched comparison between the agreement and Soviet criticisms of the British – which seems unlikely.

In the eyes of Washington, the greater offence had been to raise the dust over future base rights in Pacific Island territories arising from wartime operations. Article 16 of the agreement stated bluntly that the 'construction and use in time of war' of base facilities 'does not, in itself, afford any basis for territorial claims or rights of sovereignty or control after the conclusion of hostilities'. Dr Evatt had said that claims based on any such considerations would be 'absurd'. This provided the pretext for emotional outbursts against Australia and New Zealand in the two Chicago newspapers known for their anti-British xenophobia. The New Zealand Embassy in Washington advised that the *Chicago Tribune's* views of the agreement as anti-American were so predictable as to be of little importance. The *Chicago Daily News*, however, was owned by Frank Knox, the Secretary of the Navy. One of its correspondents reported Evatt's remarks as follows:

Claims for bases from which American submarines now leave for harassing raids against Japanese shipping and where thousands of troops, aircraft, supplies and lease-lend material have been unloaded in defence of the two members of the Empire are called 'absurd' in a direct statement by Herbert V. Evatt, Australian Minister of External Affairs.[13]

There was clearly more at stake here than small-power nationalism. Like the British before them, Americans have invested much of their national pride in their navy. After the humiliating disaster of Pearl Harbour, the US Navy became the apotheosis of American power in the carriage of the war against Japan. Big-power nationalism is as potent as any other. To this day, the United States does not take kindly to slights against the navy – as Washington's reaction, forty years later, to New Zealand's anti-nuclear stance amply demonstrated. In 1944, the provisions in the Canberra Agreement about the future of Pacific island territories offended the sensibilities of the United States Navy. Article 26 declared 'ultimate disposal of enemy territories' to be a vital interest of Australia and New Zealand, to 'be effected only with their agreement and as part of a general Pacific settlement'. Admiral King was reported by the New Zealand Minister in Washington in May 1944 to have expressed 'strong resentment' at this proposal. (Article 27 went further, to declare 'that no change in sovereignty or system of control of any of the islands of the Pacific should be effected except as a result of an agreement to which they are parties or in the terms of which they have both concurred'.) After a highly successful assault on the Marshall Islands, American forces were poised to dispossess the Japanese of the Carolines and Marianas. To the US Navy the long-term strategic importance of the Japanese mandated territories – the Mariana, Marshall and Caroline groups – along the lines of approach both to Hawaii and to Japan – would have been self-evident. Great powers brook no interference in such matters. Admiral King's reaction to the Canberra Agreement was reported by the New Zealand Minister to have been that neither country would 'have a right to a say in what is to be done with these islands on account of their having taken part in operations for the capture of them'.[14] The war in the central Pacific was to be a private affair.

Whether it was King's doing or not, New Zealand and Australia were excluded from having any further part in operations towards the Japanese mainland. By early 1944, the New Zealand Government was considering the future employment of its Air Force units prepared at considerable effort for active service in the Pacific.[15] In May 1944, air staff were told that there was 'no prospect of employment of RNZAF Squadrons in Pacific west of longitude 159 east or north of the equator', following completion of campaigning in the Bismarck Island group to the east of New Guinea. When pressed by the New Zealand Minister in Washington, Admiral King said that he would discuss the issue with the Chiefs of Staff. Nothing eventuated. There is no clear evidence that this outcome stemmed directly from the Canberra Agreement. The command area encompassing New Zealand, as distinct from Australia, was the responsibility of the US Navy, and it may well have proved difficult for the navy to absorb a relatively small component from a foreign air force into its command structures. For whatever reason, New Zealand's war effort in the Pacific was never given the opportunity to break out of the confines of the South Pacific – except for some naval activity. Units from all three services were employed on operations against residual Japanese forces in the northern Solomons and New Britain areas, but no further afield. The New Zealand Pacific army division (3 Div) was disbanded in October 1944.

British reactions to the 1944 Australia-New Zealand Agreement were of a different character. What they saw was a challenge to established procedures for doing business within the Commonwealth and the emergence of some disconcerting views about colonial policy. Nevertheless, the British held back from severely critical comment until after the follow-up meeting to the Canberra conference, which was held in Wellington in November 1944. There, they let it be known that they had 'learned with considerable surprise and concern' that the two Dominions had expressed support for an international supervisory body for dependent territories with powers to visit and report on colonial administration – a reading that went further than the notion of 'trusteeship' arrangements articulated in the agreement itself. From the first, British officials had been taken by the effrontery of the two Antipodeans in making their own agreements. On 25 January 1944, an official, Godfrey Boyd Shannon from the Dominions Office, analysed the ANZAC agreement in a minute circulated around Whitehall, 'when all allowances have been made it remains a deplorable monument to egregious amateurism in international affairs'.[16] Perhaps, it signified that New Zealand was veering more into line with Australia. (Given that Australia was widely regarded in Whitehall as being a nuisance for agitating over its strategic concerns during the earlier part of the war, this comment was surely not a compliment.) But Boyd Shannon comfortably noted that Britain took 90 per cent of New Zealand's exports before the war and that 'two agricultural islands with a population of 1.6 million must rely on the support of a stronger power if they are to resist the pull of a partly industrialised country of 7 millions'. (Nationalist-minded New Zealanders concerned that their country be drawn ineluctably into the Australian orbit, but still determined not to fall into alliance with any other power, must still contend with this paradox.)

Boyd Shannon's analysis of the Canberra Agreement is another interesting index of the attitudinal gap between the great and the small, between assumptions of great standing and the aspirations of smaller powers to have a say in matters of common concern. He had no reservations about Articles 1 to 6, which promoted closer Australian and New Zealand co-operation; he was sufficiently well informed about attitudes in the two countries to note that the reference in Article 6 to co-ordination of military efforts, 'so far as is compatible with the existence of separate military commands', was a dig at the Americans: 'Both Governments protested at the time and both have continued to dislike the division.' On Article 7, which asserted a claim to representation, 'at the highest level on all armistice planning and executive bodies', Boyd Shannon expostulated, 'If this is a claim to representation on a level with the Great Powers it is absurd. If it is not, it is not clear what it means.' Article 16, which so rankled with the Americans, drew the bland Whitehall comment, 'This is our view, though we have not found it necessary to say it so bluntly. Australia and New Zealand have become apprehensive at United States activities on Pacific Islands.' But when it came to propositions that touched more directly on British interests, Boyd Shannon was even more condescending. Article 28, which asserts support for the trusteeship concept in the administration of non self-governing territories was labelled an 'impertinent claim by two very minor countries with a few island dependencies of whose administration they have not made a conspicuous success to lay down the law to their betters'. Article 34 states the support of the two countries for convening an international conference of governments with territorial interests in the region, to consider questions of 'security, post-war development and native welfare'; Boyd Shannon described it as a 'declaration by a small country [*sic*] of an intention to convene a Conference including major powers without first consulting the other governments [which] is an extraordinary and impudent way of conducting international affairs'.

Such nonsense from a middle-level official, coupled with the readiness of a senior United States commander – not to speak of the Secretary of State – to take offence, serves once again to show that the way of smaller powers in the diplomatic field is indeed stony. Herbert Evatt, gifted and headstrong, plainly had the capacity to irritate many people incapable of seeing the world from another perspective – and he was evidently the object of much suspicion in Whitehall and Washington. His activism and ambition on behalf of Australia may well have made some of that inevitable. Nationalism of this kind, however, is not an offence. The difficulty is to fit vigorous expression of national interests into the bigger picture. The ANZAC Pact failed as a vehicle for this purpose. It is not possible to say that New Zealand or Australia were excluded from United States planning for the culminating operations of the Pacific War simply because of the Canberra Agreement. Army-navy rivalries in Washington and a powerful American disposition to turn the war against Japan into an exclusive vendetta were presumably much stronger considerations; the British too found it hard to stake their place in the final operations against Japan. And certainly, there were those on the American side who showed a perceptive understanding of the position of the two smaller regional powers. In February 1944, the United States Chargé d'Affaires in Wellington had this to say to the Secretary of State:

> I believe that both Australia and New Zealand feel Canberra agreement was good thing in expressing their stand early and perhaps in bringing themselves more forcefully to the attention of the great powers. They undoubtedly feel their position and interest in the Pacific is greater than formerly. They want to have a part in the final settlements following this war and not have everything prearranged by others for them. Australia apparently is the more aggressive partner but smaller and more distant New Zealand does not want to be forgotten either.[17]

A South Pacific Focus

The Canberra Agreement did not fail in all respects. Above all else, it succeeded, if not in quite the way intended, in giving a joint Australia-New Zealand emphasis to concerns about future developments in the Pacific. It took time. Three years after the two governments had proposed the establishment of a south seas regional commission (Article 30), the South Pacific Commission was inaugurated. New Zealand and Australia had to make concessions to get their colonial power partners with interests in the Pacific to the conference table. Their original idea was for a commission 'to secure a common policy on social, economic and political development' in the region, but they had to settle for the establishment of an advisory body. What they envisaged as an agency that would 'review progress towards the developing of self-governing institutions in the islands of the Pacific' would, in the event, be shorn of political authority. The agreement establishing the South Pacific Commission, which was signed on 6 February 1947, limited its powers and functions to 'a consultative and advisory body to participating Governments in matters affecting the economic and social development of the non-self-governing territories ... and the welfare and advancement of their peoples.'

Decolonisation slowly gathered momentum in the Pacific after the war. Western Samoa, the first independent island state, was taken by New Zealand through to independence in 1962. The other island groups followed in rapid succession during the 1960s and 1970s. Even in the French territories, the colonial period is now ending. The South Pacific Commission, set up to service and assist the colonial administrations of the region, has continued to provide advice and research assistance to island governments. Nevertheless, it has had attached to it something of the stigma of the colonial past. By the late 1960s, New Zealand and Australia were not happy with the insistence of the United States and France that the South Pacific Commission should continue to steer clear of political issues. To fit the circumstances of the time, a new regional organisation was needed. New Zealand promoted an initiative among the independent island states to form the South Pacific Forum, an informal inter-governmental consultative arrangement, which first met in 1971. Australia and New Zealand, as the metropolitan countries of the region, are invited members, sitting alongside the heads of government of the independent island states and the leaders of what are called freely associated states, which feel inhibited by reasons of size from claiming full independence. This outcome, achieved twenty-seven years after Australia and New Zealand staked their claim to involvement in regional affairs, is more than satisfactory. For all the upsets, alarms and excursions in the South Pacific in recent years, Australia and New Zealand have sought actively to play a constructive part. For both countries, but especially for New Zealand, the South Pacific is now a major focus of foreign and security policy activity: New Zealand allocates over half its external development assistance to bilateral and multilateral aid programmes in the South Pacific; Australia provides rather more money for South Pacific aid, but a smaller percentage of its overall assistance budget.

In Step at Last

In another important respect the 1944 Agreement set the tone for what has followed. Articles 35 to 42 laid down a framework for practical collaboration between Australia and New Zealand, which was over-ambitious and over-elaborate, but prescient. There was to be co-operation in defence, external policy to do with the Pacific, commerce and industrial development, the attainment of full employment and the highest standard of social security and – bringing religious zeal into foreign policy – in the encouragement of missionary work in the region. There were to be conferences of ministers at least twice a year, regular conferences of departmental officers and technical experts, meetings of standing inter-governmental committees: the respective high commissioners were enjoined to work together, exchanging information and officers, and developing institutions that would serve common purposes. To promote and monitor this frenzied bureaucratic round, a permanent secretariat was to be established in each country under the auspices of the respective departments of external affairs. Each High Commission would then designate an officer to work in 'closest collaboration with the Secretariat in which they shall be accorded full access to all relevant sources of information'.

This was a detailed framework. But would all those measures really be necessary? Would two pragmatic countries need an elaborate mechanism to keep them in touch? The framers of the Canberra Agreement were not to be blamed if they had looked at what had gone before and found it inadequate. As already noted, pre-war trans-Tasman relationships were little short of pathetic. Equally, in 1944 it was not possible to get to grips with the future ways of diplomacy. As each country developed mechanisms to carry out its international relations policies, it naturally provided for the conduct of business with one another. Informal channels were used increasingly to maintain official contacts. An elaborate system of liaison officers and secretariats soon became redundant. Each government maintained an administrative structure appropriate to the importance it accorded the relationship. The post-war world was to be the era of the international conference and hyper-active international diplomacy.

Another ministerial meeting under the Agreement was held in November 1944 in Wellington. The two governments continued to aspire to full and equal participation in armistice arrangements in the Pacific. (They yielded gracefully to their exclusion from discussions on the same topic in respect of Europe.) In what was almost certainly a counter-productive move, it was decided to send Dr

Evatt to make their case to the major powers. The conference also launched the notion of an international trusteeship authority to oversee the transition of colonial territories to self-government. The proposal that such an agency would have powers of inspection and supervision greatly alarmed the British. Peter Fraser, a man of great moral strength of mind, had very strong views on this matter and would not be put off by British strictures. He reminded the British that he had spoken forcefully on the subject at the Commonwealth Prime Ministers' meeting in May 1944, when, as McIntosh has remarked, he had 'no support whatever from John Curtin of Australia'.[18] New Zealand was by no means on all fours with Australia. New Zealand national sentiment was also easily stirred.

The November 1944 meeting also focused the attention of the two governments on the draft United Nations charter. At the San Francisco conference establishing the United Nations in 1945 the two would make strong, separate but overlapping, representations on behalf of smaller countries. Australia and New Zealand again lifted their sights to the pursuit of global as opposed to regional objectives. For a time, before the shades of the Cold War closed in, the post-war system for the conduct of international diplomacy permitted the two countries to work strenuously to preserve the interests of the small in the face of the great. Fraser and Evatt put forward many amendments to the draft charter documents. Both were staunchly opposed to vesting veto powers in five permanent members of the Security Council. Fraser had been particularly influenced by the concept of international collective action to thwart aggression, which had been enshrined in the Covenant of the League of Nations, and wished to establish it as a central feature of the new organisation. New Zealand's pre-war experience, of crying in the wilderness at the League of Nations about the need for collective action in the face of the deteriorating international situation, made him distrustful of an organisation that would be dominated by big power interests. Evatt, too, believed strongly that the draft charter gave too much authority to the five permanent members. Of course, such idealism was against the fundamental drift of the times. While the San Francisco conference was in session, the New Zealand Division in Italy was embroiled in what can now be seen as the first confrontation of the Cold War. Advancing rapidly up the east coast of Italy in the closing weeks of the European war, the division was instructed to head off Yugoslav communist forces from seizing Trieste. Both armies arrived at more or less the same time and for several weeks confronted one another in an uneasy and risky stand-off before mutual withdrawal could be organised. Fraser, while seeking a world order founded in small-power idealism, had to confront the emerging reality in which the clash of interests of the superpowers would dominate everything else – a clash in which his New Zealanders could easily have been the first victims – and which would put paid to high expectations of the United Nations system.

Perhaps of more long-lasting significance, the two countries at San Francisco were able to follow through on their commitment in the Canberra Pact to the trusteeship principle for the advancement of the non self-governing territories. This put them at odds with the British. For a time, however, they were able to work closely with the United States on these issues, until the exigencies of the Cold War began to check that country's own idealism about redressing colonialism. The US Navy's interest in bases in the Pacific prevailed over notions of decolonisation and Washington's need for close relationships with the European colonial powers became dominant as the Iron Curtain came down. The Trusteeship Council was established without the powers of overall supervision of colonial territories that Fraser and Evatt had in mind. Its authority was limited to such of the former mandated territories of the League of Nations as would be agreed. Nevertheless, the council proved to be a useful vehicle for the promotion of the interests of non self-governing territories in the Pacific. Fraser became its first chairman; three years later, in 1948, Evatt was elected president of the General Assembly.

In each country now it is the conventional historical wisdom that the one rather than the other – and certainly not both standing together – played a substantial and influential role in the foundation of the United Nations. To be in at the creation of the new international organisation was exciting for two fledgling Departments of External Affairs. A creation mythology was a necessary outcome. The conduct of diplomacy, even within international organisations, is a national affair. Indeed, nationalism is reinforced by it. The outcome may or may not reinforce international co-operation or promote harmony between the nations. In the beginning, when a whole new system is put to the touch, smaller countries may claim large victories. Such opportunities do not come again. From then on, the United Nations round became less heady and more like hard work. The brief flowering of trans-Tasman togetherness represented by the Canberra Agreement of 1944 was a product of special strategic circumstances and frustrations with big-power partners, rather than a portent of things to come. It did not translate into a close political relationship. And it certainly did not set the two countries on a course towards consolidation of their relationship. However, it did establish a pattern of close consultation which has been maintained. The Canberra Pact might have over-reached itself, but it reflected what has since become more evident: that the two countries constitute a single strategic area with overlapping regional interests. Ever since signing it, both have been trying to pin down exactly what that means in terms of genuine national commitments to one another.

The Cold War again transformed the strategic scene for the Tasman pair. With the Soviet Union well established as a Pacific power, the proclamation of the People's Republic of China in 1949 and war in Korea in 1950, the security outlook soon became, to say the least, unpromising. Sooner than either Antipodean would have thought possible when the war in the Pacific was ended at Hiroshima and Nagasaki in 1945, Japan had become a major factor in the confrontation between 'East' and 'West'. The United States wished to push ahead to conclude a peace treaty with the Japanese in order to secure the Asian nation's position in the 'western' camp. Australia and New Zealand – as necessary signatories – had some unaccustomed diplomatic leverage. Although both had qualms about Japanese rearmament, the greater concern was with securing the stability of the region as a whole. Both willingly entered into negotiations with the United States towards a Pacific security treaty. The New Zealand Minister of External Affairs observed that he would 'regard an American guarantee of our security as the richest prize of New Zealand diplomacy'.[19] Even so, the New Zealand government became alarmed when it became evident that there would be no place in the proposed security pact for the British but, in the event, accepted that the new security relationship in the region with the United States must take precedence over the old ties with London. The ANZUS Pact, concluded in 1951, represented the end of an era for the two Antipodeans. Coming on top of their own Canberra Agreement of 1944, ANZUS established the focus of their shared security concerns in the Pacific region and took the two countries away from the kind of instinctive 'kith and kin' understandings inherent in the British imperial system. For the first time, they exchanged formal mutual obligations not only with a foreign (that is, non-British) power but with one another. And the undertakings were far-reaching: 'to maintain and develop ... individual and collective capacities to resist armed attack'; to consult when a threat was perceived; and, in the event of an attack, to 'act to meet the common danger in accordance with ... constitutional processes'. This was new ground: after nearly a century in which the two Antipodeans had defined their strategic interests exclusively in terms of their instinctive – if ill-defined – relationship with an Empire centred on the other side of the world, they were signing on to formal treaty undertakings focused on the realities of power in their own region.

FEDERATION IN THE AIR.
ONE POSSIBLE VIEW OF THE POSITION OF NEW ZEALAND.

Close association with Australia will always be a wild ride for New Zealand. The question now, as it was then, is whether the smaller country can avoid getting on board.

'Federation in the Air. One possible view of the position of New Zealand', Asley Hunter, *New Zealand Graphic*, 16 September 1899. Source Ian F. Grant, New Zealand Cartoon Archive Collection, Alexander Turnbull Library, Wellington.

chapter eight

Economic Travails[1]

Colonies do not cease to be colonies because they are independent.
– *Benjamin Disraeli, House of Commons, 1863*

From the beginning of settlement, Australia and New Zealand were dependent on trade with Britain. A high degree of reliance on international trade remains a feature of both economies. From the outset, trade with one another was hampered by both countries being dependent on much the same line of primary products for export. But, through until the 1950s, both freely entered into and enthusiastically maintained an essentially colonial economic dependence on Britain. During much of the twentieth century economic diversification proceeded behind protective barriers and within the context of imperial preference arrangements. There was little incentive to focus on trans-Tasman trade and much scope to create impediments to it. Economic relations went sour between the wars and picked up only as the main props supporting the two economies – the British market and the City of London – lost dominance in the post-war world and as Britain itself turned to Europe. New Zealand concerns combined with Australian strategic condescension (a belief that the New Zealand economy would be overwhelmed by the problems of adjustment away from the British market) rather than any shared vision of mutual interest, led to a progressive reappraisal of trans-Tasman economic opportunities.

Seven Colonies, Seven Economies

In the beginning there were seven colonial economies, seven Antipodean producers of wool, timber and/or gold. Each colony was a self-starter. There was no basis for the establishment of joint or shared approaches to economic development; rather, each scrambled to construct its own trading linkages, banking arrangements and other infrastructure. The drive for local power was insistent. Separatism was, soon enough, a main theme. As early as 1836 a handful of settlers at Port Phillip (Melbourne) was pushing for separation from the mother colony of New South Wales; during the 1840s Moreton Bay (which became the nucleus for Queensland) and New England (which stayed where it was) wanted out. Each state developed its own revenue arrangements, charging one another customs duties and putting up tariff and other protective barriers. For more than a hundred years, the Australian colonies were effectively as separate from one another as they were from New Zealand. Sydney developed a rudimentary barter-style economy almost from the first day the convicts came ashore; with the accretion of wealth by the first farmers and traders, as by a corrupt New South Wales officer corps, came the establishment of a local currency, which circulated alongside sterling and notes issued on the colonial administration. The Bank of New South Wales, the first in Australasia, was established in 1817 and the Bank of Australia, also in Sydney, in 1826. The other initial economic nucleus developed around the convict settlements in what is now Tasmania: the Bank of Van Diemen's Land opened in 1826, followed by a number of others in what turned out to be illusionary expectations of prosperity. Victoria started later but, boosted by the gold strikes of the 1850s, would become the financial centre of Australia and always a rival of New South Wales. South Australia consciously set itself apart from both as free of the 'convict stain' and with a focus on large-scale agricultural development.

Agitation in the various Australian colonies to end the convict system, massive migration, gold discoveries and separate proposals for constitutional change all conspired to enshrine local politics for a further period. In the 1850s, each of the colonies, including New Zealand, established its own separate and fully representative political institutions. When dabbling with ideas for constitutional reform, the British had come up with a sketch plan for a federal system as early as 1847. Nothing further was heard of it because all proposals had first to pass the test of local politics; and the local politicians were unlikely to be capable of surmounting local issues and agreeing to federalism. Variations on the themes of natural resources, climate, history and social circumstance imposed distinctive, if hardly radical, differences of economic and political character. From the earliest days of settlement, there was high mobility of labour and capital. Banking systems soon overlapped colonial boundaries and, obviously, transport and communications links quickly developed between the colonies and, in a disconnected way, with the world beyond. Beginning their economic life at about the same time and in more or less the same circumstances, they each moved through the economic stages together; consequently, they were more likely to compete than to co-operate. Prior to 1900, New Zealand was no more agricultural then the states of mainland Australia – although New South Wales and Victoria, which had the two biggest cities and the grandest-scale squatters, had relatively smaller proportions of the labour force on the land in 1891 than the others. In the mining, manufacturing and building sectors, however, the colonies were look-alikes.[2] Rather than developing in a complementary fashion, from the first each of the seven colonies was on parallel tracks. This had obvious implications for the consolidation of separatism, rivalry and competition.

For all the temptations of nationalism, however, the tyro politicians of empire were also bound together by some singularly important scarlet threads: British inheritances in almost every aspect of life, preferential trading arrangements and membership of what was in effect a single-currency trading bloc. These were the fundamentals that made the colonies so similar and would give Australia and New Zealand a similar stamp for so long. They were the beneficiaries of an early exercise in globalisation: the empire and sterling bloc. And they clung to it, through until the mid-twentieth century. Access to the London market provided each colony with the investment for development. Capital was forthcoming for railways, agriculture and all the infrastructure of modern communities, together with the development of the Australian mining industry. Oddly, the ready supply of capital had the effect of enhancing the economic differences of the colonies during the 1890s. In Australia, the growth of major cities and a greater concentration of population in the better farming areas of the south east had already provided local markets for farm produce; before the development of refrigeration, dairy farming in Victoria was geared to local supply. By contrast, local markets for New Zealand farmers remained limited, thanks to the population spread of an elongated country. Accordingly, agricultural industry was oriented towards export of the major part of production as soon as it became possible to ship frozen, and soon chilled, sheep-meat and dairy products to the overseas market. Refrigeration was an economic breakthrough of fundamental importance to the New Zealand economy; rather less so in Australia. In New Zealand, the swing towards dairy and meat production in turn impinged on patterns of farming and rural settlement, development of livestock types to meet the demands of the British market and investment in the economic infrastructure in the shape of meat and wool processing industries and shipping.

In Australia, at around the same time, technological advances made development of large-scale wheat farming attractive – over an inland swathe of territory through Southern Queensland, New South Wales, Victoria and South Australia; Western Australia followed suit in due course. In many farming areas investment in a combination of wheat and meat production had similar economic and social consequences to investment in dairy and meat in New Zealand. However, dairy farming in Australia was of necessity confined to limited areas of comparatively higher rainfall. After scientific studies had demonstrated the need to remedy prevalent chemical deficiencies in Australian soils with fertilisers, the way was open to successful crop farming. Wheat exports soon made a major contribution to the economy; a progressive expansion in the land taken up for crop farming was a feature of Australian agriculture in the twentieth century. In time, Australian agriculture developed great diversity, responsive to the range of climate across the continent. Large-scale beef ranching in the hot northern outback, as well as sugar, cotton, tropical fruits and rice production, provided a span to the agricultural sector not able to be matched in New Zealand. On the other hand, there were massive problems with desertification and salination of the land around vast tracts of the Murray River basin, which had no parallel in New Zealand.

The breadth and diversity of Australia encouraged expansionist thinking – too much so in several colonies. Unwise capital investment in a rapid expansion of farming on to unsuitable arid land contributed to a serious Australian banking crisis in the 1890s. The economic collapse that followed led to a surge in migration across the Tasman to New Zealand. Bank failures and economic depression dampened local ambitions in Victoria, South Australia and Tasmania. Economic uncertainties – a slowing down of mining investment in Tasmania, the costs of maintaining navigation on the Murray River, the drain of expenditure involving the Northern Territory for South Australia, and a crash followed by marked social unrest in Victoria – were all helpful to the gathering cause of federation. In New South Wales and Queensland, the rise of the political labour movement fostered a growing Australian nationalism, which was underpinned by strong protectionist forces; these, in turn, helped make New South Wales the industrial centre of the country. Accordingly, federation held out the prospect of strong economic advantages – if of a differentiated kind – to the eastern colonies. On the other side of the continent, in Western Australia, these were boom years, following spectacular gold discoveries at Pilbara in 1888 and elsewhere in the early 1890s. Although its leading politicians were tempted to stay aloof from the federation movement, a referendum revealed decisive support – thanks mainly to an influx from the east of minefield workers, whose trade union connections would have predisposed them in favour. The new Australian constitution accordingly provided that Western Australia, as a special concession, might continue to impose tariffs against the other more industrialised states for an initial period of five years; a deal struck with the other premiers provided for the construction of a trans-continental railway. Economic factors, however, soon fired up Western Australian disgruntlement with the new Commonwealth; federal expenditure on transport and industrial subsidies based on population distribution was seriously unfair to a state nearly half the overall area of Australia but with a low population density, heavy emphasis on pastoral farming and a small industrial base. Discontent reached such a pitch during the depression of the 1930s that a referendum favoured secession by nearly two to one. This political hot potato was passed to the British parliament, which juggled it for so long that the moment passed, the Western Australian economy recovered – and the onset of the Second World War reminded Western Australians of their severe strategic isolation.

Behind the local ambitions and the assorted calculations of the various Australian colonies it was possible to glimpse a bright future, despite all the early travails of slumps and collapsed schemes. Investment in manufacturing, transport and mining helped the move away from the land and towards big and bustling cities. The peripheral states – Western Australia, Tasmania and South Australia –

were motivated to join the federation, whereas New Zealand was not, by continent-sized aspirations. The mainsprings of a developing Australian nationalism may have been in the east and centred on versions of history and legend that had little in common with experience in South Australia and Western Australia, but it was possible to discern economic advantages from federation that outweighed local doubts. As in New Zealand, the British connection was there as a reassurance should anything go wrong with the great experiment. Unlike New Zealand, the physical fact of living on the same continent would promote what might, in today's terms, be described as the 'global' interest of co-ordinated development and a common political destiny. The separate nationalisms of the Australian colonies could be subsumed in a larger Australian nationalism.

New Zealand, the island country, had no other focus than itself. In the absence of overlap with quintessential Australian historical experience and the developing lore of Australian-ness, the British things the two countries had in common were insufficient to light the fires of union. The structured, organised character of early settlement in Wellington, Nelson, Canterbury and Otago provided the seedbed in which a constrained, middle-class New Zealand nationalism would grow – even though it would be some time before that could flourish against the imported certitudes of a dominant British identity. New Zealand, too, had serious banking problems in 1890, but had little difficulty continuing to raise capital in London for agricultural development for the supply of produce to the British market. The 1890s were a time of growing confidence. There was no crisis, economic or otherwise, that could not, it seemed, be resolved within the expansive framework of the British Empire. By the turn of the century, the economy was already dominated by a network of owner-operated dairy and sheep farms, linked into an infrastructure of small-town dairy factories and meat works. Farming – and the production of wool, meat and dairy products for export to Britain – became the New Zealand economic staple, simply because there were few alternative opportunities for capital investment. It was an efficient system, offering relatively sure returns on investment – given the continuing demand for food in Britain – and it tied New Zealand into a drab economic monoculture for years to come. Since the Second World War, investment in extensive pine forests, planted in the depression years of the 1930s, has laid the foundations for very large soft timber, pulp and paper industries. Tourism has become a major economic factor. New investment opportunities in agriculture have been exploited, with considerable ingenuity, in deer farming, wine, kiwi and pip fruits. Deep-sea fishing has become a large-scale economic enterprise, as have mussel and oyster farming. Dependency on unstable overseas markets, protectionism and competition – not least from Australia – in these products has nevertheless exposed many new lines of production to damaging cycles of 'boom and bust'.

At the time the Australian federal system was established, there were already distinct, if not very significant, differences between the developing economies on either side of the Tasman Sea. Given the importance of rural life in both countries, such differences would come to be melded into distinctive agricultural styles, which reinforced respective notions of national identity in the two countries. The lonely New Zealand sheep farmer, his own man on his own ground, would become as much a national stereotype as the sun-seared Australian 'cockie' or the hard-driving cattleman of the sparse red north. Nationalism sprang from such notions. It was reinforced both by the necessity of economic competition, especially for the attention of the British, and the need to strain at the gnat of relatively small differences in order for each country to define itself – above all, in the aftermath of Australian federation.

The Unbalancing of Things

In economic matters, the factor of relative size would tilt advantage away from New Zealand after the establishment of the Australian Commonwealth. The question of continuing access to the larger Australian market seems not to have been given due consideration in New Zealand in the lead-up to federation. Mercantile interests joined in unusual combination with the trade unions to oppose membership of the new Commonwealth. Their concerns – protection of local markets, in labour as well as goods, against Australian imports – were not untainted by unworthy and wild thoughts about competition from 'coloured labour' in Australia. (The New Zealanders were also racist in such matters.) There was blind faith that New Zealand, in economic as in security matters, could continue to flourish under what Richard Seddon called 'the protecting wing of Great Britain'. In one sense it worked out that way: New Zealand did prosper. It did so, however, as a dependency, an outrider of the British market. What is more, from being an actor on a par with the other six Australian colonies, after 1901 New Zealand would find itself distinctly the smaller entity alongside the new unified Australia. After ranking just below New South Wales and Victoria in population terms throughout the latter part of the nineteenth century, New Zealand was out on its own – by choice – with a population of about 900,000 as against 3.8 million in Australia in 1900. (It is interesting that the population of Australia at the beginning of the century was only a shade less than that of New Zealand at its end; the Australian population is now nearly 20 million.) For many years export income in both countries would still be largely derived from agriculture, but differences of emphasis – especially in the relative weight of the wool, wheat, meat and dairy sectors – would be translated into competition in third markets rather than co-operation in building a shared Australasian regional economy. Moreover, rivalry in trade and fear of competition in the non-staple items – locally manufactured and assembled goods, foodstuffs, chemicals, building materials, and so on – would soon intensify and largely strangle trans-Tasman trade for over sixty years.

One of the new federal government's first endeavours was to establish a common Australian tariff structure – which excluded New Zealand and was regarded as hostile by New Zealanders. The essential problem was political: New Zealand now had next to no leverage in the Australian system. It could no longer play one Australian colony against another to try to influence developments across the Tasman. Both countries were still mainly concerned to transact their business at the heart of things in London. But closer to home, Australian mercantile firms actively pursued such trading opportunities as there were in the South Pacific island territories, although New Zealand too had strong interests in the islands' trade. Only relatively small shares of the two countries' respective economic interests were taken up in trans-Tasman exchanges. The goods traded – basic manufactured items and non-staple agricultural products – were nevertheless capable of generating a lot of political heat for employment reasons and, thanks to the lobbying influence of manufacturers on both governments, protectionism was an easy political response to any surges in imports. Even if it had been on the political cards – which it was not – there was little economic incentive for two unequal and smaller countries to build an interactive shared regional economy by working together rather than at cross-purposes. As in the political/security fields, so in the economic: neither country saw merit in compromising its wider 'global' interests in favour of an uncertain regional future. Each espoused the imperial preference system while wishing to provide employment and broaden the base of its economy by building up local industry behind tariff barriers. Australia, with larger prospects, could go further in this direction; with its small domestic market, New Zealand had little scope for expansion and was consequently obliged to put most of its eggs (almost literally) in the 'global' basket of the British market. In each country these very factors built up domestic political pressures that tended to push against reconciliation of economic interests. The New Zealanders had miscalculated if they ever thought life would be the same after the formation of the Australian Commonwealth.

An attempt in 1906 to patch together a preferential trans-Tasman tariff arrangement came to nothing, when the New Zealand parliament refused ratification. In-built differences of approach to tariffs and protection of domestic suppliers exacerbated the political problems. Less industrialised and with farming interests increasingly in the political driving seat, New Zealand wanted 'cheap' imports through the 'global' imperial system of preferential tariffs. Australia had a more diverse economy which it felt obliged to protect behind relatively higher tariff walls. The difference was strictly relative: both countries adopted high tariffs to protect local industry; indeed, this was virtually the universal norm at the time. The results were the same in both places. Australians were not moved to open up their larger market to New Zealand when the New Zealanders wanted to pay the lowest possible price and were not interested in buying relatively expensive products. The circular reasoning of protectionism has its own implacable logic. Accordingly, the problem for the political leadership was to reconcile a preference scheme between the two countries within the imperial preference system while responding to local protectionist sentiment and, in the New Zealand case, keeping domestic costs down through 'cheap' imports. The New Zealand tactic was to try to argue endlessly for specific exemptions to any Australia-New Zealand agreement. Alfred Deakin, the empire-minded Australian Prime Minister, wished to set things in the broader context of a preferential trans-Tasman arrangement, within the 'global' imperial scheme. He noted that the essential problem was that the 'two countries were at the same stage of development'. Yet there were, as his successor Andrew Fisher pointed out in 1912, tradeable goods on which to build a regional preference system. Vigorous and open political systems, however, gave free play to domestic lobby interests, fostering great agitation about one side pulling the wool over the eyes of the other in any proposed deal. When another attempt was made in 1913 to establish a basis for agreement on trade concessions, 'the list of complainants – New Zealand orchardists, Australian hops, oats, barley and potato growers, New Zealand manufacturers, Australian lumber firms – was as long as their woe was heartrending to politicians'.[3]

Resentment and Restrictions

The difficulties persisted and led to bad blood between the two countries in the inter-war period, especially during the trials and tribulations of the depression years. The ANZAC spirit continued to provide the rhetoric about an Australian-New Zealand partnership. In reality, that deeply shared experience proved to be, in the words of the nine-year-old Daisy Ashford, 'like piffle in the wind'[4] before the forces of local protectionism. Even before the First World War had ended, the ANZAC flame was guttering over New Zealand resentment at Australian restrictions on boots and shoes and jam. After the war, the parlous state of the British economy led to marked fluctuations in returns for New Zealand and Australian exports, pegged as local finances were to the pound sterling. It might have been expected that the two countries would find greater scope for collaboration. Relative shares of the other's market remained small: in 1921 New Zealand trade with Australia represented 4.6 per cent of exports; and Australian exports to New Zealand were 5.9 per cent of that country's total; by 1929 New Zealand's position vis-à-vis Australia had improved a little – respectively 6 per cent and 2.9 per cent. But it was still impossible for the politicians to define any sense of mutual interest. The two countries were on different tracks and there was no broader vision to bring them together. New Zealand put the emphasis on securing cheaper imports and therefore on maintaining relatively low tariffs; Australia moved increasingly to develop local industry behind high tariff walls. The differences got in the way of sustained growth in trade and led to sharp Australian pressures for protection against 'cheap' New Zealand imports. Non-tariff barriers were erected, in the form of quotas and what are now called phyto-sanitary regulations (rules to prevent the spread of plant and animal disease). There were bitter rows about the justification for Australian claims that New Zealand potatoes and oranges had to be kept out because of the perils of various kinds of blight; New Zealand in due course retaliated by banning imports of all Australian citrus fruits.

In 1921, Australia opted for a high protective tariff structure. Whereas New Zealand put all empire countries on a 'British Preferential Rate', Australia proceeded to play the 'global' against the 'regional' card by putting only Britain on this rate while erecting higher barriers against New Zealand. Outrage of outrages, New Zealand complained of being treated like 'an Asiatic country'. A more equitable arrangement was negotiated the following year. But New Zealand wanted many exemptions to suit its own delicate domestic interests, and Australia continued to press for a more broadly based tariff structure that would give its industry the kinds of opportunities in the New Zealand market which were available in Australia itself. But New Zealand could buy to better advantage in Britain the sorts of heavy industrial goods which the Australians were producing behind their tariff barriers. Australia was looking for trading opportunities in the New Zealand market that could not be reciprocated: New Zealand's interests were at the less developed end of the manufacturing chain, but the Australians with a larger domestic market were in many cases well placed to make these types of product, too. Coincidence of interest was hard to find, without a broad view of a regional interest.

During the 1920s and 1930s, the Antipodeans seemed to be living on different economic planets. Their problems were identical: collapsing prices for the agricultural products which underwrote their economies – wool, meat, wheat and dairy products. They reacted by taking stiff punitive action against one another, among other things. New Zealand complained about the 'dumping' of Australian flour and imposed duties which, in turn, sharply reduced the Australian share of its market. Australia retaliated by tripling the tariff on New Zealand dairy products, and slapping severe duties on New Zealand potatoes – New Zealand was effectively priced out of these two markets, which it had dominated in previous years. The balance of trade between the two swung heavily in Australia's favour. The balance of ill-will went New Zealand's way. A new tariff arrangement was negotiated within the British 'Commonwealth' context in 1932, as part of what became known as the Ottawa Agreements. But New Zealanders found it contained few concessions and they continued to be most indignant about Australia as the trading relationship swung further against them.

The trans-Tasman political relationship went sour in the mean-spirited years of the 1930s. In 1934, visiting New Zealand Prime Minister Gordon Coates and his trade minister were given the brush-off treatment by their Australian counterparts; planned meetings did not eventuate or were cut short by Australian ministers, who seemed always to be travelling to or from the new capital of Canberra. Underlying trading disagreements were barely addressed and the imbalance between the two countries remained a large source of grievance to the New Zealand side. The British Trade Commissioner reported to London that Coates, after being given the run-around by Australian ministers, 'was ready at once to put Australia on the foreign tariff'. The New Zealanders were not alone, at this stage, in finding Australian self-importance and introspection difficult to bear. The British representative reported that New Zealand annoyance was 'not without its amusing side thinking of all that we too have had to go through ... extreme discourtesy' on the part of the Australians had made the New Zealand ministers 'extremely angry'.[5]

New Zealand's first Labour government, elected in 1935, was motivated by a strong sense of nationalism. Perversely, an early expression of that sentiment, which would have involved complete repudiation of any kind of economic relationship with Australia, was advocacy of a total dependence on the British market. It was proposed that Britain should take all New Zealand's exports; in return, New Zealand would buy an equivalent amount, in money terms, from Britain. Fortunately for the cause of economic diversification in New Zealand and its relationship with Australia, the British were not prepared to discriminate in favour of one of their dominions against another. Trans-Tasman trading relationships were then almost whittled away to nothing in 1938 when New Zealand was hit by a serious economic crisis caused by a dramatic shortfall in foreign exchange. To conserve foreign exchange, import licensing was imposed, which enabled the government to do what it had wanted to do in the first place – protect domestic industry. An import substitution programme was put into effect. Import licences went mainly to British suppliers and Australian imports were severely constrained. It was Australia's turn to complain about being treated as a 'foreign country'. But New Zealand was already turning into something of a siege economy as exchange controls and import restrictions were applied, while at the same time the Labour government pushed ahead with far-reaching social welfare programmes at home.

As with security, some sense of community of interest was introduced to the trans-Tasman trading relationship by the exigencies of the Second World War. New Zealand, however, was on the receiving end. There could no longer be any pretence that recently introduced import substitution programmes would suffice to permit production of the kinds of heavy equipment and specialised manufactured goods required. On the other hand, Australia's policy of fostering industry – especially in steel and motor vehicles – behind tariff barriers had given it defence production capabilities which could be expanded to help meet wartime requirements. As in the development of its own navy, Australia's instinct to develop its own capacities and mineral resources to meet its own 'regional' requirements paid off. New Zealand was able to draw on Australian industry for a good part of wartime supplies, and the trade deficit ballooned out as a result. Once again New Zealand's policies of dependency on the 'global' relationship were exposed as inadequate. There could be no argument – *in extremis*, as it were – about trade imbalances. In reality, an inability to co-ordinate trans-Tasman economic development efforts in peace-time made the predicament of both countries more alarming when faced with the reality of their strategic isolation in war. As the long and exposed supply line from Britain dried up, both were thrown into reliance on the United States for military equipment and strategic supplies.

The relationship did not recover until the 1960s, when serious attention began to be given to the removal of structural barriers and to freeing up trans-Tasman trade. Ironically, the first shifts towards a more productive relationship were made possible more by Australian nationalism than by any sudden mutual conversion to the merits of partnership. Senior Australian politicians were concerned, as the free trade winds began to blow after the Second World War and Britain turned away from empire towards Europe, that New Zealand would become an economic 'basket-case'. This would undermine Australian security interests. By saving New Zealand from an economic fate worse than death, Australia's own credentials as a major international player would be the better recognised. It would take time before this negative perception of the need for a convergence of economic interests would be superseded by more positive views of the reciprocal advantages. Meanwhile, the world was changing around the Antipodean pair and it was necessary to change with it. Increasing British protectionism towards its own farming interests, loss of the comforting security blanket of imperial preference arrangements, oil crises, the effect of European economic integration, the rise of the dynamic new economies of Asia and mounting evidence of the need to increase competitiveness in both countries by reducing protectionism, gradually wore away at old attitudes. In the face of the new internationalisation, trans-Tasman rivalries began to look dated and unhelpful.

Australian restrictions on imports of New Zealand apples serve to remind a cartoonist from a fruit-growing area of a sour 'under-arm' bowling tactic once employed by Australia to win a test match.

Jim Hubbard, *Hawkes Bay Today*, 20 October 2000. Source *The Other Side Of The Ditch*, Ian F. Grant, New Zealand Cartoon Archive Collection, Alexander Turnbull Library, Wellington.

chapter nine

The Art of Building Economic Bridges

All people think that New Zealand is close to Australia, or Asia, or somewhere, and that you cross to it on a bridge. But that is not so. It is not close to anything, but lies by itself, out in the water. It is nearest to Australia, but still not near. The gap between is very wide. It will be a surprise to the reader, as it was to me, to learn that the distance from Australia to New Zealand is really twelve or thirteen hundred miles and that there is no bridge.

– Mark Twain[1]

M ark Twain would probably not have been surprised to find how difficult it has been to build trade and economic bridges across the Tasman Sea. He knew a good deal about national self-interestedness: 'It is by the goodness of God in our country that we have three unspeakably precious things: freedom of speech, freedom of conscience, and the prudence never to practise either of them.' For most of the twentieth century, Australia and New Zealand were simply not sufficiently interested in each other to provide the impetus in favour of economic collaboration. Exclusivity and introspection are at the heart of nationalism. Such sentiment between the Antipodeans was a sufficient antidote to notions of a neighbourhood. How the two countries adjusted to one another and to the wider Asian region, a process that gathered pace over the last three decades of the century, in part reflects the process of globalisation. A transformation of attitudes had also been forced upon them by the decline of empire and the British shift towards Europe. A far-reaching economic relationship, known as Closer Economic Relations (CER), was progressively forged by focusing on the overall economic advantages rather than being palsied by the narrow disadvantages. Rightly or wrongly, the relationship is still bedevilled by patronising Australian assumptions about a perpetual state of imminent economic collapse in New Zealand, from which it is the Australian mission to rescue its wayward satellite. It goes without saying that the mere echo of such attitudes is enough to stir countervailing national sentiment across the Tasman. Partly as a result, there is no sign that New Zealanders are likely to find comparable advantage in closer political relations.

On the Road to Change

As the Second World War wound down, Australia and New Zealand faced the future by turning to the past. Close dealings with the United States during the

Pacific War had laid no foundation for the development of new economic or security relationships in that direction; lend-lease trading transactions, built around the supply of food and raw materials in exchange for military equipment, were written-off. Pre-war trading patterns centring on Britain were soon re-established. At the outbreak of war, the Antipodeans had committed themselves to bulk supply agreements obliging them to export their entire surplus agricultural production to Britain and to accept British imports up to the total value of those export sales in return. New Zealand was happy to maintain this kind of economic dependency into the post-war world. Shared Australia-New Zealand membership of the sterling area and the maintenance of imperial preference trading arrangements made it natural to slip back into the British fold. New Zealand remained more dependent on the British market than Australia, and for longer, but Australia held to the bulk-supply commitment for a time to help the British overcome wartime shortages. As the world re-geared after the war, the two countries were able to secure good prices for their wool, meat, dairy products and wheat, opening up an era of growth and expansiveness, with ties to Britain providing the sheet anchor.

Both countries were in a state of denial about Britain's decline and the rise of the United States. The sense of 'Britishness' and of emotional ties to the Commonwealth had been deepened, if anything, by shared wartime experiences. The bond crossed party lines and encompassed virtually all interest groups, and loyalty to Britain remained a central tenet. In retrospect, and taking the broad view, this was hardly surprising. In Britain, it was understood and appreciated that Australia and New Zealand had made huge – even disproportionate – sacrifices in rallying to the allied cause and that they fully shared a justified British pride in overthrowing monstrous tyrannies. In London – but not in a Washington already overly absorbed in its own new-found global power – the two Antipodeans were welcome partners as successive British governments struggled to come to terms with the new post-war order. They had standing, and believed they had earned it. With Labour governments already in power in New Zealand and Australia, and in Britain from 1945, there was also an instinctive alignment. The Antipodeans backed the misplaced sentiment that the Commonwealth could become an 'almost-equal' force in the world alongside the United States and the Soviet Union. They joined in Commonwealth scientific research programmes, provided support for British nuclear weapons tests and continued to contribute to defence arrangements alongside the British – in the firm belief that shared interests were at stake, and that the British Commonwealth had a major part to play.

There was also a high degree of suspicion about the emergent new global economic order in both countries. Their free enterprise economic models had been heavily throttled back by government intervention and controls, which had become institutionalised in the aftermath of the depression and by wartime regulations. Australia and New Zealand were classic social welfare societies. Small 's' socialism was the order of the day and with it went an inherent anti-Americanism, especially strong in trade union circles. There was marked antipathy to the Bretton Woods financial institutions, introduced to facilitate use of American capital in promoting global recovery but widely believed to be instruments of manipulation of the global economy by Wall Street: Australia was able to join the World Bank and International Monetary Fund (IMF) in 1946 only after a pragmatic new Labor Prime Minister, Ben Chifley, overcame strong opposition in his own caucus; in New Zealand the issue was too hot for any government to handle and was shelved until a conservative government could bring itself to sign on as late as 1961. That the smaller and more exposed country could display economic paranoia (nationalism) of this order was no doubt a measure of dependency on, and satisfaction with, dealings across-the–board with the British – and of doubts about the Americans. At a deeper level, it reflected a pronounced insecurity about, and blinkered isolation from, the currents of change sweeping the world. In both countries, the grey conformity of tightly controlled economies dominated national life.

The British cocoon did not suddenly dematerialise – it simply faded away. Australia and New Zealand had no difficulty in tapping the London market for investment capital for a number of years, despite successive sterling crises. There was no sudden and brusque transformation from the comforts of empire to the new world of contending nation-states. The economic disaster of the depression years – which had left deep social and political scars – almost inevitably imposed caution on policy-makers. Better to stick with the devil you know. Well into the 1950s, Australian loans raised in the United States totalled less than a fifth of those raised in London. When the shift came, it was with a rush: a decade later the American share of the Australian capital market was twice that of the British.

The Antipodeans were again fortunate; they had time to adjust. Preferential trading arrangements, like those instituted by the British in the 1930s and subscribed to most heartily by Australia and New Zealand, were regarded as discriminatory by the United States. The General Agreement on Tariffs and Trade (GATT), and the global economic and financial institutions, were designed to promote economic growth by freeing up trade on a global basis. A major target of the new economic order was protectionism, which was deemed to have devastated the world economy in the 1930s (although other factors, including unrestrained American speculation and the absence of controls in Wall Street, had played their part). The GATT, which came into effect on 1 January 1948, aimed to reduce tariff barriers, remove special arrangements for supply of particular commodities and attack import quotas and controls. Yet the United States insisted on a waiver of GATT rules in relation to trade in agricultural products, which seriously compromised the organisation's usefulness to New Zealand and Australia. The IMF was intended to promote ready convertibility to head off the financial crises of the depression years; again, New Zealand's comfort with an alternative 'global' arrangement, the sterling area, served to limit its appeal. The World Bank's aims of fostering global economic growth were also beside the point.

The days of the cosy 'old' Commonwealth club with its imperial preference systems and sterling bloc financial clearing arrangements, in which the two Antipodeans still felt at ease, were numbered as sterling lost its clout in the face of the supremacy of the American dollar. Adjustment was easier for Australia: wartime needs had led to sweeping economic diversification through the growth of manufacturing industry, and further exploitation of the country's mineral wealth had opened up new economic horizons. New Zealand had no comparable glittering opportunities, although its light manufacturing had expanded as a result of the war and new industries, centred around soft-wood forestry development, soon began to give added strength to its post-war economy. The numbers of people engaged in agriculture in both countries declined, but the difference was that New Zealand had few other opportunities for earning export income. For decades, New Zealand would continue to be shackled to primary production as the principal source of its overseas earnings. This made continued dependence on the British market, which was geared to what New Zealand could produce, an inescapable fact of life .

As the Commonwealth became more heterogeneous with the independence of India in 1947, followed in steady succession by the African and Asian colonies, the point of reference became blurred; London was no longer the focus for a comfortable white club of settler societies. The system had little cohesion and British pretensions to global authority increasingly lacked credibility. New Zealand secured its agricultural markets in Britain until the mid 1950s. But it was a losing battle, as the British Empire slipped away and Britain shifted its own focus towards Europe. The British market changed as domestic farmers were subsidised and thus enabled to build up their own production, calling – inevitably – for more protection from Commonwealth suppliers. Memories of wartime partnership proved fickle.

Battling for Agricultural Trade

There is a great hypocrisy at the heart of the drive towards openness and global free trade. In matters to do with trade in manufactured goods and services, smaller powers are expected to conform to the dictates of the larger, which still retain protection for their own farmers. The United States and Japan impose protectionist regimes on many farm products, but Europe's pivotal common agricultural policy takes the prize because its methods stimulate surplus production. By contrast, prior to embarking on its slow process of engagement with Europe, Britain had maintained farmers' incomes in the face of external competition, through what were called deficiency payments, which kept production levels constant. British membership of Europe, involving acceptance of the common agricultural policy, posed two serious threats to the economic livelihoods of Australia and New Zealand. First, their traditional exports would be excluded and European production, including that in Britain, would be enhanced; second, the subsidised wheat, butter and meat 'mountains', which then built up in Europe, would be disposed of by subsidised sales on world markets – in competition with New Zealand and Australian product displaced from Europe. It was a classical demonstration of the distortion of markets through the application of subsidies and incentives.

In 1950, 67 per cent of all New Zealand exports went to Britain: in 1900 it had been 91 per cent; by 1990 it was 8 per cent (although in that year Britain still took 50 per cent of all New Zealand butter exports) – an index more of the barriers against imports of dairy products elsewhere around the world, than of any New Zealand unwillingness to diversify. (Indeed, New Zealand was by then scouring the globe and turning milk into every conceivable product in order to secure the survival of probably the most efficient dairy industry in the world.) Australia had been obliged to reduce its dependence on the British market more rapidly than New Zealand: from the late 1940s through to the late 1960s, the British share of exports of wheat, cheese and dried fruits halved; mutton and lamb sales went from 90 to 12 per cent of the total, and wool from 40 to 10 per cent. Australian mineral exports to Japan and to a lesser extent to the United States made it feasible for Australia to diversify away from Britain as a source of imports – from over 40 per cent in the late 1940s to 20 per cent in the late 1960s. During the 1950s and 1960s, New Zealand also began to diversify by trading more widely in Asia and exploiting such opportunities as there were in the United States market. In due course, trading patterns with Australia went through a fundamental shift as well. By the late 1990s, New Zealand's combined export-import trade was almost equally balanced among Australia, Japan and the United States; imports from Britain had fallen from 61 per cent of the total in 1950 to 10 per cent – by 2000, they were now about 6 per cent of total imports.

Nevertheless, during the 1960s, both countries had no options but to become heavily engaged, from rather different standpoints, in major trading battles to uphold the interests of agricultural producers. In 1959 and 1960, they mounted strenuous diplomatic campaigns to head off the threat of exclusion from the British market in agricultural products when Britain wanted to join the European Economic Community. In a curious last lap of empire, the two countries petitioned the British separately, rather than jointly, to secure stays of execution. A pronounced difference in diplomatic styles between the two countries then worked to New Zealand's advantage. Australia, like Canada, inclined towards the confrontational approach and enlisted little sympathy. Since Britain had encouraged New Zealand to continue to send as much food as it could produce to its domestic market, New Zealand could justly claim that it was a special case. It helped too that New Zealand had accepted both the logic – in geopolitical terms – of British engagement with Europe and British assurances that its interests would be protected. Less confident than Australia in its ability to earn an international living in any other way than through agricultural trade, New Zealand engaged in what has been described as a 'Thirty Years War' in Europe over market access for dairy products and lamb. With few other options and a demonstrably efficient farming system, eventually it secured agreement to a stage-by-stage phasing-out arrangement, which represented survival against vastly superior economic forces. To the critics – especially to Australians, who were less successful – New Zealand's willingness to go endlessly to bat over such mundane concerns represented cringing to the British and the Europeans. To more thoughtful students of international relations, the process was a diplomatic success of a high order for a small country, creating enough room and time for diversification of its economy with minimal disruption. By contrast, the Australian dairy and sheepmeat industries fell on hard times.

The phenomenon of nationalism appears in many, and perverse, guises. Certainly few would choose to define it in terms of diplomatic styles in pursuit of market access for cheese and lamb! But above all a small power needs to live to fight another day. Fundamental New Zealand national interests were unquestionably at play in these negotiations with Europe. The pragmatic, diligent and constructive way New Zealand negotiators pursued those interests says more than a little about the character of the country. Nationalism in New Zealand needs to be conditioned by the recognition that there are a lot of other bigger and more powerful nations and interests out there which could do the country serious damage. Even more than national survival, a sense of national worth and character flows from such challenges: it is something that a small country should show the gumption to survive against the odds.

More recently, both Australia and New Zealand have been in the van of the continuing struggle for free trade in agricultural products. In the recent Uruguay Round of negotiation for the reduction of the barriers to international trade within the GATT, the two countries were prime movers within the so-called Cairns Group of agricultural exporting countries, which was initiated by Australia. The group operated with considerable success to maintain pressure for changes to the international trading system in favour of primary producers. Again, the role ranged a number of smaller countries against large economic forces. It made diplomatic sense to co-ordinate a spectrum of smaller country interests in pursuit of the larger objective of chipping away at the domestic farm lobby interests in major markets. The major success of the Uruguay Round in achieving increased market access for farm products was nevertheless due in no small part to the recruitment of the United States to the cause. American grains and cereals producers were anxious to use the Uruguay Round to open up European markets for their own products. With the United States on side, the effort to develop improved terms of trade in agricultural products developed momentum. Yet, in the event, neither the American nor the European markets have been opened up, as expected by the Uruguay Round. In international trade it is prudent not to put too much money on biblical maxims to the effect that you would like others to do for you what you do for them.

Limited Free Trade is Not Enough

The success of the European Economic Community in facilitating regional trade prompted New Zealand and Australia to consider that the two Antipodeans could do themselves a service by opening up to one another. Both were hit by serious balance of payments crises in the 1950s and were outgrowing the economic straitjacket of tied trade. A conference of trade ministers – the first since the end of the Second World War – was called in 1956 and the respective import licensing regimes were adjusted to facilitate entry of some lines of products. But this approach was soon of dwindling usefulness, as the import licencing regime was phased out in Australia to cater for the needs of a swiftly growing population and an expanding economy. New Zealand clung to import licenses far longer, and this impeded the relaxation of constraints on trans-Tasman trade. After further ministerial meetings in 1958 and 1961, it was agreed to move to free up trans-Tasman trade, despite the heavy-handed protectionism inherent in the existing 1933 trade agreement. But substantial lobby interests had to be overcome first. Memories of wartime squabbles and mutual senses of grievance still nursed from the 'trade wars' of the 1930s did not help. The political leadership on both sides had little experience of direct bilateral dealings outside the framework of empire – in which each could play off the other. In terms of total trade, New Zealand was a small market for Australia and Australia was still – as it had been for the best part of a hundred years – only a minor market for New Zealand. The nationalism blinkers were still well and truly in place, on both sides of the Tasman.

The trade balance, so far as it went, was in Australia's favour, which imposed the need to make more opportunities available to New Zealand if Australia were to capture the openings for manufactured goods it sought in its neighbour's market. Co-ordination of trade in forestry products seemed to offer scope. There were large industries in both countries, operating under considerable tariff protection, but specialising in different aspects of forestry production. A carefully negotiated merger of the two markets would offer advantage to both. The New Zealand-Australia Free Trade Arrangement (NAFTA) agreement, which came into being in 1965, was more about limited item-by-item haggling over trade barriers than the birth of any new spirit of ANZAC economic togetherness. At a stage when former enemies in Europe were achieving, through the EEC, across-the-board economic consolidation, Australia and New Zealand were throwing caution to the winds by agreeing to dismantle barriers to the market in forest products. NAFTA rules would be extended to other products on a carefully negotiated basis. New Zealand proposed that the relationship be developed along the same lines as the European Coal and Steel Community – that is, a defined political structure devoted to joint management of particular lines of production. This was unacceptable to Australia, which was more anxious to expand the range and scope of the free trade area.

It was a start. In both countries expansion of export earnings was an urgent requirement and demand for new consumer products was high and expanding. Protection of otherwise non-competitive local manufacturing industries was unlikely to yield any significant export receipts, was costly to the taxpayer and, as likely as not, would fail to satisfy the consumer. There was, in reality, no way either country could continue to justify the maintenance of closed, inward-looking economies. This was widely recognised in Australia, less so in New Zealand. It took major effort on the part of the government in New Zealand to draw the manufacturing sector away from the traditional attitude of the camel. At the conclusion of the NAFTA negotiations, in 1965, J.R. Marshall, the New Zealand Minister concerned, addressed the Council of the Auckland Manufacturers' Association: 'I want to thank you,' he said,

> for your help in getting a good agreement. Your Council, ably backed by the majority of members, were so pig-headed and generally difficult in opposing the idea of this free trade agreement it greatly strengthened my hand. I found too that dealing with the Council over the last few years was a good practice run for dealing with the Australians except that the Australians were not quite so rough.[2]

For the first time, there was a clear reciprocity of advantage. The likelihood that the British would lose their preferential position in both markets with the phasing out of the Ottawa tariff structure opened up opportunities for both sides. It was a way for the Australians to build up exports in order to facilitate further economic expansion; a declining British share of the New Zealand market for manufactured products offered scope for penetration by Australia. By the early 1960s, New Zealand was already taking about 20 per cent of Australian manufactured exports; perhaps the trans-Tasman market could become an export platform for further expansion into other overseas markets. The New Zealand side was driven by the clear advantage of securing outlets in the Australian market for their developing wood pulp and paper industries. As well, it was hoped that Australia would provide scope for food exports and other manufactured goods. New Zealand manufacturers were, however, more concerned about whether they could compete and had to be convinced of the bigger picture: the advantages to the economy as a whole flowing from the discipline of competition and expanded opportunities for the burgeoning forestry industries.

NAFTA opened the door on a new trans-Tasman trading relationship, if not very far. Some influential Australian Ministers tended to interpret it as a 'grace and favour' arrangement, a helping hand offered with the strategic purpose of keeping New Zealand off the economic rocks. As with the EEC in its early stages, NAFTA's provisions applied only to listed categories of tradeable goods. Unlike other more comprehensive free trade arrangements, such as the EEC and its British-led counterpart EFTA, there was no commitment to progressive extension of the area of coverage and automatic reduction of duties on items not listed. New Zealand was able to keep in place the import licensing arrangements that were its principal means of protecting domestic manufacturers. NAFTA did not attempt to tackle other non-tariff barriers such as domestic subsidies, government procurement programmes or the import monopolies vested in certain of the Australian states. The opting-out clauses were unusually generous. In addition to an expected provision that items could be withdrawn from the schedule if their importation harmed domestic producers, it was permissible to withdraw or suspend trading concessions when necessary to protect new industries or to encourage economic development in either country.

The difficulty, noted earlier in the century, in freeing up trade between two countries at similar stages of development remained a large part of the problem. But the central challenge was to reconcile the concerns in the smaller country – about being swallowed up in the larger – with the broad objective of freer trade. Australian interests were keen to expand the commodity coverage of the NAFTA schedules. By contrast, New Zealand policy, according to one of the principal advocates of opening up trade between the two countries, 'seems to have been to keep out of the arrangement, at least in its initial stages, practically all manufactures, other than forest products, which are not now traded freely between the two countries'.[3] Establishment of binational panels to consider reciprocal trade in other broad categories of tradeable goods tended to produce more reasons why the agreement should not be extended in those areas than acceptance of the need to do so. The globalisation bandwagon had not yet arrived in the South Pacific. NAFTA did expand trade between the two countries; after ten years, the two governments claimed that four times as much business was being done as before 1965: of the order of $1 billion worth of two-way trade. Economists point out that much of this increase was due to inflation and that expanded trade volumes were attributable to other changes in the trading environment (import licensing and global tariff adjustments) than those provided for under NAFTA.[4]

The point is that national mindsets did not change. NAFTA did little to promote a community of interest. A law of economic nationalism can be formulated on the basis of the NAFTA experience: national interests will stymie any free trade arrangement which leaves them scope to do so. The NAFTA approach to breaking down barriers gave the national interest groups the opportunity to deny progress, as opposed to simply negotiating themselves time to adjust to change, and it bogged down in interminable haggling about 'the minutiae of trade in peas and beans, let alone horse shoes and harness bells'.[5] At another level, however, the experience showed that the smaller country did not have to get swallowed up by the larger. New Zealanders learned, through the NAFTA process, that expanded trade, rather than being a matter of winners and losers, is mutually reinforcing and beneficial to economic growth. Competition stimulates awareness of new opportunities and niches to be filled by new products. In any case, all around the world the barriers were coming down as governments and businesses alike came to understand the costs of protectionism. New Zealand overcame its diffidence and at least some of its politicians came to articulate the advantages of operating on a wider stage.

Closing Economic Ranks

Fundamental beliefs about the central role of government in the economy were being challenged by the realisation that the old ways of state paternalism may not be affordable any more. In the face of new and compelling doctrines of market economics, it was becoming obvious that protection of domestic industries and other attempts to insulate the economy and society were not only wasteful but counterproductive. The success of regional trading groupings in Europe and the dynamism of the export-led emergent Asian economies could no longer be ignored. By stimulating competition, it would be possible to proceed with economic restructuring to bring both economies out of the straitjacket of state ownership and controls. It made no sense for Australia and New Zealand to spurn the chance to redefine their overall interests in terms of the larger market gained by combining the two populations.

NAFTA was clearly inadequate. By 1980 a new approach was needed to capture the potential of trans-Tasman commerce. Australia, greatly the more self-absorbed of the two, had only a limited amount of political energy to spare for redefinition of the economic relationship with New Zealand. It was important to capture the moment. Detailed preparatory work by officials cleared the way for the necessary pressures to be put on at the political level. The domestic political stars would seem to have been in alignment – in that governments of the centre-right were in power in both countries. This factor, however, often works in counter-intuitive ways between Australia and New Zealand. Calculations of local political advantage take precedence over any notions of shared beliefs. The conventional wisdom is that relations are at their worst when leaders of the same political stripe are in office on the two sides of the Tasman, because the competition is more intense when both are coming from the same domestic political corners. Certainly in 1980 the respective centre-right prime ministers – Malcolm Fraser in Australia and Robert Muldoon in New Zealand – had little time for one another.[6] Muldoon was extremely reluctant to wean New Zealand from the import licensing approach to trade; the Australians had taken that plunge almost twenty years before and were impatient with all the minutiae of negotiation with New Zealand under this approach. Fraser delivered what was in effect an ultimatum: NAFTA would be scrapped unless trade exchanges between the two countries could be put on a broader footing by setting end goals for freeing up trade. It worked.

In March 1980 the two Prime Ministers announced that Australia and New Zealand were to develop an 'appropriately structured closer economic relationship'. What was in it for two pragmatic, if very different politicians? Obviously, there was no sudden flash of mutual trans-Tasman benevolence. Essentially, both were responding to domestic interest groups. Australian manufacturers were pressing for freer access to the New Zealand market in return for what were believed to be generous arrangements for New Zealand in the Australian market under NAFTA; New Zealand officials were seeking a way out of what was beginning to look like an economic dead end. Prime Minister Muldoon found it difficult to surmount his deep-seated protectionist instincts and was concerned to keep the manufacturers on side until after the next election. He was an old-fashioned, narrow-focus New Zealand nationalist, with no love for Australians. Negotiations dragged on. The protective nationalist instincts of the older generation of politician, brought up on the central role of the state in providing personal security and political stability, clashed with the new thinking about the need for deregulation and openness in facing the global challenges. New Zealand argued for complete phasing out of import licenses, but over a very long period – until 1995. Australia eventually conceded this point and a deal was possible. (In the event New Zealand timidity was proved unnecessary as it found that the licensing system could be killed off much sooner than the initial deadline.)

What emerged in October 1982 was called the Australia-New Zealand Closer Economic Relationship Trade Agreement (ANZCERTA); a mouthful that has since been condensed to CER. From the first, the aim was to establish a genuine free trade area. Against the background of petty nationalism between Australia and New Zealand, its negotiation was a remarkable achievement, especially for New Zealand. The objectives, set out in Article 1, are

> to strengthen the broader relationship [and develop] closer economic relations [through] a mutually beneficial expansion of free trade; to eliminate barriers to trade … in a gradual and progressive manner under an agreed timetable and with a minimum of disruption; to develop trade … under conditions of fair competition.

The preamble to the agreement also states the importance of 'strengthening and fostering links and co-operation in such fields as investment, marketing, movement of people, tourism, and transport'. New Zealand gained largely unrestricted access to a market five times larger than its own, under terms that have made it possible for the smaller economy progressively to adjust; Australia gained enhanced access to a major new market for its manufactures. From the beginning, the CER arrangement provided for a more intimate association than would have been achieved merely by a reduction in barriers to trade in goods; rather, it served as a framework for conciliation of the respective national economic interests of the two countries almost across the board. CER has turned out to be more than a free trade zone, if less than a customs union (with common external tariffs) or a common market (with joint political structures). The differences are, however, largely academic since the agreement has provided a platform for achieving many of the same aims as, for example, the European Union – without the overlay of imposed political structures.

The CER agreement has from the first had bipartisan support on both sides of the Tasman. The New Zealand Labour opposition party supported it from the first, effectively isolating the Trade Unions on the issue – just as advocacy of the agreement by a conservative government had disarmed the manufacturing lobby. The Fraser and Muldoon governments went out of office in 1983 and 1984 respectively. Their Labor/Labour successors – headed by Bob Hawke in Canberra and David Lange in Wellington – found the CER concept very much suited to the far-reaching programmes of economic re-structuring and reform over which they presided. Political relationships between the two countries sank to a low ebb in the mid-1980s, with Australian dismay at the Lange government's cavalier repudiation of central tenets of the ANZUS Security Treaty (chapter 11), but little of this flowed over into the economic arena. The two governments proceeded steadily to remove obstacles to their economic interaction. So much so that at the scheduled five-year review of CER in 1988 the scope of the agreement was broadened to provide for free trade in services except in certain defined areas (the negative list). The date for achievement of duty free trans-Tasman trade in all goods was brought forward from 1995 to 1990. This target was achieved. As from 1 July 1990, all goods meeting CER rules (50 per cent Australian or New Zealand content with the last stage of manufacture to have taken place in the other country) have been freed from tariffs, quotas and/or quantitative import restrictions; the two countries have also agreed to go further and eliminate all export restrictions on trade between them and to refrain from introducing new controls or intensifying old ones.

CER has become bedded in to economic policy-making on both sides of the Tasman and is no longer politically sensitive. It is generally reckoned that CER has become 'one of the most comprehensive, effective and multilaterally compatible free trade agreements in the world'[7] and that it is compatible with the wider multilateral trading interests of the two countries. Trans-Tasman trade in goods has grown steadily to approximately $US6 billion per year in 1996-97; two-way investment between the two countries reached about $US12 billion in the same time-scale. Australia has become New Zealand's largest trading partner, taking over 20 per cent of exports; the New Zealand market is Australia's third to fourth largest, approximately as important to Australia as the United States. New Zealand has become Australia's largest market for manufactured products (although not for goods designated 'elaborately manufactured'). Manufactured goods now dominate two-way trans-Tasman trade. It is surely an effective riposte to the protectionists, who were so concerned that New Zealand would not be able to compete, that 60 per cent of New Zealand exports to Australia are manufactured products as compared to about 75 per cent of Australian exports to New Zealand. CER provides for free trade in services, subject to some areas of exclusion, mainly in aviation, shipping and telecommunications. (Australia imposes constraints on access to broadcasting and television services and a number of qualifications on access to the domestic insurance market, while continuing to be laggardly over phasing out some export subsidies.) Services trade is, nevertheless, substantial, growing to about $US1 billion annually in 1996.

The Trans Tasman Mutual Recognition Agreement, concluded in 1996, serves to promote the free flow of goods through reciprocal acceptance of quality, packaging and testing standards. Harmonisation of qualifications and procedures for entry into professions and occupations in both countries is also being tackled under this agreement, which came into force in 1998. New Zealand suppliers of goods and services are now able to enter the contracting process for federal and state government purchases on an equal footing with Australian suppliers. The focus is now on deeper and more complex issues: harmonisation of commercial law, food standardisation, telecommunications and investment procedures, shipping issues and the establishment of an open civil aviation market. Trans-Tasman shipping and stevedoring arrangements still offer a great deal of scope for rationalisation, almost exclusively at the Australian end. Travel and migration issues are an occasional source of irritation. On the one hand, the CER approach reinforces the adage that the more you discover, the more there is to discover. That process can still cause friction. On the other hand, CER has now led into such thickets of nationalism and national control as the determination of qualifications, the setting of standards and the establishment of agreed food hygiene provisions through a joint Food Standards Authority and a single authority for trade in therapeutic products.

The central point about the CER approach to what may be described as 'regional globalisation' is that the arrangement recognises that economic issues raise political questions. Market forces may provide the horsepower for change and may help discover the things that need changing. However, the decisions about the rules for a new trading regime must be taken by governments. In this regard, CER has been built into an extensive programme for inter-governmental consultations on almost every topic coming within national oversight and control. New Zealand has membership on thirty-seven Australian ministerial councils to do with agriculture, environment, health, industry and so on down the list, and has observer status at ministerial-level bodies dealing with other issues where the Australian approach, based as it must be, on federal solutions may not necessarily mesh with New Zealand systems. The trans-Tasman relationship, in other words, has been opened up; the two governments level with one another across the board. Occasional failures to consult, as when an Australian decision to suspend progress towards establishment of a single aviation market was simply communicated by open fax, are becoming the exception that proves the rule.

Where to Now?

New Zealand has been the more forward in seeking to extend CER by attempting to hook it in to comparable free-trading relationships around the Pacific: an interesting example of the yen on the part of a smaller partner in such an arrangement to find others to diversify the mix. As the returns from the elaborately negotiated multilateral trading arrangements under the global aegis of the World Trade Organisation (the successor to GATT) have proved to be less than promised, attention has shifted to bilateral agreements. To the New Zealanders, CER should be a sort of template for forging such arrangements for freeing up international trade. A Free Trade Agreement has been concluded with Singapore and is being pursued with Chile, Mexico and Hong Kong. Australia is now on the same tack. Association with the North American Free Trade Area (between Canada, the United States and Mexico) – which now has a lien on the old Australia-New Zealand acronym, NAFTA – is a major prize for both countries. Australia has a head-start over New Zealand in negotiation of a bilateral agreement with the United States because the Bush II Administration in Washington has give a priority in such matters to its allies, a status which New Zealand has lost because of its anti-nuclear policies.

New Zealanders are committed free traders, believing that the objective must be to improve conditions for agricultural trade by reducing the impact of agricultural protectionism; equally, it has been accepted that a small country with little leverage can best persuade others to offer it concessions if it leads by example. (The Labour government elected in late 1999 rejects the latter logic and intends that New Zealand tariffs should not be at lower levels than those of competitors; as a coalition government, Labour must also contend with smaller radical parties under its wing, which have doubts about free trade.) Australians also hold strong views about persistent agricultural protectionism on the part of the major industrial powers. To them, the CER is a useful local deal, helpful to important Australian interests, but by no means a major plank in its international economic policies. As opposed to New Zealanders, few Australians seem to conceive of CER as a matter of great moment to their economy. In a very random sample, three relatively recent and comprehensive studies of Australian politics and the development of the Australian economy during the 1980s and early 1990s make no mention of CER.[8]

The advantages are plainly mutual:

CER has been of obvious economic and social benefit to both New Zealand and Australia. It has encouraged businesses to establish manufacturing and services operations on both sides of the Tasman, leading to a considerable degree of integration between the two economies. The economic activity it has generated has contributed substantially to employment in both countries.[9]

The intensity of business interaction between eastern Australia and New Zealand puts the two regions among the more active economic zones, transcending national borders, which have emerged as one of the phenomena of the new age of globalisation. In Europe, the connections between Lyons and Milan, between Marseilles and Barcelona, are being seen in the same light; north-south connections across the border between the United States and Canada, in the zone linking Vancouver with the American cities of Portland and Seattle, are now so far-reaching and deep that it has been described as a new country, 'Cascadia'. One of the most important characteristics of these new 'enterprise zones' is that they owe nothing – except the framework within which they operate – to central governments. They simply represent the economic drive to gain maximum advantages as the barriers come down. Much the same thing has happened between eastern Australia and New Zealand.

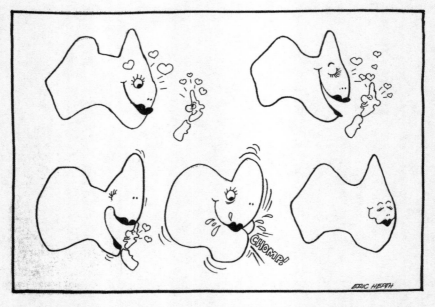

New Zealanders worry about being swallowed up by Australia, as here during trade negotiations.

'Chomp', Eric Heath, *The Dominion*, 17 August 1979. Source *The Other Side Of The Ditch*, Ian F. Grant, New Zealand Cartoon Archive Collection, Alexander Turnbull Library, Wellington.

Part II

GLOBALISM v NATIONALISM

New Zealand Prime Minister Savage wants to call in the League of Nations as the European crisis develops during the 1930s. Small power idealism does not impress.
'The Dodo', Gilmour, *New Zealand Truth*, 1937. (From *The Unauthorized Version*, Ian F. Grant.)

CALL OF THE WILD

New Zealand (and Australian) leaders revel in strutting the world stage but domestic politics calls the tune. Peter Fraser rushes back from the United Nations for a country by-election.
'Call of the Wild', Minhinnick, *New Zealand Herald*, 1947. (Source *The Unauthorized Version*, Ian F. Grant.)

YOUR DAUGHTER?

THE ALIEN WAVE

Australia was not alone in 'white' separatist thinking. In the early 1920s New Zealanders too had obsessions about being 'swamped' by Asian immigration.
Left: 'Your Daughter?' W. Blomfield, *Observer*, 1920; right: 'The Alien Wave', Ellis, *New Zealand Free Lance,* 1920. (Source *The Unauthorized Version*, Ian F. Grant.)

chapter ten

The Yearnings of Nationalism

I put for a general inclination of all mankind, a perpetual and restless desire of power after power, that ceaseth only in death.
– *Thomas Hobbes*, The Leviathan *(1651) pt. 1, Chapter* 11

The world is changing, but the world stays the same. There is no escape from the basic imperative of power and the pursuit of power, as expressed through the operation of the nation-state system. Competition and contention is of the essence. But the nation-state is not the only building block within the international system. People and nations identify themselves in a number of other ways – ethnic, cultural, linguistic or regional. The high ambition in the twentieth century was to create international structures which would not only arbitrate those differences between nations that unleashed 'the scourge of war' in the past, but create new supranational decision-making authorities. Associations of nations and peoples along cultural or civilisational lines – Islamic, Asian, Western, African, Latin American, and so on – have strong resonance. Relative wealth or industrial strength provides another basis for categorisation. So too do the regional groupings – NATO, EU, ASEAN, APEC. But the politicians and diplomats are still caught in the cage of nationalism. New Zealand and Australia demonstrate that smaller nation-states do not freely give up their separate holds on power – even when their differences are slight. The urge to do this in order, in the words of the American constitution, 'to form a more perfect union' appears to be well under control in the early years of the new millennium. Supranational organisations lack real authority and are probably losing ground in the face of new manifestations of nationalism, by big powers as well as small. National leaders do not rush to yield their autonomous power to any other agency, unless by force. Intense new pressures on the nation-state, under broad cover of globalisation, are believed to sound its death-knell. But the evidence that this is in fact happening is, to say the least, debatable.

Identity

Identity springs from basic human instincts to do with race, gender, belonging and community; it responds everywhere, around the world, to the same sorts of emotion about the character of the land, the people, history and heroes. The inspirations for nationalism are universal but, in each case, are shaped by feelings believed to be unique or intrinsic to a place or people. The force of nationalism springs from unshakeable convictions about each group's uniqueness and separateness. Yet, for all the attempts of scholars, commentators and travellers to pin it down, nationalism remains elusive in both meaning and character. Like the amoeba,, it has no particular shape. Clearly, it means something to do with a nation. What exactly is a nation? For a crisply English summing up of that difficulty, it is hard to go beyond the observation of the nineteenth-century economist and constitutionalist, Walter Bagehot: 'We know what it is when you do not ask us, but we cannot very quickly explain or define it.'[1] It is not surprising that New Zealanders and Australians respond in different ways to their physical surroundings, given the distinctive character of the two landscapes. Nor, given the prescription that the nation-state is the fundamental building block of the international system, is it remarkable that the two countries have been able easily, almost casually, to define themselves as separate nations. What is surprising is that strongly held perceptions of difference have sprung from such slight variations on the themes of western culture, history and institutions. Political separateness has been built out of very little, by way of differences of political styles, social character, history, origins or experience, and it has all happened in a very short a time.

Nationalism yokes mostly harmless notions of identity to a formal identification with a nation, and uses them – all too often – as an engine of government, the state. Nationalism of this kind moves beyond vague feelings to build native pride and commitment into political beliefs; it can then easily accommodate and help propagate notions of difference and superiority towards those who are 'not us', often leading on to disgraceful creeds of intolerance and bigotry.

A yawning gulf separates xenophobia from nationalism of the Australian and New Zealand brands. Even so, the Antipodeans have been far from reluctant to pin on themselves special qualities, especially in war and sport; there has been more than a little presumption as to European or 'white' superiority, much distasteful racism and plenty of hard dealings with their own indigenous peoples. Nationalism may not have been turned into an instrument of policy to conjure up bile against other nations, peoples or ethnic groups. Nevertheless, Australians and New Zealanders have not been above racial chauvinism and disdain for the black and coloured races; Australia has found it hard to disown its 'white Australia' heritage and is consistently accused in Asia of racial and cultural insensitivity and arrogance. New Zealanders too are in no position to point the finger at others about some of the more distasteful aspects of nationalism.

On the whole, however, in both countries nationalism is played in the minor key, more like tribalism. As such, the feelings of identity which are engaged are in almost a direct line from the simple commitments described by Homer, perhaps as much as 3000 years ago. Near the beginning of *The Iliad*, he has the muses describe the many contingents of 'the flowing haired Achaians [the Greek Army assembled before Troy which] stood up through the plain against the Trojans, hearts burning to break them'. Each troop congratulated itself about its possession of fine and productive land, its shared lines of descent, supposed battle skills and strengths as warriors and allegiance to an authoritarian leader. From the hilly coast north of Athens came those

> who held Euboia, the Abantes, whose wind was fury … of these the leader was Elephenor, scion of Ares, son of Chalkodon and lord of the great-hearted Abantes. And the running Abantes followed with him, their hair grown long at the back, spearmen furious with the out-reached ash spear to rip the corselets girt about their enemies. Following along with him were forty black ships.[2]

Such commitments derive from simple 'tribalism', pride in identity, making use of basic feelings about place and people to rally the troops. The ANZACs waiting in their ships before dawn on 25 April 1915, close to ancient Troy across the Dardanelles (see chapter five) most certainly would not have had their hair grown long at the back. But they too had strong pride in who they were and were only too eager to 'break' their adversaries on the Asiatic mainland.

A sense of belonging is one thing. Taking that simple commitment and transmuting it into a code of belief, a collective political instinct, is quite another. No longer simply a matter of tribal allegiance, nationalism is accepted in our times as a response to felt social or psychological needs. It goes beyond patriotism and love of homeland to embody notions of the rights of citizenship and self-determination; it generally rests on a common language, a shared literature and – sometimes – a religious affiliation. Because it is founded in common interests and beliefs, nationalism is easy politics. Its rhetoric comes naturally and has unstoppable resonance: the battle flags are easily unfurled. The field swirls with tantalising and elusive ideas about origins and identity; the will o' the wisp of national character constantly hovers, as does the more potent stuff of history and its twin – national mythology. Modern nationalism has many sub-texts – political, religious, ethnic, linguistic. Mindsets as much as realities are determining factors.

Several things must be taken as read. The first is that there is no nationalism gene. Nationalism is not wired into us. A few people get along perfectly well without committing themselves to any group, society or nation; many hardly even think about it – except at sports matches. With a better developed sense of common humanity, nationalism could be made redundant. With a greater sense of inclusiveness, our deep-seated, unquestioning commitments to the interests of our particular group may perhaps one day be bypassed in recognition of our shared human interest in preserving the planet. There is a long way to go. Human beings are socialised: a sense of community is fundamental. Geography and a sense of place have always made heavy imprints on the human subconscious.

Breathes there a man, with soul so dead
Who never to himself has said
This is my own, my native land
Whose heart hath ne'er within him burned
As home his footsteps he hath turned
From wandering on a foreign strand!

Walter Scott's statement on the matter is now hackneyed, but our felt need to know our place in the sun, our identity, is innocuous and natural. Such a commitment adds enjoyment and spice to life and is not to be despised. There is no escaping the division of the world into 'us' and 'them' (or 'the other'). This bipolarity is the mainspring of domestic party political struggle. Projected into the international arena, it becomes the starting point for all calculations of the national interest. Nationalism in this sense may be the lifeblood of international affairs. It springs up spontaneously; all international interactions are coloured by it, even those designed to promote co-operation and a sense of common interest.

Like St Peter, New Zealand has denied Australia at least three times: at the formation of the Australian Commonwealth (see chapter four), by deciding to stick with the 'global' strategy in 1943 (see chapter six), and by repudiating the ANZUS relationship in 1985 (see chapter eleven). On each occasion, New Zealand was articulating what it saw as its national interest as opposed to an Australasian interest. It is small wonder that Australian leaders become impatient with New Zealand protestations about the fundamental character of the ANZAC bond; the New Zealand presumption appears to be that there must be a special relationship, but not necessarily one that imposes conformity to notions of shared, overarching interests. The advancement of 'our' interests against 'theirs'– regardless of common concerns, ties of friendship or regional rapport – is at the heart of modern nationalism. Whether as a pretext for dismemberment of Bosnia in the interest of 'Greater Serbia', or in pursuit of narrowly defined national airline interests (see chapter nine), presumptions of the national interest are uppermost.

Nationalism, seen in this light, becomes truly ineradicable. The nation-state incorporates the interests of the 'nation' – the seedbed of 'nationalism' – with its governing processes, the 'state'. All international and most national business is conducted from this platform. Of course, as chapter eleven describes, there are other forces, generally encapsulated as 'globalisation', at work. The nation-states group themselves with others – for reasons to do with belonging to a region, religion or a cultural grouping – even within the United Nations and its associated agencies; any number of other supranational and non-governmental organisations provide alternative focus for international attempts to make the world a better place. Yet the reality is, decisions rest with the individual nation-states, which are guided by perceptions of their respective national interests. The nation-states are the repositories of law and the often jealous guardians of what is acceptable as international law. Smaller countries such as Australia and New Zealand tend to assume they are less inclined towards the nationalistic approach than the larger nations, and that their support for internationalist, or supranationalist, solutions to problems is evidence of a higher commitment, one that transcends mere nationalism. But it could be argued that the pursuit of supranationalist aims indicates no more than a lack of the necessary power to achieve results on one's own account. Although the effect is now often diluted, power continues to be the ultimate arbiter of the international system, no matter how much we may wish it were otherwise.

Why does it seem entirely natural for Australia and New Zealand to go their separate ways when logic points to the advantages of making common cause? The answer does not lie solely in simple feelings about separate identity, but in modern nationalism. The linkage between beliefs about separate nationhood and the apparatus of the state sets up a disposition to make differences. In both communities, a sense of 'civic nationalism' is fundamental: the state is expected, quite properly, to maintain law and order and uphold security, and the citizens are expected, in turn, to give their loyalty to the state. This is all as it should be. There is no excess in civic nationalism of this kind. But the commitment to national interests and concerns is such as to leave little room for interests other than those strictly defined in nation-state terms. The political process is entirely taken up with the concerns of the state, which means that the state has no gearing to connect everyday national interests with broader calculations of regional or supranational advantage. Introversion is an easier game to play than 'extroversion'. Antipodean brands of nationalism may be unusually low key, and the issues between the two countries innocuous, but the forces that separate are still stronger than the ties that bind. Popular attitudes – of dismissiveness on the western shore of the Tasman and rivalry on the eastern – are strong enough to have become fixed in place in a remarkably short time. If nationalism is not necessarily and always an evil phenomenon, it is also not simply a benign fancy about identity – innocent of chauvinism and divisiveness. All countries, great or small, democratic and stable or xenophobic and unpredictable, demonstrate this truth, in one form or another.

The core ingredients in the nationalism mix, which have served to set Australia and New Zealand – and all other nation-states – apart, are to do with politics, policy-making and the political processes, domestic and international. But there is nothing inherent or pre-destined about politics. It would be equally possible to move the trans-Tasman relationship in the opposite direction, towards a true sense of partnership and mutual commitment. Shakespeare puts his finger on the essence of the matter when he has Hamlet say, 'There is nothing, either good or bad, but thinking makes it so'. It is all in the mind. New Zealanders and Australians could readily give up on the cultivation of differences and work on the creation of a common Australasian identity and a merged sense of purpose.

All it would require is what is most rare: coherence, agreement, will – and leadership. The first thing to do would be for intellectuals and politicians to stop translating simple and uncomplicated feelings about identity into vacuous philosophies about 'special character', 'inherent qualities' and 'places apart'. Blanketing entire peoples or nations with generalisations about their special worth or singular worthlessness is not only intellectually silly, it is hugely irresponsible. In some parts of the world, the rage to turn myth and fantasy on such matters into dogma has become truly dangerous. The vainglories of 'national destiny' lead easily into intolerance and phobia about those 'who are not like us', and from there it is not a long step to 'ethnic cleansing'. It would be stupid to suggest that there is any of this in the Australia-New Zealand relationship. But it is necessary to dwell a little more on the mainsprings of nationalism to understand why, even at the relatively harmless end of the scale, the whole phenomenon is so unconstructive.

Nationalism and Power

The heart of the matter is very practical. Nationalism props up power – who is in charge here? Anglo-French rivalries set the ball of modern nationalism rolling. During the fourteenth and fifteenth centuries, in the 'Hundred Years' War, the English fought unsuccessfully to maintain their possessions in France and strong nationalist sentiment was stirred – on both sides of the channel; Joan of Arc and King Henry V (with a little help from Shakespeare) became standard bearers for heroic nationalism. Another dimension to nationalism was established in 1534 by Henry VIII. Henry, the English king and a devout Catholic, repudiated the authority of the Pope over what he regarded as a purely domestic and practical matter: his right to divorce because he wanted a son and heir to bolster the Tudor line in the aftermath of the Wars of the Roses. By insisting on the supremacy of national interests, he challenged the imperial political interests of the Roman Church. The famous dispute between Henry and his chancellor, Sir Thomas More, was bedded in the same issues: the king wanted unchallenged national power and territorial, as well as spiritual, independence; his scholarly chancellor could not put the king before his responsibilities to God and the Catholic Church, and was beheaded for it. Henry, the nationalist, had his hands on the levers of power; More has been described as a pre-nationalist, committed to the notion that power could reside only in God and thus in God's representatives on earth.[3] With the passage of his Act of Supremacy, making Henry the head of the Church of England, a king's divorce proceedings led, through the thickets of bitter internecine strife, to the articulation of a new national philosophy. The subsequent achievements of the Elizabethan age – Drake's circumnavigation of the globe, the advance of science and the new age of enlightenment, even the elevation of the 'Virgin Queen' herself as a national symbol, coupled with the brilliance of Shakespeare in articulating the new nationalism – consolidated the English sense of their separate and blessed state. The defeat of the Spanish armada in 1588 was the turning point: the notion of a unique nation, of a people embodying splendid and eminently praiseworthy characteristics, governed by consent, was firmly established.

One advantage of populating an island is that the territorial scope of its national identity is easy to pin down. Whereas the English drew their strong sense of themselves from a broadly based celebration of supposed national virtues, the French – whom few would regard as reluctant nationalists – also cohered, during a similar time-frame, around their own set of beliefs in their own unique qualities. The Franks emerged out of Germany into northern France around the sixth century; their kingdom became the focus for a slowly growing sense of 'France', a powerful central authority necessary to administer a territory with – at the outset – few natural boundaries. From the beginning, these feelings were Paris-based. The French language, celebrated for its expressive qualities from the thirteenth century onwards, was essentially confined to Paris or to the governing classes for several centuries. The power of the 'Very Christian' kings of France derived from the presumption that, of all the monarchs of Europe, they were especially favoured by God. Loyalty to them was spasmodic outside northern France until the English had been repelled (mid fifteenth century), the rival Duchies subsumed (in the mid-sixteenth century) and the wars of religion brought to a successful conclusion (mid-sevententh to early eighteenth centuries). The power to rule a large territory was difficult to acquire and much contested from within and without. Accordingly, French nationalism grew more out of a reverence for distinctive and special qualities of language, religious authority and political power than the more practical presumptions that led the English to assume that theirs was the chosen race.

Nationalism is not static. The tribal presumptions of Homer's day clearly no longer correspond to the political realities of modern Greece, although the famed, mountainous island of Euboea (Evvoia) continued to make a mark down the centuries. The dominance of French cultural prescriptions about reason and authority produced a counter-reaction from the other side of the Rhine in the late eighteenth and early nineteenth centuries, extolling a German romanticism founded in ideas of national individuality and character. The philosopher Johann von Herder celebrated a German culture based in a reverence for nature and a sense of a common humanity around the welfare of one's own group. Herder emphasised the social context and the need for Germans to build their own native traditions and feelings into a coherent national culture. He believed that all such cultural groupings could live together. Sadly for Herder's reputation, it is now suggested that his ideas of German-ness can be traced through to Adolf Hitler's disastrous drive to unify all German speakers in one state. Herder introduced competitive nationalism, wanting the Germans to throw off French influences and make national virtues and feelings the core of national belief. But the French Revolution changed the course of nationalism, taking it down a different and more pragmatic path. The American Revolution had already introduced the notion of the rights of the individual and of peoples to determine their own government; the French went on to associate citizens' rights to *liberté, egalité, fraternité* with the duty of allegiance to *La patrie*, the homeland and focus of government. The twin examples of the French and American revolutions have since resonated around the world. As successive groups have found the basis for assertions of their own claims to geographical cohesion, common language, cultural unity, shared traditions, history and so on, nationalistic politics have proved to be a phenomenon for all seasons.

A Taxonomy of Nationalism

Scholars have come up with concepts for the progressive development and evolution of nationalism which help explain its hydra-headed qualities. In the middle years of the nineteenth century, suppressed nationalism was unleashed to unify Germany and Italy, by force. That success triggered suppressed peoples in other parts of Europe – in Ireland, Poland, Hungary – to assert their own claims to independent nationhood. Nationalism then served to disrupt the established states and empires. The hubris of the European powers, bolstered by grandiose notions of superiority and unique national virtues, turned nationalism into a force for aggression. Presumptions of national rights to rule lesser peoples then turned into competitive imperialism and led to the collision of great power nationalisms, producing the disaster of the First World War. The well-meaning attempt set out in the Treaty of Versailles (see chapter eleven) to remake the map of Europe, on the basis of rights to self-determination, only succeeded in making the witch's brew of European nationalism worse. Meanwhile, vehement and bitter ultra-nationalists rose to power in Germany, Japan and Italy to light the fuses for another global war.

After 1945, nationalism began flowing down the different course of anti-colonialism; struggles for independence were fuelled by anger directed against this or that colonial power. At this stage, the driving force was the aspiration to the status of independence, rather than broadly based ideas about common identity. Independence represented recognition by the international community and a seat for the new nation-state in the United Nations. In many cases, the colonial boundaries were so arbitrary that it was difficult to establish a foundation for national belief systems; the establishment of representative political institutions became the touchstone for the newly independent states but, very often, these same institutions were perverted and turned into instruments of oppression against rival ethnic groups and minorities. The nationalism pot was stirred again at other levels. The ideology of the Cold War tended to add another strand to nationalism, but with its ending the nationalism trumpet has sounded another and especially divisive note reminiscent of the calls for self-determination in Europe in the middle years of the nineteenth century. Ethnic identities, long since submerged by the expansion of Russian, then Soviet, power in Eastern Europe, the Balkans, Caucasus and central Asia, have boiled up again as power has receded. The instinct to settle old scores, to redraw the maps and shuffle the deck of history once again, has been cruel.

The American scholar Carlton Hayes has explored the essential duality of nationalism: as a force for good or evil, a blessing or a curse. According to his classifications, as a focus for *libertarian and humanitarian ideals*, enshrining a pure and non-discriminatory patriotism, nationalism can contribute positively to the evolution of human societies. Nationalism as a *belief* is a horse of altogether another colour: riding with this kind of nationalism are intolerance and exclusiveness; a premium is placed on uniformity of thought and conduct; political debate is suppressed; the focus is on war and military glories; jingoism and aggressive policies, expansionism and attendant challenges to the international system are fostered. Hayes also classified the phenomenon in terms of domestic political forces prevailing at certain times in modern European history. The *humanitarian* nationalism of the Enlightenment, espoused by such thinkers as Rousseau and Herder, was founded in tolerance and regard for the rights of other nationalities. By contrast, *Jacobin* nationalism of the French Revolution was intolerant and over-zealous in its dedication to proselytising its ideals. *Traditional* nationalism emerged as a counter-balancing force, based in traditional values and an enlightened conservatism, as epitomised by the eighteenth-century English politician and writer Edmund Burke. Hayes saw *liberal* nationalism as a typically English compromise: an emphasis on individual liberty, while putting a premium on the preservation of order through the sovereign role of the national state and accepting that all nations should enjoy equal opportunities for independent development. In opposition to the liberal nationalism of the nineteenth century, what Hayes called *integral* nationalism emerged out of the age of imperialism. Arrogant, vainglorious, elevating loyalty to the national state above all other considerations and disposed to suppress individual freedoms to advance the interests of the nation and people, this form of nationalism was embraced by most of the monsters of the twentieth century. Finally, Hayes discerned that the development of global trade gave rise to *economic* nationalism: the struggle for markets and sources of raw materials, as well as to achieve national economic self-sufficiency, leading to protectionism and discrimination against the economic interests of others. Although founded in historical analysis, Hayes's classification succeeds in embracing most of the forms of nationalism on display today.

Others have categorised nationalism in terms of the response of groups of peoples to external political pressures: *oppression* and *irredentist* nationalism, reflecting the predicament of people subordinated or marginalised by other groups or within larger nations or empires; *precaution* and *prestige* nationalism emphasise the importance of competition with other nations and the demand for greater respect. The British philosopher Isaiah Berlin has given currency to the idea of a 'national wound' as a mainspring of aggressive nationalism: defeat and humiliation trigger the desire for revenge and nourish notions of injustice. In a vivid phrase, Berlin warns that the 'bent twig' will tend always to spring back. Psychologists have identified *conscious* and *subconscious* nationalism, depending on the degree of explicit assertiveness on display. Sociologists, for their part, stress factors involving group behaviour as in *hegemonic* nationalism: the motivation to augment national power at the expense of others, as in Britain, Germany and Italy in the nineteenth century and, many believe, the United States today; *particularist* nationalism, where the demand for autonomy from groups finding themselves incorporated in larger states is satisfied (for a time) by a special arrangement with the dominant power, as with the Austro-Hungarian, Russian, Soviet and Turkish empires; *marginal* nationalism, identified with the predicament of border peoples, separated by national boundaries and seeking reconciliation with their motherland; and finally (and most powerfully in our times), there is the issue of *minority* nationalism, the demand for recognition and accommodation of the cultural and political interests of minorities within a nation.

Australasian Perspectives

Where do Australia and New Zealand fit in? Both countries were certainly guilty for a time of drinking deep of the imperialism brew – but then so were most others of the western world. Equally, the two engage, along with everyone else, in prestige nationalism. As smaller nations located a long way away from the centres of power and influence in the western world to which they belong, they wish to be noticed and are greatly gratified when they are. There is – especially in remotest New Zealand – a strong impulse to believe that the world needs leadership on many of its most vexing problems and that its people are there to provide it. None of this fits classical euro-centric prescriptions about nationalism. Indeed, there is little in that approach which fits the new and dynamic forces of nationalism apparent from the generally successful nation-building in Asia over the past twenty years. Modern nationalism is not solely to be defined in terms of the experiences of major powers, in their dealings with minorities and with one another. There is a much wider current flowing. It is to do with a demonstrable need on the part of smaller communities and countries to preserve their own identities and interests in the face of the pervasive influence and pressures exerted by larger powers and the globalisation imperative. Modern networks of capital and technological power are believed to be riding roughshod over local interests and concerns. The reaction could become a factor in building nationalism of a new and perhaps radically confrontational kind. Anti-Americanism is a component in the nationalism of more countries than would care to admit. The small do not like being pushed around by the large and are even more resentful of being told that the exigencies of the 'real world' present no alternatives. Isaiah Berlin points out that 'acute nationalism is just a reaction to humiliation, and top nations don't experience that'.[4] Many observers believe that this sense of humiliation and frustration at their own comparative lack of political stability and sustained development is at the root of the anger in the Arab world about the West and the United States in particular. Since September 11 2001 the dangers of this kind of rage have become only too plain.

Of course, the sense of group identity and confrontation can go well beyond the specific framework of the nation-states. The division of the world into east and west, 'aligned' and 'non-aligned', is one example. Current Arab and Islamic anger is another. For its most enthusiastic supporters, the European Union represents an attempt to subsume the separate nationalisms of member countries into a new central authority which will not only treat with the rest of the world but become a replacement focus for loyalty and commitment (see chapter eleven). A more recent manifestation has been the attempt to create an East Asian economic caucus as a bloc, for which the membership qualifications appear to be based on exclusivity of a disturbingly racial, or at least cultural, kind. Exclusivity can plainly take many forms: the 'us' and 'them' syndrome is pervasive and sets the scene for intolerance. Yet it remains true that the more expansive and cloudy the definition of who belongs to what grouping, the less likely it is that people will commit themselves wholly to the cause. Australia and New Zealand sit at, or near, the cusp of many of these influences. By geography, present circumstances and history, they differ from both European and Asian models for the world. Their approach – pragmatic, low-key and lacking hyperbole and pretence – has much more to offer than perhaps they, or others, recognise. Sadly, common sense is not much as a rallying cry.

The Disintegrative Compulsion

At the end of the Second World War in 1945, forty-eight states, including Australia and New Zealand, signed on as foundation members of the United Nations. In the subsequent fifty-plus years, another 145 or so new nations have joined. The proud imperial powers, which signed on behalf of their subject peoples, soon lost control of their empires as scores of former colonies came to claim their separate identities as new nation-states. Since the early 1990s, the disintegration of the Soviet Union and Yugoslavia has unleashed a further, and not very comfortable, round of putting out new flags. The trend continues as rights to self-determination become a dominating feature of the international system. How far will it go? Somebody has calculated that, if every tribal and separate linguistic grouping in Africa were to achieve nationhood, there would be 440 nation-states on the continent.

Separatism is self-sustaining, as was amply demonstrated when Yugoslavia collapsed like a house of cards. Each separation, or proclamation of intent to separate, alters the power balance and the political equation within the original edifice. When one group opts out on racial or religious grounds those that remain will instinctively draw new demarcation lines according to the same criteria. Fear – for the future and for personal and family security – rapidly takes hold. Higher loyalties to a wider community go by the board as the instinct to trust only one's own kind becomes all pervasive. A rapidly spreading sense of alarm that group X will come out on top causes groups Y and Z to spring to arms on their own account. When Slovenia broke away from the Yugoslav Republic in 1991, the equilibrium between the two most powerful members in the federal union – largely Roman Catholic Croatia and mainly Eastern Orthodox Serbia – was compromised. With a bitter history between them, Croatia separated rather than remain within a federation dominated by Serbia. Bosnia then became a microcosm of the key racial and ethnic constituents in the Yugoslav mix: Catholic and Eastern Orthodox elements there had previously balanced out the Bosnian Muslims. The Muslims, fearful for their own security as the political spheres clashed around them, declared an independent Bosnia. But a majority Bosnian Muslim state would be seen as a threat to the Serbian and Croatian communities there; accordingly, Serbia seized the opportunity to encourage the separation of the Bosnian Serbs with an eye to realising a long-held dream of a greater Serbia; for the same reasons, Croatia moved to bring Bosnian Croats under its colours. Political contrivances constructed to surmount such feelings swiftly turn to dust as the different parties reassess their fundamental hopes and fears. Nationalism, which springs from the ideal of giving ultimate loyalty to one's own kind, is hoist on its own petard. One person's nationalistic meat is literally his or her neighbour's poison. Yesterday's break-aways are in their turn threatened as progressively smaller entities break away from them to proclaim their own rights to self-determination. The implications for global stability are unpromising. As the Soviet Union and Yugoslavia crashed and splintered, old, bitter ethnic and religious obsessions, which the rest of the world had long thought buried, were once again cultivated and made the stuff of war and rape and destruction. The nation-state may be the central element in the architecture of the international system. But a central question for the twenty-first century is, how stable are the nation-states in the face of such pressures?

Seventy years of practical effort in the former Yugoslavia could not withstand the siren calls of Slovenian, Croat, Serb, Albanian, Kossovan, Bosnian Muslim, and now Montenegran, nationalism. Because people do not distribute themselves in tidy, ethnically cleansed fashion and stay that way, there is nothing to suggest that the successor entities will hold. The old, shambling Austro-Hungarian Empire did better in holding the Balkans together by setting the 'nationalities question' to one side – until a few bullets fired on behalf of Serbian nationalism on 28 June 1914 brought the whole thing tumbling down. The other side to this coin, Joseph Stalin's savage political repression in the former Soviet Union reinforced by a universalist and dogmatic ideology, proved in the end to have been equally ineffective against the forces of nationalism. Around the world separatism is again in vogue. Czechoslovakia fell apart after seventy-five years as a unified state. Languid, beautiful Sri Lanka is soaked in blood from desperate ethnic and religious confrontation. Ruanda, Burundi and neighbouring states of the Great Lakes region of Central Africa teeter on the brink of further ethnic genocide. Hindu separatism threatens stability in India. Islamic extremism takes violent form in a number of countries. Separation of the predominantly Christian province of East Timor, after a prolonged struggle, suggested to many that the coherence of the sprawling Republic of Indonesia may be at risk, especially following a recurrence of long-running Muslim separatism in Aceh, in the north of Sumatra. Yet 'western' nationalist parallels may not apply to Indonesia, a nation-state founded in intricate and cross-hatched inheritances from the past, which is perhaps *sui generis*.

More moderately and subject to due democratic process, even Britain is setting itself on the course of devolution along national lines. Establishment of separate assemblies for Scotland and Wales may not prove to be the first step towards dissolution of a political union that has lasted since 1707 in the case of Scotland and 1536 for Wales. Indeed, the basic conviction is that fostering the distinctive identities and cultures of the two regions will reinforce rather than fray the bonds of commitment to a unified kingdom – although there are many nationalists in both places who see independence as both logical and necessary. The fateful relationship between England and Ireland was no doubt doomed from the start by intractable differences, especially to do with religion. But the precedent is not encouraging. Is it possible to realise deeply felt, but often confused and insubstantial, notions of difference without political disruption? In New Zealand, there are concerns that demands for Maori autonomy will scupper a carefully constructed social and political edifice designed to accommodate two communities within one nation. In Fiji, a balanced constitutional arrangement designed to protect the interests of both main races has been repudiated by a minority Fijian government. How is it possible to ensure that moderation and balance prevail on a topic that gives so much scope for the opposite?

The subsoil of nationalism is made up of yearnings for personal security in beliefs about 'being special'. These are feelings that can be accommodated in most liberal and tolerant societies. They can positively influence national political processes by prompting the need to cultivate balance and tolerance. Hopefully, in modern liberal democracies, calculations about the fundamental importance of maintaining steadiness and a sense of perspective will serve to offset undue atavism. The fluidity made possible by the global triumphs of the market economy and the progressive rise of the new individualism – whatever disadvantages may flow from these things – unquestionably also dampen the forces of 'us' and 'them'. But passionate opposition to the new globalism risks stirring up the same grievances which are at the heart of disruptive nationalism.

Even in the cause of administrative convenience or political or economic efficiency, it is not easy to make concessions of sovereignty. The idea of compromising national interests out of wider international or global concerns – even to underpin lofty political principles – is even more difficult. 'Trade-offs' are the name of the game: if 'they' give that to 'us', 'we' can give this to 'them'. The supranational idealism of the years immediately following the Second World War ('We the United Nations') has long since given way to a tightly constrained, gradual and very pragmatic extension of international co-operation. The irony is that in the now-incessant mutual interaction between states, nationalism is on the increase, rather than the reverse. There is, it seems, little progression in these matters. The many interactions between modern states do not gradually knit together a sense of a common future, of a need to merge, the better to face the challenges of the modern world. Certainly, agreements are made and new arrangements are being entered into all the time with the aim of facilitating and balancing out the exchanges between states. But sadly, the evidence seems to be that the more complex the mesh of shared interests and concerns, the greater the likelihood that one or more domestic lobby group will be affronted by developments designed in good faith to promote interactions and level out the playing field. The embassies that represent the interests of the closest friends and neighbours of the host country will often be the most embattled.[5] The advocates of 'national' interests will naturally have the ear of governments and be able to agitate against 'making concessions to foreigners'. Nationalism is a much easier cause to serve than supranationalism.

chapter eleven

Does Globalism Trump Nationalism?

For I dipped into the future, far as human eye could see,
Saw the vision of the world, and all the wonder that would be;

Saw the heavens fill with commerce, argosies of magic sails,
Pilots of the purple twilight, dropping down with costly bales;

Heard the heavens fill with shouting, and there rained a ghastly dew
From the nations' airy navies grappling in the central blue;

Far along the world-wide whisper of the south-wind rushing warm
With the standards of the peoples plunging through the thunder-storm;

Til' the war-drum throbbed no longer, and the battle-flags were furled
In the Parliament of man, the Federation of the World.
– *Alfred Tennyson,* Locksley Hall *(1842)*

The transport revolution, e-commerce, satellite communications, fibre-optic cables and the internet have mostly eliminated distance and isolation as impediments to interaction between Australia and New Zealand. Both countries, the original victims of the so-called 'tyranny of distance', have become linked into the world and 'wired-in' to one another, as never before, by the technological sea changes of recent years. Respective convictions about separate identities and differentiated national interests have not been diluted in any way. If anything, ideas about distinctive virtues and unique qualities are strengthened by familiarity. The more contact the two have with one another – in sport, the arts, business or politics – the more it becomes necessary to rehearse differences. Moreover, if distance is, in certain respects, eliminated by modern technologies then, by definition, all places everywhere are on the same footing. The new globalism in itself is no more likely to promote reconciliation and eventual merger between New Zealand and Australia than between Quebec and the rest of Canada, Canada and the United States, Singapore and Malaysia, and so on. Notions that globalisation will cause borders to disappear and the nation-state to wither away are, to say the least, unsubstantiated. Equally, fears about impersonal forces, loss of identity and control, the 'coca-colonisation' of the world, need to be re-examined in the light of the real powers still retained in the nation-states. Tennyson's vision is as delusive as ever.

The Interactive World

As we have seen, business was first transformed in Australia and New Zealand when the two countries were branched into the global cable network nearly 150 years ago. What is happening now is not new but rather a further step in the speeding up of things. Online buying and selling of merchandise and the electronic marketing of 'invisible' transactions in banking, brokerage, travel, insurance, legal and other services change the pace but not the nature of business and trade. Antipodeans these days are reported to be very much computer-literate and to make high per capita use of the internet. Being relatively wealthy, they are able to afford the technology. It remains to be seen whether that has provided them with any sort of lead in management of the new inter-connected world, or whether it will promote their mutual interaction. The two countries are already, presumably, drawing some advantage from operating in opposite time zones to major market-places on the other side of the globe. But Japan, China and most of South East Asia also operate in the same five time zones that straddle Australia and New Zealand, so there is little that is unique about the new opportunities.

It was widely thought not many years ago that the ability to work the New York market from New Zealand would be an attraction to global entrepreneurs in search of a bucolic lifestyle. The electronics revolution has undoubtedly promoted some out-migration from crowded parts of the Northern Hemisphere – as witness start-up internet companies operated by Americans from rural places in New Zealand. But, if anything, the accelerating influence, style and dynamism of the great cities and global market-places of the United States or Europe has made them even more of a magnet than before. The talented and ambitious from 'down under' still beat a path to London and New York. With the world opening up, choices about where to live will be taken on other grounds – lifestyle, environmental concerns, schooling, personal security – than the ability to plug into the internet wherever one happens to end up. The new opportunities for Australia and New Zealand lie in innovative responses to the new technologies, profiting from high education levels. Yet, despite it all, both countries are still essentially subsidiary to the focal points of commerce and innovation in the major global economic centres of the north. Devolution of the simpler forms of manufacturing and assemblage of materials, which has helped develop new production centres in low-wage economies in Asia, is not likely to be of much assistance. The global networks of multinational corporations – in the extraction of raw materials, manufacturing as well as marketing – have long since been familiar economic actors in both countries.

In a sense, the new electronic business realm begins to take on the same 'hub and spoke' characteristics as the exploitative European empires of the nineteenth century. The global marketplace is a fact of life and its effects are equally inescapable. Since the flows of information and data that establish prices and quality standards are not only massive and all-encompassing but instantaneous, the transnational corporations try to augment their leverage by increasing market share, through mergers and acquisitions around the world. The increasing power of these global enterprises is at the root of concerns about the ultimate consequences of globalisation. Protest is directed at the prospect of non-representative business enterprises, driven only by the profit motive, blotting out individual choice and undercutting the powers of the state. Massive, if incoherent, demonstrations against the operations of the multinational corporations at the World Trade Organisation summit in Seattle in late 1999, and at subsequent meetings of the World Bank and associated organisations in Washington, and meetings of the leaders of the world's major economies and the World Economic Forum are, if nothing else, indicative of widespread unease. The United States itself is vilified by critics inside and outside that country for inflicting globalisation on the world. Few are prepared to recognise the profound improvements in standards of living around the world achieved through the progressive lowering of trade barriers, nor that it is multilateralism itself – on which the small must rely to secure their interests in a contending world – they are challenging. In the last resort, the alternative to 'all for one, one for all' models is the classical realist creed of 'beggar thy neighbour'. The sting can only be taken out of globalisation, making more satisfactory provision for protection of employment and environmental standards, if the nation-states are not driven back into themselves but encouraged to make the running within multilateral fora such as the World Trade Organisation and World Bank. The multilateral ideal, as enshrined in the United Nations and associated agencies, will not be undermined by the storm of protest against 'globalisation': nationalism has already done that. Nevertheless, there is a danger that present unease with global economic pressures will simply boost unilateralism at the expense of the world's long slow march towards supranational collaboration. The consequence could be to exacerbate divisiveness and conflict, when the aim must surely be the opposite – to promote interaction.

What is going on is better called 'modernisation'. Since the Renaissance, technological change and inventiveness have progressively enlarged human capabilities and brought steady improvement in living standards. Alongside this explosion at the level of what is technically feasible, evolution in what is politically acceptable has been comparatively slow and always bitterly contested. In the twentieth century, huge conflicts were waged between ideologies loosely identified with liberalism and intolerant and aggressive versions of socialism (in the form of communism) and conservatism (fascism). Material progress has been dramatic; by contrast, moves away from the fundamental instinct to think in national as opposed to supranational terms have been hesitant and are still subject to reversal. There is no more reason to suppose that the embedded issue of nationalism in world affairs will be dislodged by globalisation of business in the twenty-first century than there was reason for the kings of Spain and France in the fifteenth century to fear for their thrones because their aspirations were backed by one of the first multinational corporations, the powerful south German bank of the Fugger family. Transnational business is nothing new.

The central authority of the nation-state still resides, as ever, in national capitals. The role of government in responsible and free societies will, as always, be to set the terms under which international transactions take place, not to monitor and control the details. Governments need to direct the process in order to ensure that maximum benefits flow through to their national society. This is very different from attempting to wall off or contain the new technologies and market pressures. Because international commerce is now almost infinitely flexible, barriers to online transactions – whether in the form of inadequate systems, untrained operators, tariffs or disproportionate taxation measures – can be immediately bypassed and the business directed somewhere else. Therefore, governments are obliged to facilitate the new technology in order to take advantage of it. If the country concerned is not to be left behind, openness to the global market place is not an option but a requirement. That consideration alone imposes new responsibilities on governments to provide appropriate legal and regulatory structures and to invest in education in order to ensure a workforce skilled in the new technologies; the provision of communications security, protection of privacy and intellectual property are also the responsibility of governments and must be addressed.

Soft Power

Almost unnoticed in the whirlwind of technological change and the extravagance of the fears engendered by the new commercial imperatives has been a truly epoch-making advance in human society. Barriers to understanding and trust – for centuries entrenched by distance, language, racial and cultural differences – are coming down as international political dialogue and business consultations, let alone ordinary human contacts, are immensely facilitated. Almost unawares, the humble telephone has become an instrument for immediate personal communication with any point on earth and for transmission of vast volumes of information as email or by the internet; imagery despatched in a moment via satellite brings home, to foreign ministries and ordinary people alike, the often painful realities of events around the world; the internet provides immediate access to information. These are among the instruments of what has been called 'soft power'. Others are to do with innovation – a capacity to make use of new technologies; to capitalise on scientific and engineering advances; to 'ride the knowledge wave'. As opposed to traditional realist power – the power of strength – 'soft power' is a leveller, offering new scope for interaction and resolution of problems regardless of the size and strength of those engaged. For Australians and New Zealanders, these new attributes of power offer huge opportunities to offset the penalities of isolation and relative smallness. A similar process transformed both societies earlier in their histories when such nineteenth-century developments as the railway, the steamship and the under-sea cable greatly reduced the effects of distance. But, in response to that stage in the modernisation process, the two countries went in opposite political directions: Australia capitalised on it to federate; New Zealand rejected federation with its neighbour in favour of consolidating its links with the major power on the other side of the world. Clearly, something more than modernisation was at work. Improved interaction is one thing, changes in political mindsets another.

Because the internet has globalised the flow and availability of information, the ability of governments to censor or otherwise control access to material deemed unsuitable or capable of undermining the national interest is weakened. Free use of the internet by Chinese students determined to let the world know what was going on during the Tiananmen Square events of mid-1989 was thought to have ended an era in human history in which governments could use a monopoly on information to hold on to power. Yet it is now evident that governments are not powerless in the face of the internet. Many states – among them Iran, Iraq and Syria as well as China – have devised ways of controlling the flow of e-information. In numerous other countries, security systems are now thought to be an urgent necessity, not only to monitor but to block access to pornography and other undesirable material as well as to safeguard networks against computer viruses. Again, the evidence is that national authorities – for good or ill – are not powerless in the face of the new globalism.

Globalisation is also impinging naturally on – but not transforming – the character of international diplomacy. Shared concerns about an impending environmental crisis make it plain that the interdependence of all peoples is real. At the time of writing, it is still uncertain whether the political responses to environmental challenges, as enshrined, for instance, in the Kyoto Protocol, will be made good anywhere. The Bush administration in the United States has formally stated it will not comply; Australia likewise. New Zealand, however, remains committed to achieving the required reductions in greenhouse gas emissions, despite fears that the key agricultural sector will be compromised. Adoption of the Kyoto standards around the world, if it happens, would signal a new readiness on the part of the nation-states to offer real concessions in terms of specifically 'national' interests in favour of broad 'supranational' concerns.

But have the nation states ever been self-sufficient and self-contained? All of them have long since consciously woven themselves into a mesh of connections with other governments, international organisations and programmes of multinational collaboration. There is no such thing as freedom of action; even for the most powerful, policy options and perceptions cannot be considered solely in national terms. The commercial world may be dominated by multinational corporations and banking institutions operating in the global marketplace; however, the terms of their engagements in the nation-states in which they operate are set by the local governments. On the social side, bands and rock groups have world-wide followings, appealing – often directly across local cultural mores – to a universal youth audience. An apparently growing conformism in dress and cultural standards suggests that a form of world-wide social levelling is also taking place. But nationalist preoccupations are not thereby eliminated. It has been remarked that terrorists plotting against the United States ('the great Satan') in Middle Eastern capitals are as likely as not to be graduates of American universities, wearing their T-shirts, jeans and Boston Red Sox caps, and devouring McDonalds burgers and Coca Cola. Surface conformity should not be mistaken for convergence of ideas and programmes. The new internationalism is more cultural and economic than political. As a phenomenon, it butts against political considerations at every turn, without changing the essentially nationalistic ground rules of international affairs. To maintain that globalisation is relentlessly imposing Western values and a western universality of thought and behaviour is to be blind to everything else that's going on. The unfocused hatred of the role of the United States and of Western influences in general in many parts of the Arab world seemingly looks past the failures and corruption of government and society at home.

Inter-governmental negotiations are shifting rapidly away from classical styles of one-on-one diplomacy. The need to maintain momentum in problem-solving, across the ever-more complicated spectrum of world affairs, coupled with the importance of keeping in step with major partners and countries important to one's own interests, introduces new qualifications on the autonomy of individual nation-states. A dawning awareness of the interdependence of issues as well as of nations makes it increasingly unrealistic and counterproductive to insist – to the point of breakdown of the negotiations – on a unique national point of view. It is still true, as was observed by Dean Rusk, US Secretary of State in the 1960s, that in international affairs 'an appreciation of the complexity of things is the beginning of wisdom'. The speeding up of business, its range and intricacy, and the increasing numbers of nations engaged, undoubtedly impose ever greater constraints on freedom of manoeuvre. Powerful international institutions such as the World Bank and International Monetary Fund are in themselves quasi-autonomous actors on the international stage. The World Trade Organisation, often these days demonised as a secretive and manipulative agency in command of global commerce, is in fact a forum at which the collective interests of member countries can be worked out. The WTO is not a new global power in its own right, so much as a mirror on the world's growing complexity. Its innovative dispute settlement procedures have for the first time set up processes that allow the small as well as the great to have their trade rows settled by international independent arbitration. Within such agencies, each nation-state is no more and no less than an individual member of an organisation, as opposed to being an independent force operating alone. The nation-states are, of course, free to opt out if they wish. But if their national interests are better served by advancing the process, even a little, they will be obliged to accept collective decision-making and multilateral trade-offs. Few – even among the great powers – are likely to get all they might hope for.

While international affairs are growing more complex, new issues are cropping up all the time – for instance, international terrorism or novel and innovative barriers to trade. Some argue that the new globalism has even changed the ground rules of diplomacy. Classical assumptions about international relations are governed by the bleak theory of 'realism', which has it that the nation-states are the only significant actors and that they cannot escape behaving in a competitive way to ensure that their own interests are upheld. Realism presumes that power is the pre-eminent consideration and protection of national security the over-riding objective; there is no supreme set of rules because the international system is not a system at all but operates in a state of anarchy. Realists conclude that, because of a predisposition towards conflict and competition, states will fail to act in a co-operative way, even when they have common interests. Modern ways of doing business within international institutions may mitigate the constraints on co-operation imposed by the essential anarchy of the system, but only in a marginal fashion.

The challenge to such austere and unpromising dogma is led by scholars who define the international realm as a 'society' rather than a 'system'; within an international society, there are groups of states (and perhaps in some areas – the environment, public health, technology transfers – the entire membership) which accept that they are bound by common rules because they share common values and objectives. By working through multilateral institutions, these countries are disposed towards co-operation rather than competition; moreover, such institutions can deliver useful advances to the interests of the nation-states without cutting across their sovereignty. The so-called 'neo-realists' accept that in matters of national security realism theory best explains the ways in which at least the great powers operate. But they would equally stress the significance of multilateral institutions and interactive diplomacy in shaping a new and more co-operative dimension to international relations – in security as in other fields. Proponents of this view note that, apart from the 'high politics' of security and strategic concerns (the domain of the grand panjandrums of foreign policy-making), there is a vast other realm of 'low politics' in which the interests of the nation-states are equally engaged, but where problem-solving between states becomes the responsibility of specialists in the field in dispute rather than the central policy-makers. For most nation-states, power and national security issues have begun to matter less, because war has become an increasingly unattractive and unpopular option. National priorities have shifted towards the attainment of goals such as faster economic growth, full employment and price stability. Within an international 'society', the nation-states thus no longer regard one another as competitors or enemies but as partners needed to secure growth and stability at home. Accordingly, their interactions are less formal and more focused on mutually advantageous goals. Of course, not all countries accept – and to the same degree – these new imperatives of engagement and collaboration to achieve foreign policy aims. There are so-called 'rogue states' and 'hermit states' which seem determined to try to set their own rules and to remain impervious to the changes sweeping the rest of the world.

Neo-Realism Down Under

New Zealand and Australia very definitely belong to the neo-realist school. As smaller actors, the two Antipodeans have, almost throughout their existence, been firmly committed to the collective approach to international affairs. Their motivation might have had more to do with recognition of their relative lack of clout than any high-minded commitment to supranationalism. But no matter. There is a lot to be said for countries which try to light candles rather than curse the darkness. A good deal of genuine international altruism has been on display in the foreign policies of both Australia and New Zealand, particularly in relation to the activities of the United Nations. A consistent record of support, on the part of both countries, for UN peacekeeping operations – in areas peripheral to direct national interests – and strong contributions to international aid and assistance are marks of comparative (qualified) generosity and high-mindedness in international affairs. The 'realist' dimension was not neglected during the years of the Cold War; through ANZUS, the Antipodeans secured an ultimate security guarantee in a region which was, at the time, very unstable. New Zealand's swerve away from this path has been based on a different approach to wider regional questions. Australian and American critics question New Zealand's understanding of the 'realist' concept; many New Zealanders cheerfully repudiate it.

For the most part, however, the two countries, jointly or separately, have keenly pursued projects for regional or other multilateral collaboration as the means to secure their own interests and to introduce a degree of stability into the international system. In recent years, Asia Pacific Economic Cooperation (APEC) has been a special focus for their foreign policy energies. APEC was established in 1989 – largely at Australia's initiative – to promote interdependence among Asian-Pacific economies. Although the gloss came off the so-called Asian 'economic miracle' with the financial crises of 1997, there is no doubting that the sense of belonging to a very productive and dynamic web of trade and exchange in the region has changed the world-view of Australia and New Zealand. A new network of regional interaction and negotiation has been established. Although APEC cannot aspire to the depth and political commitment represented by the European Union, its eighteen member countries comprise half the population of the world, most with huge potential for growth. APEC members have undertaken to achieve full free trade in the region by 2020, and in the process have engaged in intensive dialogue not only to move forward with the liberalisation of trade but to strengthen institutions – across a vast region, hitherto devoid of any structural framework – in order to promote stability and be better placed to respond to future economic challenges. What is involved is not an easy transition to a new globalised realm of open markets and transparent economies, but a steady reconciliation of divergent national interests and suspicious, jealous nationalisms. It has been what the *Far Eastern Economic Review* described after the 1998 meeting of APEC heads of government as a 'long rickety ride'; so far the train has stayed on the tracks.

The Integrative Instinct

APEC, ASEAN and the New Zealand-Australia free trade arrangement (the CER, see chapter nine) are part of a world-wide trend to promote mutual interests among blocs of countries through trade liberalisation and intensive multilateral negotiation. The European Union stands out as an example of what can be achieved. The new Europe, however, is built on the foundations of a common western civilisation. Behind all the strife that has afflicted Europe down the centuries has been the ideal of a unity of Christian society, of the oneness of common humanity in a system built on the supreme worth of each individual. Christianity, like the other great religious streams, is founded in universalist aspirations; for a thousand years and more the Church of Rome, until the revolutionary challenge led by Martin Luther and others, provided a political as well as a spiritual framework for that ideal in Europe and – by way of missionary activity – around the world. The rise of the European state system following the Treaty of Westphalia in 1648 (which formally ended the church's wars against protestantism, through its surrogate the Holy Roman Empire) cracked the universalist mould and laid the foundations for the modern competitive world of nation-states. Now the challenge for Europe is to accommodate to a substantial increase in membership as the countries of the former communist bloc are admitted and as their Union for the first time contemplates the application for membership of a strongly Islamic country (Turkey).

Wendell Wilkie's famous catch-cry of 'one world' was not invented on the spur of a moment in an American presidential campaign (which Wilkie lost). Nor was it ever entirely lost beneath the nationalistic cataclysms of the twentieth century. Since earliest times, philosophising about the nature of the world and of the human dilemma has been built on similar all-embracing conceptions. The challenge for Australia and New Zealand is to operate successfully in a part of the world which is the meeting place of many cultures and political philosophies, and where the European legacy is not necessarily regarded as genial.

Nevertheless, there is in our day a developing sense of a wider collective responsibility which is strongly felt, almost everywhere. The ideal that we are all 'our brother's keeper' not only survives but drives a large part of international effort to do with peacekeeping, aid and development assistance, relief services abroad, volunteerism and the like. In particular, the spectacular growth in the role of the Non-governmental Organisations (NGOs) reflects a widespread wish on the part of ordinary citizens to make a difference by working outside of the frame of the nation-state. Present-day world affairs are clearly not exclusively a matter of formal diplomacy on behalf of the nation-states. From the strength of the NGO communities in both countries, it is evident that in New Zealand and Australia the selfish pursuit of national interests and advantages is not regarded as the be-all-and-end-all of international relations. But it is clear that the world community has a long way to go in such matters. The wealthy nations of the G8 grouping cannot yet find the mechanisms or the political will to forgive the indebtedness of the poorest countries. Within the OECD group of the more industrialised countries, only one or two nations provide foreign economic assistance anywhere near the agreed target of 0.7 per cent of GDP. Sadly, the richest and most powerful country, the United States, gives the worst example: US assistance to less fortunate countries is a lower percentage of GDP than that of Portugal, the poorest country in the OECD. But global collective responsibility extends into other areas, such as peace operations, nation-building and disaster relief, where the United States plays a major part. 'Realism' theory is inadequate as an explanation of the behaviour of nation-states. There is a great deal else at work.

The European Movement

Does the progress of the European movement demonstrate that the dogs of nationalism can be put down by the new globalism? The European Union is unquestionably a major achievement: ancient and formerly lethal rivalries between the European states have been largely superseded by extensive and gradually deepening programmes of transnational collaboration. With acceptance of the pre-eminence of the European Court, which has established that EU laws have precedence over national laws, conceptions of European state sovereignty have been radically changed. The single currency, the euro, which came into being on 1 January 1999, under the direction and control of the European Monetary Union with its own central banking institutions, is a huge step towards full integration. Many, not least in Britain, said it wouldn't work. Now eleven participating countries (excluding Britain) have yielded national authority over this traditional function of the nation-state: the control and management of the national monetary system. The workings of the former European Economic Commission, now subsumed in the EU, have produced far-reaching conformity of policies in the broad economic sector – most notably to do with protection and support for agriculture (which is, along the way, very damaging to the economic interests of outside countries, not least New Zealand and Australia), elimination of internal tariffs, labour laws, and so on.

The EU is a confederal arrangement moving with all deliberate speed in the direction of a so far only very vaguely discerned common European future. Because no ultimate goal has been set, it has been possible to make progress through smaller discrete steps grounded in perceptions of the national interest of individual member states. National parliaments must decide whether or not to adhere to any one step in the process; not all need come on board at the same time. It could be that this game of 'softly, softly catchee the supranational monkey' will eventually yield a federal Europe like the United States. More likely, the end game in Europe is already in view, since the Treaty of Maastricht in 1992: a close association of nations, with a flexible – not all-inclusive – network of collaborative arrangements guided by common institutions, which laboriously thrashes out agreed policies and principles but which is still guided by what is and is not acceptable to national parliaments.

After fifty years of effort, there is now an unquestionable public sense of a European community and of active engagement in the regime that guides it. Politicians and bureaucrats alike are enmeshed in problem-solving within the European context; there is wide agreement that many issues are best addressed by the search for European, as opposed to separate national, solutions. Although there is little to suggest that control over those ultimate expressions of national sovereignty – defence and foreign policies – will be surrendered to central authority, common positions in these areas are continually being formulated. A great deal of bureaucratic effort goes into work – at several levels and in all EU countries – to define common foreign and security policy. Representatives of the European Union, as such, take their place in the international arena. The removal of border controls and dismantling of fortifications are evidence that there is now an internal European security community, in that the member states no longer make preparations for war against one another. This is, of course, a rather different proposition than the creation of a security community capable of generating a unified external defence policy, subsuming the separate defence and security policies of member states. The cautious beginnings of a unified European foreign policy approach to a major external problem during the early stages of the Yugoslav crisis of the 1990s were not encouraging, indeed were widely regarded as a disaster. Yet the effort continues in the monitoring and electoral work in former Yugoslavia of the Organisation for Security Cooperation in Europe. In recognition of the inadequacies of the European military response to the Kosovo crisis in 1999, and thus Europe's continuing dependence on the United States, a start has been made on defining a European security and defence identity (the delicacy of the wording is indicative of the sensitivities involved in creating what could be a large highly mobile European army corps, with Germany as a major party, capable of operating independently of the United States). For all the progress, few can yet see the day when representatives of the separate European nations will withdraw from the international arena, in favour of the representatives of the European Union.

The European movement had its origins in three hugely important strategic concerns: to prevent another war between France and Germany, to unify in the face of a demonstrable threat from the Soviet Union, and to revive a war-shattered continent through the promotion of a convergence of national economies into a single European economy. Now a recurrence of major war in Western Europe is unthinkable; the Cold War is over, and Europe has become an economic powerhouse. The present European Union has evolved over almost fifty years: from a limited, five-member Coal and Steel Community, designed to deny France and Germany exclusive use of the raw materials of war, into an integrated economic and political confederation. The EU is now encapsulated in a directly elected European parliament, a centralised European Commission with executive and limited legislative powers, and a powerful European Council, which is in effect the summit meeting of heads of state with the President of the Commission. The driving force for the whole enterprise was the original European Economic Commission (EEC). The example of the enormous strength of the United States economy, founded in a huge single market with common institutions and few internal impediments to commerce, was out there for the Europeans to emulate.

The founders of the European movement, especially the exceptional Jean Monnet (perhaps one of the most influential men of the twentieth century), believed that the economic imperative – the famous invisible hand of the market – would drive out separatism and even overcome nationalism in the economic sphere. By bringing together in a single market a large and, on the whole, ethnically homogeneous population, capable of high levels of economic performance and having high economic and social expectations, Europe could not only become wealthy again but could progressively surmount many of its inherent divisions. The lure of the expanded market would be powerful enough to overcome intractable special or local economic interests and this would, in turn, contribute to political consolidation. After the Treaty of Rome in 1957, which established the EEC on top of the original Coal and Steel Community, it proved a comparatively easy matter for the six original members (France, Germany, Italy, Belgium, Netherlands, Luxembourg) to agree to a customs union, a common external tariff and the beginnings of a common trade policy. The successes of the European movement have flowed from there. Perhaps the trigger came even earlier, when the now-forgotten Coal and Steel Community presided over a very successful expansion of those industries (production in the member countries rose by 75 per cent between 1952 and 1960). Even more importantly, the Coal and Steel Community demonstrated its flexibility and worth to national governments early on. It provided money for retraining miners (especially in Belgium) thrown out of work when the drive for greater efficiency made it necessary to close unproductive pits. The aim was to get more economical management, as well as to prevent any one country gaining exclusive control over the resources. The financial bonuses provided by the community thus helped carry national governments past the local political objections to pit closures and restructuring. The impetus may have come from fundamental 'supranational' strategic calculations to do with how best to secure peace in a continent hugely troubled by war and the consequences of nationalism. But old-time – and self-centred – 'national' politics ('what's in it for us?') still had to be satisfied before the bandwagon could get rolling.

By a process of intensive consultation and a functional approach to resolving common problems, the European movement has gone far. Against an agreed framework – Agenda 2000 – a carefully designed programme for establishment of common guidelines and procedures, the members of the European Union – fifteen, at the time of writing – have accepted ten new applicants for membership from Eastern and Central Europe, and are committed to further negotiations with Cyprus and Turkey. These countries have historically had only distant relationships with core European concerns; their inclusion will obviously not be driven by the same hard strategic calculations as with the original community. Today, the EU is embedded in elaborately worked structures to provide a level playing field across an increasingly diverse membership. Enlargement will require candidate members to conform to agreed programmes for attainment of standards of democracy, human rights performance, economic openness and structural stability; agricultural programmes and the integrity of institutions will have to conform to established standards. All this will call for a high degree of oversight and control by the organisation as a whole. The new globalism concerned with the reduction of economic barriers and the promotion of interaction drives much of this. Equally, the EU process offers important mechanisms of a broadly political kind: dispute resolution, international aid programmes, mediation, and so on. (Plainly Greece and Turkey will have to resolve their intractable dispute over Turkish occupation of Cyprus before Turkey and Cyprus can become members, for the simple reason that membership requires commitment to peaceful resolution of disputes.) The EU is not a magic wand that can wave away the bogey of nationalism. What it does do, however, is facilitate the old requirement to negotiate and find the basis for reconciliation of interests.

By proceeding in a similar step-by-step way, Australia and New Zealand have defined what has been called a 'companionable' process for the eventual creation of a single market in the two countries, which would provide opportunities for addressing other problems in their relationship as they arise.

It is not political union, but neither is the European Union. Nor is it sufficient in itself, since both countries acknowledge that their relationships, economic and otherwise, are far from being the totality of their national concerns. Indeed, the new globalism can never provide a 'one-size-fits-all' solution to international issues. Because Australia and New Zealand are so different in scale, they will, by definition, be of more or less importance, one to another. Each will have distinctive interests of varying weight with other countries. In Europe, by contrast, there is a good deal of congruence in the respective interests and concerns of member countries. Associations of nation-states – whether the CER between Australia and New Zealand, the European Union, APEC or any of the others – are based on calculations of relative advantage, not theories of new waves in international relations. They represent works-in-progress rather than demonstrable proof that nationalism can be put down. Globalisation, whether defined narrowly in terms of electronic innovation and corporate engorgement, or broadly as the entire expanding universe of the modern world, has without question promoted a more 'international' approach to international problems. Barriers have tumbled, inter-connections have multiplied and a gathering sense of economic interdependence has presumably become permanent.

Ironically, far from rendering the old barriers of national interest, identity and control redundant, these processes appear, in many instances, to have strengthened them. Nationalism is far from withering away. It is 'globaloney' of a peculiar kind to look at a world dominated by ethnic conflict and dangerous clashes of culture and conclude that diversity is on the way out, about to be supplanted by some Americanised, Anglophone world order. Indeed many observers believe the evidence is the other way: that it is western culture that is losing ground and that of the Islamic and Sinic worlds is yet to come. This, too, would hardly represent the triumph of globalisation as normally defined.

chapter twelve

A World Going Two Ways At Once

To every action there is always opposed an equal reaction: or, the mutual actions of two bodies upon each other are always equal, and directed to contrary parts.
– *Isaac Newton,* Principia Mathematica *(1687)*

Nationalism and globalisation contend. Both are profoundly changing the nature of the modern world. The one represents divisiveness and the conviction that the wagons must be circled around the community of the like-minded – however defined; the other asserts a prevailing oneness, a breaking down of differences in the face of universal forces and values. There are signs that a balance can be found; for every action there is a reaction. In the Balkans, the excesses of nationalism have led to a compensating 'global' reaction in that the international community has taken it upon itself to stabilise the situation. In reaction to a wave of protest against the unfairnesses imposed by blind forces of globalisation, the international organisations have been reminded of national interests and concerns. Whatever else is happening, however, globalisation is not depriving nationalism of meaning. There have been any number of fractionations, subdivisions and violent crack-ups in bodies politic around the world but very few examples of mergers. The independent nation-states have shown themselves remarkably unwilling to subscribe to globalisation. There is nothing new in the search for compromise and the ironing out of areas of disagreement in order to promote the broader advantage between states. The expanding universe of modern travel and communications and the extraordinary increase in the volume of interactions across the board might suggest that this process is now unstoppable. But the forces of globalisation do not sweep all before them. States can control the processes of interaction as they wish. At one extreme are the 'hermit' states – North Korea and Myanmar – which have attempted to keep the world at bay; at another are such states as Australia and New Zealand, which assume that openness to the world provides the greater advantage.

Torn Different Ways

The opposing forces of globalism and nationalism, interdependence and independence put the modern world at cross-purposes. At the beginning of the twentieth century globalism might have seemed like an impossible dream; at the end of it the very idea seemed, to many, a nightmare. International terrorism has now become a weapon in the hands of embittered opponents of the West and the globalising forces it is thought to represent. After the First World War, nationalism began to seem dangerous; after the end of the Cold War, the final struggle of the century, it was breaking out all over. What some, piously, still call the international system begins to look like topsy-turvy land. Contradictory instincts are at play, not only at the same time around the world, but within each society. The European Union represents the centripetal tendency at work; heel-dragging, on the path to union by Britain, Denmark and Norway, not to speak of sporadic separatist violence in several countries, demonstrates that centrifugal pressures are also a fact of life, even in Europe. Although the World Trade Organisation and associated regional institutions are vehicles for the reduction of barriers between the nation-states in the cause of greater international stability, the whole thrust of such integration is opposed by popular movements concerned to take back sovereign control. Pragmatism, an endless quest for mutual advantage especially in economic affairs, drives the former tendency; deep-seated instincts of self-preservation and concern about the loss of identity and power at local levels push in the opposite direction to discredit the very idea of mutuality of interests and in the end to foster separatism. But in the end, too much of separatism – as in the Serbian drive to 'ethnically cleanse' Kosovo of Albanians, produces a counter-reaction by the international community to restore the untidy balance of things. Equally, the message from the streets in protest against what are believed to be the excesses of globalisation gets through to the national representatives within the international organisations being targeted; national pressures can change the way international systems operate. Terrorism, for example, if nothing else, has obliged western countries to take note of the discontents of the Arab world. Direct military intervention to install more open, democratic regimes may not be the anticipated response, but it is a response just the same.

In an interconnected world, it is entirely possible to pursue separatism and mutuality of interests at once. Separatists in one context will be committed internationalists in another. Ireland has skilfully reinforced its apartness from Britain by unqualified engagement in the European movement. Likewise, the bitterly nationalistic and divisive states of the Balkans seek to play off their antagonisms within the wider internationalist context of Europe and the United Nations. Dedicated nationalists will use the instruments of international co-operation in pursuit of their separatist causes. The Islamic extremist enemies of the United States work within the wider Islamic world to pursue their aims. Advocates of Aboriginal causes in Australia or Maori sovereignty in New Zealand happily develop transnational networks with, say, the North American Indian Nations or within the United Nations systems (the ultimate expression of the globalist tendency) to promote separatist interests. And it is natural that Maori and Aborigine should find common cause across the Tasman in shaping communal development programmes. Modern communications and the new international agencies can serve integrative and disintegrative purposes at one and the same time. The internet, at any one moment, is serving to bring people together and being used by cyber-hackers and hi-tech vandals for anarchic or criminal ends. Equally, governments and international agencies can use the new technology to develop a sense of community; terrorists can exploit it to try to undermine the same institutions or ideas. There is a continuing tension, everywhere and always, between the felt need to assert separatism and difference and the imperative of engagement and co-operation with others, to achieve best advantage.

Balance is all. Nationalism need not be exclusive, impossible to reconcile with the expectations of others. The danger arises from unqualified commitment to one's own. Perverse and divisive loyalties can then form around vaguely defined beliefs about common blood, language, religion and culture, or in response to territorial disputes or historical, economic or political grievances – to name only the most obvious. Membership of the group then comes to transcend other loyalties to wider interests, more inclusive and tolerant ideas about society or even to common humanity. The further along the nationalism curve, and the more deep-seated the intolerance, the more dangerous it all becomes. At the end of the trail lies the totalitarian view of the world: the 'Ein Volk, Ein Reich, Ein Fuhrer' of the Nazis. More of nationalism is decidedly not better.

There is, in fact, nothing primordial about the idea of a nation as coincident with a territory or political context. The word 'nation' is an Old French derivation from the Latin *nationem*, used, not in reference to a national space but to clans and tribes. 'Native' derives from *nasci*, to be born; again, the central idea is to do with race or blood connections rather than any political or territorial context. In earlier times, the tribes may have been racially homogeneous and occupying defined – if shifting – tribal space. The intermingling of the races in the modern age leaves no justification for the identification of a race with a nation and a territory. There is no such thing now as racial 'purity' coincident with a nation-state. In any case, modern genome research demonstrates that genetic differences between races are almost infinitesimal and less than between individuals in any non-racially determined group. Even well-differentiated tribes or groups with a high sense of their own distinctive character have been able to overcome their differences as needs be. Some comparatively recent non-European examples are instructive – the Aztecs and Incas, the Iroquois Confederacy in north-eastern America – were able to surmount the problem of incessant tribal conflict by establishing forms of centralised government; the Iroquois even achieved it in a democratic form. Race was more or less coincident with state. Native American tribes have emerged as nations in the modern era, in the aftermath of a bitter retreat across the prairies in the face of oncoming European settlement, which left them with fixed – and often barren – allocations of territory within which they could establish limited self-government. Neither racial 'purity' nor tribal exclusiveness drove such movements. The collective interest was the determining factor. Tribalism and race are will o'the wisps.

Power – the power to govern – is one of the key characteristics of the modern nation-state, along with sovereignty over territory and international recognition of the authority to make treaties and deal with other states. All this has an only distant relationship with considerations of shared birth or belonging. By one means or another a national authority emerges to direct the affairs of the state. That authority is then recognised – or not – by other nation-states, dependent on a judgement as to whether it is competent to govern and is acknowledged as such within its borders. These notions, which began to gain currency in Europe only after the Treaty of Westphalia of 1648, have become, in essence, the bedrock principles of international governance. They are, to say the least, fragile. They sprang out of thirty years of bitter factional warfare (essentially to do with revolt against the authority of the Holy Roman emperors representing the out-reach of the Roman Catholic Church) which had laid waste to Germany and had pitted the United Provinces of the Netherlands against Spain for eighty years. Although the new protestant faith was at the heart of the ideological differences at stake, Catholic France was also in the vanguard of the struggle against Spain and Austria. Neither religion nor ethnicity was the central issue. The struggles were political – about power. So it has been since.

Wilson's Fourteen Points

No matter what their ideals, the nation-states, and their representatives, are largely confined within a web of nationalism and national interests. The sad fate of President Woodrow Wilson points a moral. A man of high probity and intellect, a political science professor who became president of a university, he had only a short record in state government before being catapulted into the presidency of the United States in 1912 in a divisive election. He tried and failed to bridge the gulf between theory and practice, idealism and realism, nationalism and supranationalism, in human affairs. His famous Fourteen Points, presented to the US Congress in 1918 as the basis for a post-war peace settlement, for the first time formulated broad supranational principles to govern international relations: freedom of the seas, the rights of small countries, the right to neutrality and the end to secret diplomacy. To the public of Europe, worn down by a ghastly war, such ideas had the force of revelation, offering a path out of the deadly maze of national posturing and warped parochialism that had brought only disaster.

Wilson, who also represented the rising great power whose intervention had turned the tide of the war, was hailed as the saviour of the future. His arrival in

France for the peace treaty negotiations was a triumph. But with the war over, practical national politics would again be the order of the day. At the Paris Peace Conference in early 1919, Wilson's naive pretensions to represent broad 'global' interests came up against the dogged nationalism of the war-torn European powers. At home, the central achievement of the Treaty of Versailles, the establishment of the League of Nations, was seen as undermining United States sovereignty; determined not to compromise, Wilson embarked on an arduous national speaking tour to garner support for the treaty. The political strains and fatigue brought on a physical collapse, from which he never recovered. Ratification of the treaty was narrowly defeated in the US Senate, consequently America did not join the League and the first attempt to establish a global forum to confront global problems was compromised from the start.

Ironically, the basic precept of self-determination, formally proclaimed in Wilson's Fourteen Points (and specifically formulated in four of them), was incorporated into the Versailles treaty and would help to set the clock running for the wave of destructive twentieth-century nationalism. Recognising the rights of national and ethnic groupings to run their own affairs had a certain logic. The statesmen at Versailles failed to recognise, however, that self-determination also goes hand-in-hand with divisiveness – and works against the establishment of national and international societies in which differences of race or culture or historical grievances are reconciled in the interests of a wider commonwealth. The eleventh of the Fourteen Points stepped past the fateful politics of the Balkans to proclaim – with stunning optimism (in the light of recent events in the region) – that 'the relations of the several Balkan states to one another [should be] determined by friendly counsel along historically established lines of allegiance and nationality' – and made subject to international guarantee. The Balkans wars of 1912–13 had been a depressing demonstration of the capacity of the contending allegiances and nationalities of the region to fall out: having successfully joined together to evict the Turks in the first phase of that war, less than a year later Serbs, Albanians, and Bulgarians took to fighting one another over their separate aims and ambitions. Serbian nationalism, encouraged – but certainly not satisfied – by the outcome of that fight, then set the fuse for the First World War by fostering a confrontation with the Austro-Hungarian Empire, ally of Germany. The Serbian concept of pan-Slavism was conjured, in December 1918, into the kingdom of the Serbs, Croats and Slovenes: a doomed attempt to overcome separatism among the contending tribes of the Balkan peninsula.

Serbian dominance of this arrangement, however, fed Croatian and Macedonian nationalism, unleashing a wave of political assassinations and a bitter struggle for power during the Second World War when Croats aligned with Nazi Germany, murderously to pursue their vendetta against the Serbs. The ethnic cleansings and hatreds let loose in the most recent phase of the

Balkan wars during the 1990s obviously have long roots. Students of the Balkans agree however that history is not the problem. Politics is the problem. The assertion of political expression in the name of 'felt' qualities of ethnic, racial or religious difference is a first step towards disaster. But how to avoid it, when people are conditioned, from cradle to grave, by the mores of their own particular group. The confining cage of nationalism becomes self-reinforcing when all politics and all thought are subsumed in the 'national' ethic. In the face of the new globalism, self-determination is an imperfect response; once unleashed, it has all the force of an avalanche. The twentieth century was, as a result, notable both for political violence on a vast scale and for the crack-up of states.

The Few That Went the Other Way

John Donne's famously pious proclamation, 'No man is an island, entire of itself: every man is a piece of the continent, a part of the main', is hardly a guide to practical politics. Despite all the evidence of common problems and shared issues in international life, few are inclined to follow this logic. If nationalism has transformed the international system, the reverse process – supranationalism – has not been popular for the very reason that it calls for a renunciation of nationalism, which means that politicians, generals, civil servants, judges and all who wrap themselves in national authority would have to do the almost unheard of thing and offer to give it all away. The few examples where anything remotely comparable has happened, fail to convince.

First is the European model for joining regional countries in a larger political structure. Serious compromise to the national identities and sovereign decision-making powers of member countries does not arise; decision-making is multilateral and by consensus. The national elites still hold sway. Member states may build coalitions within the EU's political institutions to try to swing outcomes their way, or may even opt out of collective decisions without forfeiting membership. Europe is expansive and inclusive, an ongoing political process. It is far from a commitment to a federal union involving renunciation of sovereignty.

Second is the case of Hawaii and Alaska, two small self-governing territories accepting full political merger with a larger and dominating power. For many years the United States had been an irresistible force in both places: Hawaii's sense of a separate Polynesian identity had been squashed beneath a heavy overlay of American commercial and military engagement early in the twentieth century; Alaska, which had attracted Americans for the Klondyke gold rushes and other mining activity at the beginning of the twentieth century, became more heavily enmeshed with the United States during the Second World War, so that there was little traction for joining Canada – the alternative to federation with the United States. Both Hawaii and Alaska signed on to the Constitution of the

United States in 1959. Tanganyika's union with Zanzibar in 1964 (after a leftist coup in Zanzibar) to form Tanzania also perhaps belongs in this category. These are very special cases.

Third is the rare instance of a state broken up by *force majeure* reconstituting itself when strategic circumstances change. In 1990, as the Soviet Union collapsed, East Germany was reintegrated into a Germany from which it had been forcibly separated after occupation by Soviet forces in 1945. Germany as such was a relatively recent creation, having been consolidated by Bismarck, essentially by force of arms, in 1870. (New Zealand is older as a separate political entity.) Germany's many vicissitudes in the twentieth century, not to speak of centuries of earlier separatism, made neither for political stability nor the creation of any enduring – and equally distributed – sense of national commitment. The circumstances of reunification were very unusual, driven by a desperate lunge for the attributes of western life after decades of failing communist austerity. Investment of a great deal of West German money has failed to iron out the differences between the 'two Germanys'. Disaffection is high. The re-unification of Korea would fall into this category, if and when it happens: the two Koreas share a deep-seated culture and a long history of struggle together; what divides them is relatively recent, and ideological, but bitter.

A fourth category of inter-state merger is the contrived creation of federations of smaller territories for reasons of governmental efficiency – or, most usually, to get over awkwardness during the decolonisation processes. The British merged its colonies on the Malay peninsula in the Federation of Malaya in 1948, adding Singapore, Sabah and Sarawak in 1963 to form the Federation of Malaysia; the colonies of Northern and Southern Rhodesia and Nyasaland became the Federation of Rhodesia and Nyasaland in 1953; and ten British West Indian colonies were conjured into the West Indies Federation in 1958. The original concept of Malaysia lasted only two years before the largely Chinese Singaporeans were obliged by the Malay majority to go their own way; the Rhodesian federation cracked up in serious civil war after ten years, and the West Indies took only three years to splinter. The Americans too have tried this approach: the Federated States of Micronesia were formed in 1991 from four Pacific Island trust territories, which had been administered since the end of the Second World War by the United States. Some of these contrived amalgamations do better than others. The United Arab Emirates, consisting of seven emirates lying along the southern shore of the Persian Gulf, apparently floats along well enough – on an ocean of oil. By contrast, the United Arab Republic, between Egypt and Syria, stands out as an example of sublime political optimism under this heading – proclaimed, after referenda in both countries, in 1958 and dissolved in 1961.

Formal inter-state alliances represent a narrow category of co-ordination of interests between sovereign states, and are as old as history. (The first recorded military alliance was concluded between Pharoah Ramses II of Egypt and Hattucillas, the King of the Hittites in 1269 BC.) The principle is familiar: joint action 'to meet the common danger'. The presumption of united action in the face of a shared threat is perhaps the ultimate expression in international relations of the maxim of 'all for one, one for all'. In 1940, as France was about to fall to the invading Germans, Winston Churchill took the precept to the length of proposing a political union between France and Britain, as though 900 years of history could be forgotten *in extremis*. The offer came to nothing and was soon forgotten amid the endless squabbling between the two countries as the war went on. In other words, alliances, in General de Gaulle's notably politically incorrect remark, are 'like young girls and flowers, they last as long as they last'. When there is no longer a shared sense of 'common danger', the states can be expected to want to go their own way.

Alliance – facing the common danger – models are of little relevance to the question of the future relationship between New Zealand and Australia. The two countries have no bilateral formal alliance commitment to one another. In point of fact, the ANZUS treaty still exists between the two countries and would provide the necessary formula if required. But it is not. The ANZACs are bound by something rare and precious – an implicit understanding and acceptance of a mutual commitment. It is no less than the conventional wisdom in New Zealand that if Australia were under threat, New Zealand would offer all the help it could; Australia, while perhaps less forthright on the issue, would no doubt take it as read that there is the same degree of obligation in the other direction. In other words, even the development of a shared threat would be unlikely to change the perceptions of reciprocal obligation between the two countries. Military and strategic differences of approach between the two Tasman countries, however, now raise other questions about the efficacy of the conventional notion that the one will always come to the aid of the other (see chapter sixteen).

The Strange Case of Newfoundland

An impoverished Newfoundland swam against the twentieth-century tide in 1948, swallowing a developed nationalism and sense of identity to enter into a federal union with Canada. There seems to be no other recent example of a self-governing people, with a history of independence, agreeing to give it all away for the greater comfort and security of merger with a larger neighbour. The island of Newfoundland is adjacent to the Canadian mainland and straddles Canada's principal sea-lane, the Gulf of St Lawrence; Labrador, the upstate territory of Newfoundland, is actually a part of the continent. In 1948 there were about 300,000 'Newfies'; there are now about twice as many. For much of the first half of the twentieth century they were, like Australia and New Zealand, a separate self-governing dominion within the British Empire. Now they are a province of the Canadian Confederation.

Newfoundland's modern history began in rivalry between Britain and France for exclusive rights to the rich fisheries of the Grand Banks. Murderous antagonisms divided the fisheries settlements from the sixteenth to the nineteenth centuries. Britain was drawn into assuming authority by the lawlessness of its own fisheries captains, who had taken to administering summary justice to curb their rivals. (The parallel with Britain's reluctant move to establish order in New Zealand in 1840 is eerie.) A resident governor was appointed in 1824 to exercise authority, through a council, over a colony which was opened to settlement; a popularly elected assembly was added in 1832 and full representative government achieved in 1855 (at almost the same time as New Zealand and the Australian colonies). Class and sectarian rivalries persisted between Catholic, especially Irish, immigrants standing for the rights of local fishermen, and a Protestant mercantile class. As with New Zealand in relation to the Australian federal movement, Newfoundland took part in the discussions leading up to the passage of the British North America Act of 1867 and formal establishment of the first Canadian Confederation in 1869. The option of joining was not taken up then and was again spurned in 1895, when negotiations were reopened at the time of incorporation of the prairie provinces into Canada. The direct relationship with London was preferred: Newfoundland as a result could detach itself from the affairs of continental Canada. Polarisation between Catholic and Protestant eased as French Catholic separatism increasingly became focused in Quebec. French-Canadian nationalism and dramatic developments, such as the 1885 rebellion of the métis (mixed blood progeny of European trappers and Plains Indians), would hardly have encouraged Newfoundlanders to join Canada. Instead Newfoundland developed its own brand of radical politics, with sharp social-political rivalry between the People's Party formed in 1907 and the Fishermans' Protective Union established in 1908.

Again, not unlike New Zealand, Newfoundland made a disproportionate contribution to the British Empire's cause in the First World War, suffering dislocating losses at Gallipoli and on the Western Front (where a number of separate memorials commemorate the efforts of the Newfoundland Regiment). Where New Zealand just managed to hold its head above the economic torrent during the great depression after 1929, Newfoundland's economy, overtaxed by the war and massive investment in railways, was completely overwhelmed. The British government assumed responsibility for its debt in 1934; the House of Assembly was suspended and the country was run by a commission appointed and controlled by the authorities in London. National finances were rebuilt while politics was put to one side. By the end of World War II, Newfoundland was satisfactorily back on the right side of the bookkeeping ledger, but politically mute. A national convention appointed in 1946 to consider the political options failed to cohere around any decisive recommendations as to either a return to the previous constitutional structure or continuation of commission government.

During the war, Newfoundland's strategic position was made evident as the United States, as well as Britain and Canada, built airfields and naval bases there to bridge and monitor the North Atlantic gap. This first brush with American power and style suggested to many Newfoundlanders that union with the United States would be advantageous. The option was never formally explored, but is believed to have had an impact on the outcome of the two referenda on the future of Newfoundland organised during 1948.

In the first round, voters were offered three choices: re-establishment of representative national government with the status of an independent British Dominion (equivalent at the time to New Zealand and Australia); confederation with Canada – an option added by London, in that it did not originate from the constitutional convention; return to administration by the commission for five years to give further time for consideration. The outcome on the first round was a victory for Dominion status which received 69,230 votes; joining Canada came next with 63,110; maintaining the commission was supported by only 23,944. For the second ballot on 22 July 1948, the least supported option (continuation of commission government) was eliminated: voters were given a straight choice between Dominion status and Canada. Confederation had it by 78,451 votes to 71,217. A majority of only 8000 votes in a poll of almost 150,000 was disturbing to observers, who believed the issues should have been fully rehearsed in a parliamentary forum before going to such an important vote. The British were accused of rigging the result by dropping the option of a temporary return to commission rule and ignoring the constituency in favour of joining the United States. The British libertarian, A. P. Herbert, was so outraged that he introduced a Newfoundland Liberation Bill into the House of Commons in London before the subsequent British enabling legislation was passed (his was the only vote in favour!).

It was all over. The referendum result was accepted in Newfoundland without recrimination. Canada signalled on 30 July that it was ready to negotiate the terms of union. A Newfoundland delegation met with a cabinet committee in Ottawa in October. Canada was generous: recalcitrant Newfoundlanders suspected that Canada had its eyes on the alluring mineral wealth – much of it discovered only post-war – of their dependency, Labrador. In any event substantial grants were offered, diminishing over twelve years, to bridge the transition to the kind of economy which would make it possible for a provincial government in Newfoundland to support the welfare and other services provided for other Canadians. Taxation structure, public administration and educational systems were to be brought into line under the same regime. Newfoundland legislation would remain in effect until repealed to accommodate Canadian law or modified as necessary. Newfoundland would have six federal senators and seven members in the Canadian House of Commons (out of 104 and 295 respectively). The terms were agreed promptly; the necessary enabling legislation was soon passed in the British and Canadian parliaments (as well as in the separate provincial assemblies) and Newfoundland signed on as a member of the Canadian Confederation on 31 March 1949.

There are some pointers in all this for those in New Zealand who imagine that it would be an easy process to pick up the wording in the Australian Constitution that is generally (if superficially) interpreted as an invitation for New Zealand to join the Commonwealth of Australia (see chapter fourteen). First, the Canadian Union is *confederal*: the states retain sovereignty, especially in revenue matters, except in respect of powers expressly transferred to the central government. In Australia, a *federal* system applies: the central government is sovereign, except for the powers devolved to the states; there would accordingly be little room for special powers to be vested in a new state wishing to accede to the Commonwealth. By contrast, Quebec was able to refuse to ratify the Canada Act of 1982, the latest attempt to upgrade the constitution by incorporating a bill of rights and equal opportunity provisions – an index of the degree of autonomy retained by the provinces within the Canadian constitutional structure. Whereas the Australian Constitution could be written for a homogeneous, essentially 'British' nation, the Canadians had perforce to reflect the regional and cultural diversity of their country. Differences between the Francophone and 'anglo' strains in communities spread across a vast land-mass have obviously been the cause of deep hostility and friction. Nationalism, founded in deeply felt differences derived from ethnic, religious and linguistic sentiment, has bedevilled Canadian national life. The accession of Newfoundland may well have been welcomed in the broader interest of preserving the precarious constitutional balancing act centring on the place of Quebec. In this regard, it is relevant that Newfoundland (and Manitoba) ultimately stymied the attempt to provide special terms for Quebec, launched by Prime Minister Brian Mulroney in 1987, under what became known as the Meech Lake Accords. In other words, Newfoundland – the last to join – has become 'more royalist than the king' in upholding the strict terms of the Canadian Confederation.

Mergers and Acquisitions

Obviously, during the course of the centuries, the factors to do with nationality and nationhood have changed for many peoples. By conquest or by monarchical choice, boundaries have been changed, groups merged with others and societies transmuted into something else. There have been many mergers – and as many fallings-out. Following a long history of interaction alternating with bitter strife – especially on the matter of religion – union between Scotland and England was finally consolidated in 1701; but Scottish nationalism did not go away, for all the deep commitment of the Scots to British Empire causes around the world and the engagement of Scottish politicians in the parliament at Westminster.

Three centuries later Scottish nationalism is, seemingly, once again on the rise and a new Scottish government has been established. Merger of the thirteen British colonies of North America into the United States was achieved on the back of a nationalist reaction to a history of oppressive behaviour on the part of the British authorities in London. A consolidated German empire – exclusive of German-speaking Austria – was brought about in 1871, largely thanks to the distinctly 'realist' brand of diplomacy practised by Bismarck. The mainspring was, however, a long-felt pan-German nationalism, founded in a common language and shared cultural resonances. Defeat by Napoleon at the beginning of the nineteenth century set the stage for a gathering nationalist response transcending the principalities and regional powers of German-speaking central Europe. Italian unification in 1861 was a product of a developing nationalism, long-thwarted by the involvement of foreign powers – Spain, France (especially under Napoleon) and Austria – in peninsula affairs.

The common thread running through these mergers was a distinctive sense of a shared cultural and political identity. Nationalism, in other words, can be a unifying force where a shared culture and common belief-systems have been artificially segmented or held back by outside agencies. Then it is possible to capture the spirit of rebellion. There is nothing like an external enemy for charging up national sentiment.

In the aftermath of the collapse of the Austro-Hungarian empire after the First World War, various combinations of national groups were patched together to make new federated states: the Czech lands (Moravia, Bohemia and Silesia) and Slovakia became Czechoslovakia; the Kingdom of Serbs, Croats and Slovenes emerged out of the contending states of the Balkans, becoming after the Second World War the Federal Republic of Yugoslavia. Czechoslovakia lasted until the dissolution of the next empire – the Soviet, in 1992 – when it split peaceably into two republics while, of course, Yugoslavia fell apart (not peaceably) at more or less the same time. In these cases contrived mergers were attempted, in the belief that national separatism could be overcome. It took time, and a severe change in external circumstances, before the bleak reality was made plain: arranged national marriages do not work.

History is also replete with examples of takeovers by force of arms. Two interesting recent examples are the seizure of the Portuguese enclave of Goa by India in 1961 and the invasion of East Timor, a similar relic of a once-proud Portuguese empire, by the Indonesian Army in 1972. Assimilation was not easy in either place and was strongly repudiated in East Timor during a long-running insurrection against Indonesia, which ended with a vote for separation and independence in 1999. In a tiny and threadbare place, for which the colonial power had done little or nothing, a spirited nationalism was crystallised out of Portuguese inheritances and Christian teachings. East Timorese nationalism is a compound of linguistic and ethnic elements, built into a colonial framework different from the Dutch version inflicted on the rest of the Indonesian archipelago; the clash of civilisations casts its shadow, since Christianity thrived under Portuguese administration, while Islam dominated across the border. It was sufficient to keep a dogged resistance to Indonesian occupation alive for nearly thirty years and East Timor has now emerged after painful struggle as a new sovereign state.

East Timor makes an interesting contrast with Kuwait, a creation of the late British imperial era, designed to provide cover for British exploitation of massive oil deposits. When Iraq invaded Kuwait in 1990, the wealthy governing classes mostly fled. In an autocratic sheikhdom there had been little room for development of an indigenous nationalism, leaving no foundation for a resistance; Iraqi occupation forces quickly stifled such opposition as there was. Kuwait was eventually relieved by an international coalition led by the United States, rather than through the efforts of the Kuwaitis themselves.

Nationalism truly comes in many guises. The Kuwaiti example is a reminder that there are often larger interests at play, which overpower the national concerns of smaller states. Kuwait was liberated from Iraq, less because of outrage at the swallowing up of a little country, than because of wider strategic concerns about the balance of power and access to oil in the Middle East. To that extent the nationalism of a small state is still – as always in the long history of the world – a sometime thing in the face of the basic, and often brutal, calculations of international power. While the 1991 Gulf War, which liberated Kuwait, was conducted by a 'coalition of the willing' (a group of states led by the United States), there was nothing about the conflict to suggest a new onset of supranational conviction within the international system. The coalition was made up of nations which had calculated the respective national advantages or disadvantages in terms of their relationships with the United States and their interests in the Middle East. The first President Bush proclaimed a 'New World Order', based on a supposed new readiness of the nations to rally against breaches of the peace. But nothing had changed. It was soon made plain, when the next humanitarian emergency occurred in Somalia, that national interests prevail over any dreams of a new era of a globalised order.

By the time the second Iraq war was unleashed in 2003, a second President Bush pushed notions of supranationalism even further to one side. When multilateral endorsement of military action failed to materialise at the United Nations, the United States, Britain and Australia pushed ahead with what was effectively a 'unilateral' invasion. The global or multi-cultural approach to the issues was in effect tried and found wanting by a super-power strong in the conviction as to where its own 'national' interests lay.

ANZAC: 1915–1985

Australians find it hard to give due place to New Zealand in the ANZAC story. On the wider stage, would Australia ever be able to accommodate New Zealand in their world-view?

'ANZAC', 1915–1985, Bill Mitchell, *The Australian*, 1985.

Part III

AUSTRALIAN AND
NEW ZEALAND NATIONALISM

Sport is a potent element in nationalism. A New Zealand cartoonist (believed to
have been the first to use the kiwi as a national symbol) laments a loss in which an
All Black team failed to score a point against New South Wales. Kangaroos and
Kookaburras rejoice.

'Nil (desperandum)' Trevor Lloyd, 1921. Source *The Other Side Of The Ditch*,
Ian F. Grant, New Zealand Cartoon Archive Collection, Alexander Turnbull Library,
Wellington.

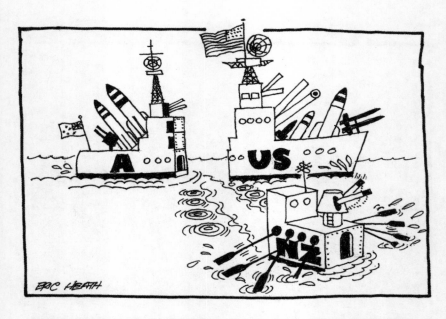

New Zealand's anti-nuclear stance causes the break-up of the ANZUS security alliance and establishes a novel notion of national independence.

'A..US', Eric Heath, *The Dominion*, 1985. Source *The Other Side Of The Ditch*, Ian F. Grant, New Zealand Cartoon Archive Collection, Alexander Turnbull Library, Wellington.

chapter thirteen

Who and Why and Which
and What Are They?

> We shall not cease from exploration
> And the end of all our exploring
> Will be to arrive where we started
> And know the place for the first time.
> *– T.S. Eliot*, Little Gidding *(1942) pt. 5*

The business of creating an identity begins at the beginning. In Australia and New Zealand, the European incomers overlooked that they were also the heirs to older native traditions; others had been there before them. The mythology of newness has been going on now for well over two centuries. Pragmatism has prevailed, and with it a kind of rough honesty and a respect for the aristocracy of hard labour. The parallel is not with British experience, but with the American frontier. As the poets explore their new circumstances, more complex notions of identity and place emerge. The land, the solitude and the sadness of the emigrant displaced from all that had gone before, the rawness of new societies, become part of the search for meaning. With wider experience and a developing interaction with the world beyond their shores, immigrant communities begin to come to terms with their new countries. That leads on to a more firmly based sense of identity and of feeling for place. Deeper analysis of human circumstances in the new setting then puts the new societies into the wider stream of history. The new communities are not places apart, after all; rather they represent yet further variants on the infinitely complex themes of human development and experience. At the popular level, the politics of identity – as represented by the need to believe in special national characteristics, which is demonstrated, not least, by the importance given to military prowess and sport – then takes over. Differences and rivalries become embedded.

Making an Identity

Maori and Aborigine had made their own art forms, songs and sacred places to establish their own identity and give meaning to the worlds in which they lived, long before the arrival of the confident newcomers from Europe. The New Zealand poet Charles Brasch has made the point:

Not by us was the unrecorded stillness
Broken, and in their monumental dawn
The rocks, the leaves unveiled;
Those who were before us trod first the soil
And named bays and mountains; while round them spread
The indefinable currents of the human,
That still about their chosen places
Trouble the poignant air.[1]

All societies, but especially New World societies, need to forge their own ideas about themselves. Identity is invented. It is a necessary invention. Since the homeland of the majority of early settlers in the Australasian colonies was Britain and all associations went back to there, a British image was naturally appropriated. It is self-evident that both countries were for an unusual length of time enthusiastic empire loyalists. From the beginning of settlement it must have been equally obvious that something different would emerge; the echoes from the aboriginal past would never be able to be suppressed and the echoes from the homelands would become increasingly faint. Immigrants have no escape from the need to shape their lives in the special – and local – circumstances which confront them from day one.

The need to pin on a national identity is more than a reaction to environment. Orderly administration proceeds from agreed beliefs about the society and shared commitments to it. A generally accepted sense of what the society is and what it stands for then sets the context for interactions with the outside world. The elements in the national-identity mix should be subject to constant re-interpretation and re-evaluation. If fixations about past glories or historic injustices are allowed to gel into something permanent and immutable, xenophobia beckons. In the Australasian colonies, British inheritances were invaluable in defining the rules and establishing the systems for the new societies. But new influences were felt from the outset. These were to do with beliefs in egalitarianism, in building new societies where Jack and Jill would be as good as their masters. Subtle influences from native inheritances took time to be worked in to the new social cloth. The Maori community's place in New Zealand life was, however, secured relatively early on; in Australia, the Aborigine had no such chance. In both countries, in the early years, the excitements of discovery and exploration, the coming to terms with unique landscapes and flora and fauna of new and sometimes weird varieties, all lent colour to the canvas of developing, and separating, Antipodean identities. Bonanzas such as the discovery of gold for a short time opened up vistas of great confidence.

Politics is, however, the key element in the mix. New and confident politicians could start out with a blank legislative page on which to build their versions of new societies. In the event, they proved unwilling – in all seven colonies – to undo comfortable constitutional inheritances from the British past. But republicanism and working-class radicalism were soon significant political strains in Victoria and New South Wales. The separate identities of the six Australian colonies obstructed a developing Australian-ness for a time, although national and continental sentiment essentially burgeoned around them.

In the class-conscious Victorian era, the New Zealanders had ideas about themselves. They imbibed middle-class values, as the British migrants poured into a country unencumbered by the rambunctious social structures on to which the Australians would have to graft their new British order. 'Convictism' was not part of their inheritance. As a result, New Zealanders could preen themselves as a 'cut above' the Australians; many still do. How ironical that the 'convict stain' is nowadays embraced as very much part of the dynamism and diversity of modern Australia. Around the world, 'middle-class values' are derided as symptomatic of dullness and conformism. Distance gave the New Zealanders another catch-cry to reinforce the belief that the country would have a separate destiny from Australia. Yet the nostrum that the 1200 miles between the two countries made 1200 reasons why New Zealand could not be part of Australia was already being undone, as advances in design of ships and marine engines were taking the burden out of distance well before New Zealanders had to decide about membership of the Australian Commonwealth. Even a hundred years earlier, long and arduous journeys were clearly no impediment to commitment to federal union in the United States. If there had been the will to join Australia, distance would have been no impediment. Instead, the ending of the New Zealand Wars and a period of prosperity during the 1890s gave scope for embroidering a native-ist sentiment around Maori lore and natural scenic wonders.

At the proclamation of the Australian Commonwealth in January 1901, an uncritical imperial fealty was reasserted in full ceremonial, to the grave disappointment of the republicans. Yet in both countries national fingerprints were all along forming – in response to the land, social attitudes, historical experience and, above all, as artists and writers began to express their feelings and interpretations of their worlds. National identities do not depend on ringing proclamations of a new order or a new birth of freedom, although these things certainly helped set the national tone in the United States. Maintenance of the British connection provided the broad backdrop to a ferment of domestic change in both countries. The rise of labour and the clamour for workers' rights, the political dynamic provided – especially in Australia – by new wealth from gold and the exuberance of the gold-diggers, then the collapse of high expectations caused by serious economic depressions and labour unrest in the 1880s and 1890s all contributed to the sense that the Australian colonies and New Zealand were striking out in new directions. The influence of reform agitation in England, especially the Chartist movement of the 1830s and 1840s, was naturally felt by the colonies, and not only by the transportation to Australia of some of the movement's ringleaders; free migrants would be, for the most part, predisposed towards breaking with the old social and political order. Working-class radicalism in the industrialising Australian colonies merged naturally with the sagas of the bushrangers and Ned Kelly and the mateship mythology inherited from rural life. With the adoption of modern technology, the rationale for separatism among the Australian colonies was weakened. The federation movement gathered strength as the railway, telegraph, and electric light overcame distance and isolation and softened much of the harshness of back-country existence. By the same means, notions of a shared Australian identity, ideas of a new destiny, were propagated across the wide continent.

Political experimentation in the late nineteenth century – notably in New Zealand in the 1890s – helped confirm beliefs that something new was being born, which in turn gave strength to ideas about vigorous and unique national personalities. Success in international sporting contests then confirmed many in the view that the Antipodeans were even evolving into new and superior physical types. It is necessary only to read correspondence from Australian or New Zealand soldiers of the South African War and First World War to understand that their sense of being different from (and better than) the British – and anybody else around – was overwhelming by that stage. This was more than petty nationalism. At a personal level, such attitudes expressed strong and important commitments to the new societies of the south. While their political masters continued to espouse loyalty to King and Empire, the soldiers in the field were looking for something different. For many, the mystique of Empire disappeared at the Somme. The problem lay in defining what came next.

Identity and Australia

The setting is the strange, harsh character of the 'great brown land' and the singular circumstances of first European settlement. Australian-ness emerges out of a long process of building on to, and adaptation of, the founding experience – as the settlers poured in and uniquely Australian legends were built around bush-ranger and emancipist, squatter and small farmer, larrikinism and mateship, the outback and the splendid cities. More recently, ANZAC, empire, republicanism, white Australia, Aboriginal issues, openness to the modern world versus persistent navel-gazing have all contributed to a feisty mix. The early arrivals were seemingly reluctant even to attempt to come to grips with a country that seemed so alien, malevolent even; they were oddly reluctant to move out beyond the first settlements. As a result, 'Botany Bay' gave Australia its first resonance in the world. Charles Dickens wove Australia, as a place of terrible punishment and of possible redemption, into his writing as early as 1837. Both the *Pickwick Papers* and *Nicholas Nickleby* (1839) have characters transported to Australia; McCawber in *David Copperfield* ends up doing well in Australia; in *Great Expectations*, the fearsome ex-convict Magwitch risks everything to return to Britain to bestow the fortune he made in Australia on Pip, the only human being ever to be kind to him.

In Australia itself the enormity of convictism was confronted most starkly with the publication (in serial form) of the novel, by English migrant Marcus Clarke, of *For the Term of His Natural Life* in 1870 to 1872.

It was already rather dated. Other, more immediate, writings of the period take up the themes of immigration, the bushrangers and the Aborigines. By that stage, great upheavals – the goldrush period, the clashes between diggers and authority, radicals and conservatives, and the social and political stirring consequent on virtually unrestricted immigration – were pushing Australian life in entirely different directions. By bush ballad and song, through affectation of a laconic and often bluntly direct personal style, by projecting a sense of disrespect for conventional values and traditions (while sticking by most of them), Australians were developing another image of themselves. Salty vividness of language was a part of it. The singularly Australian notion of mateship – the passionate innocence of sharing in the vicissitudes of the tough life of the outback – also contributed. To an unusual degree, one man – Henry Lawson – built up and established a national mythology based on the lonely battlers of the bush, toiling at the austere business of making do in harsh and demanding country. Australian nationalism was a badge which was pinned on early. The famous Sydney journal *The Bulletin* fostered it from its foundation in 1880. Radical, nationalist – and racist – *The Bulletin* popularised the work of some outstanding writers: Lawson, A.B. ('Banjo') Paterson and Joseph Furphy.

Lawson was more an itchy-footed 'townie' than a bushman. He found romance in the hardened lives of the toilers of the outback. He travelled widely, including spending some years in New Zealand; in his way he represents the closeness of experience and spirit of the pioneers of both countries in the nineteenth century. But it was Australia Lawson celebrated: the unyielding empty land, the spiritual strangeness of the ghostly gum forest, and the fellowship of ordinary working people. He touched a deep chord to do with the hopeless odds people face in their everyday lives. An early republican and a political radical, Lawson's deceptively artless short stories and poetry had wide appeal at all levels of society. When he died in 1922, after years of sad dependency on alcohol and public charity, 100,000 people turned out in Sydney for the first state funeral ever for an Australian writer. The world he revered, and for which he is revered, is long gone: the man's world of the camaraderie of the pub and the sturdy toilers in the outback, of the footloose and the fancy-free life of droving stock, while the women broke their spirits alone in the basic huts they had to call home. Although today the note is sentimental – even rather embarrassing – Lawson put his finger on the essence of the individual self-respect needed to establish a national identity:

> And though he may be brown or black,
> Or wrong man there or right man,
> The mate that's honest to his mates

They call that man a 'white man'!
The Protestant and the 'Roman' –
They call no biped lord or 'Sir',
And touch their hats to no man![2]

Lawson had also, early on, defined the essential dualism of Australian sentiment about identity. The choice would have to be made, he said, between:

The Old Dead Tree and the Young Tree Green,
The Land that belongs to the Lord and Queen,
And the Land that belongs to you.[3]

Simple romantic ballads such as 'The Man from Snowy River' by 'Banjo' Paterson were an instant success in the 1890s because of public nostalgia for a disappearing pioneering past; Paterson is also credited with composing the quintessential, and quirky, 'Waltzing Matilda'. Ingenuousness could hardly serve for long to define the character of the new country. Australian life was rapidly becoming urbanised. The foundation for a firmer tradition was laid with a handful of novels in the late nineteenth century and early twentieth centuries, examining the special circumstances of urban as well as rural experience in a raw new world. Joseph Furphy's *Such is Life* captured the rigorous regime of Australian sheep station life. Miles Franklin's sympathetic novel *My Brilliant Career* underscores the yen to escape the constraints and depressing ordinariness of life in the outback, by gaining acceptance on the wider stage. Well before federation, Australian sentiment was already strong. The movement towards political consolidation had been preceded by federation of trade unions and the church, and the development of extensive business and banking linkages. The success of sporting heroes, such as the national cricket side which won the first 'Ashes' test match against England in 1882, and the international recognition given to the opera star Nellie Melba, fired up national 'Australian' pride well before the formation of a federal union. Advocacy of the new political entity of Australia, moreover, rested firmly on continuity with the past, strengthening not severing what Sir Henry Parkes, the prophet of federation, called 'the crimson thread of kinship' with Britain and the crown. Federation was also about making more effective arrangements for continental defence, but again within the grand house of Empire. Neither radicalism nor republican ideals was given political leeway. Through Federation, Australia would become more powerful and more respected, but not less British. No violence would be done to cherished beliefs about the supremacy of the British race which, Parkes asserted, 'never had its equal on earth'.

Yet during the same period, Tom Roberts, Frederick McCubbin and Arthur Streeton, artists confident enough to work on the grand scale, were presenting vivid insights into life and character of a very different kind. They transposed the stark beauty of the outback and the hot, crackling character of the austere

Australian bush on to canvases full of light and the drama of a new and tough country. There was a paradox. Australians were at one and the same time clinging to the past and celebrating the new. It was necessary to set Australian life in the wider stream of twentieth-century history, before a strongly felt and distinctive nationalism could emerge. A lot of imperial baggage did not survive the First World War. Passionate – and compassionate – reporting from Gallipoli by the young journalist Keith Murdoch helped shape a strong sense of national pride in the resolute performance of Australian forces. So too did the on-the-spot war history writing of C.E.W. Bean (see chapter five).

But Australian literature was moving away from the celebration of solitary backblocks experience, to develop a wider focus on personal relationships in a New World. Poetry, consciously or not, turned aside from the fierce landscape to chart the even more impenetrable mysteries of the human heart. The poetry of Judith Wright and A.D. Hope and the novels of the Nobel Prize winning novelist Patrick White engage the ordinary experiences of life and love within the setting of Australia – increasingly a sophisticated urban nation. As the enthusiasms of the nineteenth century fell away, the reality of the Australian predicament obtruded, and history, the relations between men and women and the cycle of birth and death became preoccupying. Wright senses the imprint the passing human parade puts on the seemingly empty hills. In 'Bullocky', a solitary wagon-driver, the sort of bush character celebrated by Lawson as quintessential to the Australian experience, is seen simply as the heroic forerunner to the later generations:

Grass is across the waggon-tracks,
and plough strikes bone beneath the grass,
and vineyards cover all the slopes
where the dead teams were used to pass.

Oh vine, grow close upon that bone
and hold it with your rooted hand.
The Prophet Moses feeds the grape,
and fruitful is the Promised Land.[4]

If there is a common theme between Australian and New Zealand writing, it is encapsulated in a preoccupation with the impermanence of things; Wright describes it as, 'I must tread lightly the time-bomb world'.[5] In 'Australia 1970', she anticipates the environmental movement, by celebrating the land not for its mystery and timeless majesty, but for its resilience and capacity to strike back:

I praise the scoring drought, the flying dust,
the drying creek, the furious animal,
that they oppose us still;
that we are ruined by the thing we kill.[6]

In his poem 'Australia', A.D. Hope rails against:
    a vast parasitic robber-state
    Where second-hand Europeans pullulate
    Timidly on the edge of alien shores.

Strong on mythology and a vigorous critic of the second-rate, Hope, like W.B. Yeats in 'The Second Coming', looks to the very harshness and austerity of the Australian deserts for a new birth of spiritual wisdom and insight, superior to the decadence of the Old World:
    Hoping, if still from deserts the prophets come,
    Such savage and scarlet as no green hills dare
    Springs in that waste, some spirit which escapes
    The learned doubt, the chatter of cultured apes
    Which is called civilization over there.[7]

Selective quotations of this kind can present only an image of an emergent national consciousness. The aim is not to analyse the range and scope of Australian – or New Zealand – literature, but to consider some of the ways in which the peoples of these new – but old – southern lands came to terms with their environment and their developing nationhood. Few would claim that the revelation foreshadowed in A.D. Hope's imagery – as to the essence of Australian-ness – is at hand. Australia has, nevertheless, now developed a literature of monumental range and depth. Whether it represents a national identity or not, is irrelevant. The poetic and imaginative novels of Patrick White published between the 1950s and 1970s and, more recently, the sparkling work of Peter Carey and the grand themes taken up by Thomas Keneally have made a global impression. The best of Australian writing now falls well outside any regional or specifically national categories to engage in a speculative and probing way with the wider dilemmas of the human condition. In the field of drama a number of successful plays of the 1950s and 1960s – Ray Lawlor's *Summer of the Seventeenth Doll* and Alan Seymour's *One Day of the Year* – were also interesting as establishing the outlines of 'national fingerprints' over another segment of everyday life. David Williamson is a highly acclaimed contemporary playwright with a wide international reputation for getting below the surface of contemporary society, not only in Australia but more widely around the Western world.

The domestic contradictions and the vexing dilemmas faced by a smallish Western community on the edge of Asia remain. In the latter half of the twentieth century, lingering notions that this was merely a country of 'transplanted Britons' were vigorously repudiated. Robert Menzies, the last Australian prime ninister to affect an unabashed enthusiasm for things British, retired in 1966. But Menzies, as a war-time leader, had long since absorbed the lessons of Australia's uniquely exposed geo-political position. Appearance and myth are not to be confused with reality. Australia has evolved and moved on. In 1999, when

Australians found it impossible to commit themselves to designing a new model republic to replace the Crown as the centrepiece in the constitution, the problem was more to do with finding a satisfactory alternative than with nostalgia for the past. Heavily influenced by internationalism, the inroads of American culture and the interaction with Asia, the echoes from turbulent and cross-grained beginnings have faded in a modern and dynamic industrialised society.

Identity and New Zealand

The physical environment – a powerful landscape and the all-encompassing sea – have from the beginning been a constant presence in New Zealanders' thoughts about themselves. So too has been the Maori presence. Loneliness and isolation stamped itself on the European incomers from the first. Maori legend and song is now firmly established in New Zealand literature – thanks to diligent collection and recording work by a handful of enlightened early European arrivals and some of the first European-educated Maori. For Maori, there were no questions about finding a new place to stand, defining a new identity. For the nineteenth-century settlers by contrast, dependence upon Britain accentuated that difficulty. The constraints of a small society inhibited excess and stridency. There was no New Zealand equivalent to Henry Lawson, or the *Bulletin*, no Billy Hughes, fervent in advocacy of national virtues. Prime ministers of the nineteenth century – particularly Julius Vogel and Richard Seddon – were, however, nothing if not self-confident and bombastic on behalf of New Zealand interests. Their nationalism tended to be a highly coloured contribution to the imperial canvas. New Zealanders revelled in projecting a good image of themselves in London, but had more difficulty coming to terms with who and what they were at home. It was difficult to detect the establishment of a true nativism. A cosmopolitan man, William Pember Reeves, cabinet minister in the reforming Seddon governments, and himself an important political theorist, was a leading exponent of 'Maoriland' themes in his influential writings in prose and verse. There were worthy, if superficial and romantic, attempts to incorporate the heroic Maori, native trees and birds into a sense of national identity. Little of it rang true.

Some early writers, such as Samuel Butler, were simply passing through. Temporarily expatriated from England, they tried to reconstruct its patterns in the remote Antipodes. They were detached, ironical observers; what they saw was most assuredly not like home. The truer experience was that of the 'settler-exile' striving to become established but conscious always of the strangeness of the rough new place and the pull of the ordered homeland. For many of them, New Zealand was a fit place for giving effect to dreams of building a city on the hill. But the rough and raw character of the land quenched optimism. The landscape was brooding, dominant, something to be subdued, or at least put to work. To the settler, romanticising the Maori was perhaps necessary in order to forget that their resistance had to be broken as part of the process of subordinating the country to its new purpose of providing a model homeland for Europeans. Strange fancies were given credence. The Maori themselves became classical figures in a classical landscape. Their legends were assimilated with the tales of ancient Greece and Rome: Hinemoa swimming across Lake Rotorua to her lover in the enemy camp could be compared (the sex roles reversed) with Paris swimming the Hellespont to his Helen.

The deeper issue – and the deeper writing – was to do with coming to terms with the power and strength of the landscape. Even late in the 1920s, the Christchurch poet Ursula Bethell made her hill garden a metaphor of the insecurity of settlers in a new place:

> 'Established' is a good word, much used
> in garden books,
> The plant, when established' ...
>
> Oh, become established quickly, quickly, garden!
> For I am fugitive, I am very fugitive.[8]

Belatedly, there was recognition of what the Maori (and the Aborigine) had known all along – that to be at ease it is necessary to live with the land rather than pit oneself against it. Maori tribal lore and the habit of living long in one place infused every valley and hill with meaning. By the 1930s Europeans were coming to understand that, too. Charles Brasch, who wielded important influence on the development of a national literature, wrote:

> Man must lie with the gaunt hills like a lover,
> Earning their intimacy in the calm sigh
> Of a century of quiet and assiduity ...
>
> So relenting, earth will tame her tamer
> And speak with all her voices tenderly ...[9]

Early New Zealand poetry is strong on the feel of the landscape and the drama of isolation. A dominating theme is provided by the sense of stark reality that comes from living with what the poet Allen Curnow has described as

> ... the voices saying,
> 'Here is the world's end where wonders cease.'[10]

A demonstrative nationalism is rare. New Zealand writers up through the middle of the twentieth century did not celebrate so much as quiz themselves about the essential strangeness of their lonely state. Their mythic figures are loners, solitary figures in a looming landscape, doing battle with the fates. Caution reins in overconfidence. 'High Country Weather', an early poem by the influential James K. Baxter, can stand for this mood:

Alone we are born,
And die alone;
Yet see the red-gold cirrus
Over snow-mountain shine.

Upon the upland road
Ride easy stranger
Surrender to the sky
Your heart of anger.[11]

To Baxter the landscape was frightening, hostile:

In this scarred country, this cold threshold land
The mountains crouch like tigers. By the sea
Folk talk of them hid vaguely out of sight.
But here they stand in massed solidity
To seize upon the day and night horizon.[12]

This is about alienation as much as about the character of the land. Increasingly, in sombre and extraordinarily bald language, Baxter expresses his disaffection. His vision was austere and doom-laden. He found in the raw New Zealand coastline a strange meeting between the forces of nature, the sense of loss and emptiness and the world of the spirits and of legend. About the East Coast of the North Island, he wrote:

One may walk again to the fisherman's rock, hearing
The long waves tumble, from America riding
Where mottled kelpbeds heave to a pale sun
But not again see green Aphrodite
Rise to transfigure the noon. Rather the Sophoclean
Chorus: All shall be taken.[13]

The New Zealand First World War history is drab and almost unreadable in its vacuous military enthusiasm. There was no attempt, comparable to the writings of C.E.W. Bean in the Australian setting, to engage the idealism and national spirit of New Zealanders from the equally staunch contributions of their own men. Shock and the wish to put the whole episode of war out of mind seemed to be the more general New Zealand reaction when it was all over. After the ardent and full-throated enthusiasm with which the country responded to the imperial call, the almost paralysing losses left nothing to celebrate. The theme was picked up in *Soldier*, a notable war novel by a wounded veteran, John A. Lee, later a controversial politician. A female author, Robin Hyde, also turned the grim life of a soldier into a remarkable novel, *Passport to Hell*, which again is not exactly cast in the heroic mode.

A New Zealand identity floated only tentatively to the surface. The 'national fingerprints' were light at these formative stages in the New Zealand story.

Much of the impetus was given during the early twentieth century by the success in England of the expatriate writer Katherine Mansfield, whose short stories evoking her New Zealand childhood became greatly admired. By the late 1930s, however, a literary critic could say no more of Robin Hyde, now regarded as one of New Zealand's more daring and nationally conscious authors of this period, than that she had reached 'a stage of equilibrium between paralyzing subjection to the prestige of England and strident nationalism'.[14]

At about this time, the poet A.R.D. Fairburn was less than convinced about the belief that an assertive New Zealand nationhood was being defined. New Zealanders, he wrote, were

> sprouting like bulbs in the warm darkness, putting out
> white shoots under the wet sack of Empire.[15]

Yet during the 1930s a vigorous school of poets, including Fairburn, and short-story writers emerged to make a strong contribution to articulation of a New Zealand identity. The advent of the first Labour government in 1935 and moves to celebrate the centennial of the Treaty of Waitangi in 1940 gave further momentum to a growing disposition to seek national forms and models: the preoccupation was with New Zealand itself, its own particular character and the special difficulty of making sense of an incomplete society. There was a new and self-conscious search for meaning. But there were not many answers. Allen Curnow expressed it after contemplating the skeleton of the giant moa, held together by iron braces at the Canterbury Museum:

> Not I, some child, born in a marvelous year,
> will learn the trick of standing upright here.[16]

When war came again, the New Zealanders took with them no illusions but a good measure of national self-confidence. John Mulgan, an expatriate, catching up with his countrymen again in 1942, wrote:

> They were mature men, these New Zealanders of the desert, quiet and shrewd and skeptical. They had none of the tired patience of the Englishman, nor that automatic discipline that never questions orders to see if they make sense. Moving in a body, detached from their homeland, they remained quiet and aloof and self-contained. They had confidence in themselves such as New Zealanders rarely have, knowing themselves as good as the best the world could bring against them, like a football team in a more deadly game, coherent, practical, successful.[17]

An early index of a style reflecting this distinctly self-contained but mature New Zealand sense of identity is provided in the laconic celebrations of Denis Glover:

> Sing all things sweet or harsh upon
> These islands in the Pacific sun,
> The mountains whitened endlessly

And the white horses of the winter sea,
Sings Harry.[18]

James K. Baxter went on very confidently to explore essentially New
Zealand themes to do with Maori, the high country of the Southern Alps, the
sea and shore, as well as modern secularism and loss. A number of short-
story writers and novelists – including Janet Frame, Maurice Gee, Maurice
Shadbolt, Sylvia Ashton-Warner and Keri Hulme – have gained international
recognition and established once and for all a tough New Zealand
consciousness, which is generally a far cry from the soft and sentimental image
many outsiders have of the country. Modern Maori writers – Witi Ihimaera,
Patricia Grace and Alan Duff – have greatly extended the range of the Maori
contribution to a national literature, while directly confronting contemporary
social questions; Albert Wendt, a Samoan author, has similarly explored the
Polynesian element in New Zealand life. Maori art and song as well as dancing
and haka performances have developed traditional forms to add new cultural
depth. An increasingly strong – even pugnacious – sense of national difference
and an assertive independence has emerged. Having for so long struggled to
find a voice, it is as though New Zealanders now need to use the megaphone
to proclaim it.

Few Hands Across the Sea

For a time in the late nineteenth century it seemed that a trans-Tasman culture
might emerge. Australian writers were attracted to themes to do with the struggles
of the Maori, and Australian artists, including Tom Roberts, crossed the Tasman
in search of landscape subjects on the grand scale that was on offer in the New
Zealand alps. Henry Lawson, who lived and worked in New Zealand in 1893
and 1897, drew on the shared Australia-New Zealand experience of hard times
and the tough rural existence. But he came to reject what he called 'Toadyland
– New Zealand'. For New Zealand writers, the opportunities to get into print at
home were few. *Zealandia,* the only journal remotely comparable to the *Bulletin*,
lasted for just twelve issues, from July 1889 to June 1890; styling itself 'a
distinctively national literary magazine', it made no more than a start to that
end. When it failed, New Zealand writers increasingly looked across the Tasman
for publication and inspiration. New Zealand's most notable literary light,
Katherine Mansfield, whose parents were both Australian-born, published her
first short stories in Australian periodicals in 1907 to 1909. For over fifty years
New Zealand associations with the *Bulletin* were strong. Expatriated New
Zealand writers, A.H. Adams, David McKee Wright and Douglas Stewart, were
influential editors of the *Bulletin's* famous Red Page and encouraged New
Zealand contributions while doing much to maintain an idea of an Antipodean
community of letters. In the same sense of the out-migration, David Low, one

of the most influential political cartoonists of the twentieth century, graduated from *New Zealand Truth*, by way of the *Bulletin* in Sydney, to London. But the traffic was not all one way. Academics and intellectuals seem to transplant without difficulty from one side of the Tasman to the other. Several New Zealand writers, fetched up in Australia, continued to hark back to reflect on the simpler times of their homeland. Douglas Stewart drew from his New Zealand background in his short stories written in Australia, while monitoring New Zealand writing and fostering the inter-relationship in the pages of the *Bulletin*, through until his retirement in 1971. Ruth Park, born and brought up in rural New Zealand, transferred successfully to Australia and drew from both countries in her writing.

In reality, the First World War changed everything. Europe's life-and-death struggle signalled the end of colonialism and the onset of nationalism. Australia and New Zealand were carried along on the same currents. Fighting within the armies of the British Empire, the two countries developed differentiated notions of ANZAC nationhood. It was not synonymous with independence, but it was a sufficient spur to separate nationhood. National prestige, the importance of showing up well as New Zealanders or Australians, became a dominating consideration. The commanders in the field and the political leaders at home fostered beliefs that the two countries' forces had been asked to do the most difficult things, because they were the best. The troops were friendly with the Americans when they began to arrive on the Western Front, perhaps recognising that they too were representatives of the New World called in to redress the balance of the old. Australians and New Zealanders were highly competitive in inter-Allied sporting contests, carrying off the rowing (Australia) and rugby (New Zealand) trophies, for all their relatively small numbers. Out of shared experiences, each country drew its own conclusions. By the end of the First World War, both countries had an external image of imperial commitment and involvement, while inside there was another entity, growing in sureness of itself and of its own character. Australasia was out. Australia and New Zealand were in.

In the inter-war period, for all their similarities and overlapping historical experience, separateness became entrenched. Certainly, New Zealand was drawn in limited and ill-defined ways into the Australian cultural nexus. Popular magazines had a trans-Tasman appeal: so too did the adventures of certain Australian cartoon characters. (I can remember the mysteriously oblique notices in barber shops in Wellington – 'We communicate with Melbourne weekly' – which signalled that patrons could, no doubt through some shady manipulation of the exchange regulations, have a flutter on the Victorian state lottery.) This sort of ludicrously tentative interaction at the popular level has at the opening of the twenty-first century given way to a large cultural penetration of New Zealand life by Australian media: TV 'sit-coms', Australian journals of every kind and newspapers have a strong hold in the New Zealand market. New Zealanders note, wryly, that there appears to be marked reluctance on the Australian side to reciprocate by purchasing New Zealand television productions for Australian broadcasting. New Zealand had to get a ruling from the High Court of Australia that the prohibitions by Australian programming authorities on the purchase of New Zealand-produced material were contrary to the free trade agreement between the two countries. Even so, several years later, it seems that even New Zealand productions which sell around the world are apparently threatening to the Australian film production industry or likely to undermine Australian 'culture'. Perversely, convictions as to separateness become, if anything, more deeply held the more open the processes of interaction.

A growing Australian sophistication and a realisation that New Zealand may not be what it seems has produced a new skepticism and even derision. Philip Adams, writing in the *Bulletin* of 29 January 1985, had this to say of the New Zealand decision that week not to receive a visit from an American destroyer:

> we should not be surprised at anything New Zealand does. It is, under a thin veneer of respectability, a strange and eccentric country. The landscape may look as domesticated as Devon's but it trembles beneath your feet. Everywhere the suburban niceties – but is that not steam rising round the garden gnomes?

Perhaps the ideals of various founding fathers, with fine notions of new Albions or new Genevas in mind, have flourished for longer in the benign airs of New Zealand. Certainly, idealism has been and is a major influence on public life, especially on foreign policy. Great distance muffles the impact of the hard world beyond. It may well be too that the confining character of mountain ranges and encircling seas helps preserve among New Zealanders a strong sense of their own singularity. From their vantage point of great geographical isolation, New Zealanders can readily come to conceive of their country as a special, perhaps unique, piece of work. The 'God's own country' syndrome is strong – as it is in most other isolated communities. (The riposte, that 'only God knows were to find it', ruefully admitted to by people from Wisconsin and other places off the beaten track in America is, however, rarely heard.) Such conceits promote self-satisfaction and thus have the ironical consequence of restraining the more ardent spirits in pointing the way to change.

Intellectual life on either side of the Tasman has increasingly flowed in unconnected channels. New Zealand writing has its outlets at home; Maori and Pacific perspectives add a layer of cultural depth to New Zealand writing that does not necessarily travel across the Tasman. Equally, Australian cultural life has been hugely diversified and deepened by the contributions of its own immigrant communities – which have not, on the whole, made a mark on the New Zealand side of the Tasman. In the process, fundamental family similarities between Australia and New Zealand – deriving from the British inheritance – are being transformed. It is a truism now that relatively high proportions of both Australians and New Zealanders no longer share traditional cultural assumptions, based on the heritage of empire and the ANZAC tradition.

Yet these narrowly defined differences are slight when compared with the contributions of regional and ethnic writing to the broad corpus of (say) American literature. Seen in this light, there is little to suggest that the two trans-Tasman cultures do not belong in the same stream. Drawing from the same Western traditions and contending with the same circumstances of geographical isolation and sense of personal alienation from their covetous societies, writers on both sides of the Tasman have much in common. In both countries, but especially Australia, a characteristic relaxed stylishness now sets the standard: the arts flourish and a brisk, cultivated lifestyle absolutely belies smug metropolitan condescensions that the two countries are cultural deserts. To many in more fraught and troubled countries, the two Antipodean nations are indeed, both of them, places apart, havens from the frenetic onrush of the twenty-first century. Yet there is no Australasian literature, almost nothing to foster the notion of a trans-Tasman culture, or even any sense of Antipodean togetherness. James K. Baxter incorporated communications with friends in Australia in several of his poems. But the themes are more to do with separation and going different ways than of any shared experience:

> Australia I have found too flat
> And that enormous welcome mat
> Of dried-up scrub surrounding Sydney
> Killed Lawson and might well kill me.
> Thus driven by the butcher's goad,
> I turn and take the other road,
> Not out, but in.[19]

Australia continues to provide a pole of attraction for some New Zealand writers. Most, however, choose to follow Baxter's path – 'not out, but in' – and to take up exclusively New Zealand themes. *The Oxford Companion to New Zealand Literature*, published in 1999, concludes a longish entry on Australia and New Zealand literature with the observation that 'the two countries ... are now in crucial respects at greater cultural distance than at any time since European settlement, to the detriment of both. "The Growing Strangeness", to appropriate the title of one of Douglas Stewart's early poems, is to be lamented.' Perhaps making the same point, *The Oxford Companion to Australian Literature* published in 1991, finds no space at all for a section on the interactions between New Zealand and Australian writing.

Sporting Rivalry

New Zealand and Australia are old comrades-in-arms on the battlefield and ritual enemies on the sporting field. In both countries, sport has played a perhaps disproportionate part in the definition of national sentiment. The two countries were settled at a time which coincided with great English innovation in the development of field games of all kinds. Settlers brought their preferred sports with them or soon adopted the new games as they became established and popular in Britain. It was almost pre-ordained that the transplanted Britons should take to sport with enthusiasm. In small and isolated communities, sport provided community focus and a source of mild rivalry between adjacent settlements. Cricket was played between the colonies of New South Wales and Victoria as early as 1856; in New Zealand in 1864, Samuel Butler, then a high country sheep farmer in Canterbury and later celebrated as the author of *Erewhon* and *The Way of All Flesh*, wrote a commentary on a cricket match between Canterbury and a touring English team in Shakespearean blank verse. As the colonies developed and communications improved, English teams visited and Australian and New Zealand sides sallied forth to do battle with one another or to display their prowess before the inventors of their games in England itself. In due course Australian success at cricket would become legendary. When an Australian team beat England on their own ground in 1882, a traditional rivalry was initiated. The returning heroes were given a state welcome and a milestone was passed in the development of Australian national sentiment. Rugby, introduced into New Zealand in 1870, would soon carry similar national freight. A New Zealand representative rugby side swept almost all before them in a tour of Britain in 1905–6 and generated an upsurge of national pride back home in the process. They too were regarded as upholders of their national flame. It was clearly important to the definition of colonial nationalism to be able to take on, and defeat, the mother country at sport.

A study of New Zealand reporting of cricket matches between Australia and England suggests a strong bias in favour of Australia in the years up to the First World War. A shared identity as 'colonials' still survived. After the war, New Zealanders may have begun to find themselves to be not British, but they had also found they were, more decisively, not Australian. Accordingly, their cricketing sympathies turned towards support for England against Australia. Because cricket 'tests' are played against 'England' only, a less than benign history of English colonial engagement in Australia, for so many years, gave a special edge to Australian competitiveness. New Zealand nationalism, however, was not yet a flower able to bloom unsupported. Sporting rivalries require choice. Hence they would begin to favour England in matches against Australia. Like the 'loyalists' who migrated north to Canada from Massachusetts and other colonies rather than join the American Revolution against the British crown, they found it easier to identify with the old than with the new. The Australians were adjacent, louder, more crass and more numerous; New Zealanders instinctively shrank from all that and have increasingly turned to supporting Australia's sporting opponents.

Sporting success against one another also contributed in important ways to the emerging nationalism of the two young countries. New Zealand takes great delight in winning against Australia. The Australians for their part have learned to respect the dedication of New Zealanders, especially in rugby, and cherish their wins against them in that sport. In cricket, it is the New Zealanders who relish Australian dismay at losing the occasional game to their trans-Tasman rivals. Horse racing soon became a favorite pastime in both countries and New Zealanders have long taken a perverse pleasure in taking the prizes at Australia's premier event, the Melbourne Cup, first run in 1861. Australians likewise seem to New Zealanders to be prone to appropriating New Zealand-bred horses as their own. Australian enthusiasm for sport is such that, like Americans, they have invented a game of their own – Australian rules football, based on an Irish version and adopted by diggers on the Victorian goldfields in the 1850s. Although still largely confined to Victoria – and the one game in which there is no feverish trans-Tasman competition – it is hugely popular and inspires fierce suburban loyalties. There is nothing comparable to this fierce club loyalty in the New Zealand sporting scene. Perhaps it could have been otherwise if Australian rules had flourished in New Zealand. Before World War I there were a hundred clubs; after it the game virtually died out in New Zealand. Yacht racing and water sports of all kinds have long figured prominently in the Antipodean scheme of things, and in 1983 an Australian syndicate became the first to uplift the cherished America's Cup from the New York Yacht Club. An immense surge of national sentiment was unleashed. New Zealand put in its own challenges and won the cup back from the Americans in 1996. Australia then seemed to lose interest, mounting only a lack-lustre challange to New Zealand in 2000 and none at all in 2003. Although New Zealanders and Australians are generally very competitive when playing one another, they seem to prefer the role of giant-killer. New Zealand is plainly not in the 'giant' category for Australians; which may explain Australia's boredom with the America's Cup when it is held by New Zealand.

For New Zealanders, by contrast, winning against the Australians in almost any sport gives the pleasure of the under-dog. With rather less than a fifth of the population of Australia, New Zealand prides itself disproportionately on its successes and uses relativity as an excuse for its failures. The scope for competitive joke-making at the expense of the opposing Antipodean is seemingly boundless. When the Australian challenger in an America's Cup series broke in half and sank, the New Zealanders said that for the next series they would get a glass-bottomed boat – because it was always important to keep the Australians in sight. When New Zealand won twice as many gold medals as the Australians at the Olympic Games in Los Angeles in 1984, the Australians were not fazed. The Kiwis, they noted, won their medals sitting down – in rowing, equestrian sports, canoeing and yachting – whereas theirs had been won in the serious events. In recent years, Australian focus on sport, coupled with the careful nurturing of athletic skills and a strong sense of national confidence, has brought outstanding international success. Few would now doubt the importance of sport as an ingredient in Australian nationalism. The New Zealanders have been able only to admire.

International competition in sport is widely reckoned to be a modern substitute for war, so intense are the feelings of national commitment involved. In this regard, trans-Tasman sporting contests have undoubtedly played their part in enshrining separatism and competition between the two countries. In the last few years, the growth of professionalism has opened up another possibility. In the sport of rugby league, a New Zealand team, the Warriors, has become a participant in the regular national competition played between Australian sides. It might be expected that engagement at the non-international level would permit national rivalries to be set aside. But the reverse has happened. The Warriors, although not a fully representative New Zealand side, are strongly backed by many New Zealanders, who previously had little interest in the game of rugby league, simply because they are playing against Australian teams. In the same way the 'Super 12' – a very high profile rugby competition involving top teams from the two countries plus South Africa – fires up national sentiment even though national teams as such are not involved. Sporting nationalism, like any other form of the virus, will break out at any level and in almost any circumstances.

Earlier in the twentieth century, Australians and New Zealanders were able to join to send teams to the 1908 and 1912 Olympic Games, competing as Australasia. Two world-class tennis players, Norman Brookes of Australia and Anthony Wilding of New Zealand, were the core of a combined team, Australasia, which won the international competition, the Davis Cup from 1907 to 1909, 1911 and in 1914, and again in 1919 (without Wilding, who was killed in the war). Periodically the wistful aspiration surfaces that if the now deep-rooted traditional sporting rivalries between New Zealand and Australia could be set aside and the two competitors could again join forces as Australasia, the combination would again be formidable – in almost any sport. The newspaper *The Australian* had this to say on 18 July 2000:

> The result of the Bledisloe Cup rugby union match between Australia and New Zealand has highlighted a long-standing ambition among Australian sportsmen. It is now clear that even at their best it is a rare thing for the Wallabies to beat the All Blacks, so we can either accept continuing defeat by the men from a country of only 3.5 million people or do what was first proposed more than a century ago: make New Zealand Australia's seventh state. If you can't beat 'em, make 'em join you.

But quite simply, the primitive joys of sporting nationalism are too sweet to allow any such thing.

THE SPIRIT OF ANZAC

Where New Zealand is shaping defence forces focused on United Nations peace operations, Australia takes up arms in the conventional military manner, in alliance with the United States.

'The Spirit of ANZAC', Alan Moir, *Sydney Morning Herald*, 9 May 2001. Source *The Other Side Of The Ditch*, Ian F. Grant, New Zealand Cartoon Archive Collection, Alexander Turnbull Library, Wellington.

chapter fourteen

Differences

I shall be telling this with a sigh
Somewhere ages and ages hence:
Two roads diverged in a wood, and
I took the one less travelled by
And that has made all the difference.
– Robert Frost, *Mountain Interval* (1916), Road Not Taken

Although political attitudes and philosophies on the two sides of the Tasman are closely related and similarly relaxed, the actual political constructs are different. Those New Zealanders possessed of the notion that their country should sign on as a state of the Australian Commonwealth should know that the power of the federal government has been augmented over the past 100 years at the expense of the interests of the separate 'sovereign' states. A New Zealand political society accustomed to independence would find the constraints of the federal constitution seriously inhibiting. Without full recognition that the two countries have a shared destiny and that their interests powerfully converge, there is little point in grappling with the details about how political union might work. New Zealand's insistence on its own strategic stance towards the United States effectively scuppers the idea from the outset. Major commitments of political will and energy, as well as the development of an entirely novel sense of common purpose, would be needed to get the two countries on the same path. Nothing of the kind is visible in either political firmament at present. The divergent roads chosen over a century ago have now taken the two countries some way apart.

Westminster Models

Australia is a federal, New Zealand a unitary, state. Both have held to British constitutional norms by way of the Westminster system of government, with the executive directly responsible to – and deriving its authority from – the parliament. Governments in both countries hold office for only three years before elections must be held. The rule of law is firmly entrenched through legal and judicial systems founded in the common law of England; human rights, race relations and equal opportunities commissions are established elements in governmental systems; ombudsmen, national press councils, and so on help ensure citizens' rights and freedoms. In the conduct of external relations,

Australia and New Zealand have been independent, self-governing states since the early years of the twentieth century. Having signed the Treaty of Versailles in 1919, both were among the forty-eight foundation members of the United Nations when it was formed in 1945 and they were original signatories of the United Nations Declaration on Human Rights in 1948.

British constitutional symbols are perpetuated, in part because an indefinable nostalgia for the British civilisation still lingers, but mainly because, having had no radical cause to make a break with the past, there has been no good reason to repudiate inherited British trappings of government. The Crown remains as the symbol of state; governors-general, acting as the British monarch's local representatives, assume ceremonial roles as heads of state; the prefix 'royal' is incorporated by many institutions; British honours and awards were discarded in Australia in the 1980s and in New Zealand only at the turn of the twenty-first century; the British Union Jack embellishes one quadrant of both national ensigns, while barely distinguishable representations of the Southern Cross adorn the rest. Many, on both sides of the Tasman, would like to see all this swept away. Debate about giving more national purpose not only to the symbols but to the structures of sovereignty is becoming urgent. The sentiment is strongest in Australia, where a constitutional convention led to a referendum in November 1999 on the question of whether to establish a republic. In the proposition put to the voters, the essentially Westminster character of constitutional processes was to be retained: a president would be selected by majority vote of the two houses of parliament, and the prime minister would continue to exert executive power on the basis of authority derived from parliament. The key feature of the American Constitution – separation of the administrative, legislative and judicial powers – was not contemplated. Since the governor-general has for several decades now been an Australian, appointed on the recommendation of the government, with the tacit support of the parliament, there was less in the proposed changes than met the eye. To no great surprise, the voters rejected them.

Some commentators believe that there would have been majority support for a change to a directly elected president, with defined powers independent of the government of the day. To have gone so far would have required a major re-jigging of the constitution. A wide-ranging and open-ended national debate would have been needed, with the outcome by no means clear. Politicians are notoriously reluctant to embark on such unknown waters. The key issue is that a directly elected President would have political authority of his or her own, which would unbalance the mainspring of Westminster-style constitutional arrangements. The Australian electorate seemed to be taken up by the idea that the politicians were simply trying to maintain their control in refusing to contemplate change on this crucial constitutional point. There are ways of finessing the problem: by electing the president through an electoral college, for instance, or confining the choice of candidate to nominees chosen by the parliament. Without the spur of a defining moment in history when it might be possible to capture a national mood, there proved to be no impetus in these directions.

The tetchy quality of such debate as there is about constitutional questions in New Zealand suggests an unwillingness even to consider how to broach such flamboyant issues as the relationship with the crown, or the establishment of a republic. Most accept that the changes have to come, while asking whether such things really matter. Many find New Zealand's low-key and pragmatic constitutional arrangement, a monarchy-at-one-remove, an appropriate reflection of an unassertive, non-vainglorious nationalism. More thoughtful Australian commentators are pointing to a similar vein of practical conservatism, even common sense, in the results of the Australian referendum: 'If it ain't broke, don't fix it.' Both countries are easy-going – and because the fundamentals of democracy are unshakeable, it is hard to work up steam about questions to do with the outward form of things. Deeper down, there are challenging issues – for both countries, but perhaps especially for New Zealand – about how to redefine and give new purpose to their isolated societies in the new global age. Most, it seems, would prefer not to have to plunge into such thickets just yet.

The Australian Constitution

So much for the similarities. What about the differences? The architects of the Australian Commonwealth produced a constitutional horse of both British and American colours, with a nod at Canadian experience. As in the United States, the Australian Constitution vests certain defined powers in the central government, leaving residual powers in the jurisdiction of sovereign states; the Canadian Constitution, by contrast, specifically divides legislative and executive powers as between Canada and the provinces. Although the core Australian institutions derive from the Westminster system, there are constraints on political processes and layering to decision-making that are entirely at odds with the flexibility to which New Zealand is accustomed. The High Court of Australia is charged with interpretation of the constitution; with resolution of disputes about its meaning and about the intent of acts of the federal parliament. The Commonwealth of Australia comprises the federal government in Canberra and the governments of the six states – the former colonies of New South Wales, Queensland, South Australia, Tasmania, Victoria and Western Australia – plus two self-governing territories, Australian Capital Territory (Canberra) and the Northern Territory. As in the United States, each state is equipped with a replica of the federal governmental structure – its own governor and a two-chambered parliament – with the exception of Queensland, which has a unicameral parliament. In the two territories the executive has rather less power than in the states. In theory, all are sovereign and equal; as in the United States, they administer matters of direct concern to the citizen – health, education, welfare, police and justice, local government and transport. Again, as in the United States, an overlay of federal administration in these fields has been imposed as power has shifted ineluctably to the centre. Regardless of size, all states have equal representation in the federal Senate – a provision needed to reassure the smaller states that the new Commonwealth would not be dominated by New South Wales and Victoria; each state presently has twelve senators with two each from the two territories. The number of members each state may send to the federal House of Representatives (which, at present, has 148 members) is determined in proportion to the numbers of their people; the constitution stipulates that the House of Representatives shall, as nearly as practicable, have twice the membership of the Senate and establishes a formula for a quota in order to achieve the right balance.

The politics of the constitution bulk large. Federal-state relations are bedevilled by the complexities arising from the High Court's constitutional rulings down the years. Arrangements for distribution of revenue have been at the heart of efforts to preserve state powers. At federation, it was agreed that the federal government would return to the states three-quarters of all customs revenue (the principal source of funding at the time), in compensation for loss of their own rights to levy customs dues on inter-colonial as well as external commerce. This deal, however, was to apply for ten years only. Since then, progressive loss of control over their revenue income has undermined the autonomous capabilities of the states. In 1942, under cover of the exigencies of war, the federal government took the power to collect all income tax and to redistribute it to the states according to an agreed formula. There have been numerous – unsuccessful – challenges to the 1942 legislation, but central authority in fiscal matters has become permanent. The annual federal-state conferences on budgetary allocations are a powerful political weapon in the hands of the federal government of the day and, without question, reinforce the dominant role of Canberra in the Australian political system.

A quarrelsome separateness among the Australian states has often been noted. In 1901 the federated Commonwealth of Australia inherited a legacy of separatist decision-making, which created problems for the future. Most notoriety has attached to the different gauges of railway track laid in each colony, which impeded the development of a national railway system for the next sixty years. After federation, the states, which owned and operated their own railway systems, were also in a position to suppress or regulate competition from road transport. Various state government practices restricting inter-state road transport were finally declared unconstitutional only in 1954. States maintained their own traffic rules and regulations until 1999, when a national road code was introduced. On the other side of the ledger, the states soon had cause for complaint about the federal government. For the smaller, less developed states at the margins, the federal system was weighted in favour of the urban, industrialising states of Victoria and New South Wales, and commissions were appointed in 1925 and 1928 to investigate the concerns of Western Australia, Tasmania and South Australia. The central issue was the establishment of financial equity. Road and rail construction and other development costs fell more heavily on taxpayers and governments in states of wide geographical extent and smaller population compared with those in the more populous and compact states of the south-east. Tariffs and subsidies, introduced to protect industry in Victoria and New South Wales, were an unfair charge on rural states, largely dependent on agricultural products, which had to be sold at world market prices. Western Australia had been the most reluctant entrant to the Commonwealth and for a long while believed the whole thing counter-productive. 'An economic island separated from sister-States by a sea of solid ground',[1] Western Australia voted to secede and become a separate British dominion in 1933. The state was divided over the interests of the farming and industrial/mining sectors; the latter had strong ties to the industrial east. Unlike their counterparts in Massachusetts 150 years earlier, Western Australia's 'embattled farmers' were not prepared to take up arms for their rights. As in the early years of the United States, it was soon found that the answer to states' complaints about governance in a federal system is to augment federal powers vis-à-vis the states. Commissions were appointed, with powers to administer and reconcile conflicting interests. Application of the emollient of federal money then eased the pain. Before long the stark clash of interest between unificationists and advocates of states' rights would be softened; more subtle variants on the theme of federal-state relations evolved. It did not help Australia in the long run that the solutions were usually to be found by augmenting government intervention and establishing procedures that had little to do with cost efficiency.

Australia has a famously big superstructure of government. What has been called the Australian Settlement[2] – building in basic principles of egalitarianism, state paternalism (a 'fair-go' for all), and imperial benevolence (Empire defence and free trade) – called for extensive bureaucratic controls. The Commonwealth, according to this interpretation, was founded on an implicit national bargain, enshrining a white Australia, protectionism, and arbitration of industrial disputes. Most of all this, of course, went by the board in the 1980s when market reforms were implemented and bureaucratic structures dismantled or reorganised. Analysts and politicians alike, however, still find that the political machinery grinds exceedingly slowly, with much overlap between Canberra and the state capitals and a top-heavy bureaucracy. New Zealand, too, had a long history of state intervention and control. The objectives were much the same – egalitarianism, paternalism and Empire – although there was never any notion of enshrining it all in national dogma. In both countries, state engagement was, for most of the twentieth century, the dominating prescription for all social and political ills. The difference was that these basic subtexts for politics had to be worked out in the very different environments on either side of the Tasman; whereas federalism ensured that Australian politics would be labyrinthine and tough, the simpler political context in New Zealand made for a comparative straightforwardness and ease of manoeuvre.

Australian politics at state level encompass the same basic left-right party political split (Labor Party versus Liberals) and significant coalition partners (the Australian Democrats and the National Party) as in the federal parliament. There has not been a necessary correlation between the parties holding power in Canberra and those in power in the states. Except for a brief – and tempestuous – Labor tenure in the 1970s, a Liberal-Country (now National) coalition held office in Canberra from 1949 to 1983, yet Labor governments were in power in many of the states for much of that time. Again, Labor held power at the federal level for thirteen years, from 1983 to 1996, while several states maintained Liberal or more conservative administrations. Liberal Party political structures for much of this time relied on strong organisations at the state level; by contrast, the Labor Party has for many years built up a national constituency. Occasional exotic blooms in state politics of factional or narrow-focus interest-based parties – such as One Australia, which sprouted in Queensland in 1998 and as suddenly wilted – have not flourished when transferred to the federal level. Similarly, leaders whose political base is concentrated in only one state have difficulty when transferring their ambitions to the federal stage. In other words, federal politics has a life of its own.

Section 92 of the Constitution stipulates that there shall be free commerce between the states. Well and good in today's terms. But that provision, written in the high days of external protectionism and minimal government engagement in the economy, was for years a major obstacle to governments of the left seeking, for example, to nationalise industry or develop government monopolies. In the 1930s, a Labor government held referenda on constitutional amendments to enable it to set up marketing monopolies and a national airline system; both were rejected. When the High Court ruled against attempts to nationalise airline services in 1946, the Labor government had to contrive another airline and a manipulated, tightly regulated airline system to establish the necessary levels of 'free commerce'. When New Zealand governments chose to nationalise they simply did so – and with abandon. In the same way, when New Zealand went in the other direction to dismantle the structures of state enterprise, they could do so without constitutional challenge.

New Zealand: Unitarism Rampant

In New Zealand, no powers are devolved to subordinate assemblies. For over fifty years, New Zealand has had a uni-cameral democracy, the entire national political process taking place within – or around – a single legislature, from which the government of the day derives its authority. There is no written constitution. Constitutional principles are, as in the Westminster system, embodied in common and statutory law and in the practices and traditions of the parliament. There has been no break with the British constitutional past, although of course local norms and practices have established a distinctively New Zealand system of government, unusually centralised, pragmatic and uncomplicated. There is no formal provision for judicial review of acts of parliament – the conventional assumption being that parliament is sovereign and that the role of the judges is to interpret the legislation as they find it. This presumption has been challenged in recent years, especially in regard to issues arising from the Treaty of Waitangi. New Zealand has had no separate or free-standing bill of rights to reflect the basic principles of a social contract between governed and governors. A Bill of Rights Act was, however, passed in 1989 to make formal provision in law for these basic freedoms.

New Zealanders can, with good cause, claim the advantages of flexibility and quickness of adjustment for their system. The absence of a senate to provide a balance of representation and a further check on legislation has nevertheless left the executive holding virtually unbridled power. There have been concerns – unjustified on the New Zealand historical evidence – that without a written constitution, a small democracy is dangerously exposed to would-be tyranny. More tellingly, a decade of sweeping and uncomfortable social and economic reforms, beginning in 1985, driven through with no other consultation with the electorate than the regular general elections, left many lamenting that the New Zealand political system simply did not provide sufficient checks and balances to serve as a counterweight to untrammelled executive power.

In 1994, after two referenda on the matter, the electorate sanctioned the introduction of a proportional representation system which would make it difficult for any government of a single party to gain a decisive majority in the parliament. The expectation was that it would be necessary to build and maintain coalitions of different party and interest groupings to carry on the business of government and that this would put a brake on the power of the executive. The intense politicking, claim-jumping and switches of political loyalties inherent in coalition government have, however, proved to be unpalatable to many New Zealanders. After only one parliament under the new system, there were calls for further changes. A further round of consultations on how best to achieve balance is now contemplated. New Zealand, then, is in constitutional flux. But this is no novelty in a system without the definition provided by a formal written constitution. The contrast with Australia's ponderous system, evidently very difficult to alter, is telling. After a hundred years of federation, the gulfs in political experience are almost as wide as the Tasman Sea.

The Politics of Difference

Dismantling the 'Australian Settlement' and restructuring New Zealand political and economic life began at more or less the same time in the 1980s, in response to the gales of globalisation. Both countries needed extensive changes to create adaptable, modern market economies, but neither wished to do away with the welfare state. New Zealand's Labour government could ram through its reforms. By contrast, in Australia the constitution gets in the way of speedy adjustment. A more complicated political scene, with federal-state calculations to be made at every turn, ensured that the process not only took longer but required more careful adjustment and calibration of the political forces at work. Party political processes and entrenched interests at the state as well as the federal level had to be accommodated. Causes taken up by the federal leadership, such as tariff reform and protection of the environment, ran head on into local concerns. Construction of a controversial dam by the state government in Tasmania was blocked by the federal government in 1985 through the application of the 'external affairs power' in the constitution. The High Court upheld the federal government's stand with a wide interpretation of the parliament's powers under this heading – which stand undefined in the Constitution. Advocates of the separate rights and interests of the states can only have been dismayed. Similar use of federal power made it possible for Canberra to stall a large mining project on land set aside for the Aboriginal people in the Northern Territory. A progressive shift in power away from the states and towards the centre may be inevitable – and is certainly consistent with experience in other federal systems – but as a trend it is hardly an incentive for a sovereign country such as New Zealand to throw in its lot with the Commonwealth of Australia.

The most serious political crisis in Australian politics in recent times – the dismissal of the Labor government of Gough Whitlam by the governor-general in 1975 – also had its roots in dispute about the meaning of the constitution. By way of a literal reading of the Constitution, the governor-general of the day, Sir John Kerr, assumed powers which were widely believed to have been devolved to the elected government. A written constitution, in other words, became the vehicle for displacing an elected government based on a set of presumptions about executive power, long since put to one side in other countries with the Westminster system. The Whitlam-Kerr confrontation exposed a huge gulf between the egalitarian, pragmatic and democratic instincts of ordinary Australians and the arbitrary power derived from a constitution that had not kept up with the times. Because the governor-general derived his authority as a representative of the British crown, the entire constitutional framework was shaken. The New Zealand reaction was to institute a little pragmatic tinkering with the reserve powers of its governor-general in times of political crisis. This has no doubt established a sufficient bulwark against such happenings in the future. But perhaps a showdown, a confrontation of this kind, is necessary to refresh and recharge a system? The cause of republicanism in Australia was boosted by the 1975 crisis and with that came stronger beliefs in the need to build exclusively Australian institutions and a stronger Australian sense of identity. The unflustered New Zealand response to the Kerr-Whitlam crisis may have reflected the low-key national style, but it also did little to focus national feelings and beliefs about constitutional issues.

New Zealand's adoption of a proportional representation parliamentary system, based on two different kinds of member of parliament, may also have set the two countries on different political tacks. New Zealand voters now have two votes – for their constituency representative and for the political party of their choice. Thus the parliament is made up of directly elected representatives and members chosen from lists drawn up prior to the election by the political parties; the better the party does in the election, the more members it will be able to draw from its 'list' . Should New Zealand ever decide to join with Australia, the electoral system would have to be altered again – to meet Australian provisions for election at both state and federal levels, which are based exclusively on single-member constituencies. Australia also has the 'single tranferable vote' electoral system: each voter lists all candidates in priority order; candidates getting 51 per cent or more of the vote are elected; if this does not happen the voters' 'preferences' for the various candidates are counted and distributed until one gains an absolute majority. To complicate matters further, the Australian Senate is elected on a proportional representation basis. Australian procedures seek to avoid constant boundary changes by ensuring maximum stability in the vote for each electorate in the lower house, while offering opportunities for third parties in elections to the Senate. Australia was a pioneer in electoral reforms, introducing the secret (or Australian) ballot, and has made voting in general elections compulsory.

The more each Antipodean country defines its own political system and develops political models reflecting its own political and social environment, the more they become impenetrable and odd, each to each. The two countries have never dealt with one another on the intimate plane of domestic politics. On the other hand, New Zealand now participates in meetings that bring together federal and state authorities to canvass issues arising in particular areas of government authority. This gives New Zealand politicians and officials a greater awareness than ever before of the inwardness of Australian politics. By all accounts, they are well able to play the federal-state game to secure New Zealand policy objectives in the fields under consideration. But these are advisory bodies. The nub of Australian politics is elsewhere, and New Zealand has no place.

New Zealand and the Australian Commonwealth

Article 6 of the Preamble to the Constitution of the Commonwealth of Australia first defines the Commonwealth, then specifies that:

> The 'States' shall mean such of the Colonies of New South Wales, New Zealand, Queensland, Tasmania, Victoria, Western Australia and South Australia, including the northern territory of South Australia, as for the time are parts of the Commonwealth and such Colonies or Territories as may be admitted into or established by the Commonwealth as States, and each of such parts of the Commonwealth shall be called a State.

The door is – to that extent – ajar to New Zealand. Part VI then establishes the procedures; Article 121 specifies 'The Parliament, may admit to the Commonwealth or establish new states, and may upon such admission or establishment make or impose such terms and conditions, including the extent of representation in either House of Parliament, as it thinks fit.' Article 122 authorises the federal parliament to 'make laws for the government of any territory surrendered by any State to the Commonwealth'. Article 123 authorises the federal parliament, 'with the consent of the Parliament of a State and the approval of a majority of electors of the State [to] increase, diminish or otherwise alter the limits of the State'. Part V of the Constitution sets the roles of the states of the Commonwealth and the powers they may or may not have. Most are predictable. There is no room for equivocation about forfeiture of sovereignty: states may not raise or maintain their own naval or military forces, nor may they make their own currency; 'Every law in force in a Colony which has become or becomes a state shall continue in force until provision is made in that behalf by the Parliament of the Commonwealth'. The member states of the Commonwealth are listed in the Constitution itself only in the context of allocation of seats to the first parliament; thus, the addition of New Zealand as a new state or states would in itself seem not to call for formal amendment to the Constitution.

If it all seems stilted and rusty that is because it is. The machinery for accession of a new state has never been tested. Western Australia became an 'original State' only in the nick of time – and is accordingly not listed in the preamble to the Constitution as a 'people' agreeing 'to unite in one indissoluble union'. (The Western Australians had not signed on before the Constitution Bill was enacted by the British parliament in May and July 1900. They did so, however, before the Constitution was proclaimed on 1 January 1901; Western Australian representatives accordingly took their place in the first federal parliament which opened on 9 May 1901.) Most importantly for New Zealand, there is no precedent for the negotiation of special terms. If it were found necessary, for example, to make special provision for the position of Maori in relation to New Zealand constitutional concepts, amendment to the Australian constitution would be required, presumably in terms of part V. The issues would have to be thrashed out first – perhaps within some kind of joint constitutional convention, before submission to the Commonwealth parliament. Article 128 states:

> This Constitution may not be altered, except in the following manner: the proposed law for the alteration thereof must be passed by an absolute majority of each House of the Parliament, and not less than two nor more than six months after its passage … [it] shall be submitted in each State and Territory to the electors qualified to vote for the House of Representatives.

The proposal must be upheld by both a majority of the states (four) and a majority vote in a national referendum before it can be incorporated in the Constitution.

There might be times – of serious external threat to both countries, for example – when Australians would cheerfully go through these hoops. By the same token, a New Zealand application submitted at a time of profound national crisis – or even a collapse of confidence in the New Zealand future – could cause many Australians to wonder whether accession of a broken-backed New Zealand would be in the interest of the Commonwealth. Depending on the matters at issue, New Zealand may have difficulty raising the political clout needed to generate the necessary levels of support. Where would the necessary constituencies be which could give New Zealand the weight to be able to negotiate to advantage on such matters? Could an Australian electorate, long since attuned to regarding New Zealand as beyond the pale, be persuaded to vote seriously on the matter?

Once admitted to the Commonwealth, would New Zealanders be able to swing things their way by operating as a national bloc in a reconstituted federal House of Representatives? If the merger took place now, New Zealand, with a population of 4.0 million, could expect to have about the same proportion of seats as Queensland. New South Wales has fifty seats in the current house, Victoria thirty-seven and Queensland (population 3.4 million in June 1998) twenty-seven – out of a total of 148 seats at present. Queensland is one of the fastest growing states in Australia and is predicted to surpass Victoria as the second most populous state by about 2035. By 2050, when Queensland's population is projected to be about 6 million, New Zealand's seems likely to be no more than 4.7 million. New Zealand would then rank, in terms of numbers in the House of Representatives in Canberra, no more than fourth out of seven states. It has been suggested that New Zealand could increase its political weight in the Australian Commonwealth by applying for membership as two states – North and South Islands. This would give them more clout in the Senate, but not in the House of Representatives, where it counts – because the same numbers of people would be involved.

Federal politics will usually be played along party lines, rather than between regional blocs. Calculating the relative weight New Zealand political parties would add to the mix in Canberra would obviously be uppermost in the minds of party strategists (on both sides of the Tasman) if a merger were ever contemplated. In the same way, party political alignments (not national or regional commitments) would be decisive in getting results in the negotiations. Adjustment would be laborious. Harmonisation of laws and practices – not to speak of attitudes – would take time and effort. The Australian political scene is heavily influenced by strong pressure groups, such as the Australian Council of Trade Unions and the Employers' Federation; New Zealand entities would no doubt wish to amalgamate with their Australian counterparts, but the politics involved, in which New Zealand had neither weight nor experience, could be daunting. The established place in the Australian 'settlement' of the system of industrial arbitration adds another dimension in which New Zealand would be an outsider. Commitment to a federal system, the loss of sovereignty in foreign affairs and defence, the need to concert with the other states against the centre and, with that, the requirement to come to terms with the nitty-gritty of Australian political life would transform New Zealand. This may be no bad thing. If the national autonomy of smaller states is being eroded by the processes of globalisation, why not align with the devil you know?

But what would Australia gain? An augmentation of overall national weight by something of the order of a fifth to a sixth would be no minor consideration. Nor would the broader base and augmented security achieved from consolidation of interests and assets across the board. The immediate hurdles, however, would be political – without consensus in Australia, any New Zealand promptings on the issue of union are beside the point. New Zealand's occasionally flagrant disregard for Australian interests has from time to time caused profound irritation among the Canberra political classes. Equally, it is difficult – short of a disaster – to see where any New Zealand government that wished to push union with Australia would find a sufficient constituency at home. The issues would be highly divisive. As much to do with perception as substance, on both sides of the Tasman they would nevertheless go to the heart of politics; as between long-established societies, they are also of the essence of nationalism – and separatism.

The Treaty of Waitangi

New Zealand's foundation stone, the Treaty of Waitangi, is a deceptively simple compact. It formally recognises the authority of the chiefs (tino rangatiratanga) in respect of lands, homes and taonga, tribal assets or 'treasure'; at the same time, sovereignty (tino kawanatanga) is transferred to the crown. At least that is how the arrangement was interpreted by the crown and – for well over a hundred years – by successor New Zealand governments. Only in recent years has it been recognised that 'sovereignty' is virtually untranslatable into Maori: kawanatanga implies not so much sovereignty as 'governance'. It is now asserted that the chiefs would have assumed that the Governor, with whom they signed the treaty, had undertaken to 'govern' in ways that would uphold Maori rights and property against the European incomers. Certainly, there is little cause to believe that proud chiefs would have willingly signed away their own authority and powers. Moreover, recognition of chiefly authority, implicit in the concept of tino rangatiratanga, carries to Maori the wider meaning of a guarantee of chiefly autonomy and mana, as opposed to the limited interpretion of authority over lands and tribal treasures. (Mana, which has gone into the English language to convey the notion of prestige and power, retains to Maori a sense of the intangible attributes of strength and authority embodied in people, artefacts and places.) The treaty unquestionably glossed over complex issues of the autonomy of the chiefs and traditional Maori assumptions about tribal rights. European presumptions of untrammelled sovereign rights vested in the government of the day were soon at odds with Maori beliefs in the continuing authority of their own institutions. The tragic history of the New Zealand Wars that followed (see chapter three) sprang from just this clash of interest and belief. Governor William Hobson's well-meaning remark at the conclusion of ceremonies at Waitangi, 'He iwi tatou' ('We are one people') has equally bedevilled relationships for its implicit paternalism and assimilationism. Maori have never ceased to assert the separate and special character of their culture and society.

Yet the treaty also established a framework for dealings between two distinctive communities within the one nation and has ensured that Maori issues would remain at the core of New Zealand life. As well as a foundation stone, it has ever since been a touchstone for Maori concerns about their place in a bicultural society, and provides the basis for a continuing process of adjustment and conciliation between the two races. In 1976, the authority to determine its meaning and effect was vested in the Waitangi Tribunal, which also provides a forum for claims by the tribes against the consequences of legislation, policies or practices of the Crown that are inconsistent with the spirit of the Treaty. Accordingly, there is now in place a treaty regime capable of adaptation to meet changing circumstances. The Treaty of Waitangi has become, in other words, a fundamental constitutional instrument, with which much that is positive in New Zealand has been built.

For the same sorts of reasons, the treaty is generally assumed to be a principal obstacle to union with Australia. Not only is there no similar compact in regard to the Aborigine, but there is a question as to why an Australian parliament would wish to import the ethnic, political and constitutional issues with which New Zealand must contend in giving life to the treaty. To many modern Maori, the treaty has become a basis for vehement assertions of Maori nationalism and sovereignty. Boldness, compassion and generosity on the part of the European majority are now being called for to establish a new concept of partnership between the two communities. A political system that has provided for active Maori participation for over 130 years is being reminded that something more is needed than the application of simple parliamentary majorities to settle complex issues of tribal inheritance and custom. To embark on what the Chief Judge of the Waitangi Tribunal has called a 'bi-cultural development in partnership' is calling for a delicate adjustment between traditional concepts of governance in the European sense and notions of Maori authority.

New Zealand has moved in new directions in the definition of its national identity. National life has been diversified and given important depth by being merged with Maori traditions, language and cultural precepts. Maori ceremonial and social norms are incorporated into public occasions. The Maori term Aotearoa – meaning 'the land of the long white cloud' – is now preferred by many as the name of the country. There is a strong sense of association with the Polynesian world of the South Pacific. While most Maori would not regard the process as either adequate or complete, many European New Zealanders may already see it as going too far. Nevertheless, the political commitment is there and there is every reason to expect that it will continue to be honoured. Without reassurance that the Treaty of Waitangi would continue to be at the centre of the accommodation between Maori and Pakeha New Zealanders, there is no way an accommodation could be fashioned between New Zealanders and Australians. Yet there is no inherent reason why this special dimension – in respect of New Zealand as such – should be inimical to a closer relationship with Australia. It would simply be a separate issue, which on the face of it could be resolved by establishment of a special position for the 'state' of New Zealand.

Aboriginal concerns are so far from the mainstream of Australian life that many Australians have been surprised, even offended, by the protest movement that sprang up in the 1970s and 1980s, with the establishment of Aboriginal 'embassies' in Canberra and a series of demonstrations against celebrations of the Australian Bicentennial in 1988. Visions of Australian multiculturalism, with a full part accorded the Aborigine, have tended to be swamped by divisive issues in the national debate to do with Asian immigration and the character of 'Australia'. Despite a powerful combination of mining interests and large landholders that has effectively dampened down any enthusiasms on the part of the politicians about land rights of Aborigine, nasty political problems have continued to surface. An official policy, over some eighty years, of separation of some Aborigine children from their parents in the 'interest' of educating them in the mainstream system, has been labelled cultural 'genocide'. A High Court ruling to the effect that Australia was not *terra nullius* – a land free of prior property rights held by the traditional occupants when the Europeans arrived – has become a political timebomb. Aboriginal claims to sacred places and tracts of central Australia over which they roamed for so many millennia have been revived and become divisive. The federal government is baulking at calls that it must apologise for past injustices done to Aborigine. (Interestingly, in New Zealand, a formal process of apology has been adopted as part of settlements of Maori grievances achieved under the Waitangi Tribunal process.)

The official Australian foundation stone is a federal constitution promulgated over a hundred years after settlement began. For the mass of Australians, as for the British and – except in Maori matters – New Zealanders, civil rights and political freedoms were secured in the corpus of law and judicial interpretation that provides the underpinning of the Westminster system of government. There was no one touchstone, other than the workings of a vigorous democracy. Can that kind of pragmatism be reconciled with the demands for specific solutions and for redress of grievances to the problems that have arisen from the clashes of civilisation on both sides of the Tasman? Could a formula devised to secure an accommodation with Maori, in the special national circumstances of modern New Zealand, be vested separately in a 'state' of New Zealand within an Australian federal Commonwealth? Without understanding on this issue there is no way New Zealand could, or should, pursue a closer political relationship with Australia.

Justice: Separate, Equal and Different!

Law and justice in Australia are essentially in the hands of the separate sovereign states. Police authority also rests with the states. In each state, there are levels of jurisdiction, culminating in a state supreme court. All matters falling within the purview of the states, and most issues ultimately to be determined at federal level, come up through the state judicial system. The High Court of Australia, sitting in Canberra, is the pinnacle of the Australian judicial system and stands, alongside the federal parliament and the executive power, as the third principal component in the Constitution. In addition, there is, a Federal Court of Australia with jurisdiction in matters formerly dealt with by the Australian Industrial Court and the Federal Court of Bankruptcy.

There are few significant procedural differences in police or judicial functions between New Zealand and Australia. The judicial hierarchy in New Zealand, from district courts through to the High Court, would presumably fit readily with the Australian system at the state level. If New Zealand were to become a state or states of Australia, there would appear to be few problems of reconciliation of legal systems because the country would have accepted the provisions of the Constitution, establishing the High Court of Australia as the court of last resort. New Zealand now has its own national Court of Appeal, from which appeal is still allowed – in recognition of the relative smallness of the New Zealand body of law – to the Privy Council sitting in London. This is about to change. Australia abolished appeals to the Privy Council in 1967 – so far as this could be done without infringing constitutional rights – and has now done so without qualification. Legislation was introduced into the New Zealand

Parliament in late 2002 to establish a national Supreme Court and bring to an end appeals to the Privy Council.

The cause of a 'greater Australasia' would be boosted if it were possible to establish an integrated trans-Tasman final appeals process. The High Court of Australia has jurisdiction over all federal courts and in respect of the supreme courts of the states; the federal parliament may also, by law, confer jurisdiction in the Court on matters to do with the Constitution or arising from any law made by parliament. In view of these constitutional functions and the High Court's role in respect of Australian legislation, there is no way the New Zealand Court of Appeal, as at present constituted, could be merged with the High Court of Australia if New Zealand had not first endorsed the Australian Constitution. The European Court of Justice, established as long ago as 1958, does not constitute a precedent. That body has jurisdiction in respect of specifically European, as opposed to national, law; the Court's function is to ensure uniformity of application of the treaty obligations assumed by member countries. In the absence of a mutually acknowledged corpus of transnational law between Australia and New Zealand, it is difficult to find a foothold for New Zealand within the Australian judicial system at present. Over twenty years ago the Federal Court of Australia Act 1976 enabled the Federal Court of Australia to exercise limited jurisdiction to the extent of taking evidence in New Zealand; the High Court of New Zealand was authorised to act likewise in Australia. For these purposes, then, the two courts may sit in the other country; but it seems not to have happened. Extradition arrangements between the two countries are handled with special flexibility. Otherwise there is little by way of common processes.

The now highly integrated character of trans-Tasman commerce and the specialised jurisdiction of the Federal Court of Australia in industrial and bankruptcy matters may yet drive a closer integration of legal and judicial systems. The Trans-Tasman Mutual Recognition Arrangement, 1996, concluded in the context of Closer Economic Relations negotiations, set up reciprocal obligations designed to promote the free flow of goods and movement of people between the two countries. Any goods sold in New Zealand may, as a result, be sold in Australia and vice versa – irrespective of labelling and other criteria established by the receiving country. Australia has gone on to enshrine in federal domestic law these treaty obligations to New Zealand in the Trans-Tasman Mutual Recognition Act, 1997; New Zealand has formally acknowledged that the treaty obligation in CER provides the necessary set of sovereign obligations in terms of its own domestic law. (That the two countries used different methods to make formal their obligations under the Trans-Tasman Mutual Recognition Arrangement is in itself an interesting reflection of the divergences between their political systems.) Harmonisation of business law between the two countries has also been driven by CER; as a consequence a series of regulatory laws and practices in such fields as taxation, customs and excise, quarantine provisions, trade practices, competition and commercial laws have been brought together and reconciled. Without raising questions of political sovereignty, practical realignments of procedures are being made. There remains the issue of whether some kind of joint tribunal may have to be established, in due course, to reconcile disputes in these fields. The Mutual Recognition Arrangement also opens the way to reciprocal acceptance of qualifications. People required to meet certain criteria in order to register to practice an occupation in one country are able to seek automatic registration to practice in the other, without having to submit to further examinations or checking. Nevertheless, the maintenance of separate jurisdictions in each Australian state complicates mutual recognition of legal qualifications. There is no across-the-board Australasian arrangement as yet. New Zealanders wishing to take cases in Australian courts must, like Australians, have the requisite qualifications in the state concerned, in addition to their New Zealand qualification. In other professional fields, such as medicine, there is a ready acceptance of the professional qualifications of New Zealand practitioners in Australia, and vice versa. The medical professions in the two countries are in fact in the vanguard in the promotion of integration within their disciplines across the Tasman. Australasian colleges of surgery, public health, pediatrics, and so on have been maintained for many years to sustain the highest standards in advanced medical qualifications across the two countries.

In the search for an alternative to the New Zealand practice of reference of higher appeals to the Privy Council, it has been suggested that a review panel could be established drawing together justices from the High Court of Australia, the New Zealand Court of Appeal and perhaps other jurisdictions. Some proponents seem to have in mind the establishment of a wider Pacific jurisdiction, bringing the island states in on a higher appeals process. Others suggest that to offset the danger of introversion in a small jurisdiction like New Zealand, the highest court of appeal should empanel Justices from Australia or elsewhere, with comparable qualifications. Questions arise, of course, as to whether Australian or other outside appointees would be sufficiently familiar with, or sensitive to, the legal and social issues within the New Zealand system. A high proportion of cases referred from New Zealand to the Privy Council are brought by Maori against the crown or involve disputes within Maoridom itself. The Privy Council path has been favoured by Maori because it has allowed their concerns to be aired in a broader forum than that available within a strictly New Zealand judicial structure. Maori also contend that since the original compact, the Treaty of Waitangi, was concluded with the Crown, appeals to do with Maori rights stemming from that treaty should go back to the ultimate judicial authority of the Crown, the Privy Council. One of the strongest arguments against maintenance of that appeals channel is that British law lords, for all their expertise in matters of the common law, are no longer in touch with social and political circumstances in New Zealand.

Once again the issues boil down to matters of strictly national interest and concern. Nationalism – Maori nationalism and New Zealand nationalism – lurks beneath that surface. Short of a wholesale national commitment to entering into a federal political union with Australia, it is hard to see how piecemeal engagement – by involving Australian High Court judges in an expressly New Zealand appeals process – could be a satisfactory alternative to the present system, which involves British judges. Judicial systems are at the heart of national sovereignty; an alternative appeals process cannot be conjured up out of theory. Nor can it be half one thing and half another. Appeals to the Privy Council survived for so long in the New Zealand legal system because of concerns that a small society could not produce either the body of law or the judges with the necessary qualifications to maintain a national jurisdiction. With gathering maturity and sophistication and the expansion of the national body of law within the common law system, these arguments lose force. A legal system has to be a mirror of society. If New Zealanders were disposed towards ever-closer political convergence with Australia, then it would make sense to begin on a process of adjustment to Australian legal systems. Without that commitment the country will have to stand on its own feet – in judicial as in all other matters.

The Alliance Dilemma

On the fundamentals of strategic policy, Australians and New Zealanders do not see eye-to-eye. In the Australian mind-set, recollections of Japanese attacks and of acute vulnerability during the Second World War have given defence and security issues a high profile. From the beginning of the twentieth century, the new Australian Commonwealth set out to build continent-wide military capabilities responsive to regional challenges and to promote an Australian role in the world founded on its regional circumstances. For over fifty years successive Australian governments have firmly endorsed the ANZUS alliance with the United States. The essential rationale would be that ANZUS enhances national security because it obliges any potential adversary to take the probability of American assistance into account when planning an assault on Australia or on Australia's direct national interests. Moreover, it would undoubtedly be calculated that Australia benefits from an alliance relationship through access to policy-makers in Washington as well as to advanced technology, intelligence exchanges, preferential logistic support arrangements, joint military training and exercises, and industrial and scientific co-operation.

New Zealanders are perhaps increasingly seeing the world through a different lens. There is little or no sense of threat. The prevailing belief that New Zealand is a country of the quiet South Pacific has seemingly not been shaken by the political and economic fragility, violence and intolerance now on display in many of the new states of the South Pacific. Asia weighs less heavily than in

Australia. A small, isolated and sea-girt country finds it difficult to accept that the quiet south is co-extensive with the dynamic, fast-changing world of emergent Asian nationalisms and of serious great power confrontation in the North East Pacific. After the 11 September 2001 terrorist attacks destroyed American notions of invulnerability, New Zealand remains among the very few countries in the world never to have been directly attacked by anybody. The closest to offensive action ever was German mine-laying off Auckland and Wellington harbours during the Second World War, which sank one ship without loss of life; in 1985 French sabotage also sank a ship (*The Rainbow Warrior*) and killed a man. (Maori presumably see things differently; the European occupation of the country in the nineteenth century would surely have brought home to them that the country enjoys no immunity from invasion and usurpation.)

Absent any lively concerns about their own national security, many New Zealanders have taken to preachiness and moralising about the security and strategic concerns of others. Americans in particular find to their amusement an echo in New Zealand of Tom Lehrer's song about the US peace movement of the 1960s: 'We're the folk song army, every one of us cares; / We're for peace, freedom and justice – unlike the rest of you squares!' Where the troublespots are far away, it is easy to gloss over the security concerns of others.

At least until the mayhem in East Timor in 1999, Asian regional affairs seemed remote from everyday concerns. The popular presumption is that New Zealand will work out its defence arrangements alongside Australia. Serious commitment to national defence is however far from being a political priority. Debate is exiguous and cranky and has become tangled up with presumptions of 'independence'. There is resistance to the notion that New Zealand and Australia constitute a single strategic entity, because this would require closer co-ordination of policies and commitment to expenditure on interactive military capabilities. New Zealand nationalism, barely strong enough to endorse the need for effective national defence forces, is too strong to support close co-ordination of military effort with Australia. Where there are no immediately discernible threats, the easier course is to stand up for multilateralism and arms control and to distance the country from engagements with others which could have strategic implications.

Australia was more directly engaged in Indonesia in the immediate post-war period than New Zealand. Both countries accepted military roles in Malaya and Singapore during the 1950s and 1960s – in a British Commonwealth context, alongside the British. Australia made a serious commitment in support of the United States in Vietnam in the 1960s, sending conscripts to fight; New Zealand was more tentative, committing only small numbers of professional forces. Both countries entered into, and continue to support, the Five Power Defence Agreement involving Britain in a continuation of its former defence links with Malaysia and Singapore. Engagement in American global strategies through the establishment of joint facilities for communications with strategic submarines, surveillance of missile launches and monitoring of satellites has been regarded in Australia as an acceptable price to pay for the ANZUS alliance. New Zealand has no such facilities and rejected a proposed low-frequency broadcasting system for transmission of navigational data to ships at sea after protesters claimed it would be used by strategic submarines; Australia accepted the system. Australia, moreover, endorsed the broad proposition that such contributions to nuclear deterrence strategy constitute the country's best protection against the threat of nuclear war. New Zealand has long been more guarded.

In 1985, New Zealand committed anti-nuclear heresy and was excommunicated from the ANZUS church. A new generation of politicians of the left wished to nail a radically different national credo to the door – to do with opposition to the nuclear confontation, but also – at root – a determination to strike out in new national directions. It was an interesting assertion of nationalism; the assumption being that it is necessary for a small country to assert its individuality and sense of difference. In the process New Zealand changed the character of its relations with Australia as much as with the United States. Canberra and Wellington had been at odds on foreign policy and security issues before (see chapters four to seven), but this time they were at complete cross-purposes. An Australian Labor government, elected in 1983, had headed off anti-nuclear activism in its own ranks; Prime Minister Bob Hawke had made plain his disapproval of New Zealand's stance and his insistence that the relationship with the United States was of fundamental importance to Australia. In 1985, a leaked letter from Hawke to New Zealand Prime Minister David Lange stressing that Australia could not accept any notion that the terms of the ANZUS Treaty had more than one meaning, or that members of the alliance could pick and choose their obligations, was resented as a gross intrusion in New Zealand affairs.

There may be few better examples of the perversity of the nationalism phenomenon than that of New Zealand and Australia seizing on opposite interpretations of alliance with the United States to bolster their respective beliefs about themselves. Many New Zealanders still believe their anti-nuclear stance to be a light in the nuclear darkness and that rejection of port visits by the ships of an ally was an act of national virtue and moral leadership. They believe the New Zealand stand has won admiration around the world. So it did – among the many of diverse political stripes whose principal rationale is to be opposed to the United States and all its works. At government level, only Vanuatu followed suit. Australian officials and commentators, by contrast, maintained that staunchness and worth lay in sticking with an ally, because the wider view of security interests must prevail over narrow or local interpretations. (In 1943 the boot was on the other foot: it was New Zealand which endorsed 'global' alliance policies and Australia which believed regional concerns should prevail (see chapter six). New Zealanders saw themselves striking a blow for national independence, whereas Australians bluntly pointed out that the anti-nuclear policy confined New Zealand even more severely than before, this time as a dependent on Australian goodwill for exercising and training its armed forces. New Zealanders revelled in plucking a feather from the eagle's tail, but Australians were not amused at what they understandably believed was blatant disregard for their own national interests.

There can be little doubt that external criticism bolsters nationalism. Polling evidence suggests that New Zealanders were at first equivocal about the fourth Labour government's commitment to anti-nuclearism. At the time, there was a majority (slim) in favour of retaining the security relationship with the United States – even if that meant giving up on opposition to port calls by ships that may be nuclear-armed. Tough reactions from Washington and Canberra, more than the policy itself, then boosted nationalistic sentiment. Nations that feel themselves put upon by the rest of the world will fall in behind the flag. Defiance may not be much of a motive for foreign and security policies, but it provides a glue for holding a community together in the face of outside disapproval. It was notable that prominent and conservative leaders of the New Zealand community rallied to the anti-nuclear cause in the face of what they perceived as bullying by the United States of a loyal ally which simply took a different view of an important global issue. Nationalism flourished in New Zealand more in the aftermath of ex-communication from the Western alliance, probably than ever before.

A watershed had been crossed; an anti-nuclear New Zealand would in future have a different world-view from Australia and would become, in the minds of many Australians, both a black and a lost sheep. (Sheep jokes again.) Ten years after the policy was introduced, in 1995, a leading Australian foreign affairs commentator could still write,

> Real national independence involves dealing with reality, taking responsibility for your own situation, maximising your effectiveness and pulling your weight. That New Zealand chose not to do this in the 1980s was a sign not of independence but of insouciance and irresponsibility … An irreplaceable skein of [New Zealand] credibility and respect was torn in Washington and in Canberra.[3]

Equally, a New Zealand leader could still claim, thirteen years after the rift, that the crusade against nuclear weapons had given a small country special authority and leadership. In 1998, the then Leader of the Opposition, Helen Clark, who had been a prominent anti-nuclear activist in the 1980s and would become prime minister in 1999, wrote that in China, a nuclear weapons state,

> it was apparent to me that New Zealand's independent stance on nuclear issues enabled our voice to be heard on issues like human rights in a way which would not have been possible were we seen to be closely tied into an alliance with major western

powers … It is important that we preserve our reputation as a small nation which makes up its own mind on these issues.[4]

(China, of course, would have its own reasons for registering approval of countries that break with the United States on fundamental security issues to do with the Asian-Pacific region.) In 1999, John Howard, Liberal Prime Minister of Australia, saw things the other way round: alliance was what made it possible for Australia to contribute in the world. Australia's consistent support for the United States in the past warranted a return commitment by way of a solid American contribution to an international peacekeeping force in East Timor; a regional role of this kind by Australia, with American support, was a logical extension of United States global roles, with support from Australia. (The implication that Australia would be a perpetual, loyal and unquestioning deputy to the United States caused a media storm in Australia and in South-East Asia. The Prime Minister's office speedily denied the notion of a 'Howard doctrine' and subsequent statements on the matter were more qualified.)

The ANZUS breakdown skewed the Australia-New Zealand relationship in other ways. The United States not only formally suspended its security obligations to New Zealand but also ruled out all military contact; bilateral and multilateral military exercising and training with New Zealand defence forces were stopped. New Zealand turned to Australia for assistance in these areas. The Australians accepted that their interest lay in ensuring that New Zealand was not left completely isolated and that the New Zealand defence establishment should not wither on the vine through the loss of training and exercising opportunities. Canberra initiated an awkward balancing act – maintaining defence links with the United States while going through the motions of what became known as a Closer Defence Relationship with New Zealand. Trilateral military exercises along ANZUS lines were ruled out, and Australia set up additional separate bilateral exercises and training for the New Zealand defence forces to help maintain military expertise while continuing with its own programme of exercising and training with the Americans. Extra costs were imposed on a hard-pressed defence vote and extra demands made of the Australian defence forces. Australian dismay persists with concerns that New Zealand is slipping into a limp, insular escapism, or even non-alignment. This is very unlikely. But Australians fret about unwonted strategic problems with their contrary associate on the eastern flank.

Effective inter-operability has been maintained – as demonstrated when New Zealand took a proportional part in the East Timor operation. The first phase of a UN-sanctioned peacekeeping force to East Timor in September 1999 was carried out under Australian leadership and involved putting approximately 4000 Australian, 850 New Zealand and 200 or so British troops on the ground, with significant and vital American intelligence and logistic support and the back-up of a major sea-borne force of US marines available if the operatione went sour. Canadian, Fijian and Irish companies were soon added. Regional contributions from Thailand, the Philippines and South Korea followed until there were eventually 11,500 troops on the ground – from twenty-two nations. New Zealand unquestionably earned high marks in Canberra for its prompt and effective contribution to the East Timor operation. It is readily acknowledged in Australian defence circles that New Zealand's immediate offer of a trained, operational infantry battalion helped make the operation seem feasible in the early stages.

Defence issues, however, are never static. One swallow does not make a summer. The awkward consequences of the two-level approach imposed by the rupture of New Zealand's security relationship with ANZUS partners linger in trans-Tasman discrepancies in equipment and experience. The New Zealand Labour government's decision in 2000 not to proceed with purchase of F16 ground attack aircraft disappointed Canberra, which had seen them as a useful addition to regional capabilites. The follow-up decision in 2001 to drop the air combat wing of the Royal New Zealand Air Force altogether again nettled the Australian defence establishment, since extra funding and training would be required to replace the New Zealand aircraft, which had for a number of years provided close air defence training for the Australian navy. A programme, useful to both countries and of demonstrable value in terms of integration of defence capabilities was summarily dropped by Wellington. However, the Australians came out the winners, as skilled air and ground crew trained at great expense by New Zealand moved across the Tasman to join the Royal Australian Air Force when their squadrons were closed down in New Zealand.

There have also been consequences of a diplomatic kind. A tripartite ANZUS gave diplomatic leverage to the two southern countries in their dealings with the United States. One could play off against the other. National interests could be leveraged in a tripartite forum. In 1985, New Zealand's expulsion left Australia with the inside running over any New Zealand manoeuvres to improve its own relationships with the United States. New Zealand efforts were, in any case, severely compromised because – for the best part of nine years – direct high-level New Zealand political contact with Washington was disallowed. The Australians were stringent in insisting that all parties must play to the same rules. If New Zealand were to be let off lightly by the United States, Australians would soon conclude that there was no cause for them to stay the course either. Accordingly, Australian representatives in Washington were enjoined by the government in Canberra to be exigent in ensuring that there was no relaxation of United States sanctions against New Zealand. The Clinton Administration took some steps to retrieve New Zealand's position in Washington. New Zealanders are again attending military training courses in the United States; joint military exercising is contemplated, if only in the strictly limited context of specific peacekeeping deployments. The political dialogue is restored;

President Clinton visited the country in association with the 1999 APEC (Asia-Pacific Economic Cooperation) meeting. But the ANZUS triangle remains broken and probably any attempt to rebuild that kind of security relationship in current global strategic circumstances (not to speak of the politics of the matter in New Zealand) cannot be made.

There are regular meetings of senior politicians of Australia and New Zealand – annually at prime ministerial and minister of defence levels, and every six months between the foreign ministers, at which defence issues are discussed. There is continuing and close collaboration among military planners and officials, from both defence and foreign affairs departments, on a day-to-day basis if necessary. Australian experts have expressed the view that current New Zealand defence policies are understandable in New Zealand's circumstances and acceptable to the extent that the uncertainties have been removed. Australia now knows where New Zealand is coming from and appreciates what it can – and cannot – do. The implication is that New Zealand – in the absence of an agreed, integrated approach to defence issues – is no longer a strategic partner. Meanwhile Australia, under a Liberal government, has continued to build a focused bilateral relationship with the United States.

The United States for its part continues to place a premium on its relationships with those partners willing to share the burden of global strategic roles. Australia is promoted to the status of 'principal ally' in the Asian-Pacific region – along with Japan, Korea, Taiwan and Singapore. (New Zealand belongs to a 'second tier' of countries of the region with which the United States has favourable relationships; the rubric is that New Zealand is a friend, but not an ally.) The United States holds regular executive-level discussions with Australia, but not with New Zealand. Of course, this positive security relationship does not provide Australia with trouble-free dealings with the United States. Allies have no overriding claim. (Canberra was at first disconcerted that the United States was unwillingly overtly to join the East Timor deployment; further consideration would have demonstrated that it was very much in Australian as well as American interests for Washington to maintain flexibility in its dealings with Indonesia. As indicated, American assistance in the background proved invaluable.)

The more important point is that an alliance commitment represents a fundamental strategic alignment. Australia has maintained that basic compass bearing. New Zealand has not. Australia committed forces to war with Iraq; New Zealand has contributed to anti-terrorist operations outside of the Gulf, but held back from any commitment to the invasion of Iraq, in the absence of a Security Council directive on the matter.

Present New Zealand defence policies are to shape defence forces around peacekeeping and regional surveillance roles, while retaining effective operational capabilites, directed in particular towards peacekeeping and United Nations roles. While New Zealand and Australian forces can remain interactive and even maintain a degree of inter-operability within this concept, it leaves little room for development of a combined, integrated approach to the defence issues of the region. A basic premise up till now has been that that a New Zealand contribution to combined effort would be useful because it could fill gaps in Australia's own inventory. If New Zealand forces are to be equipped and trained only for circumscribed, less militarily intensive, roles while Australia shapes its military establishment around inter-operability with the United States, the very idea of an ANZAC security partnership is jeopardised. The two countries are developing very different world-views. For the one, the premium is on alliance to offset strategic isolation; for the other, nationalism seems to require a repudiation of alignment and to pin faith instsead on a hazy multilateralism. In foreign and strategic policy terms, Australia is, without question, the most important country in the world to New Zealand. It is surely fascinating that even on the most fundamental of all issues, security policy, nationalism – the determination to insist on being different – should leave the two adjacent countries stranded, so far apart.

ANZAC Frigates

The advantages of defence collaboration are obvious: the development of integrated, interactive forces capable of meeting in an efficient and shared way the strategic challenges of a far-flung region. Cost savings and enhanced self-sufficiency from harmonisation of logistics support arrangements for the two defence forces, and sharing of training and force development programmes would follow. An integrated defence industrial base would have spin-offs by way of economic progress, jobs and the introduction of higher technology and skill levels, while serving the overlapping strategic interests of the two countries, adding to their sense of regional self-reliance and extending the scope and spirit of the CER agreement. Overall, the armed forces of the two countries would be more firmly embedded in their economies and better integrated into their respective communities.

The ANZAC frigate programme was an attempt to move in this direction. In March 1986, the Review of Australia's Defence Capabilities concluded that a 'light patrol frigate' was needed to meet Australia's maritime interests across a wide zone from South-East Asia through to the South Pacific. Such a vessel would be of lesser military capability than the Australian Navy's two existing classes of destroyers and modern frigates of US type. New Zealand, at the time, was considering replacements for its own fleet of British-type frigates. The logic in favour of designing and building vessels suited to the needs of both navies was accepted by both governments. The aim was to build a maximum of twelve ships: eight for Australia and two, plus an option to take two more, for New Zealand. All ships would be built in Australia with maximum Australian and New Zealand industrial involvement; there would be integrated logistic support for the completed ships and as much commonality of equipment and spares as possible. Three support facilities were to be established, at least one of them in New Zealand.

It was no coincidence that a New Zealand Labour government joined this programme in the immediate aftermath of the ANZUS breakdown. The Australian relationship was the necessary – indeed the only – peg on which to hang the semblance of a credible defence policy. In a remarkable bi-national exercise, the two countries worked closely together through all the intricacies of drawing up specifications. Major construction and shipbuilding companies around the world were asked to register interest in late 1987. Evaluation of tenders for a project of this scale and complexity will normally be detailed and extensive. With the joint ANZAC ship, it was that much more intricate. Australian and New Zealand officers were made co-leaders of the tender evaluation teams. From the start, the ANZAC ship project lifted defence industrial collaboration between New Zealand and Australia to new levels of practicality and common sense. At the defence policy level, it was shown that, with goodwill and sustained application, sensitive questions of force development and equipment policy could be reconciled between the two countries. The ANZAC ship project pointed the way towards the development of a significantly closer defence relationship – to match the CER. The professional military and major corporate interests on both sides of the Tasman could not only work to overcome obstacles to the development of a large-scale joint project, they gave it their sustained support. The New Zealanders involved could more than hold their own in determining beneficial returns for New Zealand from the project.

In sharp contrast, the political debate was almost pathetically caught up in suspicions, recriminations and arrogance. There is an insight here into the way the world-wide contention between the trend towards globalism and the opposite option of nationalism may play out. On the one side the argument was about interdependence. A joint Antipodean design and construction project would not necessarily be the cheapest way of getting new ships for the two navies, but it would trigger wider investment, employment, technology transfer and industrial advantages to both countries that would add a decisive overall benefit. In military terms, operation of the same ship-type with integrated support systems and closely linked command and control arrangements would give the two governments cost-efficient and more flexible capabilities to achieve effective interdependent maritime coverage over the vast area over which they had, respectively, assumed authority. On the other side, the concerns were about loss of independence. New Zealand opponents pounded the petty nationalist drum. 'The chief function of these useless frigates,' wrote an activist in the 'No Frigates' campaign, 'will be as a constant reminder of the need for New Zealanders to work for an independent foreign policy if we are to avoid becoming a satellite of Australia.'[5] An 'independent foreign policy' meant, to opponents of the frigate project, disengagement from all 'entangling alliances'. It also meant an unwillingness to work out how a small country – perhaps the most isolated in the world – could provide for its defence interests without working with others. From the outset, the project was beset by addled thinking from the New Zealand side about the capabilities of the warships themselves. Lightly armed patrol frigates of a modern type, specifically designed for the oceanic environment of New Zealand and Australia, were represented as 'incredibly sophisticated',[6] intended to re-incorporate New Zealand in US war planning.[7] (The briefest look at US naval operations would show that only American ships have the sophisticated weaponry, plus the command and control equipment, and their crews the training, to be able to work in a coordinated way in the battle-fleet environment.) Concerns about a return, by the back door, to ANZUS and about dependency on Australia were, nevertheless, not the only causes of complaint about the project. The costs, and associated preferences for the money to go to social programmes, were obviously a part of it; much of the clamour would have come from opponents of any military expenditure. The fact that the project earned substantial returns for New Zealand industry and created jobs for New Zealand workers seemingly could be discounted.

Nationalism, in the shape of a rejection of dependency – on Australia, the United States, or anyone else – was what this strange uproar was all about. The advocates of the frigate programme thought they were arguing for Australasian self-reliance and independence; the opponents believed it offered the opposite because New Zealand would be harnessed to Australia. Those in favour found carefully managed collaboration with Australia to be sensible and advantageous to New Zealand – in defence as well as industrial terms; those against saw it as the loss of an opportunity to cut New Zealand's coat from truly independent cloth – independence being defined in constrained terms of non-alignment. The Australian Prime Minister Bob Hawke didn't help with some rather heavy-handed advocacy; nationalism has sensitive corns. American defence officials were reliably reported to believe that if the New Zealanders stuck with the ANZAC frigate programme, it would at least show that the country had not entirely slipped its Western moorings.

There was plenty of wrangling in Australia too. Rivalries between New South Wales and Victoria about where the work was to be done, between the navy and the other services over the stretch the project would impose on the defence dollar, and arguments with New Zealand about price and division of the industrial spoils between the two countries, all added to the political temperature. The Australian peace movement was also full of complaint about the project; an unexpected and ironical spin-off from the whole exercise was enhanced collaboration on tactics between peace groups on either side of the Tasman. The Australian Minister of Defence, Kim Beazley, kept off the rhetoric and argued cogently for the shared trans-Tasman advantages of the project; he no doubt also indicated that New Zealand participation would be seen in Washington as a positive signal.

In the event, and for whatever reasons, both governments went ahead. In September 1989, Australia announced that eight ships to the agreed design would be built for the Australian navy; New Zealand followed suit and committed to the purchase of two frigates while retaining the option to take up to two more at a later date. The first New Zealand ship came into service in 1997, the second in 1999. When the first New Zealand ship was launched in 1995, the cost of the two-ship project was assessed as NZ$931 million, of which the main contractors had been obliged to place at least NZ$531 million worth of work with New Zealand industry. By 1999, New Zealand businesses had been successful in bidding for over 500 separate sub-contracts within the overall frigate programme. Defence industrial production, from almost a zero start, was producing export earnings of over NZ$130 million a year (more than the annual export returns at the time from the much-acclaimed local wine industry) and among the strongest supporters for the frigate programme was the Engineers' Union, a bastion of the New Zealand Labour Party. Despite such positive returns, a minority National (centre-right) government in 1999 was unable to gather the parliamentary support needed to take up the option to order a third ANZAC frigate. (The idea of New Zealand taking four frigates has been quietly discarded; the consequent abbreviation of the programme has added to the overall costs per ship.) Many of the arguments used ten years earlier were rehearsed again; indeed many of the old campaigners against the project re-emerged. The New Zealand national imperative is not yet in any danger of being overwhelmed by the evident advantages of economic and military/industrial collaboration with Australia. The inference must be that the political bandwagon in favour of moving closer to Australia has yet to even begin to roll. Nationalism wins.

chapter fifteen

The Antipodean Skein

Men are not tied to one another by papers and seals. They are led to associate by resemblances, by conformities, by sympathies. It is with nations as it is with individuals.
– *Edmund Burke*

Antipodean differences are offset by multitudinous interconnections. The resemblances and conformities between Australia and New Zealand are so extensive and instinctive that there is no need for formal treaty ties as a platform for co-operation. Where there is an accepted need for collaboration, the way is immediately and readily found. Transport and communications developments now largely invalidate the traditional New Zealand 'distance' excuse against joining Australia. The economies have become largely inter-dependent. For financial and commercial trading purposes, the two markets are, effectively, one. Cross-investment, business mergers and joint marketing programmes are constantly thickening up the already intricate trans-Tasman skein. Monetary union has been suggested – and merger of stock markets. Political, personal and professional links are close and constant – springing, as they do, from unique ties of history and sentiment. Yet, the parochial view still colours mindsets. Separatism makes more noise than similarities. Political management of the interactions, the daily business of government, in effect reinforces separateness. Nationalism is an easy winner over the new world of interactivity in politics as in commerce. The Antipodeans cannot take their natural affinities and their tight skein of connections to the logical end of amalgamation, because they have each persuaded themselves they are different.

The Die is Cast

A dispersed, mini-federal system of government based on six provincial assemblies was established in New Zealand in 1852. It took only twenty years for it to be accepted that there was simply no basis for such separatism; power was transferred to the centre. Yet, in the 1870s and 1880s, exactly the same issues arose in the wider context of the federation of the seven 'Australasian' colonies. New Zealand was unenthused. Why? New Zealanders and Australians thought and looked the same; the informal styles of the American colonists had soon spread through the Antipodes. Disrespect for the establishment and unconfined informality so noticeable in early New South Wales reproduced itself naturally across the Tasman. Travellers from Britain found, often to their dismay, that 'Australian' styles in dress, attitude and language prevailed. Antipodean colonists were almost at one in discarding not only the prejudices and discrimination but the hocus-pocus of the class system, as soon as they stepped off the boat. They had established themselves in new lands for the same sorts of reasons – to better their lot. The communities they built – from the 1850s onwards – were virtually identical, with very similar political systems in which the state would dispense openness of opportunity and egalitarianism, subject to tight rules and extensive governmental intervention.

After New Zealand declined to join the Australian federation, shared British inheritances still kept the two countries on the same track. The professions, the military, the universities continued to operate under very similar (British) standards and methods. Until after the Second World War, advanced professional qualifications – for example, in medicine and the law – were obtainable only in Britain. Education systems were modelled on the British, and British examinations were used to determine Antipodean standards. Eventual progress through to entry to Oxford or Cambridge represented the ultimate in educational ambition. All this provided a foundation for interaction between Australia and New Zealand perhaps unmatchable between two adjacent countries anywhere else. Apart from the inter-colonial conferences already discussed (see chapter four), there soon sprang up exchanges on matters of practical administration. After Federation, New Zealand began to take part in the Standing Committee on Attorneys-General in Australia, the Australian Agricultural Council and meetings dealing with quarantine, public health, road transport, railways and education.[1] This network of contacts has progressively and naturally expanded. Well before CER systematised the connections, officials were crossing the Tasman to attend conferences with their counterparts on topics as diverse as civil service administration, sea and air transport, education, tourism, welfare and prison reform. All this was very much in the tradition of 'British' informality and practicality of administrative style. It represented a pragmatic response to the need to co-ordinate policies and to adjust to changing circumstances.

Trade Union politics also set the stage for later trans-Tasman collaboration. From the earliest days, the classical clash of interests between capital and labour was part of the stuff of politics in New South Wales and Victoria – with a strong dash of radicalism and challenge to the social and political establishments thrown in. In the 1870s, when official strategic thinking about how best to concert the interests of all the Australasian colonies was deficient, Australian trade unionists were crossing the Tasman to promote an integrated approach to the struggle for workers' rights. This might have been a 'first' – Australians and New Zealanders acting in concert. If so, it was a disaster for the labour cause in New Zealand and for political dreams of Australasian unity. As the prolonged economic depression in the late 1880s, on both sides of the Tasman, was coming to an end in 1890, a group of seamen's and watersiders' unions in New Zealand joined together as the Maritime Council and participated in a major and damaging maritime strike in Australia. Shipping from both countries was affected and the economic dislocation was severe as waterfront workers and shearers joined in. When the strike was defeated, the New Zealand Labour movement had lost so much ground that pursuit of separate representation as a 'Labour party' in Parliament was abandoned in favour of the rising Liberal Party. Moreover, suspicion of a trans-Tasman link-up of organised labour and concern about the effects of the maritime strike helped undermine such small enthusiasm as there was for pursuit of federation with Australia. The Liberals dominated New Zealand politics for the next twenty years. The New Zealand Labour Party, bringing 'socialist' and 'labour' wings together in pursuit of effective parliamentary representation, did not emerge until 1916. When it did, trade unionists with Australian connections soon rose to the top; the first Labour leader, Harry Holland, and the first Labour Prime Minister of New Zealand, Michael Savage, were Australian-born and raised. John Christian (Chris) Watson, the first Labor Prime Minister of Australia (1904–05) came to New Zealand as a young boy – from Chile – and was educated there before entering Trade Union politics in Sydney. The close connection between the trade union movements on the two sides of the Tasman has proved enduring, especially in the maritime and transport industries.

With the Liberals, New Zealand politics also took on the 'rough-and-tumble' style already well established across the Tasman. Their dominant leader, the combative, self-made Richard Seddon, in himself represented the convergence of experience between the Australian and New Zealand colonies; Lancashire-born, he spent three years on the Victorian goldfields and married an Australian. Ideas for some of the advanced 'world-first' legislation for which his government was renowned – such as the establishment of an arbitration court to resolve labour disputes and techniques for breaking-up large landed estates – first surfaced in Australia; other New Zealand leads, on votes for women and old age pensions, were soon taken up across the Tasman. Yet Seddon was a vociferous, parochial, colonial nationalist and under his leadership New Zealand gave short shrift to the notion of joining the Australian Commonwealth.

Economic Interdependence?

For over sixty years after Federation protectionism remained an article of faith; as a result, trans-Tasman trading connections were rudimentary. There was enough to sustain a useful shipping link. But it is perhaps a measure of the relative importance the Australians attached to the New Zealand trade that the main shipping company on the route was New Zealand-owned and operated. Cargoes were mainly bulk supplies for New Zealand industry in one direction and such New Zealand products as could gain entry to Australia in the other. Yet, in fundamental ways, the two economies and societies were already convergent. Banking and insurance sectors had been closely intertwined almost from the beginning, because of mutual dependence on British capital and the City of London. The same currency – the pound sterling – was in circulation. Both countries operated within the one international trading environment – the British preferential system – so far as concerned their major exports and imports. For the best part of a century, Australasia was thus effectively a single economic unit. Like the political and security fields, the lines of force were all oriented towards London. Each established differentiated and independent controls over monetary policies, in reaction to the economic stresses of the 1930s. Two separate national economic jurisdictions were set up. When reciprocal protectionism was abandoned, with the CER during the 1980s, a new level of economic interdependence could emerge (see chapter eight). The economic relationship would henceforth be based on mutual market interpenetration, not membership of a global trading bloc.

By June 2001, almost twenty years after CER, New Zealand exports to Australia were worth NZ$6 billion a year, an increase of 600 per cent from 1983. Australia had become New Zealand's most important trading partner, taking 20.0 per cent of total exports, while imports from Australia were 22.1 per cent of all imports. Two-way trade had increased by 485 per cent to a value of $NZ12.8 billion. New Zealand was Australia's fourth most important export market. Australian exports to New Zealand were valued at A$6.8 billion (NZ$8.0 billion) representing 6 per cent of total Australian exports; while imports from New Zealand were 5 per cent of total Australian imports. For Australia, the New Zealand market yielded not only a large trade surplus but had become the principal external outlet for manufactured products and a platform for expansion of this trade into other countries. Thus, each is important although hardly of preponderant weight, for the other country. Historically the trade balance between the two countries favoured Australia, rising from two to one in the 1930s and reaching four to one in the 1950s; since the mid-1950s the trading accounts have been more or less at par, although in the last two or three years the balance of advantage has been strongly in Australia's favour. As CER agreements have taken hold, each country's share of the other's import markets has progressively increased. New Zealand's early timorousness about closer economic engagement with Australia has proved to be unfounded, as its share of that country's imports has progressively risen from 4.2 per cent in 1990 to 4.5 per cent in 1995 to 5 per cent in 2001.

Little of the old economic patterns remains. In the early 1950s, two-thirds of New Zealand's total trade (imports and exports) was with Britain; in 2001, 5 per cent of New Zealand's imports were from Britain and approximately 6 per cent of exports went to Britain. Britain remained Australia's largest trading partner until 1966, when it was overhauled by Japan; the British market now takes no more than 3.5 per cent of Australian exports; imports are approximately 7%. The trading scene for both countries was transformed by the rising prosperity of Asia. Australia's principal export commodity is coal (11 per cent of total exports); in 1998–99 42 per cent went to the Japanese market, 11 per cent to Korea, 9 per cent to Indonesia and 6 per cent to Taiwan. The second most valuable export product was gold, of which Singapore took 20 per cent of the total, Korea 17 per cent and Hong Kong 6%. Almost 50 per cent of exports of iron ore (Australia's third most important export item) went to Japan; China took 20 per cent and Korea 15%. Australian and New Zealand trade is now locked in to the Asian-Pacific region; in the space of less than thirty years the economic centre of gravity of both countries has moved from Britain and Europe to Asia and the Pacific. Australian exports and imports to and from the member countries of the APEC grouping in 1998–99 were each 70 per cent of total trade: Japan (20 per cent of exports and 15 per cent of imports) was Australia's most important trading partner; the United States (10 per cent of exports and 20 per cent of imports) came next; New Zealand competed with Korea for third place. The New Zealand picture is similar, except that Australia dominates both exports and imports); the United States came next, taking about 14 per cent of exports and sending 19.3 per cent of exports; followed by Japan (12.7 and 12.5 per cent respectively), Korea, and China, while Germany and Belgium remain important participants.

Prior to CER, the conventional wisdom was that the Australian and New Zealand economies were similar and therefore bound to be in competition. With predominantly agricultural economies and struggling and protected manufacturing sectors, the two countries were thought to offer little scope for interactive development and trade. Neither tried hard. The agricultural sector, dominated by pastoral farming (dairy products, beef, sheepmeat, wool) remains dominant in the New Zealand economy, bringing in about 55 per cent of export income; in Australia a very broad-ranging agricultural industry, producing wheat, barley, rice, sugar and cotton as well as wool, meat and cheese, earns approximately 18.2 per cent of export income. Direct competition between the two economies in dairy products and beef in the past is increasingly being offset by diplomatic co-ordination in opposing barriers to agricultural trade, by effort to phase out uneconomic producers (notably in the Australian dairy industry), and by trans-Tasman cross-investment and thus harmonisation of production and marketing. Australian apple and pear growers continue to fight tooth and nail to keep New Zealand fruit out of that market by invoking the spectre of a disease called fireblight, which is not known ever to have been transmitted by trade in the fruit. This has been going on now for about seventy-five years. In other sectors – grains, wool and tropical products – specialisation largely eliminates competition.

The manufacturing sectors occupy much the same relative position in the two economies: Australian manufacturing exports earn about 16 per cent of commodity trading income; New Zealand approximately 18 per cent. Australia has shown significant growth of about 11 per cent a year over the past decade in export of ETMs (Elaborately Transformed Manufactures) such as scientific, medical, and telecommunications equipment, assembled motor vehicles, etc. New Zealand too has advanced in this sector. Again, product specialisation, along with niche marketing and development, gives new scope for economic interdependence. For example, joint contracting and construction of components for the ANZAC frigates (see chapter fourteen) produced real economic benefits on both sides of the Tasman. In contrast, Australia is among the world's leading suppliers of coal, gold, iron ore, bauxite/alumina, aluminium, crude and refined petroleum and natural gas. In 1998–99 this sector accounted for about one-third of exports, earning Australia A\$35.5 billion; of which the simple digging and despatch of coal, A\$9.2 billion, gold A\$6.3 billion and iron ore A\$3.8 billion contributed almost A\$20 billion. New Zealand is simply not in this league. Of major commodity exports, the only mineral items on the New Zealand list are 'iron and steel articles' and 'mineral fuels' which were worth in the 1998–99 year, respectively A\$405 million and A\$395 million. New Zealand mines ironsand as the raw material for its iron and steel industry and oil – which could supply approximately 60 per cent of national requirements, but because of its quality is more profitable to sell abroad; natural gas is also exploited for domestic consumption and as CNG.

Tourism is now New Zealand's major earner of overseas currency and accounts for approximately 10 per cent of Australia's external income. New Zealand's resources, in fisheries and the potential to exploit a land and climate almost ideally suited to temperate agriculture and forestry, are generous. (Protectionist barriers nevertheless make it difficult to add value to agricultural products in world markets awash with the subsidised production of the wealthier countries.) The New Zealand forestry industry goes some way towards redressing the balance between the two countries; although Australian production is equal to or greater than New Zealand's in most categories, greater domestic consumption and slower growing times for exotic timbers mean that a relatively smaller proportion of the Australian product is available for export. New Zealand, by contrast, earns important foreign exchange from forestry and paper products. This industry is the foundation for two of the more important New Zealand multinationals. A small domestic market and the inherent limitations of an economy based on farming, fish and forestry nevertheless make it difficult and arduous to develop alternative sources of wealth. It will remain that much more important to New Zealand to develop and extend the economic relationship with Australia – making it no mystery why New Zealand has made the running on CER. There are self-evident advantages in securing access to a market five times that of New Zealand.

Twenty years on, free trade is a two-way street. New Zealand holds its own. Migration of businesses and jobs has, nevertheless, become a fact of life that can only concern the advocates of national direction and control over national assets. An effectively integrated market will, of course, prompt New Zealand businesses to consider their options: either to move their operations across the Tasman or, at least, to invest in Australian enterprises of a complementary kind. Australian business will equally obviously seek to build market share by investment in New Zealand. New Zealand is Australia's fourth largest outward investment destination, accounting for 5 per cent of the total, while being Australia's eighth largest source of foreign investment. Business migration is, effectively, globalisation at work. The New Zealand Dairy Board (the largest exporter of dairy products in the world) has recently merged its operations in Australia with Australia's second largest dairy group, to make the first trans-Tasman dairy operation; Qantas established a joint venture with New Zealand interests to buy the second major domestic airline in New Zealand, Ansett NZ. (For more on this saga, see chapter sixteen). Telecom, New Zealand's largest and most successful company, has progressively increased its stake to full acquisition of AAPT, Australia's third largest telecommunications company. (As an example of the smaller country's business operating to advantage, Telecom has 50 per cent of a joint company, 40 per cent owned by Cable-Wireless Optus, Australia's second ranking telecommunications company, to lay fibre-optic cables across the Tasman and on to the United States; the joint company sold sufficient rights of usage of the cable to pay for construction, long before it was completed.) Seventy per cent of group assets of Lion Nathan, New Zealand's largest brewing company, are in Australia, where the company holds 41.6 per cent of market share; the head office has moved from Auckland to Sydney. New Zealand's second largest forestry group, Carter Holt, could follow. Four of the five major banks in New Zealand are Australian-owned and controlled; the fifth is British. There is no inevitability about business migration from the smaller to the larger. Heinz Corporation's investments in food production and processing in Australia have been managed from New Zealand, which is a main source of Heinz supply. Fisher & Paykel, the major New Zealand whiteware company with a substantial share of the Australian market, is content to continue to have its production and management focus in New Zealand.

The scale of business mergers and interleaving under CER will inevitably bruise nationalist sensitivities, in view of the obvious discrepancies in size and economic clout. But the process is far from being a mere predatory snapping up of New Zealand trifles. New Zealand companies, seeking expansion, may often find it difficult to raise the necessary capital in the smaller market. The scope for expansion in Australia combines with readier access to capital in the larger market, causing a high volume of listings of New Zealand companies on the Australian stock exchange or at least dual listings on the two exchanges. It is estimated that 70 to 80 per cent of major New Zealand business is now Australian-owned or merged with Australian interests. The management structures adopted to run businesses with this degree of overlap and incorporation by one economy of the other will in large measure set the comfort level in the smaller country with its increasingly subsidiary position. Devolution of responsibility for New Zealand operations to wholly owned New Zealand companies or subsidiaries will at least ensure regional corporate identity is preserved. By contrast, usurpation of regional businesses, with management incorporated into a distant hierarchical enterprise, seemingly unmindful of local interests and concerns, can only stir local resentment at foreign ownership and control.

Both styles are on display in the New Zealand business realm vis-à-vis Australia. The flagship New Zealand bank, the Bank of New Zealand, is now 100 per cent owned by National Australia Bank with headquarters in Melbourne. Local operations are subsidiary to central management and control from across the Tasman; there is no separate share ownership in the New Zealand segment of the business, although there is a New Zealand board with responsibility for New Zealand operations. By way of contrast, the Australian mining enterprise Comalco Ltd, itself a subsidiary of the Rio Tinto Group in London, has adopted the federal model. Comalco NZ is a New Zealand registered company, listed on the New Zealand exchange, with specific responsibility for New Zealand operations within a truly Australasian enterprise. Comalco Ltd mines bauxite in Northern Queensland, which is processed into alumina near Brisbane and shipped to Bluff in the south of New Zealand for smelting into aluminium, using hydro-electric power. Comalco's operations in New Zealand are and always will be politically sensitive, in that the smelter consumes around 20 per cent of national energy resources. New Zealand sovereign concerns are accordingly recognised through delegation from the central board of specific responsibilities for the New Zealand role in company affairs, with the chairman of the New Zealand company holding designated responsibilities (not confined to New Zealand affairs) on the advisory committee to the Australian board of Comalco Ltd. Through delegated responsibilities, as in a federal constitution, the New Zealand branch contributes to the operation of the whole. As New Zealand business becomes increasingly intermeshed with Australian, the character of the day-to-day relationship and the degree of residual New Zealand control will become that much the more important, in strategic and political terms, in determining the national future. Globalisation offers scope as well as pain. Since few countries are likely to respond to it by choosing the 'hermit' option, the answer is to be in a position to compete and to adjust and to define the terms of engagement. There is very little to suggest that New Zealand's increased economic interaction with Australia has been other than beneficial all round.

The facts of economic life for both countries suggest that the widest view may be needed; the future does not necessarily look bright. Real GDP per capita in both countries has steadily declined over the last fifty years in relation to other OECD countries: New Zealand ranked third on the putative list of the most wealthy in 1950, now it is twentieth out of twenty-nine member countries; Australia has declined on this list from eighth in the 1950s to sixteenth. Australia's net national savings as a percentage of GDP was 3.6 per cent in 1998 and New Zealand's was 6.3 per cent; the OECD average was 9.8 per cent. Neither country is exactly an economic giant: Australia generates 1.6 per cent of world trade, New Zealand about 0.4 per cent. For New Zealand, such statistics are the more concerning; for the last twenty-five years its GDP per capita has been sinking relative to Australia's and is now about 80 per cent of that across the Tasman. Even a full economic interdependence, such as the constituent Australian states have with one another, does not guarantee that all will perform at the same level; in the Australian setting, Queensland right now is doing better, Tasmania and South Australia worse. The generators of economic productivity lie in the innate capabilities of each unit. The removal of all barriers to interaction will help dispose of the product, but not necessarily augment the means to create wealth. For that, a country must look to its education systems, capacity for innovation, savings rates, investment arrangements, among other things.

The key to successful management of business interactions – as with keeping a sense of balance in government-to-government dealings – in this sort of unequal relationship lies in the creation of a sense of strategic unity. If Australia and New Zealand could forge a true sense of partnership, of 'we two against the multitude', nationalistic difficulties would slip away. Then it would be a matter of working to secure the overall best advantage. Where would the necessary breadth of vision come from? How is it possible to overcome the parochial perspective? Without a genuine sharing of hopes and fears, of co-ordinated planning at the most intimate levels of governmental policy-making, there can be no strategic foundation to relationships between New Zealand and Australia.

Monetary Union?

Money may or may not be the root of all evil, but it is surely close to the soul of nationalism. A national currency warms the national blood. Yet in a world of instantaneous switching of finance and investments, differing exchange rates can only be an impediment to trade. Therefore, the formation of currency blocs with major trading partners has strong commercial appeal. Most of the continental Europeans have now managed the transition to the Euro, with all that entails by way of changing everyday calculations of value and consigning traditional national currencies to the waste basket of history. The abandonment of national jurisdiction in the fiscal realm is in the end a profoundly political decision. Attachment to one's national symbols on banknotes may be important to the nationalists. The more important consideration is surrender of direct national control over the money supply and interest rates. By this means the nation-states can make adjustments to the national economy in reaction to external and internal pressures, including export price fluctuations, switches in currency trading, the domestic inflationary curve, and so on. The role of the national central bank is crucial to the maintenance of a steady environment for economic activity.

The two prime ministers put the issue of currency union on the Australia-New Zealand agenda in March 1999. Officials were directed to look at whether a common currency should be pursued as a means to extend the CER. No firm conclusions were published and no moves have been made. New Zealand manufacturers have more recently expressed strong support for the idea. Their interest is understandable: elimination of transaction costs would facilitate access to the Australian market; moreover, trans-Tasman trade in manufactured goods is a growth area, through which both countries can develop greater economic depth and sophistication in their manufacturing output. The problem is that the interests of the broader Australian and New Zealand economies will not necessarily coincide at any one time or in respect of their different productive sectors. The staples of the two economies are not the same. The Antipodeans are buffeted by different external economic waves. Demand for Australian coal and minerals will not necessarily be in line with international interest in New Zealand dairy products or timber. An ANZAC exchange rate, determined in response to Australian circumstances, would put the smaller economy in for a wild ride. Whether New Zealand were to enter a monetary union as such – in which it would have some minority say in the management of what would essentially be a new trans-Tasman currency – or simply adopted the Australian dollar, the arrangement would inescapably reflect the interests of the larger economy. With the best will in the world, would that be possible without wider political arrangements to fit New Zealand firmly into the commonwealth system?

Where a large part of total trade is taken up within a bloc – as is the case with most members of the European currency union – the argument in favour of monetary union is strengthened. When there is also a strong strategic sentiment in favour of political amalgamation, again as in Europe, the case develops further momentum. The United States dollar, for example, has long since been backed by a powerful political union with a huge and – despite recent difficulties – very potent American domestic economy, in which a relatively small part (about 12 per cent at the time of writing) of all transactions is taken up with external trade. By contrast, Australia and New Zealand are global traders, not largely taken up with one another. With New Zealand's trade with Australia representing about 20 per cent of total national trade and Australia's with New Zealand only about 6 per cent of the total, a common currency would have little impact on transactions with the rest of the world – although both would presumably benefit from trading as members of a currency 'bloc' embracing a marginally greater share of global trade than each can capture separately. Political calculations, however, might well oblige the two countries to re-think even that aspect of the conundrum. Both are interested in developing their CER relationship as a springboard to other expanded free trading arrangements, especially in the Asia-Pacific region. A common currency could offer an additional incentive to regional partners to deal with the CER 'bloc'. Again however, this consideration suggests that the logical course would be to re-jig not only monetary arrangements but the entire relationship. If the overall aim is to provide a more secure foundation for dealing with a dynamic region, then the answer is to develop an integrated 'Australasia', combining resources, programmes and political processes. Small chance!

Would the better monetary option be to link in with a major global currency – the US dollar? A number of countries do not have their own national monetary systems or tie their currencies to another: the Argentine peso was pegged to the US dollar for over ten years, squeezing the inflation out of the economy but introducing a punitive internal cost structure, as the US dollar strengthened. The precedent is unpromising. The arrangement so distorted the Argentine economy that when parity could no longer be held, the resultant collapse had disastrous social as well as economic and political consequences. Australia and New Zealand have experience of this way of proceeding, which was also not encouraging. For many years both maintained a single currency, the pound sterling, and both found that the stresses of conformity to an externally imposed financial discipline could be severe. Australia established the Commonwealth Bank as early as 1911, giving it some powers of a central bank to control the money supply in 1924. Yet, in the huge financial turmoil of the depression years, challenges to the banking system – and in particular the determination of the Premier of New South Wales, Jack Lang, to repudiate debt to British bankers rather than suspend civil service pay – caused an eruption in Australian political life. The Labor Party split and a coalition government held to 'orthodox' monetary policies. The pieces were not tied together until the 1950s, when the present structure centred on the Reserve Bank of Australia was established. New Zealand was similarly buffeted around in the depression of the 1930s by the disciplines of a tied currency – and was similarly resentful of hectoring advice about management of its economy from officials of the Bank of England. An early action of the Labour government elected in 1935 was to establish a central bank, the Reserve Bank of New Zealand.

Today, with far more complex economies and broader based national trading interests, the sterling area precedent is irrelevant – except as a reminder of the difficulties of sticking with such arrangements when the economic sledding gets rough. As globalisation gathers pace, the advantages of adopting a truly global, freely traded currency – the US dollar – may become apparent. They are not so at present. The sterling area precedent will not be encouraging to Australian or New Zealand central bankers. The smaller members of a currency bloc can have little influence on the large; their threshold of economic pain will inevitably be lower than for their larger partner and will likely be brought on by differing economic pressures. Moreover, it is a fiction to suppose that the wealth of a major economy such as the United States will transfer to a smaller country that adopts the dollar as its national currency. It didn't happen to Argentina or Panama – where the currency has also been pegged to the US dollar. Such a realignment would also pose formidable strategic problems for Australia and New Zealand. Each has one foot in the Asian-Pacific realm, and the other in the West. The idea must be to keep things that way – to avoid making a choice. Linking with the dollar would not only cause loss of independent control over national policies but would raise serious questions about the sincerity of the two countries' commitment to Asia. The potential for doing political as well as economic damage would be high.

The case has yet to be made for a trans-Tasman monetary union. Ironically, since this was the group most opposed to federation with Australia at the beginning of twentieth century, most of the enthusiasm is coming from New Zealand manufacturers who are now very much persuaded of the advantages of doing business there. The alarm bells ring for those who worry about how best to manage and nurture a small economy in very unpredictable times. To New Zealand nationalists, monetary union would carry the adverse freight of loss of sovereign control and identity in matters to do with money and the symbolism of the national currency; Australian nationalists would scoff at the very idea that the increment of the mere 'Kiwi' dollar could add to their splendid sum of things. On both sides of the Tasman, the more sobering questions are to do with how best to secure and maintain economic growth in two relatively small economies – in a world of very large economic forces well able to destabilise them. Without a solid political commitment to unity, it's hard to see how a side merger of currencies or monetary arrangements would help.

The merger of stock markets on the two sides of the Tasman has also been considered, as a means of attracting investment and building the market base in the two countries. From the New Zealand side, the cry was that the capital needs of smaller companies would be lost from sight if the local exchange were to lose its autonomy. Nationalism for the small will automatically require that the interests of the smaller actors be protected. The question is whether the maintenance of separate institutions is in fact the way to promote small business initiatives. There is nothing to suggest that small start-up businesses in large markets such as the United States are in any way stymied for want of capital. On the contrary, a higher level of day-to-day business interaction through access to larger markets for investment capital and as a basis for developing potential outlets, provides the spur. Again, nothing has eventuated.

Reciprocal Arrangements

Pushed along by a deep inter-leaving of popular culture and virtually interchangeable societies in recent years, New Zealand and Australia have progressively drawn closer together – without much noticing it. Economic convergence is a fact of life. Already the degree of inter-penetration of business on the two sides of the Tasman provides reciprocally interwoven career paths for many people. With only unexceptionable restrictions on entry, to do with the health and criminal records of applicants, nationals of the one country are free to travel and work in the other, although New Zealanders must present passports that are screened before entry. For young New Zealanders, Australia is a springboard to the wider world. Each is the other's largest source of tourists.

Although it has not always been that way, migration is now heavily in Australia's direction; New Zealand is Australia's biggest source of permanent immigrants (15.2 per cent of the total in 1997, with Britain second at 11.3 per cent). It is hardly surprising or exceptional, in an increasingly interactive and sophisticated global environment, that the flow of people should be mainly from the smaller to the larger; the brighter lights will never lose their allure. It is the same for Australians and Europeans vis-à-vis the United States; the same for the young of Colorado or South Dakota vis-à-vis Chicago and New York. Although depressing for New Zealanders, this 'down under' replication of a global trend makes the point about the vanishing significance – especially for the young – of borders and separatism.

An almost unqualified invitation to New Zealand ministers to join in official federal-state discussions in Australia takes that process further. New Zealand is now a full member, or a participating observer, in twenty-seven Australian ministerial councils dealing with health, social welfare, transport policy, prison systems, ethnic affairs and the full range of other issues to do with day-to-day governance. A Trans-Tasman Food Standards Authority has been established; arrangements are being made to establish a single authority governing recognition of standards and sales procedures for therapeutic goods. A far-reaching agreement on mutual recognition of qualifications and generous provisions in both countries for emergency medical collaboration and specialist treatment for nationals of the other country further promote reciprocal exchanges of people. In terms of practical administration, New Zealand is already, to all intents and purposes, a state of Australia – without the political discipline.

The trans-Tasman journey is now hardly an obstacle to interaction. The return day trip is commonplace. To Americans, this is completely unremarkable; the time shift from the East Coast to most of the mid-West is the same as Auckland to Sydney; there, the equivalent distance – 1800 kilometres – is not regarded as the slightest impediment to business.

Defence Co-operation

According to the 1999 annual report of the New Zealand Defence Force, 'to not work together with Australia in response to security challenges in our neighbourhood would defy logic'. There is a marked convergence in training, in military institutions and force development concepts between the armed forces of the two countries; Australian and New Zealand forces readily serve under the command of the other as appropriate; there is much consultation, a great deal of joint exercising and training and a high degree of overlap between roles and missions. There has been some harmonisation of major equipment purchases, such as the ANZAC frigate project, and the adoption of the same basic infantry weapon, manufactured in Australia. Perhaps no other two nations could invest such reciprocal trust and confidence in one another as to be able to form a joint infantry battalion, as Australia and New Zealand did in Vietnam. Most recently, the ease with which the two defence establishments were able to mesh together and deploy forces capable of effective and closely integrated shared military roles, has been demonstrated once again in East Timor. There has, however, never been doubt about the capacity of the two countries to co-operate at this military-to-military level.

The issue now is whether there is still a foundation for what was called the Closer Defence Relationship; the term coined in the 1980s was obviously intended to mirror the Closer Economic Relationship. Such a concept can, however, rest only on a shared appreciation of what is required to meet the security concerns across the entire Australasian strategic area and a reciprocal undertaking to commit resources to meet that requirement. Separate, unco-ordinated decision-making doth not a closer defence relationship make. The famed and justifiably proud ANZAC military record in many battlefields has not, as we have seen, been matched by any comparable, shared strategic vision. Twentieth century efforts to promote the kind of far-reaching collaboration required for an integrated approach to an Australasian strategic area were largely nugatory. No political thought has ever been given to establishment of joint operational commands, or effective integration of defence policies and planning across the Tasman; barely a word is breathed of military merger. Even pooling certain basic requirements, common to both, such as pilot training programmes, has proved too difficult. By insisting on a lonely strategic perspective oriented towards the South Pacific, New Zealand has effectively shut the door on prospects for military development in tandem with Australia. Notions of a closer defence relationship have not yet even begun to chip away at traditional concepts of national sovereignty as expressed through the ownership and control of national armed forces.

The key concept – that the two countries constitute a single strategic entity – continues to frighten the horses, at least on the New Zealand side of the Tasman.

It implies, according to the New Zealand Prime Minister Helen Clark, that 'the decisions would not be ours alone and, deeply as we love [the Australians] we are not prepared to take that step'. This rationale puts the premium on separatism at the expense of analysis of what could best be done jointly with Australia in response to the strategic environment the two countries share. The starting point should be a commitment to working out how best to co-operate to overcome isolation and promote stability and security in the wider east Asian and Pacific region. The ultimate consideration is acceptance of a reciprocal responsibility for the survival and good fortune of the other partner. Australians, remembering their Second World War history, have for many years been putting major resources into the development of defence capabilities across the north of the country. Many New Zealanders find it difficult to share this degree of engagement, and some even interpret it as misplaced. In the words of Clark, after a visit to Australia in March 2000, 'the Indonesians have had centuries to invade and have never done so'. Jibes are no substitute for strategic thought. The issue is not about Indonesian 'invasion' but about guarding against any tilt in the balance of power in the region, which would shut out the Western countries – a matter of vital importance to New Zealand, as much as Australia. Miss Clark pins her Western colours to the mast; she is in no doubt that New Zealand is a country of the 'West'. But at this point doctrine gets in the way of analysis. New Zealand and Australia have been, she notes, 'on different security tracks for some time'. New Zealand politicians, without exception, aver that if Australia were to be attacked they could rely on New Zealand assistance. This is, by definition, a statement of a shared strategic interest. New Zealand nationalism, however, seemingly makes it impossible to draw from that conclusion the need for a co-operative approach to a vast region of shared, indeed overlapping, strategic concern.

Air New Zealand is about to fall out of the sky as its Australian subsidiary ANSETT collapses. The Captain seems unwilling to acknowledge an emergency.

'This is your Captain', Alan Moir, *Sydney Morning Herald*, 10 September 2001. Source *The Other Side Of The Ditch*, Ian F. Grant, New Zealand Cartoon Archive Collection, Alexander Turnbull Library, Wellington.

chapter sixteen

The Parochial Streak

The tendency since the end of the war in 1945 has been for nations to solidify their nationalism, rather than to build an interdependent world. The parochial streak in people is perhaps the strongest streak in human nature, and I have no idea how it can ever be eradicated sufficiently to allow a better state of affairs.[1]
– E.B. White, American essayist

In New Zealand and Australia systems and beliefs, sufficient to separate closely similar peoples and societies have been built over the relatively short space of two hundred years. Both countries are committed multilateralists in foreign policy – meaning that, in theory, they accept the need to qualify strictly national concerns in the interest of the wider collective. Such accommodations in their own mutual affairs, where national identity might be compromised, are seemingly beyond them. Their many interactions do not point to an eventual merger. Nothing except a great fright from a shared external danger is likely to overcome their separate parochial streaks – unless the smaller partner were to lose all confidence in its ability to manage as an independent nation. Otherwise, Australia and New Zealand will jog along, working the same side of the street but not in harness, standing reminders that even sensible, practical nations, with almost all things in common, cannot be deaf to the siren song of nationalism, even when the notes are low key and lacking in vainglory.

The Prickly Pair

Parochialism surely springs eternal. The interest in the case of Australia and New Zealand lies in the essential triviality of the differences out of which separatism has been fashioned. Societal mixes are only mildly differentiated; the local glosses on a common culture are of slight significance; the respective lessons taken from a mostly shared history are hardly on the same scale as, for example, those drawn by Scots and English in the 'United' Kingdom or northerners and southerners in the 'United' States of America. The only conclusion which can be drawn is that because Australia and New Zealand are so similar it is necessary to stretch the point to accentuate the differences or, to put it the other way, to invalidate notions of over-arching, collective interests.

The modern nation-state is obviously founded in perceptions of national interests, national identities and national ideas about national roles in the world. It is another truism that the concept of the nation-state has ballooned out in the years since the Second World War until it now fills almost the entire international space. So much so that notions that smaller states might do better by pooling their sovereignty in Empires, federations or other trans-national collectives have begun to seem fantastical – belonging to a distant past. Even the central multilateral organisations of the United Nations function according to the whims of the nation-states. Official transactions, even routine dealings, become enfolded in sensitivities about sovereignty. As we have seen, the attempt, following the ANZAC Pact of 1944, to establish informal collaborative arrangements for the management of the foreign policies of New Zealand and Australia was soon overpowered by the wave of national sovereignty which became the be-all and end-all of international life in the years following the Second World War. The informality remains: Australian and New Zealand diplomats operate in a relaxed and open way in their day-to-day dealings with one another; access is easy and protocol largely absent. Essentially however, the two countries now maintain the same context and the same diplomatic structures for the conduct of reciprocal affairs as with any other nation. Sovereignty is the determining factor; national interests are the touchstone. Notions of a collective, trans-national set of interests are difficult to sustain. Rows are frequent and often bitter.

Over the same period, since the end of the Second World War, Australia has begun to take itself seriously: 'The Lucky Country', with size, mineral resources, a new sense of drive and national pride, conflated to confer notions of destiny and splendour among the nations. Its off-shore island neighbour has no place in this picture of grandeur. Indeed, chauvinistic Australians have been known to slight the very idea of a linkage out of concern that their own national image may thereby be diminished. For its part the smaller country has never wavered from the belief that relative size does not matter and that its own unique qualities entitle it to equal standing. New Zealanders are not tempted by aspirations to grandeur. Smallness imposes its own reality checks. Instead, New Zealanders like to believe that their national speciality lies in showing the way to others: 'Guide her in the nations' van,' the national song says, 'Preaching love and truth to man.' At the onset of the twenty-first century, a hundred years after New Zealand declined to join the Australian Commonwealth, it has seemed sometimes that nothing could be more remote than the possibility of trans-Tasman amity and respect. Sharp disputes over airline operations and financing, immigration, social welfare payments, defence policies and even over the staging of the 2003 Rugby World Cup have caused deep resentments – on both sides of the Tasman Sea. In New Zealand it occasionally seems that a vein of serious animosity towards, and distrust of, Australia and Australians has been tapped. In Australia, disdain for New Zealand and belittling of the efforts of New Zealanders begins to look like a national pastime. Brief surveys of some of the clashes of the last three or four years may illustrate how easy it is to misinterpret the signals, to overlook the collective advantages, to be dismissive of the 'other'. Nationalism grows there.

The Airline Business

In the modern world airlines carry more freight than just passengers and cargo; they have become – for perhaps all countries, except the United States, which seems to have grown out of this particular brand of nationalism – symbols of national accomplishment and pride. They are flag-carriers. For a number of countries, perhaps especially New Zealand and Australia, the national airline also represents an important strategic factor. Isolation brings with it an understandable preoccupation about transport linkages – for commerce and more broadly to overcome the limitations of distance. The importance of retaining in national hands the airline component of the network of communications linkages accordingly ranks high with governments. Airlines obviously can be maintained by private operators. Airline industry economics have, however, become increasingly fragile; isolated governments cannot entertain with equanimity the possibility of vital links with the world being abandoned by private operators finding better prospects elsewhere. At the same time demand for travel and for fast transport for goods, domestically and internationally, has increased exponentially while the costs of aircraft and the associated infrastructure has continued to escalate. In the face of an insatiable demand for capital and for decentralisation of control most 'national' airlines have been 'privatised' long since, not least Qantas and Air New Zealand. Finances have become diversified with a mix of government and private, national and international investment. National symbolism and national control are accordingly far from clear-cut. Yet the potency of the symbols – the kangaroo on the tail plane of Qantas aircraft and the Air New Zealand koru, representative of the fern frond – remains virtually unchallengeable.

In the real world, however, the strategic importance of the two airlines to each government and their iconic status in the national scheme of things in both countries – in economic as well as cultural terms – come hard against the inexorable pressures of globalisation. Qantas and Air New Zealand are significant commercial actors in the region; Air New Zealand is about a third the size of Qantas and thus represents more than its proportional share of the major airline operations of the two countries. But on the world scene, the two airlines, even lumped together, are minnows, representing about 4 per cent of global airline activities. The problem is: how to hold heads above water in the face of intense competition, mounting costs and a global down-turn in profitability in the airline industry worldwide? As early as 1961, Australia and New Zealand entered into an air services agreement in the attempt to regularise respective air transport interests. In pursuit of the open market principles established under CER (see chapter nine) a Memorandum of Understanding creating a single aviation market was concluded in 1992. In 1994 Australia unilaterally withdrew access to its domestic aviation market, along with the offer of additional 'beyond' rights (carriage of passengers and freight from Australian airfields to third countries). New Zealand was hugely offended, not only by the abrogation of a previous undertaking but by the off-hand, seemingly contemptuous way the Australian decision was communicated (by fax). The issues, however, could not be so summarily waved away. The agreement formally establishing the single aviation market was finally signed in 1996, with exceptionally liberal provisions allowing airlines from each country to fly unrestricted within the other's territory and across the Tasman. A further MOU on open skies between Australia and New Zealand was concluded in November 2000.

Air New Zealand – and Australia-New Zealand relations – then took a terrible drubbing. Instead of expanding its base of operations by taking up domestic rights in Australia directly, the New Zealand airline moved to acquire ownership of Ansett, Australia's second major airline operator, announcing the intention to take a 50 per cent holding in September 1996 and the remaining 50 per cent in 2000. They sowed the wind and reaped the whirlwind. The Ansett operation was in poor shape and Air New Zealand did not have the financial strength to keep it afloat. Almost at once, things began to go wrong: ten of Ansett's largest aircraft were grounded for safety reasons; Air New Zealand was obliged to write off Ansett investments, causing it to record a NZ$1.4 billion loss; the Australian government pressured Air New Zealand to accept responsibility for a further A$400 million for Ansett staff entitlements; in September 1991 the New Zealand Prime Minister's aircraft was blockaded at Melbourne airport by Ansett workers worried about pensions and other benefits; it was claimed in Australia that Air New Zealand had made misleading statements as to its financial position. Everything that could go wrong did. Ansett ceased flying on 4 March 2002 – one of the largest corporate failures in Australian history. Bitter things were said: the Australian Minister of Transport claimed,

> Their (the Air New Zealand Board's) incompetence destroyed one of Australia's great icons. If they were men and women of honour they must immediately meet their obligations to their customers and former employees.

New Zealand and New Zealanders were held up to ridicule and contempt in Australia.

There are lessons here, both about corporate decision-making and about nationalism. It is perilous for a smaller partner to try to increase market share by take-over of an established operator; if things go wrong the accusation of destroying a national icon will surely be run up the mast. A more carefully controlled and monitored approach is needed, paying careful regard to shared interests. These remain the same: the national airlines of the two countries need capital and both face the likelihood of direct competition from outside operators which can pick the eyes out of their businesses. Where a full services (international and domestic) national flag-carrying airline must provide an extensive infrastructure in engineering services, etcetera, and far-reaching, often unprofitable, networks, alternative airlines have freer rein. Accordingly the key issue for the two national airlines was to find a way to protect their interests, while continuing to provide the services needed by their two countries and to survive in an intensely competitive environment. What they propose is uncomfortable to the nationalists and has raised immediate alarm in New Zealand on that score. But as a rationalisation of the issues confronting two major businesses in the two countries and a way to manage their interactions to best mutual advantage the concept may well prove to be a model for the conduct of trans-Tasman relations.

Qantas and Air New Zealand announced, in December 2002, the intention to form a Strategic Alliance to be managed by an Advisory Group with three representatives appointed by each airline; decisions to be unanimous. Qantas would take a 22.5 per cent holding in Air New Zealand with two directors on the Air New Zealand Board; the latter would be entitled to appoint one director to the Qantas Board, even though it would not be subscribing for shares. NZ$550 million in cash would be injected over three years. In the wake of the Ansett disaster the New Zealand government had taken an 82 per cent holding in Air New Zealand at a cost to the taxpayer of $885 million; the Qantas proposal would eventually reduce the New Zealand government holding to around 64 per cent. On the operational side, the Strategic Alliance will create a Joint Airline Operations network, to be commercially managed by Air New Zealand. All Air New Zealand flights will be part of this network and all Qantas flights into, within and out of New Zealand; there will be coordination of pricing, capacity and all other aspects of business operations in respect of the Joint Airlines Operations network and 'where it is efficient and effective to do so' on non-JAO networks as well; the two airlines will also provide 'extensive reciprocal rights for codesharing on each other's services'. The advantages to New Zealand, in terms of improved efficiencies, additional tourist flows, more jobs, especially in the engineering and maintenance fields, improved freight capacity, etcetera are real and quantifiable. Nevertheless the arrangement merges Air New Zealand interests into those of Qantas; it immediately raises obvious concerns about competitiveness: the temptation to eliminate competition could well push up air fares. As mentioned, nationalism has already reared its head: New Zealanders are being told that their representatives will be unable to hold their own, that the Aussies will be out to do them down; that Qantas in the past has made it clear that it would like to 'take-out' Air New Zealand. Australian workers are being told that it will deny them jobs to the advantage of New Zealanders. What has changed?

First came the realisation that the long-term survival of the two national carriers may be at stake in a world aviation market where even the biggest companies have become vulnerable. Old shibboleths about the purity of national control and maintaining national identities began to carry less weight against the imperative of survival. What the two airlines have produced is a carefully worked-out and structured approach to overall financial and management problems and strategic challenges which appears to balance their respective interests. The ability of the New Zealand segment in the alliance to influence decisions and to retain power over what goes on in respect of their own interests has not been compromised. The Strategic Alliance between the two airlines looks to be a first: a serious attempt between the two countries to develop a formal management scheme for an area of joint and interlocking concerns. Like the ANZAC Frigate programme (see chapter fourteen) as originally conceived, the Strategic Alliance provides for effective New Zealand engagement in day-to-day administration and development. More than that project, this alliance looks to harmonisation of operations of the two airlines on a basis of shared strategic interests. In effect Air New Zealand will manage some 10 per cent of Qantas operations. For the first time since the conclusion of the ANZAC Pact in 1944, the two countries (or a significant sector of their respective commercial concerns) propose to join together on a 'we two against the world' basis. The proposal has yet to be approved by the respective commissions on the two sides of the Tasman charged with passing judgement on proposals which appear to inhibit competition. Meanwhile, it is noteworthy that Australian and New Zealand interests have been able, at this mature stage in their national development, effectively to suppress national jealousies and doubts in favour of a concerted approach to an 'Australasian' set of problems.

It's Only a Game

Negotiations towards staging the World Rugby Cup in Australia and New Zealand in 2003 produced a debacle which ended up with the Australians gaining sole rights to host the competition. New Zealand, as a major rugby playing nation and a former holder of the championship, was hugely affronted. Instead of a trans-Tasman sharing of the competition, all games will be played in Australia. An agreement with the Australian Rugby Union in 1997, with New Zealand to act as a co-host, became unravelled in 2002. Bitterness among rugby fans towards Australia, and the principals who negotitated for Australia, was – and remains – deep. There is, unquestionably, a sense of betrayal. Yet, as a subsequent enquiry made clear, it is also obvious that the New Zealand negotiators were outclassed and made a number of serious misjudgements. The co-hosting arrangement promised to bring in substantial returns to New Zealand from overseas visitors to watch the games. Yet no financial guarantees were secured from government to back up the negotiating position of the New Zealand Rugby Football Union. New Zealand's special circumstances were apparently not appreciated by the international organising committee for the World Rugby Cup. With a relatively small market for advertising purposes – and the difficulty a small country has in meeting revenue-raising requirements based on the huge stadia, and the large crowds to fill them, in other countries – the New Zealanders found themselves negotiating at a disadvantage. Rugby is a big money sport. The World Cup is an important opportunity to raise large sums of money for the promotion of the game worldwide. Yet, at the same time, sport, as much as other inter-actions between countries, is a huge repository of nationalism.

In the event a small country came to feel aggrieved, both with its own Rugby Football Union and with its own circumstances – seemingly become too small to take part in hosting a major world sporting event. But again, the old maxim, if you can't beat 'em, join 'em applies. The New Zealand Rugby Union made no attempt to enter into a strategic partnership with Australia within which the two countries, through continuous and committed interaction, could iron out their problems together in order to negotiate to best advantage with the international organising committee. Again, the issue is one of power, and relative power. In order to secure its wider interests the smaller country has to try to add strength to its negotiating arm. Separatism, bolstered by nationalism, is not good enough. Driven by hubris about New Zealand's respected position in the rugby world, the New Zealand negotiators found themselves out of their depth in a pool full of bigger fish, with sharper teeth. Unfortunately the legacy is one of animus towards the country's natural ally and most important partner, in the rugby sphere as in so many others.

Combat over Combat Aircraft

In December 2001 New Zealand summarily severed a ten year association with the Australian Defence Force when it withdrew Skyhawk combat aircraft from a joint training arrangement with the Royal Australian Navy. The New Zealand jets, based in Australia, had flown low-level attack practice runs at Australian ships to sharpen their defensive capabilities. In May, the New Zealand Labour government had decided to disband its air combat arm and put the aircraft – 17 A4 Skyhawks and 17 Aer-Macchi jet trainers – up for sale. Refusal to continue to sustain a limited force of strike aircraft was in line with the New Zealand Government's general belief that national defence forces should be shaped more strictly to meet regional needs and United Nations peacekeeping roles. It was plainly not in line with any strategy shared with Australia, either by way of pooled training arrangements or any meeting of minds about the defence requirements of the region. Australian Ministers were reported to have been incredulous – that any country could simply give away a strategic asset in which it had invested so much. At the same time there was marked annoyance that New Zealand should again cause Australia to ratchet up defence expenditure. Instead of building on the training association with the Australian Navy and cementing it into a wider shared vision about defence needs in the Australia-New Zealand part of the world, the New Zealanders chose to go their own way. It was, as already noted (see chapter fifteen) not a surprise to the Australians. In Canberra, New Zealand is regarded as having for many years paid only lip-service to defence collaboration with Australia while assiduously building-in its own unorthodox views of defence requirements. Rather than deciding – in collaboration with Australia – how best to develop limited defence capabilities the better to serve the wider strategic interests of the two countries, the emphasis has been on unilateralism. The point, again, is about the relative advantages of nationalism or of sharing and pooling resources and assets in the common interest.

The New Zealand decision could hardly have surprised Australian Ministers. In security perceptions and defence commitments there are now solid differences between the two Antipodeans; New Zealand has long since been shaping a unique anti-nuclear nationalism in defence and security matters, viewed with suspicion and some distaste in authoritative circles in Australia. The Australians politely noted that the New Zealand Government was entitled to decide that its defence interests could be served by aligning its forces with peacekeeping requirements. The web-site of the Australian Department of Foreign Affairs is more blunt.

> Australia regrets New Zealand's decision not to maintain at least some competent air and naval combat capabilities. Such forces would allow a more significant contribution to be made to protecting our shared strategic interests, especially in view of the essentially maritime nature of our strategic environment.

Australian commentators have also noted that New Zealand's failure to continue to maintain effective air and naval combat capabilities will mean that New Zealand may have to rely on other countries (i.e. Australia) should the need arise in those areas. Neither country has the independent clout or weight in the world, lightly to discard solid connections and commitments to co-operation one with the other. Nationalism is two-edged: if there is no shared commitment, there may be no commitment at all.

Immigration and Social Welfare Woes

No topic raises the nationalism hackles more swiftly than immigration. No matter how strenuously the experts may insist on the economic advantages brought by systematic skills-based migration programmes, the political temperature is easily raised by alarmist claims that foreigners do not assimilate, disrupt conventional social and cultural values and are a drain on resources because of undue demands on the welfare budget. In two countries with such close connections, failures of co-ordination in immigration and refugee policies and disproportionate flows of people from one side of the Tasman to the other, have precipitated acute political problems. The base document is the Trans-Tasman Travel Agreement 1973, which allowed Australian and New Zealand citizens to enter each other's country to visit, live and work without the need to qualify for authority to enter under normal immigration procedures. Associated with entry to the other's country came entitlement to its social welfare provisions. Over the past twenty years as New Zealand has struggled to maintain its standard of living, while Australia has steadily gained in comparative terms, migration flows have become markedly unbalanced.

In 2000 it was calculated that 450,000 New Zealanders were living in Australia compared to 50,000 to 60,000 Australians living in New Zealand (about one-and-a-half times the respective relative proportions of population). In the

1999–2000, year 43,000 New Zealanders came to Australia as permanent settlers or long-term visitors. Permanent New Zealand settlers (31,600) accounted for 31.3 per cent of all settler migrants. Studies show that Australia has been making a net gain from migration of New Zealanders across the Tasman; New Zealanders resident in Australia on average are better educated and earn higher incomes – and accordingly pay higher levels of tax – than the average of Australians.

The Trans-Tasman Travel arrangement, like similar provisions for free movement of people across the national boundaries within the framework of the European Union, established a common labour market for Australia and New Zealand. This was a strategic asset for both countries, a pooling of labour resources. In this sense, any obstruction to the free flow of people, as of ideas, across the Tasman is a disaster, especially for the smaller country. For generations, from colonial times, two-way freedom of movement across the Tasman has been seen as a right arising from a common inheritance. The connection is indispensable to New Zealand's need to ensure that its people have wider options than can be provided within a smaller society; put simply, it is a safety valve permitting people to move when employment opportunities dry up.

It had earlier been agreed that each government would reimburse the other for welfare payments to its nationals in the other country. By 2000 the costs of this arrangement to New Zealand were predicted to rise to intolerable levels. Australia – short-sightedly – was insistent on punitive rates of compensation. The New Zealand government was faced with an unpalatable choice: continue to pay Australia for New Zealanders who had chosen, at least temporarily, no longer to live and work in New Zealand, or agree to constraints on the entitlements of New Zealanders to Australian welfare benefits. The latter would amount to a major abridgement of the principle of a strategic approach to shared labour and employment issues. The Clark Government chose to negotiate a new agreement and to give away that ideal. As from February 2001, New Zealanders arriving in Australia will no longer be able to claim unemployment or single parent family benefits until they have obtained permanent residence (which involves a waiting period of two years). The upshot is expected to be a further inducement to New Zealanders to move permanently to Australia, to take out citizenship in order to qualify. Rather than promoting flexibility, the free movement of people from one side of the Tasman to the other, migration will be permanent. Another prop to the notion of a strategic community of interest between the two countries has been removed.

Refugee policies and policies on entry of certain Pacific Island nationals have also generated political heat. New Zealand is believed in Canberra to be unduly lenient in its interpretation of criteria for acceptance of refugees and to have taken in Pacific Island and Asian migrants who could potentially move on to claim entry to Australia under the Trans-Tasman Travel Agreement, but who would not have qualified under standard Australian immigration criteria. Australia in fact can rightly claim to have done more than its share, since the Second World War, in accepting and providing for genuine refugees. Nevertheless, when Canberra decided, in early 2002, to intercept refugee boats (apparently organised by migration racketeers) and transfer the hapless passengers to various Pacific islands, where their applications for refugee status could be processed, much of this good record was forfeited in a wave of adverse publicity. New Zealand helped relieve some of the pressure by taking a hundred of them into a processing centre in Auckland, while generating the suspicion in Canberra that it was mainly motivated by the wish to play the part of the good international citizen alongside the regime adopted by Australia. (No refugee boats have yet attempted the long voyage to New Zealand. Geography confers advantage in this case.)

These are some of the frictions generated by modern issues to do with movement of peoples. Somewhat the same considerations apply in respect of policies needed to redress the grievances of native peoples and restore imbalances between communities within the two countries. Innovative, integrated solutions could be worked out – to the advantage of both countries if a sense of common purpose could be generated. Adoption of common policies, establishing an agreed external border to the two countries for management of immigration/refugee policies would in theory be the way to go. Unfortunately, nationalism needs protestations of difference. There is not a chance that the politics of separatism and exclusivity, which are at the heart of migration debates, will be abandoned in favour of inclusiveness in a greater Australasia. Rather than fostering the notion of the common good the political emphasis is increasingly on trans-Tasman people flows as a problem for the two governments, in terms of separate national interests.

Strategic and Security Challenges

Australia and New Zealand are awkwardly placed. The strategic setting is one of unusual maritime isolation: two essentially western communities, both highly dependent on international seaborne trade with mainly distant markets. Without land borders, and indeed lacking any identifiable potential enemies, the two countries have been at the margins of the great strategic confrontations of the twentieth century. Yet both have been deeply engaged. Remoteness from the centres of power and cultural influence, to which both traditionally looked, remains a constant theme. Foreign and security policies call for a high-class trapeze act, which has not always been successfully brought off. In the cultural or civilisational context, the trick is to look backwards and forwards at one and the same time. The western connection is undeniable but the need to be established members of an Asian-Pacific community is irrefutable. It is not easy to be neither one thing nor the other.

Isolationism as such has never been an option. Commitment to collective security has been a guiding principle, at least since the beginning of the twentieth century. Both countries are the keenest of multilateralists. Both have played an extensive part in United Nations peace operations around the globe. Both are strong supporters of international agencies for consultation and the better ordering of affairs in the broader Asian-Pacific region: for example, APEC, the Antarctic Treaty, the Pacific Islands Forum, South Pacific Nuclear Weapons Free Zone, the 'dialogue' process of engagement with ASEAN, the ASEAN Regional Forum, and United Nations Convention for the Law of the Sea (which established the ground-rules for delineating New Zealand's only border – where its Exclusive Economic Zone meets that of Australia's, in the northern Tasman Sea). In the environmental field, the two work closely together, although there are significant differences of perception and of policy interests. For instance, implementation of the Kyoto Protocols looks attractive to New Zealand, which can hope to generate carbon credits from extensive forestry interests, but less so to Australia, which has a major economic stake in minerals exports which are greenhouse gas intensive. The smaller country finds comfort in international treaties and undertakings where the larger is wary of making commitments which may compromise its more complex economic and other interests. Since the end of the Cold War, both countries have operated actively within the new, more informal context of the 'coalitions of the willing' – the sometimes disparate groupings of countries convened mainly by the United States to tackle particular problems, usually in the field of international peace operations. Both joined the Cairns Group of agricultural exporting countries put together to pursue major reductions in barriers to agricultural trade during the Uruguay Round of multilateral trade negotiations. New Zealand is a member of a 'new agenda coalition' seeking progress towards implementation of pledges by the major powers to achieve comprehensive nuclear disarmament, within the context of the 2000 review of the Nuclear Non-Proliferation Treaty; Australia, mindful of its security relations with the United States, has declined to join.

Both emphasise across-the-board engagement with Asia. In the process it is almost inevitable that issues will arise which challenge their own non-negotiable commitments to Western principles of political practice and values. Glib proclamations to the effect that they are 'Asians now', or at least the 'white tribes' of Asia do nothing to help bridge the gap – for either side. A tendency to drum up the connection with the United States, plus its obviously greater salience, has made Australia a target for resentment on the part of some Asian countries. New Zealand, less prominent, generally escapes such attention but is not content simply to tuck in behind its larger neighbour; it has its own interests to pursue in the wider Asian-Pacific setting. Without compromising their key commitment to globalised multilateral agreements on reduction of trade barriers, the two countries are exploring the scope for proceeding with bilateral arrangements, which would not only enlarge areas of commitment to free trade but serve to solidify the ties between the two Antipodeans and Asia. Asians cannot be expected to recognise either of them as anything other than Western countries. But regional partnerships and close, responsible engagement in the affairs of the region will serve to blur the boundaries. There is, moreover, evidence that some Asian countries are interested in dealing with Australia and New Zealand because of, not despite, their Western connections; their linkages give the two countries an importance – as bridges to the wider world of Europe and the Americas – out of all proportion to their actual weight. The issues are delicately poised. But the fundamental policy objective for both countries – the importance of heading off any prospect of a breach in Asia and the Pacific between East and West – cannot be doubted. The explosion of Japanese frustrations and ambitions in the face of Western and colonial pressures in 1941 is a constant reminder of the dangers of such a rift. In the face of such a dominating concern, minor variations between the Antipodeans on the nationalism theme are of little account.

The Asia-Pacific Arena

New Zealand and Australia live in a very complex and challenging neigh-bourhood. Many streams flow into the Pacific. On the religious front alone, Islam, Buddhism, Christianity and Hinduism have all been profoundly influential. The racial admixture is complex; ethnic stresses are pervasive. Political and philosophical inheritances from several branches of Western colonialism – British, French, Dutch, American, Hispanic and Portuguese – along with those other European imports, communism and capitalism, have played on various parts of the region. Beneath it all lie the powerful inputs of the major Asian civilisations – Indian, Chinese, Japanese and their hugely diverse subcultures and empires, including Javanese, Vietnamese, Korean, Malay and many others. The Asia-Pacific region brings almost the full gamut of human experience together. There is little wonder in the absence of political structure and cohesion. The two southern countries must define their own place in this kaleidoscope.

Six of Australia's ten largest trading partners are now in east Asia; Japan is Australia's largest export market. Some 60 per cent of New Zealand's trade is with Asia (excluding Australia). The Austral-Asians are not alone in this degree of involvement with the region: external trade of the United States across the Pacific is now almost twice that across the Atlantic and European countries, too, are increasingly conscious of their economic stake in Asia and the Pacific. For Australia and New Zealand, however, relative proximity and their dissimilarities, relative to the countries of the region – their entirely different cultural, ethnic and historical inheritances – introduce special challenges.

The new engagement of China with the world, its growing economic and political weight, coupled with the strong bridging role of Japan, the emergence of dynamic market economies in many east Asian nations and the development of regional collaboration and a sense of shared interests are all indices of a growing confidence and spirit among the countries of Asia and the Pacific. Astounding patterns of growth in regional trade and a new awareness of economic interdependence, following a collapse in confidence in several Asian economies in the late 1990s, have stimulated co-operation and the drive to reduce trade barriers. Security concerns are being engaged through interactive dialogue (especially within the ASEAN Regional Forum) and the development of communities of mutual interest and support among the nations of the region. South-East Asia, from being almost a by-word for instability and disruption in the 1960s and early 1970s, became a region of rapid growth and confidence by the 1990s. Their quick recovery from the economic crisis of 1997 has again demonstrated the new-found strengths of many Asian societies.

Plainly, Australia and New Zealand are neither powerful nor populous in the regional context; presumptions that even acting together their concerns would weigh heavily in the regional balance are unrealistic. Both have developed constructive relations with the region's major actors, Japan and China. For a number of reasons to do with suspicions of Western engagement in the region and resentment of Western criticisms in matters to do with human rights and respect for the rule of law, the going has been rockier in South-East Asia. The Prime Minister of Malaysia has been critical of the Australian role in the region and has advanced the notion that Asian regionalism should be limited to 'Asian' countries, exclusive of the countries of 'Western' interest – essentially the United States, Australia and New Zealand. It would plainly be disastrous if nationalism in the region became based on ethnic or cultural separatism. Doctrines of the primacy of certain values, be they 'Asian' or 'Western', are counter-productive in an area of huge diversity and overlapping interests.

The difficulties of accommodating ideals and beliefs confronts the Austral-Asians most directly in Indonesia. From its position across their communications links with Asia and as a dominant member of ASEAN, Indonesia is of fundamental strategic importance to both countries. There is little in history that indicates the archipelago is predestined to unity – or stability. Converging currents of Buddhist, Hindu and Islamic thought, Chinese and Western political influences and centuries of rule by Java-based European empires have left their mark in a colourful diversity which bears an only distant relationship to political coherence. The proclamation of the Republic of Indonesia by Sukarno in 1945 followed several decades of anti-colonial struggle; there was prolonged and bitter civil strife between the Dutch and pro-independence factions before the republic could come into its own in 1949. The geographical spread of Dutch colonial rule, as opposed to any sense of unity, determined the borders and sense of national identity of the new state. Sukarno's authoritarianism and penchant for playing the East against the West, together with the instability of institutions in a new and politically unconsolidated country, led to an anti-communist coup and great blood-letting in 1965, which ushered in thirty years of personal, increasingly despotic and corrupt rule by General T.N.J. Suharto, strongly backed by the Indonesian armed forces. With the unruly deposition of Suharto in 1998, the way was opened for a renewed attempt to establish democratic political processes. Representative institutions have been established; political power has changed hands without undue discord; open judicial systems are in place. Yet indebtedness is at record levels and corruption endemic. In addition to long-standing disaffection with the central government in Aceh and West Papua and religious strife in the Moluccas, Indonesia is now challenged by Islamic extremism and terrorism.

At the beginning of the twenty-first century, Australia and New Zealand were – properly and conspicuously – upholding human rights and helping with nation-building in a small corner of the Indonesian archipelago, East Timor. A frenzied response by Indonesian military and paramilitary forces to East Timorese moves to independence had left the territory in ruins and the population traumatised, with the majority forced to flee while many hundreds were killed. Australia, in particular, became the target of Indonesian resentment; in a lurid and heated atmosphere, intervention to uphold the human rights of people in a small country was interpreted as a replay of white, Western and colonial extension of power. The risk of disruption of state-to-state and multilateral links with the region remains very real. A bilateral security treaty and another determining arrangements for joint surveillance and exploitation of oil and gas resources in the Timor Gap between Australia and Indonesia were, at least temporarily suspended by Djakarta.

Terrorist bombings of a Bali nightclub, frequented by Westerners, on 12 October 2002, introduced a new element of insecurity. At least 191 people were killed, nearly ninety of them Australians. For the first time since the Second World War alarm about security became a major issue in Australia; a renewed commitment to the US-led war on terrorism and the associated campaign against Iraq followed. Australia and New Zealand have had to get to grips with the realisation that radical anti-Western sentiment, as represented, for example, by the Indonesian fundamentalist group Jamaah Islamiah, had taken root in their largest and most potent neighbour.

The Unquiet South Pacific

Pacific affairs, meanwhile, have presented the two South-landers with yet another reality check. The South Pacific is its own place and increasingly unpredictable; South Pacific countries have their own agendas which, again, are not necessarily identifiable with the ways of Western democracy. De-colonisation led to the establishment of independent island nations, some miniscule in population and exploitable resources; deep-seated tribal, ethnic or regional rivalries were often merely papered over. Traditional elites have proved impervious to change. Development issues rank high; substantial outside assistance is provided, notably by the European Union and the United States, as well as New Zealand and Australia. Both countries have also been active in promotion of regional co-operation through the Pacific Islands Forum and its agencies. There is co-ordination of shared commitments to development assistance. Both have also accepted substantial flows of migrants from the region.

With the best will in the world, Australia and New Zealand are finding themselves not well placed to control Pacific events. The island nations were unwilling to echo New Zealand's anti-nuclear activism by adopting the South Pacific Nuclear Weapons Free Zone Treaty enshrining a commitment to ban visits by ships and aircraft that may be carrying nuclear weapons. Instead, they opted for a milder version of the treaty (one acceptable to Washington), which left such questions to the discretion of individual governments. Nationalism is a two-way street. More potently, the virus of separatism has long been well established. The region is beset by ancient antagonisms and historic grievances, founded in ethnic differences and regional or tribal rivalries. Rather than progressing towards open and balanced democratic government, many of the new island states are unsettled by local power struggles, corruption, and administrative ineptitude. Indigenous island peoples, unbalanced by disturbance of traditional tribal ways under colonialism and now faced with the pressures of globalisation on land, forestry and other resources, have begun to react with violence against the post-colonial order.

In Fiji, in May 2000, an ugly hi-jacking of power – holding an elected prime minister and parliamentarians hostage – has highlighted divisions and intense power struggles within the ethnic Fijian community, and racial hostility towards an economically powerful minority Indian community. Two military coups in 1987 had unseated one attempt to establish an ethnically fair constitution. A radical re-balancing of the constitution, under the chairmanship of a former governor-general of New Zealand, ushered in the multiracial government in 1999 that was repudiated a year later. Fijian nationalism is generating a paranoia that will be difficult to appease. In Solomon Islands, ethnic intolerance between inhabitants of adjacent islands has unleashed fatal violence and civil insurrection. In Bougainville, a prolonged struggle for power among rival tribal groups seeking independence from Papua New Guinea has resulted in thousands of deaths, and been brought under control only with substantial diplomatic and peacekeeping assistance from New Zealand and Australia. The Bougainville example of successful defiance of the post-colonial order has proved highly contagious in the neighbouring Solomon Islands. Elsewhere in the Pacific, corruption in Western Samoa led to the assassination of a cabinet minister, while an oddball feudalism holds back progress and responsible government in Tonga. Financial scams and money-laundering schemes have become almost endemic. Far from following the Australian and New Zealand examples, the South Pacific has become a source of instability and intolerance.

Although the countries concerned are small and, to a degree, off the beaten track, there is no escaping the fact that the phobias of nationalism and tribal separatism so prevalent elsewhere in the world have arrived. For Australia and New Zealand, the consequences – aside from denting presumptions of aloofness from trouble – in terms of increased migration pressures, demands for military assistance and peacekeeping deployments and stepped-up development programmes are now serious. Australia, in August 2003, has taken up the challenge. Under Australian leadership, a major police/military peace operation, supported by New Zealand and other Pacific countries, has been mounted in Solomon Islands. Other Australian initiatives include promotion of a regional police training centre and a new emphasis on fostering good governance.

An Absence of Proportion

Obviously Australia and New Zealand are and will always be out of balance. New Zealanders have difficulty coming to terms with the dimensions of space and time imposed by living in Australia – 4000 kilometres wide and 3750 kilometres from top to bottom. Australia's challenges for national defence of occupying a continent empty at the top end, hard against a very different and crowded Asia, tend also to elude New Zealanders. Their own splendid land mass – off to one side and so much smaller and oceanic – helps them pretend to ignore the challenges which face Australia, as it were, in their own backyard. Their cousins across the water are in turn contemptuous or dismissive of New Zealand's determination not to come to terms with the realities of the Asian-Pacific world in which both countries must live. New Zealanders are able to see eye-to-eye with east coast Australia on a relatively cosy, trans-Tasman basis. It is more problematic for New Zealanders to feel engaged with those living on Australia's western seaboard on the Indian Ocean, or to project themselves northward to the Arafura and Timor seas. From Auckland to Perth is nearly 6000 kilometres, over a quarter of the way round the world; from Dunedin to Darwin the span is similar, about 5800 kilometres. Perhaps these distances count for less in populous contiguous countries such as Russia, China or the United States. With relatively small populations and a still strong sense of competitive isolation, Australians and New Zealanders seem to have more difficulty thinking about their asymmetric shared region in collective terms.

The inherent tensions were noted over fifty years ago by American diplomats. New Zealand, reported the State Department in 1948,

> is much less prestige conscious and desirous of individual recognition than Australia. While no serious differences have arisen between the two countries, there has been an increasing reluctance on the part of New Zealand to accept unquestioningly Australian leadership in the Pacific, particularly where Australia has opposed the policies of both the United Kingdom and the United States.

From the other perspective, the State Department noted,

> Australia sees herself as spokesman for the British Commonwealth and senior member of the ANZAC partnership in all matters relating to the Pacific area ... Australia's occasional assumption that it speaks for the ANZAC powers has not been accepted without reservation by New Zealand. We should respect New Zealand sensibilities in this respect and not assume that a single approach to Canberra will suffice for both Dominions.

For all the close patterns of Antipodean consultation and collaboration, the trans-Tasman relationship is peripheral for Australians and far from all-absorbing for New Zealanders. Both have other fish to fry. The absence of symmetry manifests itself in another important way: since the inter-relationship for both countries is only a relatively small part of the total span of their engagement with the world, the platform for building a constituency for merger or even closer strategic collaboration is that much the smaller. European countries are spurred to engage with one another because, for the most part, their respective inter-relationships rank high in the scheme of things for each country. Similarly, the Europeans are more likely to be able to create the necessary political foundation for notions of a common (European) identity simply because their overlapping histories, geographical propinquity, interactive economies and labour markets and the underlying strength of their cultural connections constitute such a large part of the national life of each country. Even in Britain, which tries the hardest to escape the logic of the 'continental commitment', the range and depth of the European dimension is undeniable. By contrast, New Zealanders can acknowledge a high degree of economic interdependence with Australia and that their neighbour is important, while continuing to pretend to a national independence and a future as a place apart. By the same token, from Canberra, peripheral vision is needed to take in New Zealand at all.

New Zealanders find it hard to accept that – in population terms at least – their country is of the same order of importance to Australia as Fiji is to New Zealand. (Fiji's population is about one-fifth that of New Zealand's.) But many New Zealanders compensate by getting high on the belief that their moral leadership is admired and influential in the world at large. Isolation confers its own delusions. Immunity from the pressures and risks to which others are exposed fosters presumptions that a little tutoring will make them see the error of their ways. The much grizzled-about Canadian relationship with the United States offers an important parallel. Most Canadians concede that their most cogent definition of who and what they are is 'not American'. New Zealanders revel in the same formula; they insist on being 'not Australian'. At the same time, great numbers of New Zealanders choose to live in Australia – again like the Canadians in the United States – and 'Kiwis' naturally band together with 'Aussies' when travelling abroad. Both relationships in fact confer a great deal on the smaller partner. Canadians gain security alongside a superpower and, through a comprehensive free-trade arrangement, the opportunities which flow from sharing a productive continent and having access to a huge and prosperous market; a remarkably transparent and open border confers huge advantages. Although Australia is no superpower, New Zealanders prefer not to acknowledge that their country gains in similar ways from their relationship with their own larger partner.

Relative smallness begets greater prickliness and sensitivity to slights, real or imagined. New Zealanders are always leery of compromising their independence. New Zealand nationalism takes aim at Australia, because New Zealanders have difficulty coming to terms with Australia's greater prominence in the world and its more abundant natural resources; Australians make New Zealand into a convenient Aunt Sally, using it – when the facts of the matter permit – as a measure of their own comparative success and achievement, quite overlooking the disproportion in size and scale. Interestingly, in their dealings with Australians, New Zealanders often find they have more in common with Tasmanians and south and western Australians than with the folk from New South Wales or Victoria, who carry with them the hubris of the central power and influence. So it has ever been between Scots and the Welsh and London, or the Plains states and New York or California. For their part, New Zealanders reject the notion that they might be another Tasmania in the grand Australasian scheme of things.

Alliance ties with the United States encompass global and Asian-Pacific political and economic issues as well as those bearing on international security. In forfeiting this relationship, New Zealand also lost a vital counterweight to its relationship with Australia. In a strategic and civilisational sense, there is now no way around the need to take account of Australia. The smaller country cannot find comfort in greater numbers; without other partners there are no ways of marshalling support for courses of action other than those that might be determined by Australian interests. In such circumstances, New Zealand feels obliged to insist the more stridently on national control over key processes of government. An unbalanced pairing of this kind leaves little room for manoeuvre. The smaller partner keenly pursues notions of a 'natural relationship', seeing such things as reflecting equality of standing, a working partnership which puts the two countries in the same league, shoulder-to-shoulder. Romantic fancies of an ANZAC freemasonry – we two against the multitude – still resonate among many New Zealanders. Most, secure in the presumptions of a settled and narrowly focused society, do not want to recognise that the caravan has moved on, population patterns in the two countries have changed and ancient ANZAC history means little to the migrant communities of Australians. More than that, New Zealanders tend to make light of the many ways in which they get off-side with Canberra, especially in defence and strategic matters. For Australians, the anger of a few years ago about the cavalier way New Zealand flouted Australian interests, by separating itself from the ANZUS alliance, has probably settled into resignation. It is understood that New Zealand is determined to be different. But there is little comprehension as to why. Many New Zealanders feel the same. Australians have tended to see the burgeoning economic interaction with New Zealand as a mark of their own generosity, an act of charity, admitting a pauperish New Zealand to the rich stalls of the Australian marketplace: New Zealand should be more grateful for having been thus saved from going belly-up in the world economy. New Zealanders, noting weaknesses in Australian economic and social systems, have long since concluded that their trans-Tasman partner simply doesn't 'get it'. Australians cannot take seriously New Zealand pretensions to partnership, and New Zealanders would settle for nothing less.

chapter seventeen

The Aerial Fabrick

Blew fresh all day but carried us round the point to the
total demolition of our aerial fabrick called continent.
– *Joseph Banks, Journal. 10 March 1770*[1]

No Republic of Australasia

By circumnavigating New Zealand, 1769–70, James Cook finally disposed of
the theory that there must be a 'Great South Land' in the Pacific. Any thought
that New Zealand might unite with Australia to create a new Great South Land
– a republic of Australasia, woven together from mutuality of experience and a
shared strategic predicament – must prove equally illusory. Careful cultivation
of the similarities rather than the differences between the two peoples could
have brought it off during the Federation debates in the late nineteenth century.
Sadly, and unlike the celebrated authors of the American Constitution working
through a hot Philadelphia summer in 1787, the Antipodeans lacked the vision
to create something original. Another New World state, determined to strike out
on its own, independently of the Old World it had left behind, was not to be.
High comfort – and confidence – levels under the umbrella of Empire ensured
there would be no ringing 'Declaration of Antipodean Independence'. Australia
and New Zealand proceeded without considering how to take advantage of all
that they had in common, the better to cope with their situation. It had nothing
to do with a rational sifting of the issues, along lines Captain Cook would have
recognised, and everything to do with the emotional instinct of nationalism.

Since the Empire umbrella blew inside out, little by way of a sense of shared
momentum and Antipodean common purpose has emerged. The CER lacks a
political dimension. Except perhaps for a year or two at the end of World War II,
New Zealand and Australia have never shared overlapping assessments of
reciprocal advantage from close co-ordination of their interests. The disconnects
may be irrational, but they may also be growing. The 'fabrick' of shared political
commitment which might knit New Zealand and Australia together begins to
look increasingly 'aerial'.

New Zealand Alone?

The 'man alone' is a staple of the New Zealand imagination. Notions of the
small battler, the doughty under-dog scorning to hunt with the pack, have strong
appeal. In fact, of course, New Zealanders are highly dependent on a complex
skein of interconnections with the wider world. New Zealand is an instinctive

and committed multi-lateralist; a small country must gain weight by working with others towards overlapping goals. A remarkably active diplomacy is deployed to bolster such linkages. Yet the theme-song is often a determined rendition of 'I'll do it my way'. In one sense this is all well and good, even necessary, to show that the little guy is not to be taken for granted. In another it is self-deceiving and counter-productive. A determination to show independence is important, but not for its own sake. The calculus must always be to do with securing best advantage.

Smallness and isolation are not, by definition, disadvantages. In a congested, unstable world, New Zealand has a lot going for it; a 'clean, green' environment and an uncluttered lifestyle in an uncrowded, quiet, beautiful land make it a privileged place. A small body politic is easier to manage and to turn in new directions than a large; problems can be managed. Governance is relatively straightforward and responsive. A smaller community confers a sense of belonging and engagement in the issues of the day. By striving for an independent, non-aligned stance in international affairs New Zealand can be active in pursuit of pragmatic solutions; the role of 'honest broker' appeals and can, in fact, sometimes be turned to practical advantage. Without close partners and allies, a smaller, independent country can determine its own courses based on its own assessments of its own interests.

On the other side of the ledger there are real challenges. It is hard to garner substantive and effective influence when you are small and isolated – especially where there is even a hint of a self-preening righteousness. Smallness gives the economy little shelter against all the winds of the globalised world: the effects of conflicts or epidemics elsewhere, fluctuating investment flows or oil prices, market collapses, protectionism or currency movements. A small taxation base and limited availability of investment capital makes for a constant stretch to meet steadily rising expectations. Long distances mean high transport costs and, with a small and scattered population, infrastructure is expensive. Isolation has never conferred security for New Zealand, even less so now that terrorism has become the weapon of choice of the aggrieved. A curiously blinkered view of the world skews thinking about defence and the place of the military in modern society. Continuing high trade deficits, a debilitating exodus of trained people and sky-rocketing social costs add to the concerns. The politics of the parish pump can readily take over; insularity and inwardness loom. An outward show of confidence masks apprehension and uncertainty about the way ahead.

Yet New Zealand is unquestionably its own place. Students of these things recognise a distinctive national style and character. Convictions about a unique New Zealand destiny have taken deep root. The belief that a small country's worth is measured by a lonely stand on an odd issue like anti-nuclearism is widely held. Many are convinced it is of the essence of New Zealand nationalism. Nationalism, however, should not be an unwavering, fixed commitment for all seasons. (Only the most dangerous kind of social engineer would insist otherwise.) A society brings together all kinds of beliefs, attitudes, cultural predilections and biases. As circumstances change so, too, should attitudes and notions of what is wise and proper. Adaptability, the capacity to turn in new directions if necessary, should outweigh blind nationalism. For Australia, stolidly British up to that point, the world changed when Japan went to war in the Pacific in 1941. The Prime Minister, John Curtin, promptly and very publicly turned to the United States as the arbiter of things in the Pacific. Australia has effectively stuck with that course. New Zealanders, as we know, have not. Now Australia's stance towards the United States is, for many New Zealanders, an obstacle in the way of close trans-Tasman ties.

Such stands have consequences. Australia has cheerfully elbowed New Zealand aside in pursuit of a Free Trade Agreement with the United States. Washington has given the inside running to Canberra, in recognition of Australia's staunchness as an ally. New Zealand, it has been made clear, forfeits any claim to special negotiating advantage by what is seen in Washington as a perverse anti-Americanism, thinly disguised behind the proclaimed nuclear allergy. An Australia-US Free Trade Agreement may or may not meet all the expectations of all sectors of the Australian economy. But, for New Zealand, it seems inescapable that even modestly improved Australian access to the crucial United States market will cause investors to take advantage of opportunities across the Tasman that are not available to New Zealand exporters. The economic impact could be severe.

There are suggestions from Canberra that a Pacific basin community should be created, centered on Australia, perhaps with a common market and a single currency, the Australian dollar. Predictably, New Zealand hackles have again been raised. New Zealand sees itself as rather more than one among a number of lesser satellites of Australia. Currency union – on Australian terms – has been shown to be unachievable. The smaller Pacific island states are themselves divided by history, colonial experience, ethnicity and culture. New Zealand and Australia, as the two developed members of such a Pacific grouping would – almost by definition – have similar interests but be rivals in pursuit of them. Would the weight of the island states be sufficient to help New Zealand secure real trade-offs in dealing with Australia? If not, where would the advantage lie for New Zealand, which has its own well-developed linkages with the Pacific?

At the time of writing, New Zealand is indulging in another fit of hand-wringing about Australia because Canberra has chosen to push a firm line in the Pacific over the risks to the region from failures of governance and economic management in the island countries. Australians are accused of pursuing a 'Howard Doctrine', of having the ambition to lord it over the South Pacific. The presumption is that this is all at the behest of the United States. Lost in all the dark suspicions about excessive Australian 'muscle' deployed in the region is any sense of alliance and shared interest. It is elementary in international affairs that nothing comes for nothing. To have influence on Australian policy-making,

New Zealand will have to show willingness to contribute meaningfully to joint enterprises. Commitment is required. Sideline critics have no impact on outcomes. First comes the need to agree on a ground-plan, on the key strategic objectives, to establish mutual confidence. The dominant presumption in Australia, however, would be that New Zealand could bring little to the Australian table. Consequently, it will be up to the New Zealanders to persuade Australians of the need for a change in mind-sets.

A New Birth of Regionalism?

Australia has long since defined itself without New Zealand. For its part New Zealand will not give up its independence for a subordinate bit part in a federal system centered on Canberra. The central issue lies elsewhere. In a globalising world, sovereignty as such is not the be-all and end-all of relations between states. National preoccupations from as little as twenty years ago are everywhere being jettisoned in the face of pressures to lower barriers and augment transparency and openness. Two countries with as much in common as Australia and New Zealand could surely ride this wave. Forget about New Zealand joining the Australian Commonwealth. What is needed is a deeper and formal commitment to an Austral-Asian regionalism.

Many New Zealanders would relish the wider opportunities and challenges implicit in increasingly close engagement in the bigger system provided by the Australian Commonwealth. Numbers have already gone to live there for that reason. There is wide admiration for modern Australia. At the same time there is concern that Australia's greater economic weight is progressively reducing New Zealand to economic dependency. Without a positive sense of Austral-Asian interests, a 'road map' if you will, this process will only compound New Zealand's sense of insecurity and uncertainty. With mutual political commitment to redefinition of the relationship absent, snidery and bickering set the tone.

It plainly is possible – even for countries steeped in dire antagonisms from the past – to rally to regional integration. The Europeans are showing that in certain circumstances nationalism can be shrugged off. By working away to promote a mutuality of interests something new is being achieved, which begins to put the nation-state in the shade. Caution is called for; too much should not be made of what has been done in Europe. The doctrine of 'subsidiarity' – what does not need to be decided at European level is the prerogative of the national parliaments – demonstrates that nationhood is alive and well. Moreover there is, as noted earlier, something of a backlash, especially in some smaller countries, against the loss of identity implicit in the European project.

Nevertheless, the die has been cast. The counterparts of New Zealand, with comparable small populations and aspirations to the highest standards of living and economic development – Denmark, Sweden, Finland, Ireland – can embrace European regionalism. Proud individualistic nations have been able to calculate the odds and to accept that advantage lies in progressive consolidation of their interests within a larger regional entity. Even within the little-regarded Nordic Union, Denmark, Iceland, Norway, Sweden and Finland have achieved mutual abolition of visas, common law enforcement arrangements, the creation of a common labour market, mutual recognition of academic degrees and an airline consortium. (The trans-Tasman drift in several of these fields is in the opposite direction.) The Nordic Council funds joint institutions and projects in the areas of investment finance, scientific research and development, culture, education and social welfare and health. Australia and New Zealand plainly live in a different universe to Europe. The unequal trans-Tasman partnership severely limits the scope for the smaller country. The smaller players in Europe can readily form alliances to achieve their ends against their larger partners; they have scope for state-craft and cunning. As things stand, New Zealand has no such options vis-à-vis Australia.

Nevertheless, the European experience shows that integration and co-ordination of effort can be brought off without subordination or political merger. New Zealand and Australia have, in typical pragmatic style, already created an extended skein of more or less *ad hoc* interactions which permit co-operation in most of the key fields of modern endeavour. The two countries face identical challenges: how best to meet the high expectations of their peoples; how to secure their respective precarious footholds on the margins of the Asian-Pacific world? Both are constrained not only by distance from the sources of innovation and change, but by relatively small technological and population bases. At present, New Zealand assets and talent migrate to Australia to contribute to the development of that economy without compensating advantage to New Zealand. This begins to make conventional Australian assumptions that New Zealand is destined to be a basket-case look self-fulfilling. How much more sensible to achieve maximum mutual advantage by pooling programmes and skills to achieve defined Antipodean aims? A combination of political and economic forces would strengthen the capacity of both to develop their place in the region. It is necessary to build a firmer foundation for the relationship, with a formal commitment to such ends.

Nationalists will no doubt spring to their swords to guard New Zealand virtue against the very idea of getting into bed with Australia. Belief-systems, founded in convictions about national history, character and worth, would be outraged. But the argument is not about loss of sovereignty – or even such a serious matter as giving up the All Blacks. It is about the establishment of a new sense of regional identity and mutual commitment. It is about reaching beyond sterile arguments to define a more compelling basis for an interactive regional partnership.

More Than Just Good Friends

Each country can be proud of what it has achieved in a relatively short history. Both are decent, profoundly democratic, individualistic nations. The long march of New Zealand and Australia has worked out pretty well so far. The smaller country is by no means a surrogate of the larger and the larger does not dominate the smaller in a way which blots out the sun. Both countries weigh off their mutual relationship in other directions. This will continue. A fast-changing region and a world rapidly becoming more economically integrated, nevertheless, puts a new complexion on these things. There is already a generational shift. Young New Zealanders and Australians are highly mobile and assume – almost without question – that they can and should be able to make their lives in the other country across the Tasman, or in Britain or the United States; many are already at home in Japan, Hong Kong, Singapore, France or any number of other places. Petty nationalism must look pathetic to them. The action is elsewhere, out there in the big world.

The smart money is always on emphasising distinct and separate qualities and virtues, rather than the interactions and the things held in common. Perhaps it is after all truly impossible to get beyond what a Canadian writer Joyce Marshall (who lives in Quebec but writes in English) has called, 'the rub and bite of difference which keeps us all alert and alive.' No doubt New Zealand will always be the butt of provincial jibes in Australia and Australians will always be regarded in New Zealand as over-bearing and plain silly with their ridiculous sheep jokes. Does it matter?

A look at the map should make it plain that such irritants fade into insignificance against the need for a new world-view – an 'Austral-Asian' perspective of shared and fully inter-penetrating, vital national interests. The old myth about New Zealand having a South Pacific focus and Australia a South East Asian has to be jettisoned, now that Australia is picking up the pace in the South Pacific. With Australia taking up the cudgels in Solomon Islands and asserting its leadership in the Pacific Islands Forum, and New Zealand actively engaged in East Timor, this distinction between the strategic outlooks of the two countries no longer makes sense – if it ever did. The two are Austral-Asians together, although the penny might not yet have dropped.

Nationalism is a hardy growth. Putting it to one side – thinking outside of the national frame – will call for political leadership of a kind which seldom appears. Whatever the singularity of the push behind the European movement, there is a shared vision for the future. A lot of work has to be done and ultimate success may be unattainable, but out there, gleaming in the future, is the idea of a united Europe – from the Atlantic to the Black Sea. New Zealand and Australia share nothing of this kind. The two countries will continue actively to co-operate and to be constructive partners in regional affairs. But nationalism has done its work. In the short space of two hundred years a largely fictitious book of differences has been written. Australia and New Zealand have developed distinct and self-regarding views of themselves. As with the famous English newspaper billboard: *'Fog in Channel – Continent isolated'*, the view of the whole is being blotted out.

There is a pressing need to make sure that doesn't happen. As the former New Zealand Prime Minister and Director-General of the World Trade Organisation, Mike Moore, has said 'Always remember, the Australians are our best friends, even if we don't like them.'[2]

Best friends find ways to surmount their differences in order more effectively to present a united front to the world. The two countries are the sole shareholders in Austral-Asia Inc. No partnership can work without undertakings as to shared interests and objectives. Formal marriage may be out, but a modern partnership agreement – an exchange of commitments based on a vision of a common destiny – is very much needed; a Declaration of Interdependence perhaps? The real truth of the matter was best expressed by the late Robert Menzies, long-time Prime Minister of Australia: 'The world interests of Australia and New Zealand are, properly viewed, not identical, but inseparable'.[2]

Notes

chapter one

1   Edward Heath, *Travels, People and Places in My Life,* 1977.
2   Keith Sinclair, *A History of New Zealand,* Penguin Books, Harmondsworth, 1959.
3   Horace Walpole, 'I do not dislike the French from the vulgar antipathy between neighbouring nations, but for their insolent and unfounded airs of superiority.' 1787.

chapter two

1   A.R.D. Fairburn, 'Elements', *Collected Poems*, Pegasus Press, Christchurch, 1966.
2   William Shakespeare, *Coriolanus*, III, 2.
3   K.R. Howe, *Where the Waves Fall*, George Allen & Unwin, Sydney and London, 1984, p. 47.
4   *Ibid.,* citing Golson, *The Pacific Islands and Their Prehistoric Inhabitants.*
5   Manning Clark (ed.), *Sources of Australian History*, Oxford University Press, London, 1957, p. 6.
6   Daniel J. Boorstin, *The Discoverers, A History of Man's Search to Know His World and Himself,* J.M. Dent & Sons, London and Melbourne, 1984.
7   Allen Curnow, 'The Unhistoric Story', *Selected Poems, 1940–1989*, Penguin Books, Auckland, 1990.
8   Manning Clark, *A History of Australia, Vol I: From the Earliest Times to the Age of Macquarie*, Melbourne University Press, Carlton, Vic., 1979, p. 317.
9   J.C. Beaglehole (ed.), *The Journals of Captain James Cook*, Vol. 1, Cambridge University Press for Hakluyt Society, Cambridge, 1955, Thursday 23rd August 1770.
10   Bernard Smith, *European Vision and the South Pacific, 1768–1850,* Oxford University Press, Oxford, 1960, p. 87.
11   Clark (ed.), *Sources of Australian History, op. cit.*, p. 75.
12   Robert Hughes, *The Fatal Shore*, Pan Books Ltd, London, 1988, p. 109.
13   Drawn from Judith Binney, 'Tuki's Universe', in Keith Sinclair (ed.), *Tasman Relations: New Zealand and Australia, 1788–1988*, Auckland University Press, Auckland, 1987.

chapter three

1   Isak Dinesen, *Out of Africa*, 1937. 'A herd of elephants ... pacing along as if they had an appointment at the end of the world,' part 1, chapter 1.
2   Smith, *European Vision and the South Pacific, 1768–1850, op. cit.*, pp. 134–5.
3   *Ibid.*
4   Thomas Keneally, Patsy Adam-Smith and Robyn Davidson, *Australia, Beyond the Dreamtime,* London, BBC Books, 1987, p. 22.

5 A.G.L. Shaw, '1788–1810', in Crowley (ed.), *A New History of Australia*, William Heinemann, Melbourne, 1974, p. 43.

6 Robert Hughes, *The Fatal Shore*, Pan Books Ltd, London, 1988, pp. 87–88.

7 *Ibid.*

8 James Belich, *Making Peoples: A History of New Zealanders from Polynesian Settlement to the End of the Nineteenth Century*, Allen Lane, Auckland, 1996.

9 Keith Sinclair, *A History of New Zealand,* Penguin Books, Harmondsworth, 1959, p. 41.

10 Judith Binney, 'Tuki's Universe', in Sinclair (ed.), *Tasman Relations: New Zealand and Australia, 1788–1988, op. cit.*, p. 24.

11 Peter Adams, *Fatal Necessity: British Intervention in New Zealand 1830–47,* Auckland University Press/Oxford University Press, Auckland, 1977, p. 250.

12 Michael Roe, '1830–50', in Crowley (ed.), *A New History of Australia, op. cit.*, p. 102.

13 Russel Ward, *The Australian Legend*, Oxford University Press, Melbourne, 2nd edn, 1966, chapters II and III.

14 Hughes, *The Fatal Shore, op. cit.*, p. 331.

15 Belich, *Making Peoples, op. cit.*, p. 129.

16 Hughes, *The Fatal Shore, op. cit.*, p. 273.

17 Beaglehole (ed.), *The Journals of Captain James Cook*, Vol. 1, *op. cit.,* August 1770, p. 399.

18 Hughes, *The Fatal Shore, op. cit.*, p. 95.

19 Augustus Earle, *A Narrative of a Nine Months' Residence in New Zealand in 1827*, p. 258, cited in Smith, *European Vision in the South Pacific, 1768–1850, op. cit.*, p. 251.

20 John Molony, *The Penguin History of Australia.* Penguin Books, Ringwood, Vic., 1988, p. 61.

21 Claudia Orange, 'James Busby', *Dictionary of New Zealand Biography,* Vol. 1, Allen & Unwin NZ Ltd and Dept of Internal Affairs, 1990.

22 A.H. McLintock (ed.), *An Encyclopaedia of New Zealand*, Vol. 1, Government Printer, Wellington, 1966, p. 279.

23 Manning Clark, *A History of Australia, Vol. 2: New South Wales and Van Diemen's Land, 1822–1838*, Melbourne University Press, Carlton, Vic., p. 199.

24 W.C. Wentworth is another, like Samuel Marsden, whose reputation on one side of the Tasman does not square with the view on the other. In Australia he is the founder of Australian nationalism; in New Zealand, a ludicrous pretender to squatters' rights.

25 Sinclair, *A History of New Zealand, op. cit.*, p. 53.

26 A.H. McLintock, *Crown Colony Government in New Zealand,* Government Printer, Wellington, 1958.

27 Manning Clark, *A History of Australia, Vol. 3.* Melbourne University Press, Carlton, Vic., 1979, p. 156.

28 Ward, *The Australian Legend, op cit.*, pp. 16–17.

29 Belich, *Making Peoples, op cit.*, vol 1, p. 278.

30 Ward, *The Australian Legend, op. cit.*, p. 112.

31 Anthony Trollope, *Australia and New Zealand*, George Robertson, Melbourne, 1873, p. 632.

32 J.A. Froude, *Oceania, England and Her Colonies*, Charles Scribner's Sons, New York, 1886, p. 25.

33 In America these were the 'sod-busters'.

34 'Ranchers' in the United States.

35 I acknowledge my debt in this section to Erik Olssen, 'Lands of Sheep and Gold, The Australian Dimension to the New Zealand Past 1840–1900', in Sinclair (ed.), *Tasman Relations: New Zealand and Australia, 1788–1988, op. cit.*

chapter four

1   Cited in Lawrence James, *The Rise and Fall of the British Empire*. St Martin's Press, New York, 1994, p. 210.

2   The American spelling of 'Labor' was deliberate – in recognition of close links with the labour movement in the United States, as represented in particular by its populist spokesman, Henry George.

3   André Siegfried, *Democracy in New Zealand*. G. Bell & Sons, London, 1914, p. 227.

4   Keith Sinclair, *A History of New Zealand*, Penguin Books, Harmondsworth, rev. edn, 1969, p. 218.

5   Manning Clark, *A History of Australia, Vol. IV: The Earth Abideth For Ever*, Melbourne University Press, Carlton, Vic., 1978, p. 242.

6   Geoffrey Blainey, *The Tyranny of Distance*, Sun Books, Melbourne, 1966, p. 226.

7   I am indebted for both information and citations in this section to Raewyn Dalziel in '"Misunderstandings Rather than Agreements", Intercolonial Negotiations, 1867–1883', in Sinclair (ed.), *Tasman Relations: New Zealand and Australia, 1788–1988, op. cit.*, p. 71.

8   William Pember Reeves, *A Colonist in his Garden*, Grant Richards, London, 1898. In one of life's little ironies, Reeves departed from New Zealand to serve as Agent-General in London and never returned. The attractions of the intellectual life in the metropolis soon overcame the joys of nation-building on the other side of the globe. He was later instrumental in founding the London School of Economics.

9   Clark, *A History of Australia, Vol. IV, op. cit.*, p. 99.

10 *Ibid.*, p. 338.

11 Henry Lawson, *Collected Verse, 1885–1900*, edited by C. Roderick, Sydney, 1967, pp. 54–7.

12 Allen Curnow, 'Landfall in Unknown Seas – on the three-hundredth anniversary of the discovery of New Zealand by Abel Jantzoon Tasman, 13 December 1642', *The Penguin Book of New Zealand Verse*, Penguin Books, Harmondsworth, 1960.

13 Geoffrey Blainey, 'Two Countries: The Same But Very Different', in Sinclair (ed.), *Tasman Relations: New Zealand and Australia 1788–1988, op. cit.*

14 Manning Clark, *A History of Australia, Vol. V: The People Make Laws*, Melbourne University Press, Carlton, Vic., 1979, p. 36.

15 *Sydney Morning Herald*, 28 August 1989.

16 Richard Jebb, *Studies in Colonial Nationalism*, London, 1905, cited in Keith Sinclair, 'Why New Zealanders are not Australians', in Sinclair (ed.) *Tasman Relations: New Zealand and Australia, 1788–1988*, Auckland University Press, Auckland, 1988.

17 Clark, *A History of Australia, Vol. V: The People Make Laws, op. cit.*, 183.

chapter five

1   William Shakespeare, *Henry V*, IV, 4.

2   G.L. Buxton, '1870–90', *op. cit.*, in Crowley (ed.), *A New History of Australia, op. cit.*, p. 210.

3   Thomas Babington Macauley, 'Von Ranke', in *Essays contributed to the Edinburgh Review (1843)*, Vol. 3.

4   F.K. Crowley, '1901–1914', in Crowley (ed.), *A New History of Australia, op. cit.*, p. 271.

5   André Siegfried, *Democracy in New Zealand, op. cit.*, pp. 361–3.

6   Rudyard Kipling, 'The Islanders', in *The Definitive Edition of Rudyard Kipling's Verse*, Hodder & Stoughton Ltd, London, 1940, p. 301.

7   M.R. Wicksteed, *The New Zealand Army: A History from the 1840s to the 1980s*, Government Printer, Wellington, p. 8.

8   Byron Farwell, *Queen Victoria's Little Wars.*

9   Clark, *A History of Australia, Vol. V: The People Make Laws, op. cit.*, p. 210.

10 See Chapter 14 on the ANZAC frigate agreement of 1989.

11 I am indebted for much of this section to I.C. McGibbon, *Blue Water Rationale: The Naval Defence of New Zealand 1914–1942*, Government Printer, Wellington, 1981.

12 John Molony, *The Penguin History of Australia, op. cit.*, p. 206.

13 Major Fred Waite, DSO, *The New Zealanders at Gallipoli*, The New Zealand Popular History Series, Whitcombe and Tombs, 1919, p. 17.

14 Clark, *A History of Australia, Vol. V: The People Make Laws, op. cit.*, p. 390.

15 Waite, *The New Zealanders at Gallipoli, op. cit.*, p. 22.

16 'The Gallipoli Diary of William George Malone', in *The Great Adventure: New Zealanders Describe the First World War*, Jock Phillips, Nicholas Boyack and E.P. Malone (eds), Allen & Unwin/Port Nicholson Press, Wellington, 1988.

17 Christopher Pugsley, *Gallipoli: the New Zealand Story.* Hodder & Stoughton, Auckland, 1984, p. 81.

18 'Tpr C. Pocok, Canterbury Mounted Rifles', diary, 25 March 1915 in *ibid.*

19 Pugsley, *Gallipoli: the New Zealand Story, op. cit.*

20 'The Letters of Randolph Norman Gray', in Phillips, Boyack and Malone (eds), *The Great Adventure, op. cit.*

21 W.P. Morrell, cited by Keith Sinclair in *A History of New Zealand*, Penguin Books, 1959, *op. cit.*, p. 232.

22 Alexander Aitken, *Gallipoli to the Somme, Recollections of a New Zealand Infantryman*, Oxford University Press, 1963, p. 47–8.

23 Major General Sir Alexander Godley to Sir James Allen, New Zealand Minister of Defence, letter dated 10 January 1915. Cited by Christopher Pugsley in *Gallipoli: the New Zealand Story, op. cit.*, p. 82.

24 Pugsley, *op. cit.*, p. 115.

25 Phillips, Boyack and Malone (eds), *The Great Adventure, op. cit.*

26 Clark, *A History of Australia, Vol. V: The People Make Laws, op. cit.*, p. 389.

27 Richard White, *Inventing Australia, Images and Identity, 1688–1980*, George Allen & Unwin, Sydney, 1981, p. 126.

28 Clark, *A History of Australia, Vol. V: The People Make Laws, op. cit.*, p. 422.

29 *Ibid.,* pp. 424–45.

30 'The letters of Alec Hutton', in Phillips, Boyack and Malone (eds), *The Great Adventure, op. cit.*, p. 254.

31 Capt. the Hon Aubrey Herbert, *Mons, Anzac and Kut*, cited in *ANZAC, The Story of the ANZAC Soldier*, by John Vader, New English Library, London, 1970, p. 33.

32 O.E. Burton, *Spring Fires,* cited in Pugsley, *op. cit.*, p. 23.

chapter six

1 Australia sent 331,700 troops to the battlefields, all of them volunteers. This represented 6.8 per cent of the total population of 4,875,300; 68.5 per cent of them were killed or wounded. New Zealand made use of conscription: 98,950 New Zealanders went to the war from a total population of 1,099,450 (8.9 per cent of the population); 58 per cent of those who served were killed or wounded. The comparable casualty rates for Britain were 52.5 per cent of troops engaged, for France 55 per cent, for Germany 54 per cent and for Canada 51 per cent. Looked at another way, 5.32 per cent of the total population New Zealand were casualties; 1.5 per cent died. Of the total population of Australia, 4.41 per cent were casualties; 1.2 per cent died. By comparison 5.29 per cent of the population of the United Kingdom were casualties, of whom 1.2 per cent died. The United States had made the extraordinary effort of deploying 1,250,000 troops in 18 months of active involvement in the war. Australia, however, with about 1/25th the population of the United States at the time (over 100 million) lost more killed or died of

wounds (59,342) in total in four years than the Americans (49,000).

2 William Ferguson Massey, Prime Minister of New Zealand, 1912–25. Notebook. National Archives, New Zealand, Bay 14, Reform Party Correspondence.

3 Foreign Office documents, *The Armistice and Peace Negotiations, 1918–19,* June 1943, Public Record Office, London.

4 By 1918, of just under two million British soldiers under arms, 500,000 were from the Dominions or India. On the Western Front, there were 154,000 Canadians, 94,000 Australians and 25,000 New Zealanders, with smaller contributions from South Africa and Newfoundland. In the Middle East, 92,000 Indians and 20,000 Australians and New Zealanders were under arms and in Mesopotamia, 102,000 British troops and 120,000 Indian. 702,000 British soldiers were killed in the war and 205,000 soldiers from the Empire.

5 'There is another consideration rightly to be borne in mind when enquiring into the characteristics of these principalities: and that is whether a prince's power is such that, in case of necessity, he can stand alone, or whether he must always have recourse to the protection of others.' Niccolo Machiavelli, *The Prince. X: How the power of every principality should be measured,* translated by George Bull, Penguin Classics, Penguin Books, Harmondsworth, (2003).

6 McGibbon, *Blue Water Rationale: The Naval Defence of New Zealand 1914–42, op. cit.,* p. 206.

7 Robin Kay (ed.), *The Australian-New Zealand Agreement 1944*, Documents on New Zealand External Relations, Vol. 1. Dept of Internal Affairs, 1972, p. 1.

8 *Ibid.*, p. 4.

9 F.L.W. Wood, *The New Zealand People at War: Political and External Affairs.* Historical Publications Branch, Department of Internal Affairs, Wellington, 1959, p. 76.

10 Kay, *The Australian-New Zealand Agreement 1944, op. cit.,* p. 5.

11 Sir Geoffery Whiskard, UK High Commissioner to Australia, Dominions Office, 24 November 1939. Document 386, Australian Foreign Policy Documents.

12 Kay, *The Australian-New Zealand Agreement 1944, op. cit.,* pp. 6–7.

13 'The first time we saw a bren gun was on the wharf at Suez', Rt Hon. David Thomson MC, personal communication.

14 Dominions Office Records, WG 110/2/20, Public Records Office, London.

15 *Ibid.*

16 Documents relating to New Zealand Participation in the Second World War, Vol II, War Histories Branch, Department of Internal Affairs, Wellington, 1949, p. 4.

17 Paul Freyberg, *Bernard Freyberg VC, Soldier of Two Nations*, Hodder & Stoughton Ltd, London, 1991, p. 235–7.

18 *Ibid.*, p. 257.

19 D.M. Horner, *High Command, Australia and Allied Strategy 1939–1945,* Australian War Memorial, Canberra, George Allen & Unwin, Sydney, 1982, p. 53.

20 The first bombing raid on Darwin on 19 February 1942 caused 243 deaths, sank eight ships and inflicted severe damage on airport, harbour and city. Darwin was attacked sixty-three more times during 1942–43; Broome, Wyndham and Townsville were also bombed repeatedly; some seventeen vessels to a total of 80,874 tons were sunk by raiders or mines off the east coast, causing the loss of 503 lives. Three Japanese midget submarines entered Sydney Harbour, and Sydney and Newcastle were shelled from submarines.

chapter seven

1 The Pacific War Council was established in March 1942 and met in Washington. The membership was the United States, Australia, Britain, Canada, China, the Netherlands, New Zealand and (later) the Philippines.

2 D.M. Horner, *High Command, Australia and Allied Strategy 1939–1945, op. cit.,* pp. 206–14.

3   Samuel Eliot Morison (ed.), *Military History of United States Naval Operations in World War II*, Vol. IV, Boston, Little, Brown, 1983, p. 246.

4   Roger J. Bell, *Unequal Allies, Australian-American Relations and the Pacific War*, Melbourne University Press, Carlton, Vic., pp. 146–7.

5   Kay (ed.), *The Australian-New Zealand Agreement 1944, op. cit.*, p. 47.

6   Alister McIntosh, 'The Origins of the Department of External Affairs', in *New Zealand in World Affairs – Volume I*, New Zealand Institute of International Affairs, Wellington, 1977, p. 21.

7   Curtin took part in the opening meeting and signed the final agreement. However, Evatt had the running of the conference. Curtin later admitted in an interview with President Roosevelt in May 1944 that he had given Evatt his head. 'Some people had wanted to consider post-war affairs.' He had been preoccupied with 'immediate war problems', but had seen no harm in giving them pleasure of concerning themselves with post-war problems in which they were engaged. Roosevelt commented the 'whole thing must be very largely a bit of Evatt'.

8   'Though Australia and New Zealand were neighbours with so much in common, especially on trade and economic issues, their relationship was more often a matter of rivalry. Relations had, in fact, been more distant than close and, following New Zealand's decision, conveyed to John Curtin in May 1943, to keep the 2nd Division in the Middle East, relations became distinctly cool.' McIntosh, *New Zealand in World Affairs, op. cit.*, p. 21.

9   McIntosh, *New Zealand in World Affairs, op. cit.*, p. 23.

10   Kay, *The Australian-New Zealand Agreement 1944, op. cit.*, p. xxxii.

11   Dominions Office Records, DO 35/1214/WR 227/11, Public Records Office, London.

12   Kay, *The Australian-New Zealand Agreement 1944, op. cit.*, p. 159.

13   *Ibid.*, p. 181.

14   *Ibid.*, p. 209.

15   As well as making up a second infantry division for service in the Pacific, New Zealand, from very exiguous resources, went to considerable effort to build a Pacific Air Force 40,000-strong which would eventually deploy fourteen squadrons forward for active service in the Solomons/New Guinea areas.

16   Dominions Office Records, *op. cit.*

17   United States Department of State, *Foreign Relations of the United States, Diplomatic Papers 1944 – Volume III*. US Government Printing Office, Washington DC, 1965, pp. 181–2.

18   McIntosh, *New Zealand in World Affairs, op. cit.*, p. 25.

19   New Zealand Minister of External Affairs to New Zealand Ambassador, Washington, 9 May 1950, in Robin Kay (ed.), *The ANZUS Pact and the Treaty of Peace with Japan: Documents on New Zealand External Relations*, Vol. III., Historical Publications Branch, Department of Internal Affairs, Wellington, 1985, p. 546.

chapter eight

1   Slogan coined for Presidential election campaign of W.J. Clinton, 1992.

2   Gary Hawke, 'Australian and New Zealand Economic Development from about 1890 to 1940', in Sinclair (ed.), *Tasman Relations: New Zealand and Australia, 1788–1988*, Auckland University Press, Auckland, 1987.

3   Keith Sinclair, 'The Great ANZAC Plant War, Australia-New Zealand Trade Relations, 1919–39', in *ibid.*, p. 125.

4   Daisy Ashford, *The Young Visiters or Mr Salteena's Plan*, chapter 5, Chatto & Windus Ltd, London, 1988.

5   Sinclair, 'The Great ANZAC Plant War, Australia-New Zealand Trade Relations, 1919–39', in Keith Sinclair (ed.), *Tasman Relations: New Zealand and Australia, 1788–1988, op. cit.*, p. 138.

chapter nine

1   Mark Twain, *Following the Equator: A Journey Around the World*, Dover, 1989 (first published 1897), pp. 251–2.

2   Sir John Marshall, cited in Alan and Robin Burnett, *The Australia and New Zealand Nexus*, Australian Institute of International Affairs, Canberra, 1978.

3   Frank Holmes, 'Free Trade with Australia', Discussion Paper No 10, New Zealand Institute of Economic Research, Wellington, 1966, p. 11, cited in P.J. Lloyd, 'NAFTA to CER', in Sinclair (ed.), *Tasman Relations: New Zealand and Australia, 1788–1988, op. cit.*, p. 146.

4   *Ibid.*, pp. 150–54.

5   Doug Anthony, Deputy Prime Minister of Australia, March 1979, cited in Hugh Templeton, *All Honourable Men: Inside the Muldoon Cabinet, 1975–1984,* Auckland University Press, Auckland, 1995, p. 130.

6   A senior New Zealand official, witness to the first meeting between Fraser and Muldoon, reported that 'They took an instant dislike to one another, with total justification on both sides!'

7   *Growing Closer Together, Australia and New Zealand*, compiled by the Australian High Commission Wellington. First published September 1996, revised August 1998.

8   Paul Kelly, *The End of Certainty: The Story of the 1980s*, Allen & Unwin Sydney, 1992; Peter Kriesler (ed.), *The Australian Economy: The Essential Guide,* Allen & Unwin, Sydney, 1995; *State of Play 8: The Australian Economic Policy Debate,* Allen & Unwin, Sydney, 1995.

9   *Growing Closer Together, Australia and New Zealand*, compiled by the Australian High Commission Wellington. First published September 1996, revised August 1998

chapter ten

1   Walter Bagehot, *Physics and Politics*, Kegan Paul, Trench and Co., London, 1887, pp. 20–21.

2   *The Iliad and the Odyssey of Homer*, Book Two, para 540. Translated by Richmond Lattimore, Encyclopaedia Britannica Inc., Chicago, London, 1990.

3   Liah Greenfeld, *Nationalism: Five Roads to Modernity*, Harvard University Press, 1992, pp. 29–31.

4   Isaiah Berlin and Ramin Jahanbegloo, *Conversations with Isaiah Berlin: Recollections of a Historian of Ideas,* Charles Scribner's Sons, New York, 1991, pp. 101–2.

5   See Allan Gotlieb, *'I'll be with you in a minute, Mr Ambassador': The Education of a Canadian Diplomat in Washington*, University of Toronto Press, Toronto, 1991.

chapter thirteen

1   Charles Brasch, 'Forerunners', in *Collected Poems*, edited by Alan Roddick, Oxford University Press, Auckland, 1983.

2   Henry Lawson, cited in Clark, *A History of Australia, Vol. V: The People Make Laws, op. cit.*, p. 225.

2   *Ibid.*, p. 5.

4   Judith Wright, 'Bullocky', in *Collected Poems, 1942–1970*, Angus & Robertson Publishers, Sydney, 1977.

5   Judith Wright, 'Letter to a Friend', *ibid.*

6   Judith Wright, 'Australia, 1970', *ibid.*

7   A.D. Hope, 'Australia', in *Collected Poems*, Angus & Robertson, Sydney, 1966.

8   Ursula Bethell, from 'Time', included in *From a Garden in the Antipodes*, 1929, republished in *A Book of New Zealand Verse 1923–50*, chosen by Allen Curnow, The Caxton Press, Christchurch, 1951.

9   Charles Brasch, from 'The Silent Land', republished in *ibid.*

10 Allen Curnow, 'Landfall in Unknown Seas', in *Collected Poems 1933–1973*, A.H. & A.W. Reed, Wellington, 1974.

11   James K. Baxter, 'High Country Weather', in *Collected Poems*, edited by J.E. Weir, Oxford University Press, Wellington, 1981.
12   James K. Baxter, 'The Mountains', *ibid*.
13   James K. Baxter, 'Elegy at Year's End', *ibid*.
14   E.H. McCormick, *Letters and Art in New Zealand*, Department of Internal Affairs, Wellington, 1940, p. 178.
15   A.R.D. Fairburn, 'Dominion Album Leaves' and 'Imperial', in Allen Curnow (ed.), *The Penguin Book of New Zealand Verse*, Penguin Books, Harmondsworth, 1960.
16   Allen Curnow, 'Attitudes for a New Zealand Poet (III): The Skeleton of the Giant Moa in the Canterbury Museum, Christchurch', in *A Book of New Zealand Verse 1923–50*, chosen by Allen Curnow, *op. cit.*
17   John Mulgan, *Report on Experience*, Oxford University Press, London, 1947, pp. 14–15.
18   Denis Glover, 'Themes', in Allen Curnow (ed.), *The Penguin Book of New Zealand Verse*, *op. cit.*
19   James K. Baxter, 'Letter to Max Harris', in *Collected Poems*, *op. cit.*

chapter fourteen

1   W.K. Hancock, *Australia,* Jacaranda Press, Brisbane, reprinted 1961, p. 84.
2   Paul Kelly, *The End of Certainty: The Story of the 1980s*, Allen & Unwin, Sydney, 1992.
3   Greg Sheridan, Foreign Editor, *The Australian,* 4 October 1995.
4   Helen Clark, 'Finding the Military Middle Ground', *The Dominion,* 30 March 1998.
5   Nicky Hager, 'No Frigates Campaign', letter in *The Dominion*, 4 October 1989.
6   Ruth Dyson, *The Dominion*, 30 September 1989.
7   Nicky Hager, *New Zealand Herald*, 5 December 1989.

chapter fifteen

1   Alan and Robin Burnett, *The Australia and New Zealand Nexus*, The Australian Institute of International Affairs, 1978, p. 12.

chapter sixteen

1   E.B. White, letter to Robert S. Palmer, 4 December 1964, *Letters of E.B. White,* Harper & Row, New York, 1976.

chapter seventeen

1   Beaglehole (ed.), *The Journals of Captain James Cook*, Vol. 1, *op. cit.*, p. 262.
2   Jim Weir, *New Zealand Wit and Wisdom: Quotations with Attitude*, Tandem Press, Auckland, 1998.

Index